FIRE ANTS

NUMBER THREE
Texas A&M University Agriculture Series

Fire Ants

Stephen Welton Taber

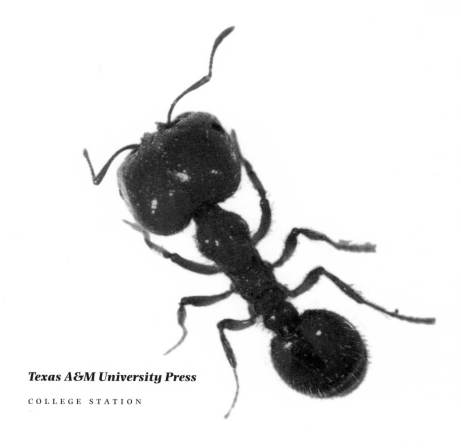

Texas A&M University Press

COLLEGE STATION

The paper used in this book meets the minimum requirements
of the American National Standard for Permanence
of Paper for Printed Library Materials, z39.48-1984.
Binding materials have been chosen for durability.
∞

Library of Congress Cataloging-in-Publication Data

Taber, Stephen Welton, 1956–
    Fire ants / Stephen Welton Taber. — 1st ed.
        p. cm. — (Texas A&M University agriculture series ; no. 3)
    Includes bibliographical references (p.).
    ISBN 0-89096-945-0 (cloth)
      1. Fire ants.   I. Title.   II. Series.

QL568.F7 T2347 2000
595.79′6—dc21

595.796

00-026346

To Elaine

And why should they stop at tropical South America? . . .
Suppose they go on spreading! Suppose they come down the
river to the sea and send off an expedition in the hold of some
eastward-travelling ship! What could one do?

—H. G. Wells, "The Empire of the Ants" (1905)

The ant will be restricted to an ever-decreasing area until
eventually it is "driven into the Gulf"—presumably making its
last stand at its central port of entry, the Mobile Bay area.

—J. L. George, *The Program to Eradicate the Imported Fire Ant* (1958)

Contents

List of Illustrations   xi

Preface   xv

Chapter 1.   Introduction   3

Chapter 2.   Invasion   15

Chapter 3.   The Red Imported Fire Ant *(Solenopsis invicta)*   25

Chapter 4.   The Black Imported Fire Ant *(Solenopsis richteri)*   58

Chapter 5.   The Tropical Fire Ant *(Solenopsis geminata)*   66

Chapter 6.   Fire Ants Native to the United States   87

Chapter 7.   Fire Ants Endemic to South America   101

Chapter 8.   The Origin and Evolution of Fire Ants   105

Chapter 9.   Nest Symbionts of Fire Ants   117

Chapter 10.   Medical Importance of Fire Ants   128

Chapter 11.   Chemical Control and the Pesticide Issue   141

Chapter 12.   Enemies and Biocontrol of Fire Ants   159

Chapter 13.   Fire Ants Pro and Con   194

Chapter 14.   Conclusion: Prospects and Questions   216

Appendix 1.   Fire Ant Species of the World   229

Appendix 2.   How to Identify U.S. Fire Ants   230

Appendix 3.   Preserving Fire Ants for Study   234

Glossary   237

Bibliography   243

Index   301

Illustrations

1.1. Red imported fire ant stinging author's hand   4

1.2. Jaws and sting of red imported fire ant   4

1.3. Sting of black imported fire ant   5

1.4. Pustules produced by imported fire ant stings   5

1.5. Pustules at higher magnification   6

1.6. Section through a pustule   6

1.7. Massive response of nestmates to intrusion   7

1.8. Red imported fire ant major worker   8

1.9. Black imported fire ant major worker   9

1.10. Tropical fire ant major worker   9

1.11. Southern fire ant major worker   10

1.12. Golden fire ant major worker   10

1.13. *Solenopsis amblychila* major worker   11

1.14. Thief ant   13

2.1. Pine seedling growing from imported fire ant mound   19

2.2. Nursery stock growing from imported fire ant mound   19

2.3. Imported fire ants tending aphids on a plant   19

2.4. Red imported fire ants dispersing during a flood   23

3.1. Natural range and accidental distribution of red imported fire ant   27

3.2. Red imported fire ant mounds   29

3.3. RIFA mounds dotting pasture   30

3.4. Honeycombed interior of red imported fire ant mound   30

3.5. Foraging trail of red imported fire ant colony   31

3.6. Gaster-flagging red imported fire ant worker   35

3.7. Red imported fire ants subduing corn earworm caterpillar   36

3.8. Red imported fire ants tending queen and brood of
     monogyne colony   42

3.9. Red imported fire ants dragging dead queen of polygyne colony   43

3.10. Virgin RIFA queen about to take flight   46

3.11. RIFA male about to take off for nuptial flight   46

3.12. RIFA nuptial flight begins   47

3.13. RIFA nest queen, wingless and mated   50

3.14. Wing scars of RIFA queen   50

3.15. RIFA larvae   51

3.16. RIFA male   53

3.17. RIFA sperm cell   54

3.18. Castes and sexes of the RIFA   56

4.1. Natural range and accidental distribution of black imported
     fire ant   59

4.2. BIFA winged queen   63

4.3. BIFA male   64

4.4. South American BIFA nest queen, a larva, and parasitic
     nematode worm   64

4.5. BIFA worker   65

5.1. Natural range and accidental distribution of tropical fire ant   67

5.2. Tropical fire ant nest   70

5.3. Seed of arrowroot plant *Calathea microcephala*   74

5.4. TFA major worker, winged queen, and male   79

5.5. TFA male   79

5.6. TFA queen surrounded by workers and brood   82

5.7. TFA eggs at high magnification   83

5.8. TFA eggs and larvae   83

5.9. TFA larva in feeding position   84

5.10. TFA larva   84

5.11. TFA major worker pupa in advanced stage of development   85

5.12. Developing jaws of TFA media worker pupa   85

6.1. Range of southern fire ant   88

6.2. SFA winged queen   92

6.3. SFA male 92

6.4. Range of golden fire ant 94

6.5. Castes and sexes of golden fire ant 96

6.6. GFA male 96

6.7. GFA gynandromorph 97

6.8. Range of *Solenopsis amblychila* 98

6.9. *Solenopsis amblychila* winged queen 99

6.10. *Solenopsis amblychila* male, major worker, and media worker 99

8.1. Genetic relatedness among U.S. fire ants 106

9.1. A thysanuran (silverfish) taken from RIFA nest 118

9.2. *Myrmecophila nebrascensis* feeding on secretions of
harvester ant 119

9.3. Houseguest beetle *Myrmecosaurus ferrugineus* 119

9.4. Houseguest beetle *Metopioxys gallardoi* 121

9.5. Houseguest beetles *Hippeutister solenopsidis* and *Dinardopsis*
plaumanni 122

9.6. Beetle *Poecilocrypticus formicophilus* 123

9.7. Remains of *Poecilocrypticus formicophilus*, recovered from
RIFA nest 123

9.8. Blind houseguest beetle *Anillus affabilis* 124

9.9. Houseguest bug *Atrazonotus umbrosus* 125

9.10. Houseguest scuttle fly *Commoptera solenopsidis* 125

9.11. Phorid fly with useless wings 126

10.1. Sting apparatus of imported fire ant 129

12.1. Daguerre's fire ant (queen) 161

12.2. Daguerre's fire ant (male) 161

12.3. Comanche harvester ants with prey, a winged RIFA queen 163

12.4. Little black ant *Monomorium minimum* 163

12.5. Fire ant's natural enemy: *Pheidole dentata* major worker 164

12.6. Blind army ant *Labidus coecus* 164

12.7. *Aphaenogaster* ant 165

12.8. *Orasema* wasp 166

12.9. Tiger beetle 167

12.10. Larva of the beetle *Pseudomorpha* 167

12.11. Adult male strepsipteran 168

12.12. Larva of strepsipteran *Caenocholax fenyesi* 169

12.13. Phorid fly *Pseudacteon litoralis* 170

12.14. Phorid fly larva and pupa occupying mouth of fire ant 171

12.15. Green darner dragonfly *Anax junius* 172

12.16. Ant-lion and fire ant 173

12.17. Female black widow and egg sac 173

12.18. Parasitic nematode *Tetradonema solenopsis* 175

12.19. Fungus *Beauveria bassiana* growing on cicada 176

12.20. Parasitic fungus *Metarhizium anisopliae* and spores 177

12.21. Legume of the genus *Sesbania* 179

12.22. Fire ants and *Pheidole dentata* 183

12.23. Queen army ant *Neivamyrmex nigrescens* and worker 184

12.24. Red imported fire ants and tropical fire ants in battle 185

12.25. Phorid fly *Pseudacteon crawfordi* 187

12.26. South American paper wasps defending nest against
fire ants 192

13.1. RIFA nest at edge of asphalt road 200

13.2. Horn fly *Haematobia irritans* 204

14.1. S-shaped growth curve showing IFA infestation over time 218

14.2. Expected U.S. distribution of red imported fire ant 221

14.3. Range of RIFA x BIFA hybrid in United States 224

A2.1. Red imported fire ant worker 231

A2.2. Two-segmented club of fire ant worker's antenna 231

A2.3. Clypeal teeth of imported fire ant major workers compared
to those of native fire ant major workers 231

A2.4. RIFA major workers have a reddish spot 232

A2.5. BIFA major workers have a yellow spot 232

A2.6. Head of TFA major compared to winged queens and male 232

Preface

The prophecy of H. G. Wells quoted at the opening of this book was fulfilled thirteen years after those words first appeared in *Strand Magazine*, a now-defunct British periodical better known as the showcase for so many Sherlock Holmes stories. This real-life invasion began when the South American black imported fire ant came ashore in Mobile Bay, Alabama. Its close relative the red imported fire ant followed two decades later. The second prophecy, J. L. George's vision of the fire ant's last stand at its port of entry, will never materialize. The red imported fire ant is presumably here to stay and is currently *expanding* its range into the southwestern United States. The fact that fire ants are "hot climate specialists" (Andersen 1997) should be considered when pondering the potential extent of this expansion. Indeed, Wells's question "What could one do?" has been asked by entomologists for the last seventy years. Effective but controversial chemicals have been tried and abandoned (one of them might have done the job), and new insecticides have taken the place of old without eradicating the invader. Some experts gave up on eradication very early in the game (Allen 1958). Now the United States Department of Agriculture has abandoned its eradication efforts altogether and is attempting to hold the insect in abeyance with biocontrol.

My own purpose is a synthesis of the enormous literature on the fire ants of the world. The red imported fire ant in particular has a fascination and importance—medical, agricultural, and ecological—unrivaled by any other. Yet until now there has been no comprehensive book on the subject. This is no oversight. Most fire ant experts are engaged in original research and have no time to step aside long enough to compile a synthesis of what has already been done. State and federal money (and pressure) abounds, and these myrmecologists are just too busy discovering. As S. B. Vinson has said: "Another truth is that when funds are limited, competition, not collaboration, rules." I have tried to fill the resulting void in a way that is useful to the general reader and to the harried specialist as well.

Research has generated thousands of articles, many of them in major peer-reviewed scientific journals, and these are supplemented by untold numbers of stories in newspapers and popular magazines. It was neither feasible nor appropriate to use them all, nor would the market bear such a massive tome. Instead, I have emphasized information of the first kind, professional papers covered by *Biological Abstracts* from its inception in 1926 until the time of this writing (2000). These works are hardly error-free, and the authors' conclusions are sometimes contradictory. Nevertheless they comprise the best and most reliable sources of information. I attempted to obtain and read every article on fire ant biology referenced by this resource. Even that limitation failed to reduce the mass of text to an acceptable level. Further sifting and filtering of the major articles was required.

I did obtain valuable information from the few scholarly books that include chapters on fire ants and from state agricultural extension service bulletins specializing in the practical matter of fire ant control. Occasionally I drew upon a newspaper or magazine with a fire ant cover story or upon some other popular article if it contained believable information never published in the primary literature. But fire ants have been studied longer than *Biological Abstracts* has been in print, so I found myself reaching back in time, 122 years beyond volume 1, until I came to the beginning of it all. The short description of the tropical fire ant by Fabricius (1804) is the first word on the subject.

Sorting of a second kind was required. Reports on imported fire ants had been published for more than forty years before it was suddenly discovered that two different species were involved, not merely a single ant with a disconcerting amount of color variation. I disentangled one from the other wherever possible, using locality data, year of publication, and any other information that might help determine which of the two species was the subject of a given report. These two species are the red imported fire ant and the black imported fire ant. Occasionally I found it impossible to decide between the two and had to settle for "imported fire ant" with no further distinction. From 1972 onward, most authors made the distinction themselves.

Separate chapters are dedicated to the basic biology of those two species. Subsequent chapters are devoted to the biologies of other species, medical importance, pesticides, evolution, animals that share the nest, and enemies and biocontrol. The plan was to start with basic biology and conclude with interactions between ant and human, to supply a reference that is easy to consult in a hurry. A manuscript reporting a new species of fire ant was being prepared elsewhere while this book was in production, but I was unable to obtain specimens for examination and inclusion here. Some material in the book is entirely my own. For example, photos of two fire ants native to the United States *(Solenopsis aurea* and *S. amblychila)* have never to my knowledge been published before.

The scientific names of some ant species appearing here will be unfamiliar even to specialists. These seemingly novel word combinations are due to my adoption of certain changes listed in Barry Bolton's authoritative 1995 revision entitled *A New General Catalogue of the Ants of the World.* I followed this excellent work except as regards the New World harvester ant genera *Pogonomyrmex* and *Ephebomyrmex.* The chosen scientific names of those species are based upon my own work (Taber 1998). Readers will find explanations of many unfamiliar terms in the glossary. A less sober side of the fire ant coin bears a title nearly identical to that of the present volume: for that mixture of fact, fantasy, and even erotica, see Saul Wernick's 1976 novel *The Fire Ants.*

I thank Roy R. Snelling of the Los Angeles County Natural History Museum for a loan of hard-to-find fire ants and for help with etymologies of scientific names. I thank Brian V. Brown of the same institution for a phorid fly of the type being used in biocontrol efforts against the red imported fire ant in the United States. I am also grateful to Barry Bolton of the British Museum for checking the list of currently recognized fire ant species. Mark Trostle of the Texas Department of Agriculture and S. B. Vinson of Texas A&M University loaned photographs and gave permission to use them, a selection process greatly aided by Karen Dickie, also of the TDA.

FIRE ANTS

CHAPTER I

Introduction

What about this Argentine fire ant? In
many quarters it is painted as the blackest of
villains and a threat to the life and economy of
man. Let's look at some facts.

—*R. H. Allen, Jr.* (1958)

THE fire ants comprise a group of eighteen to twenty insect species native to the New World (Trager 1991), where entomologists have traced their origin to an ancestor arising tens of millions of years ago in tropical South America (Wilson 1986). The origin of the common name *fire ant* is obvious to all who have been stung, for the sting—not the bite—feels like a burning match held against the skin, and the insect is quick to employ its pyrogenic weapon (figs. 1.1, 1.2, 1.3).

A white pustule resembling those of smallpox in size and shape usually appears within twenty-four hours if the culprit is one of the two imported species (figs. 1.4, 1.5, 1.6). But pain and pustule are only two prongs of the imported fire ant's triple-threat attack. The third facet is its massive and instantaneous retaliation against all intruders. When the mound itself is disturbed, the flames are fanned by hundreds or even thousands of sterile female recruits responding to airborne alarm chemicals secreted by nestmates at the scene of the attack (fig. 1.7). These signals provoke one and all to bite and sting in defense of the

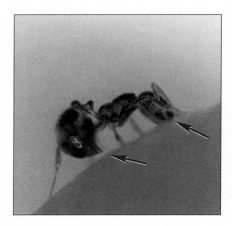 

Fig. 1.1. A red imported fire ant stinging the author's hand. *Left photo:* The insect bites with the jaws at one end to obtain an anchor (right arrow), allowing the sting to be driven into the skin at the other end (left arrow). Soon it will curl into a ball as the weapon is pushed deeper *(right photo).*

Fig. 1.2. The jaws and sting (arrow) of a red imported fire ant.

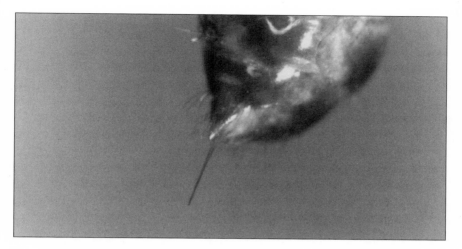

Fig. 1.3. The sting of the black imported fire ant.

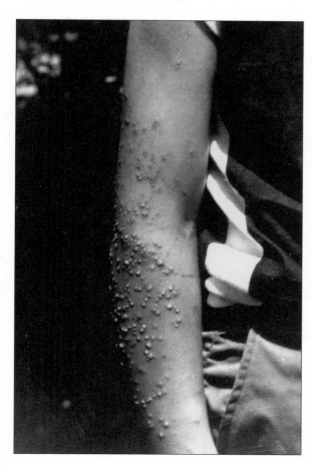

Fig. 1.4. The pustules produced by multiple imported fire ant stings resemble the symptoms of smallpox. Reprinted from Vinson and Sorensen 1986. By permission of the senior author, Texas Department of Agriculture, and United States Department of Agriculture.

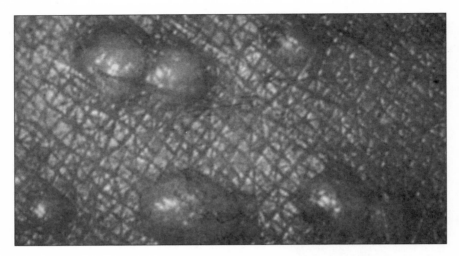

Fig. 1.5. Pustules at higher magnification. Reprinted from Vinson and Sorensen 1986. By permission of the senior author and Texas Department of Agriculture.

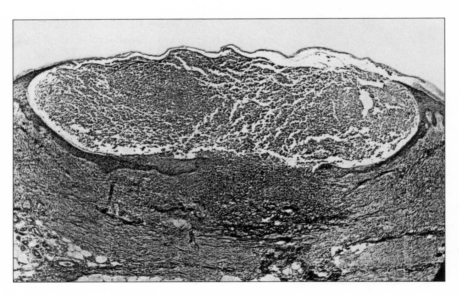

Fig. 1.6. A section through a pustule at still higher magnification, showing the internal anatomy of the blister and the underlying dead cells. Reprinted from *Archives of Dermatology* 75, p. 480, 1957. Copyright 1957, American Medical Association.

Fig. 1.7. The painful sting of a single fire ant is amplified a thousandfold by the massive response of its nestmates to even the slightest intrusion. The ruler on this styrofoam block is five inches long.

egg-laying queen(s), though the defenders themselves lack functional ovaries and will never have offspring of their own to protect (Oster and Wilson 1978). It is this formidable arsenal that sets fire ants apart from less bellicose relatives. In fact, the ardor of the fire ant's retaliation sometimes increases to an audible level. As swarms of major and minor workers attacked the styrofoam block pictured in figure 1.7, the rustle of scurrying bodies could be heard from five feet away. Fire ants make a second, very different sort of noise known to specialists as stridulation. I deal with it in chapter 3.

Fire ant is only one of many common names applied to this insect. In South America it is known in Spanish as *hormiga colorada* (red ant) and as *hormiga brava* (fierce ant) and in Portuguese as *formiga de fogo* (fire ant), *formiga lave-pé* (wash-foot ant), *formiga rúiva* (red ant), and *formiga toicin-*

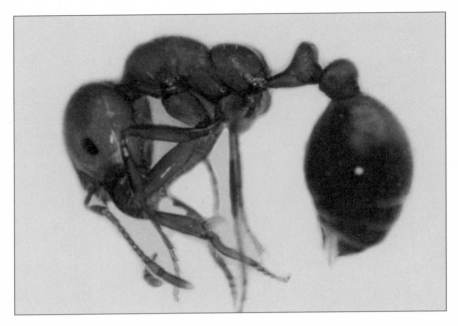

Fig. 1.8. A red imported fire ant major worker.

heira (lard ant) (Gonçalves 1940; Trager 1991). German scientists use a literal equivalent of the English common name—*Feuerameisen* (Reichensperger 1935). To the native South Americans who have known the fire ants of that continent longer than have any others, it is *pucacuro-kuna* and *aracaras.* Over time, hunting dogs in the Amazon Basin become blinded by fire ant stings; their clouded corneas have prompted a local saying that "the dog with white eyes is always a good hunter" (Hogue 1993). True fire ants such as these must not be confused with the little red fire ant *(Wasmannia auropunctata).* It too is famous for a painful sting, and it too has been accidentally introduced into ecosystems far from its home base. The little red fire ant is said to be harming fragile wildlife in the Galápagos Islands (Lubin 1984), the Ecuadorian archipelago famous for its role in the formulation of Darwin's theory of evolution.

In this book I focus on the six true fire ant species that occur in the United States, both introduced and native (figs. 1.8, 1.9, 1.10, 1.11, 1.12, 1.13). These are the red imported fire ant *(Solenopsis invicta)*, black imported fire ant *(S. richteri)*, tropical fire ant *(S. geminata)*, southern fire ant *(S. xyloni)*, desert or golden fire ant *(S. aurea)*, and *S. amblychila*, an almost entirely ignored species with no common name. Focus is necessary because

Fig. 1.9. A black imported fire ant major worker.

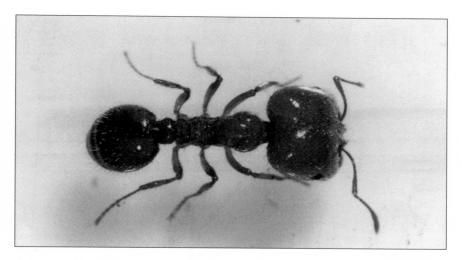

Fig. 1.10. A tropical fire ant major worker.

the enormous literature summarized here is primarily concerned with economic impact, something that imported fire ants generally seem to lack in their homelands south of the equator, where defoliating leaf-cutter ants are far greater pests than are fire ants (Wilson 1986). In fact, some entomologists once believed that leaf-cutters arose evolutionarily from fire ant–like ancestors when those ancestors began cultivating fungi, which infected the seeds stored within their nests. Eventually the impurity replaced the origi-

Fig. 1.11. A southern fire ant major worker.

Fig. 1.12. A golden fire ant major worker.

nal item in the ants' diet (Goetsch and Grüger 1942). This hypothesis is not widely held today. Nevertheless, modern red imported fire ants are attracted to dallis grass infected with a species of the fungus genus *Claviceps*. This sac-fungus produces a nectar-like substance (Vinson 1972), and consumption of this honeydew causes hallucinations in humans.

Fig. 1.13. A *Solenopsis amblychila* major worker.

The most famous of the six species featured here, the red imported fire ant, has a solid reputation in the United States as a noxious pest. Yet some see it as a mere nuisance, and others see the Brazilian native as a fortuitous ally in a war on other pests plaguing the fields, farms, and homes of the southern United States. Both the Brazilian red and the Argentine black imported fire ant arrived by accident on U.S. soil so recently that some among us in the year 2000 were born before the ants jumped ship near Mobile, Alabama, in the early part of the twentieth century. At least three and perhaps all four of the remaining species are native ants: the southern fire ant, golden fire ant, and *Solenopsis amblychila* probably evolved in what is now the United States or in nearby Mexico. The continental origin of the tropical fire ant remains shrouded in doubt. Either it is a U.S. native with a wide natural New World distribution or it was accidentally introduced hundreds of years ago when the ship that ferried it north was fashioned from wood and powered by sail. International commerce has carried this tramp species far and wide, even into the Old World, a distinction that has so far eluded the red imported fire ant.

The stay-at-home southern fire ant, like the tropical fire ant, is economically important or pestiferous, depending upon the circumstances. The desert fire ant and its close relative *Solenopsis amblychila* are stay-at-homes too. Yet neither is considered to be harmful or beneficial. Continuing westward expansion of the red imported fire ant at the expense of the three confirmed

United States natives threatens to coin a phrase that may leave some people incredulous—"endangered fire ant." Accidental importations have so far been unidirectional, and it is the flora and fauna of northern latitudes that must come to terms with expanding southern invaders.

For convenience I often refer to the six North American insects by acronyms. This has a dual utility because it also minimizes the confusion and controversy surrounding a recent discovery that *Solenopsis invicta*, a scientific name used since 1972 for the red imported fire ant, is an invalid name by the rule of priority (Bolton 1995). The previously overlooked name *Solenopsis wagneri* is older and therefore has precedence over a label with almost mantra-like familiarity and usage among entomologists. This is, after all, "the most studied ant species in the world" (Lofgren 1986a). Because *invicta*, "the unconquered," has been burned into the literature so deeply, many professionals would prefer to keep the name alive, even though there seems to be no analogous protest to a similar name change in the case of the infamous Argentine ant. This pest, which happens to be an enemy of fire ants, was best known until 1992 as *Iridomyrmex humilis*. Since then it has been referred to by the certainly less familiar name of *Linepithema humile*. To do differently in the case of the fire ant—to reject its proper name for the sake of convenience—is to embrace a double standard. Scientific names were originally conceived to *avoid* confusion and disagreement; the red imported fire ant has been a pest here, too. At this writing, a petition to conserve the familiar name *invicta* was under consideration (Shattuck et al. 1999). Four opinions, including my sole dissenting voice in favor of *wagneri* (Taber 1999), were published while this book went to press.

The scientific genus name of the fire ant, like the creature itself, is here to stay. *Solenopsis* means "pipe face" or "pipelike" (think of the cylindrical shape of the electromagnetic device known as a solenoid). Perhaps J. O. Westwood chose the name in 1840 because the slender bodies of the smaller worker subcastes brought to mind the shape of a pipe. It is rare for the same scientific name to appear in two different kingdoms of life, but there is a *Solenopsis* among the plants too (Crespo et al. 1996, 1998). A member of the lobelia family, it has a Mediterranean distribution that has so far ensured that plant and animal *Solenopsis* species do not overlap in a geographic sense. If the priority of scientific names ever becomes an issue at the kingdom level, the animals will lose out—*Solenopsis* was a plant name four years before it was first applied to a fire ant.

I leapfrog over the *invicta/wagneri* fray by referring here to the red imported fire ant as the RIFA, an acronym that was in use long before the controversy arose. Likewise the black imported fire ant is the BIFA, the tropical fire ant the TFA, the southern fire ant the SFA, and the desert or golden fire ant the GFA. I prefer to emphasize color over habitat in the latter case because the golden color of the smallest workers is striking; the ant's scientific name refers to this color, not to one of its several habitats; and the species is not confined to deserts at all—it was discovered in Austin, Texas, which seems dry but is no desert. Also for convenience, I refer to the red imported and black imported species as such, even when discussing them in their South American home. (Reading the names as "riff-uh" for RIFA, "tiff-uh" for TFA, and so on eases the flow.)

All this considered, it is a relief to find that the vast majority of the roughly two hundred species comprising the animal genus *Solenopsis* are not fire ants at all. They are smaller, inconspicuous creatures, many of them known as "thief ants" for their habits of nesting near or within the colonies of other ants and for taking food from the stores of their hosts (fig. 1.14). This food includes the other species' young. By that device a few thief ants became natural enemies and biocontrollers of their fire ant relatives. Thief ants are said to be equally aggressive but unable to pierce human skin with their tiny stingers (Creighton 1950). Like their more famous kin, they are unusual among animals in that their venom contains alkaloids. This class of chemicals is far more common among plants. In fact, the defensive alkaloids in the skin of certain frogs may derive from a habit of eating thief ants (Jones et al. 1996, 1999).

Fig. 1.14. A thief ant.

Distinguishing characteristics and genetic relationships within *Solenopsis* have not been satisfactorily determined (Bolton 1987, 1995; Gorman et al. 1998; Trager 1991). This problem has bedeviled experts for decades. William Steel Creighton hammered away at it (1930) and soon repeated Carlo Emery's (1921) description of *Solenopsis* as the *crux myrmecologorum* —the cross that the ant specialist must bear. Barry Bolton of the British Museum of Natural History has described this state of affairs as "appalling." In the absence of a clear explanation of how fire ants are distinguished from all other members of their genus, I offer two short appendixes to clarify some matters. Appendix 1 is a list of the fire ants of the world. Appendix 2 shows how to recognize every species known to occur within the boundaries of the United States as of 1999. The glossary and the distribution maps prepared for each of these six species will aid in their identification.

There are reasons to believe that this rather short list will lengthen in the future. First, one or more species yet unknown to science might be foraging even now in the deserts of the southwestern United States. And second, there is always the chance of another invasion from South America.

CHAPTER **2**   Invasion

This ant has for several years done considerable
damage to young satsuma orchards and nursery
stock by girdling the trees just above the union of
stock and graft, evidently to get the oozing sap.

—H. P. Löding (1929)

H ENRY PETER LÖDING is credited with having
registered the first complaint in the United States
regarding the newly introduced or imported fire ant.
This was the black imported fire ant, the more famous red one not yet having landed on the Gulf Coast
shore. He reported it as *Solenopsis saevissima richteri.*
Löding first noticed the invader in 1918, when the
South American ant was discovered in the area of
Mobile, Alabama. Oddly enough, the actual report
eleven years later was either overlooked or disbe-
lieved by some early fire ant researchers, for they
commonly rejected the claim that fire ants consume
vegetable matter as well as meat. One such study
found no evidence that the imported fire ant fed on
plants, and this early underestimate of its pest potential was highlighted by an Alabama state health
officer who knew of no medical problems worthy of
record. The ant's sting was often mistakenly called a
bite. One Alabama zoologist believed the imported
ant to be a nuisance but no economic pest (Allen
1958). Time and experience would alter these views.

Most Americans plagued by fire ants today have
never heard of or dealt with the original import. They

15

know instead the red imported fire ant (RIFA). By far the heavier hitter of the two accidentally introduced species, this second arrival was destined to back the BIFA into a northern refuge within the southeastern United States while itself fanning out in every direction. We are still dealing with the consequences of these accidents today and will do so into the foreseeable future; entomologists agree that the RIFA is here to stay. The fate of the original, the black imported fire ant, is more precarious. It is under simultaneous attack from humans, from its close relative, and from a hybrid of the two bona fide species. Ironically, the BIFA may have paved the way for the success of the RIFA by being the first to deal with competing ants native to the southeastern United States (Lofgren et al. 1975).

There is also agreement among fire ant researchers about the mode of entry. Both insects arrived in Mobile, Alabama, by accident from South America, and by ship, though each species might have arrived on more than one occasion. The BIFA came ashore around 1918, the RIFA between 1933 and 1945 (Callcott and Collins 1996). It is interesting that the arrival time of the red imported species cannot be pinned down with greater precision. The ants were probably stowaways concealed in cargo or in ballast soil taken from a South American riverbank. If they were in ballast soil deep inside the hold of a ship, how could they possibly find their way ashore? Vinson (1997) offered a solution. Lightweight agricultural goods arrived from South America, and heavy machinery was loaded for the return trip, requiring removal of ballast soil from the vessel. Or perhaps the BIFA arrived with fruit (George 1958), and the RIFA arrived with a shipment of cattle (Trager 1991). Genetic evidence suggests that between five and fifteen mated RIFA queens made this initial landing (Schmidt 1995), and there may have been multiple invasion episodes (Ross et al. 1985). There is another mystery here. Why did two kinds of fire ants disembark in Mobile while never invading other Gulf ports during these early years, especially the much larger cities of Houston and New Orleans?

Clandestine entry is not always the case with exotic insect pests. The gypsy moth was brought into the United States on purpose, with the intention of producing caterpillar silk commercially. Its escape and subsequent defoliation of native forests was accidental, and it remains a pest 130 years later. The Africanized "killer bee," like the RIFA, came to the southern United States from Brazil by accident, but the bees journeyed slowly, overland, and without further human assistance. Their original introduction into Brazil from Africa in 1956 was a conscious effort to increase honey production. The values of these and all other insects are thus in the eyes of the beholder. I develop this theme for the fire ants in chapter 13.

At least one student of the RIFA has wondered whether it will take a thief to catch a thief—effective biocontrol might require the introduction of even more exotic ants, perhaps as many as thirty different kinds, preferably species that do not sting and that are not pests in their own right. Together they would outcompete the red imported fire ant (Buren 1983). This is a daring proposal, and one can imagine how at least some environmentalists would react. Yet it might succeed. And it is important to remember that *native* is usually a relative term. For example, the Native Americans of the modern United States are descendants of Asian immigrants who arrived long before the Europeans who displaced them. Evolution's legacy is a history of colonizations, conflicts, successions, and environmental disturbances, beginning millions of years before humans came onto the scene. Clearly alterations of native ecosystems by new arrivals are not intrinsically bad.

Before treating the two imported fire ant species individually, I use the early ignorance of their separate identities to advantage by drawing upon those reports for a general introduction to imported fire ant (IFA) biology as witnessed by those who studied them first. The reports are historically important and they set the stage for what follows.

The first extensive publication on the IFA to appear in a major North American journal dealt with both species unknowingly (Lyle and Fortune 1948). The ants were once again identified as *Solenopsis saevissima* var. *richteri*. This name was widely used early on for the two species that eventually became known separately as the BIFA and the RIFA. *Solenopsis saevissima* is now recognized as a valid species but as of this writing it is found only in South America. The other two species were considered in these early days to be a mere variety of *S. saevissima,* much like a race or subspecies.

Lyle and Fortune discovered that imported fire ant mounds grew to heights and widths of three feet. The interior was hard and honeycombed. Each colony remained close to the top of its mound in winter but moved below with the arrival of summer's heat. Brood (eggs, larvae, pupae) were moved about inside the mound to keep up with changes in soil water level, and colonies nested near a source of water, mostly in low-lying areas. The ants preferred meat to carbohydrates, but tended mealybugs (the sugar-rich excretions of which are also a source of carbohydrate), and in the southern part of Mississippi, fire ants (possibly the RIFA) destroyed a cornfield by eating the embryos within the seeds. Citrus trees were damaged and newborn livestock were killed; this last contention became one of many controversies. Painful stings made potato harvesting so miserable that laborers refused to enter the fields. The net result of all this trouble was a program of eradication begun by the State of Mississippi, when some of the first pesticides used against imported fire ants included DDT, chlordane, toxaphene, and a substance with the ominous name of 666 (gamma benzene hexachloride). Chlordane was particularly effective.

Lyle and Fortune's seminal paper was followed one year later by a report dealing more extensively with control efforts (Eden and Arant 1949). The earliest damage known to the authors occurred in 1935, when the IFA attacked a cornfield adjacent to Mobile Bay, and it had reached Florida by the time their paper appeared. Young plants and germinating seeds were killed by foraging ants. Mound-building activity was at its seasonal height from May to July, and the hard nest structures damaged farm machinery in the fields. Alabama began dealing with the invader as early as 1937, using cyanogas and labor from the Works Progress Administration (WPA). State prisoners lent a hand in 1949 when DDT, toxaphene, benzene hexachloride, aldrin, dieldrin, and chlordane were used. All of these pesticides became infamous.

In the same year, an extremely young E. O. Wilson, who eventually became the world authority on ants in general, became one of the first to publish on the IFA (Wilson and Eads 1949). This important study was undertaken for the Alabama Department of Conservation and is very difficult to find. I have seen the original report complete with photos of mounds, the small black-and-white prints still in their little frame pockets (figs. 2.1, 2.2), and I have photographed specimens collected by Wilson at that time. The authors were able to distinguish a black "ecotype" and a red one. Nest tunnels or galleries of these IFAs extended to a depth exceeding five feet. The insects tended pine scales, aphids, and mealybugs for their honeydew excretions (fig. 2.3), and they constructed protective soil shelters over their "cows." Surprising items in the omnivorous diet included leaves of ash trees, fertilizer, and soiled clothing.

Fiery aggression, voracious feeding, and prolific nest building combined to make the invader a pest of cotton, potatoes, cucumbers, pecans, cantaloupes, tomatoes, okra, beans, peas, cabbage, rutabagas, collards, fruit trees, and pastures. Calves and piglets were killed, and bee colonies were destroyed overnight. Yet Wilson and Eads were among the first to recognize that imported fire ants have a beneficial side. The accidental introductions were killing boll weevils in the cotton fields, and nursery stock growing from mounds seemed healthier than stock not growing from mounds (fig. 2.2).

Additional benefits were identified by Hays (1959). Mound construction aids the turnover, formation, and aeration of soil. In this capacity the

Fig. 2.1. Pine seedling growing from an imported fire ant mound. Near Stockton, Alabama, April 13, 1949. Courtesy of Dr. E. O. Wilson.

Fig. 2.2. Nursery stock growing from an imported fire ant mound. Near Phillipsville, Alabama, April 12, 1949. Courtesy of Dr. E. O. Wilson.

Fig. 2.3. Imported fire ants tending aphids on a plant. Reprinted from Vinson and Sorensen 1986. By permission of the senior author and Texas Department of Agriculture.

work of fire ants resembles that of the earthworms. Water channeling into nest tunnels replenishes the water table and is drawn upon by plants; the effect also helps prevent erosion. Much later, Herzog et al. (1976) discovered that IFA colonies alter the chemistry of soil. Phosphorus and alkalinity are high in the mound area whereas organic matter is reduced. Even more recently, it has been shown that Mississippi mounds are higher in clay, phosphorus, and potassium than is the adjacent soil. These same mounds have less organic matter and sulfur than the soil nearby, and the soil dries out more rapidly than uninfested soil (Green et al. 1998, 1999). The authors believe that entire landscapes might be altered as colonies grow and move about. Whether this is seen as a beneficial change will depend upon the attitude of the landowners.

Focus shifted at least temporarily from natural history and control to an evolutionary viewpoint emphasizing the existence of a black form *and* a red form (Wilson 1951): "During the spring survey of 1949 there was observed an unusual amount of variability in color from nest to nest." Wilson noticed the red form as early as 1942, in the Mobile area, and was perhaps the first to do so. This paper launched the incipient sorting process culminating twenty-one years later in the recognition of two distinct species, the RIFA and the BIFA (Buren 1972). During the early period of investigation, Wilson recognized six worker color-types ranging from dark to light, though all males were black, and he concluded that the red form had either originated from South America, like the black form, or arisen in the United States as a mutation from the black form. For the time being he favored the mutation origin, though his position soon reversed to the second-introduction theory, at which time he also predicted that temperature would ultimately be more important than moisture for the expansion of the fire ants in North America (Wilson 1953). The red form's introduced populations existed in densities as high as seventy mounds per acre, and it had already pushed the dark form to the edges of the IFA range. Native ants, including the southern fire ant, the tropical fire ant, and the Florida harvester ant, were becoming scarce where the fire ant was abundant. The dark form built the largest mounds, sometimes covering them with vegetation, charcoal, or pebbles. Wilson noted something else that became a topic of intense research decades later: IFA colonies sometimes adopt queens from outside the nest. He found that chilling the workers beforehand increased the chance of successful adoption. The IFA had entered Louisiana and Georgia by the time of this important publication.

The unexpected hardiness of South American fire ants in northern climes was demonstrated in nearby Mississippi when colonies survived winter freezes, though many individuals died and were later piled up outside the mound in masses by surviving nestmates (Green 1959). I want to emphasize that freezing temperatures were recorded in the area. Ants that happened to freeze probably died as a result. Green discovered a chain reaction of events that exacerbated winter mortality. When an early frost killed plants that would otherwise have reinforced the integrity of the mound, the structure collapsed and the ants near the top of the nest died. Green also believed (1967) that gallery-riddled mounds provided protection against cold because they were filled with insulating air, though later writers suggested the opposite—that they are drafty, and hence a liability rather than a benefit (Francke et al. 1986). It would be interesting to test these conflicting ideas at the northern limit of the RIFA's range, where the cold winters kill off colonies that are not sheltered by windbreaks. Either way, activity stopped well above freezing, at 48°F (Hays 1959). Such temperatures caused the ants to cluster around the queen (Hays and Hays 1959). Green discovered a waxy lining of the galleries that could function as waterproofing, and he found colony waste heaps outside the mound. These are known to myrmecologists as kitchen middens. Middens were often found in a depression on the south side of the mound.

A preference for insect prey over crops and other vegetation was inferred from an early Alabama study (Hays and Hays 1959). In fact, imported fire ants chose cannibalism over a diet that offered nothing but plant tissue. Insects alive or dead were found to be fair game, and prey were often eaten outside the nest. Nevertheless, seeds, including those of pine and peanut, were collected and eaten. Some seeds were carried to the mound overland, but presumably there was much traffic well out of sight, within the subterranean tunnels that are so characteristic of fire ant nests. Storage cells within the mound contained food or even living termites. One mound contained cells filled with disemboweled weevils. Fly larvae were found to be a favored food, and apple-infesting aphids were tended even under laboratory conditions.

The effect of fire ants on native bird populations became another topic of controversy, this time embracing the "native" tropical fire ant as well. Chicks were killed by the IFA when blood exposed during the hatching process attracted foragers. Their thief ant relatives were already known to kill hatchling bluebirds while the parents fluttered about without helping their young (Hays and Hays 1959; Laskey 1940).

The chemicals that attract IFAs to feed upon their prey were found to be of the lipid or fatty type (Vinson et al. 1967). Different fatty acids stimulate very different responses. Soybean oil (from plants, of course) is so attractive to fire ants that it became the standard attractant for poisoned baits. Yet objects containing oleic acid or palmitic acid were carried to the trash heap as though they were dead workers. Soybean oil was therefore a "phagostimulant" (feeding stimulant) whereas the other two were stimulants of "necrophoresis" (carrying of the dead). Oil was found to be a bigger part of the IFA diet than either protein or sugar. Larvae received the greatest amount, adult males the smallest amount (Vinson 1968). This is no surprise, for ants do not grow once they assume their familiar adult form, and males have a limited (though important) use to the colony.

Early experimental work on the sensory organs of the IFA did turn up one surprise. This insect was found to be sensitive to red light as well as ultraviolet (Marak and Wolken 1965), an unexpected result because the honey bee cannot see red, nor is it common for other insects to see in this part of our visible spectrum (Borror et al. 1989). Though the IFA was said to have small eyes for an ant (Wilson 1962), it reportedly can learn to find food in a maze without relying on the chemical cues so important to ants in seemingly every activity (Stratton and Coleman 1973). The "Glagolewa-Arkadiewa mass IR radiator" device demonstrated the RIFA's ability to detect light beyond the reaches of our own visible spectrum. This includes infrared, which is detected with the ant's antennae (Callahan 1971). Tested individuals moved their appendages vigorously when the switch was thrown.

Imported fire ant reproduction and development is understandably a major topic of research, and this is an opportune time to explain certain terms that can be otherwise confusing. Each adult female is either a sterile, wingless worker or a reproductively capable queen or "gyne." Queens start out with wings and are known at this point as unmated or virgin queens. They shed their wings after mating in the air with a winged male and become fertile queens that often begin a nest of their own. Early studies reported a simultaneous nest exit for the winged males and winged females as they embarked upon the nuptial flight (Fincher and Lund 1967). Later studies conflict with this generalization, allowing the males an earlier exit (e.g., Vinson 1986). After mating, the queen lays about twenty eggs within two days.

The adults of the queen's first brood are all workers and are smaller than those of all later broods. They are known as minims. Unmated sexual females sometimes shed their wings and begin laying male eggs even if they never fly in a nuptial swarm. This phenomenon discovered by Fincher and Lund (1967) stimulated much later research.

IFA development (presumably for workers in this case) required a total of from three to four weeks. The queen carried her brood about in a clump produced by a sticky saliva coating (Green 1967). The youngest larvae hatched from the egg in about nine days, spent the same amount of time as larvae outside the egg, and completed the pupal period in about a week. At this time they emerged as adults (Wilson 1958). Males often took twice as long to develop into adults as did workers. Green reported that queens occasionally left their incipient nests.

The nuptial or mating flights of the IFA serve a dual purpose, for this is one natural mechanism that reduces competition between nests, a mode of dispersal facilitated along the Gulf Coast by southerly winds prevailing during the nuptial flight season (Green 1967). Northerly winds would have blown the reproductives out to sea instead. For example, Cat Island, seven miles off the Mississippi shore, was infested by a flight from the mainland, and a queen landed on a fishing boat six miles away (Markin et al. 1971). Queens also disperse by landing on the surface of moving waters (Morrill 1974b). In this manner, and via overland flights, the range of the invader increased by about six miles per year (Markin et al. 1971; Vander Meer 1996). Humans have since taken to the air after them, using airplanes and special infra-red film to spot fire ant mounds from the air (Anonymous 1978). Another dispersal mechanism is the formation of a ball of floating ants during floods (fig. 2.4). Floating colonies were seen on the Alabama River as early as 1957 (Hays 1959). Hays believed that colony juveniles

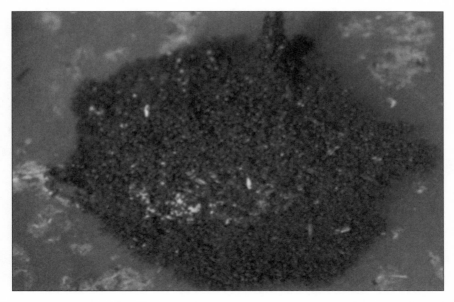

Fig. 2.4. Red imported fire ants dispersing during a flood as a mass of floating adults and brood. Reprinted from Vinson and Sorensen 1986. By permission of the senior author and Texas Department of Agriculture.

were abandoned when this happened, though the tropical fire ant maintains and protects its brood within these living balls when riding out the storm (Wheeler 1910). A floating ball has two obvious adaptations—the trapped air provides buoyancy and the rotation of the ball prevents any individual ant from spending too much time underwater (Rhoades 1977).

IFA colonies were known to abandon their mound for no apparent reason. The queen and her brood were seen in the train of ants streaming along the ground, where there was no sign of stored food being taken in tow (Hays and Hays 1959). In a more recent South Carolina study, most observed RIFA colonies moved several times over a three-year period. The cause was again unknown (Hays et al. 1982). One colony moved a mere four feet over the course of twenty-four hours (Favorite 1958). Queens of the polygyne social type (see glossary and chapter 8) disperse to begin nests of their own by simply leaving the colony in an overland march with a contingent of workers. This is dispersal by a kind of "budding" that calls to mind the asexual reproduction of yeasts or protozoa. Wilson (1962) never saw workers transporting nestmates from one point to another. Yet this is a common behavior for some species of ants.

Early on it was discovered that people extend the range of fire ants by transporting infested nursery stock (Wilson and Brown 1958). This is responsible for modern spot-infestations discovered from time to time well outside the southeastern United States, from Los Angeles to Virginia. It was also responsible for much of the early spread because the Mobile area happens to be famous for its azaleas and camellias (Green 1967). The red imported fire ant queen's habit of seeking areas near reflective surfaces (e.g., a body of water) when landing after a mating flight causes unknowing dispersal in the protective beds of pickup trucks where water sometimes collects (Vinson 1997). Transport on the surfaces of cars and trucks was blamed for an infestation at Fort Benning, Georgia in 1956. Most of the sting victims were small children who thought they were playing with sand piles (Olive 1960).

CHAPTER 3   The Red Imported Fire Ant

(Solenopsis invicta)

Eradication is not a viable alternative.

—*Official position of the Texas Agricultural
Experiment Station* (1998)

WHAT is now called the red imported fire ant
became known to science in the early years of the
twentieth century when E. R. Wagner collected the
first specimens in Argentina (Santschi 1916, p. 380).
Felix Santschi never considered the creature to be
anything more than a variety of the well-known species *Solenopsis saevissima*. He therefore named it *Solenopsis saevissima* variety *wagneri* in honor of the
collector. More than half a century later, W. F. Buren
was studying the red form of the fire ant accidentally introduced into the United States when he de-
cided that it was a completely different species from
the black form. So he christened it *Solenopsis invicta*
(Buren 1972), unaware that Santschi had already
named the RIFA. A typographical error gave hint
of what was to come—the fire ant's second, super-
fluous name was misspelled in Buren's paper as *in-
vica*. For twenty-three years the oversight went unnoticed while *Solenopsis invicta* went on to become
one of the most widely used binomials in the world of
entomology. Bolton (1995) eventually corrected the
error and dropped *Solenopsis invicta* Buren in favor of

25

Solenopsis wagneri Santschi, according to the rule of priority. Nevertheless, *invicta* has its advantages, and I will adopt it here. The name is euphonious, it means "unconquered," and it is well entrenched by decades of constant usage. Many specialists prefer to keep the newer name.

As already noted in the discussion of the early days of the invasion, Edward O. Wilson recognized the presence of a red fire ant in the United States three decades before Buren's paper was published (fig. 3.1). This was in the summer of 1942, in a vacant lot in Alabama, and it led to his first formal work on ants (Wilson 1994). At the time, Wilson suspected that the red form was a mutation of the black imported fire ant, but he later came to believe that it was a light-colored variant of a well-known South American species and that its presence in North America was due to a second introduction (Wilson 1952). He did not suggest that the red form was a previously unrecognized species, as Buren would propose two decades later. Whether mutant, second introduction, or species new to science, the RIFA was hybridizing extensively with the black form even then, and the BIFA, TFA, and SFA were all being extirpated by the advance of the newest invader (Wilson and Brown 1958). Later work showed that these North American red imported fire ants did not come from the Argentine region where Wagner had made the original collection of the species. Chemical analysis indicated their homeland as the Cáceras region of southwestern Brazil (Vander Meer and Lofgren 1990).

Nesting Sites

The Brazilian RIFA came ashore in a cultivated and urbanized southeastern United States, which had been a forest only a few hundred years earlier. Native ants are not as well adapted to cleared areas and other disturbances produced by humans. The fire ant was and is able to dominate these altered habitats (Buren 1972; Stiles and Jones 1998), though it also does well in the other extreme of South American rain forest (Trager 1991). Its nesting tolerance probably explains why it was able to make passage in a ship in the first place. For these reasons the RIFA can be described as a "weedy" animal (Tschinkel 1986). Weeds reproduce early in life, have high reproductive rates and efficient dispersal, and colonize and dominate disturbed habitats. Human disturbances favoring the spread of the RIFA include clear-cutting, road building, and urbanization in general. Tschinkel summed up this comparison to weeds by noting that "man is the fire ant's greatest friend, even though the sentiment may not be returned."

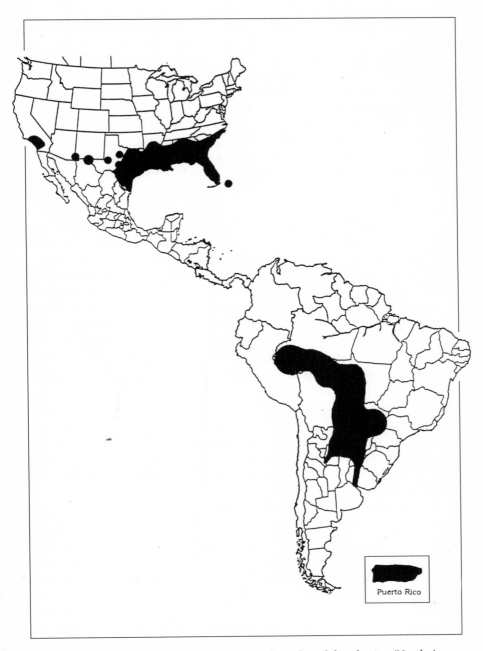

Fig. 3.1. The natural range (South America) and accidental distribution (North America) of the red imported fire ant.

When RIFA nests are found in disturbed and developed forested areas, such as certain state parks, they are especially abundant along roadsides and trails and near buildings. The tropical fire ant is then found deeper in the woods, having been pushed aside by a superior competitor. Tschinkel has seen this phenomenon in Florida and I have seen it among the loblolly pines of Central Texas.

Commercial orchard development requires disturbance of a different kind from that experienced when clearings are made in naturally forested regions. In this case the native vegetation is cleared away to make room for trees that, like the troublesome ant, are imported from elsewhere. Citrus growers are all too aware of the RIFA's tendency to build nests where tree trunks rise from the soil (Banks et al. 1991).

Pastures are favorite targets for newly mated RIFA queens. Colony densities in Georgia pastures average about twenty-seven per acre (Diffie and Bass 1994). A single acre of recently disturbed land can harbor more than a thousand colonies (Lofgren et al. 1975). In the sugarcane fields of Louisiana the RIFA prefers weedy soil rich in clay (Ali et al. 1986), but it will tolerate sand (Wangberg et al. 1980; pers. obs.). Some fire ant nesting sites are nearly unbelievable. On one occasion a queen and her eggs were discovered inside an insectivorous pitcher plant (Vogt 1996). She made her nest there atop the piled remains of the plant's insect prey. This could easily end in disaster for an incipient ant colony, though wasps and some other insects do nest safely in pitcher plants.

When nesting indoors the RIFA will crawl into drawers, boxes, and walls or under rugs and will even invade personal computers, bringing soil in every case (Vinson 1997). Outdoors the ant has been known to nest in boats floating at dock (Arkansas Cooperative Extension Service 1998). The titleholder for extreme tolerance was a colony living on a Florida sandbar: that nest was covered twice a day by tides (Rhoades 1977).

In its native South America we might expect to find the primitive preferences of the RIFA. Natural nesting sites in the Brazilian state of Mato Grosso are limited to moist or protected areas, including soil, logs, and the nests of termites. But here too the fire ants take up residence with humans in the walls of their homes (Allen et al. 1974), and they are common enough along roadsides on both continents. The RIFA does seem less abundant on a local scale in its primeval home than in the recently infested areas of the United States (Gilbert 1996), where fire ant densities are about five times as high as in South America (Porter et al. 1997a). Reasons for this difference, which may seem surprising at first, are given in discussion of the fire ant's natural enemies (chapter 12).

Fig. 3.2. Red imported fire ant mounds. *Left:* In the wild, with beverage container for scale. (Reprinted from Vinson and Sorensen 1986. By permission of the senior author and the Texas Department of Agriculture.) *Below:* On the University of Texas campus, with numerous exit holes indicative of a coming nuptial flight. The ruler is six inches long.

The Nest

Only the fire ant's sting is more famous than its mound (figs. 1.7, 3.2, 3.3). The mound is an above-ground portion of the nest that allows the brood to be moved about in order to track temperatures and humidities suitable for their development. Nest size, shape, and internal anatomy depend upon soil type and vegetation. Clay soils allow mounds to reach heights and widths exceeding three feet. A hard outer crust encases the structure over time. Its interior becomes riddled with galleries and chambers (fig. 3.4), and a mirror image of the cone-shaped edifice develops well

Fig. 3.3. Large RIFA mounds dotting a pasture in Central Texas.

Fig. 3.4. The honeycombed interior of a sun-baked red imported fire ant mound.

below ground. Galleries or tunnels can occupy more than half of the total volume, so that a mound can be said to be mostly air (Tschinkel 1993a). Some colonies have more than one mound and are described as "poly-domic" or "polycalic" because of the satellite structures, which alternate between periods of activity and inactivity (Hays et al. 1982; Hölldobler and

Fig. 3.5. The partially covered foraging trail of a red imported fire ant colony.

Wilson 1990). Ants leaving the nest to forage and those returning with food
are not as conspicuous as one might expect because much of their movement is through horizontal subterranean tunnels lying within one half
inch of the surface (fig. 3.5). In this respect their behavior is like that of
certain army ants.

Each RIFA mound has several main, horizontal tunnels radiating up to
one hundred feet into the surrounding area. These in turn have smaller side
branches with openings reaching to the soil surface. There are vertical tunnels too, some plunging six feet or more to the water table (Lofgren et al.
1975; Vinson and Sorensen 1986; Markin et al. 1973).

Casual observers seldom notice the beginnings of a red imported fire
ant nest. This occurs when a recently mated queen or queens (up to five in
a group) begin digging a vertical tunnel in the soil to a depth of about three
inches. A cell or chamber is constructed at each end. Within one day the
entrance will be closed from the inside and the queen or queens will begin
laying eggs in isolation from the rest of the world (Markin et al. 1972). This
behavior is called "claustral founding." Within three years such a nest can
grow from a tiny burrow to a mound roughly one foot high and two feet
wide at the base. A special caliper was devised to measure these physical dimensions (Morrill 1976b). The combined volume of visible mound and subterranean nest eventually grows to about ten gallons (Markin et al. 1973).

In Brazil, mounds are smallest in the dry season, largest in the wet season, and generally not as large as in the United States. Roughly one quarter of these are found to be abandoned at any given time (Wojcik 1986).

RIFA mounds in the area of Tallahassee, Florida, were found to be oval in shape and oriented in a particular way with respect to the directions of the compass. The long axis of the oval was oriented in a north-south direction, allowing the mound to warm up more efficiently beneath the sun's rays (Hubbard and Cunningham 1977). If the heat is too intense, as in the hottest part of summer, mounds are sometimes entirely absent because the ants cool off by retreating into the depths of the soil and do not maintain the structure. Changing seasons or substantial rains will signal the return of mound-building activity (Bartlett and Lofgren 1961; pers. obs.)

Nest Population

The maximum colony size of about 220,000 workers can be reached five years after a nest is begun by a queen or queens (Tschinkel 1988b). Males and sexual females (the mated queens and especially the virgin queens) often comprise nearly half of the colony's weight, though only about 4,500 sexuals are produced each year (Tschinkel 1986). Other fire ant specialists estimate maximum colony sizes of 260,000 (Lofgren et al. 1975), or even 400,000 (Vinson 1997). Under ideal conditions in the laboratory, the RIFA society can approach this size in a mere three months (Vargo 1990). The variation among these estimates may reflect the existence of the two social forms of this species (see chapter 8). Polygyne colonies do have the potential to grow larger than monogyne colonies.

There are about as many males as sexual females in a given population of nests, so that the total sex ratio is 1 : 1 sexual female to male, but each colony tends to produce more of one sex than the other. Texas populations of the polygyne social form have female-biased ratios that could be explained if workers assassinate excess males, as some other social insects are known to do (Bhatkar 1990). The sex ratio would be enormously biased in favor of females if the hordes of sterile workers were included in the calculations.

Foraging Behavior

Foraging, or searching for food, ranks with nest founding as one of the most dangerous jobs a fire ant can undertake. It requires brutal exposure to enemies and the elements and is reserved exclusively for the oldest members of the worker caste. Indeed, no more than one-fifth of the colony's workers are engaged in this activity at any given time (Tschinkel 1986). They use their famous sting to subdue prey, to kill or discourage enemies that interfere with their work, and to lay a chemical trail back to the nest when a windfall is discovered that is too large for one hunter to handle. As dedicated as the RIFA forager is, she returns home with food on only one half of the trips she makes into the world outside (Tennant and Porter 1991).

Queens never forage, and the colony's first foragers will be the adults of the first brood. These are the smallest workers the colony will ever produce, and they begin their all-important task several days after reaching adulthood (Markin et al. 1972). Future workers, those of later broods, must progress through a series of stay-at-home employments before passing into the final, foraging phase of their lives.

Outgoing ants leave the nest through subterranean tunnels and enter these once again upon their return. They hunt alone unless they are part of a recruitment party, as discussed later (Lofgren et al. 1975). Such behaviors are unlike those of many familiar ants native to the United States (e.g., harvester ants) in that fire ant foragers do not necessarily travel in the open along conspicuous surface trails, nor do they leave and enter the nest through a conspicuous hole in the mound (Zakharov and Thompson 1998b).

E. O. Wilson (1962) was among the first to describe foraging behavior in detail. The insect walks in loops as part of its exploratory strategy. If a manageable item is encountered, the ant picks it up or drinks it and returns immediately to the nest. If there is more food than the forager can handle on its own, it must lay a chemical trail back to the nest so that others might follow. Trail layers move slowly, keeping the body close to the ground while swinging the front end from side to side. The chemical being applied from the sting to the substrate is the "recruitment pheromone" of the Dufour's gland, located in the ant's abdomen. The pygidial gland may be a second source of the same substance (Billen 1990). The sting touches the ground only occasionally during this operation, though trail layers can amplify the result by backtracking on their own work. Sometimes trails are protected with a roofing of soil. There is disagreement about the information conveyed by the recruitment pheromone. According to the earliest reports, the trail indicates food position but not quality or quantity. Later reports attributed more to the trail than just positional information. In any event, the ant can be forced to run in a circle by painting that geometric shape onto a surface with the substance of Dufour's gland (Wilson 1962).

It is not known how these pioneers find their own way back to the nest. Perhaps they rely on vision (Vander Meer 1986a), though other possibilities exist. Some papers report that the RIFA is attracted to electric and magnetic fields (Vinson and MacKay 1990; MacKay et al. 1992a, b; Anderson and Vander Meer 1993; Slowik et al. 1997b). Other papers dispute this in one way or another (Slowik et al. 1996; Klotz et al. 1997b). Iron particles have been located inside the bodies of fire ants (Slowik and Thorvilson 1996; Anderson and Vander Meer 1993; Esquivel et al. 1999), and honey bees and monarch butterflies do possess internal magnetic material thought to aid in navigation (Slowik et al. 1997a). But the apparent attraction of fire ants to electric fields may be explained by chemical attraction instead. It seems that foragers occasionally cause short circuits in electrical wiring when looking for food, and as they die they release alarm chemicals that attract their nestmates to the scene (Slowik et al. 1996). One person was killed when a fire started after such an incident (Brenner et al. 1994). Research was under way in 1999 to develop an electrical device that would prevent fire ants from damaging more conventional equipment nearby.

A farnesene chemical and a homosesquiterpene named C-1 are among the components of the Dufour's gland secretion (Vander Meer et al. 1990). About 200,000 workers—roughly the population of a mature nest—were steam-distilled, and from about one gallon of this raw material came a mere two milliliters of secretion (Walsh et al. 1965). One teaspoon could be used to paint a functional trail two millimeters wide that would circle the earth five thousand times (Vander Meer 1996). Components of the glandular secretion have been synthesized in the laboratory (Alvarez et al. 1987).

Various chemicals alone or in combination draw the recruited ant to the trail, make it receptive to following the trail, and stimulate it to proceed along the trail. More specifically, the three phases have been described as: (1) attraction of the recruited ant (by farnesene and an unidentified sesquiterpene), (2) "orientation induction" (chemical stimulus unknown), and (3) orientation (by farnesene alone) (Vander Meer et al. 1990).

The farther the food is from the mound, the greater the recruitment rate to it (Horton et al. 1975), though much of this activity occurs out of sight within the tunnels. The colony's foraging area in some regions is greater at night than during the day. For example, foraging in Texas is said to occur mostly after dark. This might be partly driven by the fact that daytime heat occasionally kills hunters that are caught in rising temperatures while looking for food (Claborn et al. 1988). Yet the schedule does vary with habitat. Foraging in soybean fields can be more intense during the day than during the night (Kidd and Apperson 1984). The greatest activity seems to occur when the tunnels are between 70°F and 97°F, though it continues as long as temperatures remain between 50°F and 109°F (Porter and Tschin-

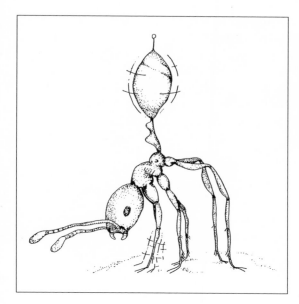

Fig. 3.6. A gaster-flagging red imported fire ant worker, with a droplet of venom at the tip of the sting. Reprinted from Obin and Vander Meer 1985. By permission of the senior author and Plenum Publishing Corporation.

kel 1987). Seasons also have their effects. Foraging occurs to some extent through fall and winter, though rain inhibits workers from doing their job (Markin et al. 1974c; Porter and Tschinkel 1987).

There is a definite foraging territory around the mound where other fire ants are not tolerated (Wilson et al. 1971). Territories in weedy sugarcane fields change in size every day and are smaller than territories elsewhere because the weeds provide excellent hunting grounds (Showler et al. 1989). Territories of the monogyne social form (see chapter 8) can now be estimated by simply calculating the volume of the mound (Tschinkel et al. 1995). To drive competing ants away from a food source, foragers raise their abdomens, extrude the sting, and vibrate it until venom is dispersed directly into the air (Obin and Vander Meer 1985), as shown in figure 3.6.

All in all, the red imported fire ant is surely an ardent forager (fig. 3.7). Bait set down in infested areas is usually discovered within ten minutes (MacKay et al. 1994; pers. obs.). Workers of one colony brought back more than fifty items per hour (Wilson and Oliver 1969), and during tests of the effectiveness of a chemical to be used against the RIFA, workers built bridges of sand over treated paper to reach their food (Troisi and Riddiford 1974). The ants have no problem entering fresh dung to get the maggots within (Hu and Frank 1996), and they will climb at least thirty feet into the heights of pecan trees to collect aphid excretions that have fallen onto the leaves (Tedder et al. 1990), though in soybean fields they do spend more

Fig. 3.7. Red imported fire ants subduing a pestiferous corn ear-worm caterpillar *(Heliothis zea)*. Reprinted from Vinson and Sorensen 1986. By permission of the senior author and Texas Department of Agriculture.

time on the soil than on the plants themselves (Kidd and Apperson 1984). The ants hunt below ground on the roots of crops (Smittle et al. 1983), and they defend above-ground nectaries from other insects (McLain 1983). When foraging in cotton, the RIFA sometimes builds mud shelters over its boll weevil prey (Agnew and Sterling 1981). Ticks are also processed in a distinctive fashion. The legs of blood-engorged females are first bitten off, and when recruited workers show up, the team eats the blood and viscera, leaving only a shell behind (Fleetwood et al. 1984). Stranger still, the remains are sometimes buried (Harris and Burns 1972). This may be a response to a chemical repellent produced by the tick (see chapter 12). Yet the RIFA is not so impressive when its foraging abilities are compared to those of an equal number of ants of certain native North American species (Phillips et al. 1986a).

One might ask how it is that only workers search for food when the nest commonly has thousands of queens and males at the ready. The reasons are anatomical and behavioral. First, every forager must possess the all-important sting apparatus (which served an original and entirely different function in some distant ancestor—the laying of eggs). Second, this tool must be used in both offense and defense. The male of course lacks a sting and would be worse than useless if the colony wasted resources in the production of ill-equipped hunters. The queen, being a female, does have a sting, and one might imagine her employing it as the worker does. But she does not (Vinson and Sorensen 1986). She has very different uses for it, all or at least most of them applied only within the confines of the nest. These functions are described later in this chapter. The versatility of the fire ant's sting is nearly as impressive as its power in the defensive role so familiar to our own species.

Diet

There has been much confusion about the diet of the red imported fire ant. Some early authors believed that plants were never eaten. The animal was supposedly entirely or mostly carnivorous. Part of the misconception was due to the fact that foraging fire ants often collect liquids from animals or plants, rather than a solid fragment that can be easily seen in their jaws. That is, they commonly drink their prey in the field (Tennant and Porter 1991). This behavior is evident from a swollen abdomen, which betrays the presence of a filled crop within. It is hard to know just what has been collected if it cannot be seen from the outside. Yet an early study of the RIFA queen's digestive tract provided evidence that the diet was indeed largely liquid. Her pharynx is built like a muscular sucking organ (Walker and Clower 1961). That fire ants do feed by extracting the liquid from their prey was demonstrated in a dramatic fashion by the reduction of a hard-boiled egg to dry powder within a few hours (Rhoades 1977).

It seems best to describe the RIFA as omnivorous, and the foragers themselves as more scavengers than predators (Young 1984). The insect utilizes an enormous variety of animal, plant, and even fungal and bacterial food (Vinson 1972; Jouvenaz et al. 1996). Because this activity is responsible for much of the species' economic importance, I treat it in more detail in chapter 13. The following examples suffice to indicate the breadth of the diet: tree leaves, bark, nectar, sap, fruit, roots, stems, leaves, herbaceous plants, and birds (Adams 1986); insects and other arthropods (Reagan 1986); reptiles (Whiting 1994); insect excretions (Tennant and Porter 1991); and even mammals (Mitchell et al. 1996; Scott et al. 1987). Mammals are usually scavenged but are killed when the ants are able to do so.

Favored insect prey include springtails, beetle grubs, and termites (Tennant and Porter 1991; Waller and La Fage 1986a). Fire ants eat their own kind too, including their own nestmates and a variety of materials produced by nestmates. Larvae and eggs are cannibalized (Voss et al. 1988; Vinson 1997), as are dying adults (O'Neal and Markin 1973), and dead queens are eaten by living ones (Tschinkel 1993b). Cast-aside skins and anal excretions are recycled in the same way (O'Neal and Markin 1973). The larvae eat trophic (inviable) eggs produced by the queen for just this purpose. Such eggs cannot develop into ants in any event because they have abnormal mitosis spindle fibers that lead to the destruction of their own gene-bearing chromosomes (Voss et al. 1987). Also on the larval diet are regurgitated secretions from the newly mated queen. These are the breakdown products of flight muscles that are no longer useful once she sheds her wings and begins laying eggs (Markin et al. 1972).

The RIFA colony requires the nutrients found in its natural insect prey if it is to produce brood in the lab. A combination of sugar and insects was found to be better than typical artificial diets (Porter 1989), though lab colonies survive on a mixture of honey, water, fly pupae, ground beef, eggs, and vitamins (Williams et al. 1980b). The worker caste can get by on sugar water alone, and workers prefer this to amino acids. Larvae have more exacting requirements and a preference for amino acids over sugar (Cassill and Tschinkel 1999b). When they are raised without insects in their diet, their adult exoskeletons are soft and so transparent that food can be seen moving through the gut. They are abnormally light in weight and their stingers are too soft and flexible to penetrate human skin (Williams et al. 1987b).

In Brazil as in North America, arthropods are the preferred food of the red imported fire ant, though rice grains and other seeds are collected and stored within the mound before consumption (Wojcik 1986). When eating seeds such as those of corn and sorghum the ants generally prefer the embryo itself to the carbohydrate-rich endosperm (Drees et al. 1991). Investigators discovered that carbohydrate bait is preferred over protein in cool seasons but that the converse obtains during warmer times of the year (Stein et al. 1990). Foragers can detect nutrient shortages in the colony diet, and they alter their hunting strategies to compensate for the missing items (Sorensen et al. 1985b). The magnitude of all this feeding activity can be expressed by an estimate of the amount of food consumed by the ants of thirty-six mature RIFA mounds on a single acre of land. They consume thirty-five pounds of insects and sugar every week during the summer (Macom and Porter 1995). Yet there are some seeds, especially those of certain legumes, that are simply not acceptable to the ants (Ready and Vinson 1995).

Studies of the RIFA diet have yielded a few surprises. For example, symbiotic yeasts were discovered living within the bodies of the insects, where they probably provide some form of nutrition to their hosts (Ba and Phillips 1996), as certain bacteria are known to do within the human intestine by synthesizing important vitamins.

Sometimes the red imported fire ant's diet reveals a lighter side. One investigator came upon a band of normally nocturnal smokybrown cockroaches *(Periplaneta fuliginosa)* that were acting strangely in the broad light of day. Their bodies were vibrating and they were secreting defensive chemicals. Closer inspection revealed the cause of their alarm. They had been rousted from their hiding places by fire ants intent upon collecting their feces (Appel 1986).

Feeding Behavior

All colony members are able to eat liquids but only a select group of larvae can process solid foods. Liquids stored within the returning forager's crop are digested internally to some extent and then regurgitated to nestmates. Queens are also able to store food in the crop. A liquid diet is forced upon adult fire ants because they have a filter near the mouth that screens out particles larger than 0.88 micrometers. For comparison, a typical bacterium is about that size, and many are too large to enter the insect's digestive tract. Solids strained out by this sieve accumulate in a pocket and the resulting pellet is fed to the oldest larvae, which do not filter their food (Glancey et al. 1981).

Nutrients tend to become equally distributed among the adults because workers beg from one another until their crops are equally filled. The sharing of food by regurgitation in this way is called trophallaxis. Most of the protein brought into the nest is fed to the larvae and to the queen, though as noted, the only colony members able to process solids—protein or otherwise—are the oldest larvae. These are known as fourth instar larvae because they are in their fourth and last stage of larval development. Fourth instar larvae feed upon particles cradled in a special "food basket" (the praesaepium) located on the belly. While eating, the grub lies on its back and is curled into the shape of the letter C, resembling a sea otter with its shellfish dinner. Some of the food in the basket is of course used by the larva or eventually excreted. The remainder is returned to workers after further processing. For the larva to provide a worker with processed, digested food, two regurgitations are required: one to digest the solids lying on its belly-basket with its own enzymes, and a second to feed the worker with the imbibed results (Vinson and Sorensen 1986). At this point, at least three regurgitations are likely to have occurred since the food was collected outside the nest. Amino acids produced by older larvae from the breakdown of proteins are directed back to the queen via worker intermediates, and the more fourth instar larvae a colony has, the faster the queen can lay her eggs (Sorensen and Vinson 1982; Vinson 1986). Four digestive enzymes have been isolated from these grubs (Whitworth et al. 1998). The gene for one enzyme was cloned in hopes that chemical control of fire ants might someday target the species by inactivating it with an inhibitor molecule (Whitworth et al. 1999). In keeping with its unique ability to process solid food, the fourth instar grub and no other possesses hardened mandibles (Petralia and Vinson 1979). Fire ant larvae are big eaters but they never defecate until they reach the pupal stage because the front part of their gut is not connected with the back part until that time (Vinson 1997).

Younger larvae, those lying in a pile of eggs and brood, also receive regurgitated meals as part of their feeding regimen. When they receive food they seem to suck it from the nurse worker's mouth (Cassill and Tschinkel 1996). But they also fend for themselves when they "rotate their heads until they locate a trophic egg to eat" (Lofgren et al. 1975). These small larvae do not limit themselves to eggs that cannot hatch. They also devour embryonated eggs that might have developed into sisters and brothers (Vinson 1997). Mated queens can lay all three varieties of egg—trophic, female, and male—though they cease laying the food-egg as they age. Virgin queens usually, or perhaps always, lay only trophic and male eggs (Voss et al. 1988).

The relative abundances of the adult female castes being produced in the nest (workers and virgin queens) can dictate the feeding program for female larvae, so that the number of adult workers and queens can be adjusted. High-quality diets tend to channel female larvae into becoming queens. Because the sex of an ant is genetically determined, it cannot be changed by a simple alteration in the feeding program. Excess male larvae must be killed off by the workers (Vargo 1990; Vinson 1997).

The largest workers of the red imported fire ant colony seem to function as storage units like the famous "repletes" of the desert honeypot ants, only to a lesser degree. This was discovered when the large workers (known as "majors") were fed with a blue dye that they retained one full year later (Glancey et al. 1973b). Trophallaxis is known to occur between individuals of different nests. Foragers that have strayed from their own colony might be adopted in this way (Bhatkar 1979). It also seems that food can be exchanged on a very large scale indeed. This was concluded when dyed food buried inside one nest was discovered some time later in twenty-two nearby mounds (Lofgren et al. 1975). Or perhaps it was a single large polygyne colony. Multiple-queen (and multiple-mound) nests were just being discovered by fire ant researchers at the time of that report.

The complexities of RIFA feeding behavior require a great deal of interaction between colony members. Each larva must be contacted by workers nearly 120,000 times during its development, ten times as often as honey bee larvae are contacted by the caretakers of the hive (Cassill and Tschinkel 1995). It appears that, in general, small workers (known as "minors") tend to groom these larvae while large workers act as repletes. Medium-sized workers ("medias") seem to be more versatile in the range of their behaviors (Cassill and Tschinkel 1999a).

Communication

Communication among ants is largely chemical. One important chemical communicator is the trail or recruitment pheromone already discussed under "Foraging Behavior." A different kind of recruitment is elicited by the alarm pheromone. It summons the workers to defend individuals and the colony itself when these are attacked, it gathers them in the defense of food, and it encourages workers to protect the sexual forms when these leave the nest for the mating flight. The chemical structure of the alarm pheromone and even its gland of origin remained unclear at the time of this writing, though the mandibular glands are a likely source (Billen 1990; Vinson 1997). An early report on fire ant chemistry suggested Dufour's gland as the site of synthesis (Wilson 1962). Chain-reaction secretion of this chemical explains the massive sting response suffered almost immediately by humans who disturb a fire ant nest (Vinson and Sorensen 1986). Sometimes there is a display associated with alarm; workers can signal distress by raising the gaster (the rounded back end), and therefore the stinger at its tip, to a near-vertical position, a gesture called "gaster-flagging" (Wilson 1962). In the case of the alarm surrounding the mating flight, it is the winged sexuals that are largely responsible for secreting the chemical (Alonso and Vander Meer 1997).

It is fair to say that the nucleus of the colony is the queen and her ongoing reproductive functions. Communicatory chemicals play an enormous role here too. First, the queen must be recognized if she is to be tended

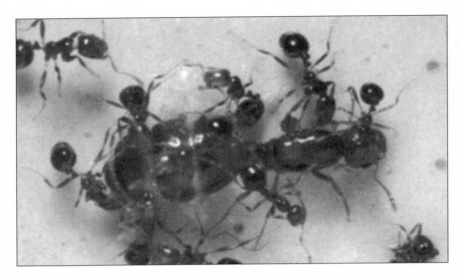

Fig. 3.8. Red imported fire ants tending the queen and brood of a monogyne colony. Reprinted from Vinson and Sorensen 1986. By permission of the senior author and Texas Department of Agriculture.

by her workers (fig. 3.8). An attractant pheromone or a mixture of such chemicals makes this possible. Known as the "queen recognition pheromone," it consists of a set of lactones called invictolides, which have been synthesized in the lab (Mori and Nakazono 1986). The venom apparatus produces the substance (Billen 1990), which is dispensed from the queen's sting (Vander Meer et al. 1980), and the odor is specific to the individual (Fletcher and Blum 1983a). Glancey (1986a) recalled the discovery of this substance when a jar containing queens was opened. Workers were attracted to the spot, presumably by chemicals dispersed into the surrounding air. The unknown material was present in relatively large amounts in the queen's abdomen. This causes workers to drag their queen about if she will not follow, and the signal is tenacious enough to keep the abdomen of a dead queen attractive to workers for eight months (fig. 3.9). When the recognition pheromone is painted onto distantly related ants, even those of different species, it affords temporary protection within the fire ant nest.

Less well known is the chemistry associated with egg-laying behavior. When the queen lays an egg she draws her sting across it, applying venom that contains an antibiotic or perhaps a signal for the workers to carry it away to the egg pile (Glancey and Dickens 1988). Queens reduce the rate of egg production if the oldest larvae are removed from the nest (Tschinkel

Fig. 3.9. Red imported fire ants dragging a dead queen of a polygyne colony.

1988c). One might have predicted the opposite—that more eggs would be laid to replace the lost juveniles; but as noted earlier, old larvae are important food processors for the colony. Another queen pheromone (or pheromones) can direct nurses to feed larvae in a manner that produces workers instead of queens (Vargo 1988b).

When more than one functional queen is present in a colony, a social condition known as polygyny, the recognition pheromone of one appears to be more attractive to workers than that of any other queen (Chen and Vinson 1999), and each queen produces inhibitory pheromones that cause the other queens to lay fewer eggs than they otherwise would. The more queens present in the polygyne association, the stronger the effect (Vargo and Fletcher 1989). In a similar fashion, the poison gland of a mated RIFA queen produces an inhibitory pheromone that prevents virgin queens in the same nest from shedding their wings and laying eggs (Vargo 1997). These are ways of holding nestmate competitors in check. The signal is detected with the antennae (Vargo and Laurel 1994). If the mated queen is removed, the virgins shed their wings, lay eggs destined to become males, and begin secreting the inhibitory pheromone themselves. In a monogyne nest (where a single mated egg-layer is the norm), all but one of these potential successors is likely to be executed by workers, which compare levels of a queen-fecundity substance produced by the virgins. Those producing the lowest amounts are killed (Fletcher 1986). In polygyne colonies, workers single out certain queens for execution based upon a product or products of one particular gene (Ross 1992; DeHeer et al. 1999; Goodisman et al. 1999). The outward signal has been described as a "green beard" because it gives its bearer away. The phenomenon is treated in more detail later in this chapter. Yet polygyne-colony workers are very tolerant of intruding workers from other RIFA nests, whether these are from polygyne or monogyne societies. The resident workers of a monogyne nest tend to attack any intruder, no matter what its caste or sex (Vander Meer and Morel 1998).

The factors that allow nestmates to recognize one another are more complex than one might expect. Environmental odors comprise part of the signal, which changes over time (Vander Meer et al. 1989b). A second factor is the presence of hydrocarbons on the outer surface of the exoskeleton. Differences in amount rather than kind are critical (Vander Meer 1986b). In a related manner, the RIFA chooses soil from its own nest over soil from other nests when these are offered in a preference test (Hubbard 1974). Laboratory-reared workers lack an identification substance possessed by workers reared in the wild (Obin 1986).

The brood have their own attractive chemicals (Vinson and Sorensen 1986), for they must be fed when hungry and assisted when the time comes to shed the skin (Vander Meer 1996). The sexual brood (the immature gynes and males) have been noted to possess the pheromone "triolein" (Bigley and Vinson 1975; Vinson 1997). The nature of these chemicals, and whether they are true pheromones, has been debated (Walsh and Tschinkel 1974). Perhaps there is an attractant in the skin of the brood that belongs to some other class of substance (Vander Meer and Morel 1988; Vander Meer and Alonso 1998). In any event, when brood extract of a given colony is painted onto small objects, the workers place these among the real brood, and they will accept young from other colonies if these are painted beforehand (Glancey et al. 1970a). The Dufour's gland appears to play a role in the transport of brood by workers (Wilson 1962).

The chemistry of Dufour's gland does more than stimulate brood collection, recruit nestmates to food sources, and raise the general alarm. It also stimulates the emigration of the colony from its nest to a new location, and it causes nestmates to come together as a group or aggregation. Certain glands near the tip of the legs secrete an adhesive material, but the function of the RIFA metapleural gland (within the front part of the abdomen) is unclear (Billen 1990). This is especially interesting because that structure is nearly a defining feature for members of the ant family. The chemical stimulus for the licking movements associated with grooming behavior remains unknown (Wilson 1962). Even the last gasp of the RIFA is signaled by chemicals. When the insect dies, "necrophoric" substances are formed by decomposition, causing workers to discard dead nestmates on a trash heap outside the nest (Vinson 1997).

There seems to be no signal, chemical or otherwise, to allow reductions in the populations of the various size-determined worker subcastes (minors, majors, etc.). For example, major worker production does not decline as more and more majors are added to the colony (Porter and Tschinkel 1985a). This is unusual because most biological systems have some form of negative feedback that slows down production as materials begin to accumulate.

Finally, there is the matter of stridulation. Red imported fire ants, like many other ant species, can produce sounds by rubbing abdominal plates together. In the case of the RIFA the frequency is said to be too high to hear (Rhoades 1977). The significance of stridulation for communication among fire ants remains unknown, though queen *Pogonomyrmex* harvester ants stridulate to end the mating process.

Reproduction

The prodigious reproductive ability of the red imported fire ant lies behind its notoriety as a pest. It is therefore somewhat of a shock to find that the complete mating process has never been observed in nature. Shocking, that is, until one learns that it usually, perhaps always, occurs on the wing and high above ground, probably at heights of about a thousand feet. The idea of animals mating on the wing is astounding, especially when the rest of their lives is spent entirely underground. Walter Gehring, the discoverer of the homeobox regulatory genes so important for the embryonic development that follows the aerial mating of fire ants and the earthbound mating of our own species, described in-flight copulation as "the zenith of evolution" (Gehring 1998). Airplanes fitted with nets have captured copulating pairs at altitudes just below one thousand feet. Flying males increase the likelihood of finding a mate by forming in the sky a layer that females above them must pass through if they are to reach the ground (Markin et al. 1971). The queen lands after mating, sheds her wings, and begins digging a nest. The male dies. It is not surprising that males have the highest metabolic rates in the colony. They are adapted for nothing more than a brief, highly energetic mating flight outside the nest (Vogt and Appel 1999).

Approximately one hour before the nuptial flight begins, workers bore

Fig. 3.10. A virgin
RIFA queen about
to take flight from
vegetation near the
nest. A mite, per-
haps a parasite, is
attached to a seta
or hair of her head.
Several protective
workers scurry
about in the back-
ground, out of
focus here.

Fig. 3.11. A RIFA
male about to take
off for the nuptial
flight.

numerous exit holes in the mound so that the virgin queens and the males
can escape (figs. 3.10, 3.11, 3.12). Alarm pheromones released by waiting
sexuals probably induce this activity (Tschinkel 1998a). Workers then pa-
trol the area around the nest in an aggressive fashion, fanning out to form
an ever-widening circle of protection. Anyone standing in the area is likely

Fig. 3.12. The RIFA nuptial flight begins. Above all the rest is a wingless male, which attempts in vain to fly (arrow). Next is a queen with mites on her back. Just below and to the right is a normal male. Other sexuals and protective workers are on their way up.

to be stung. The sexuals begin leaving the nest at rates of up to one hundred per minute, with an average total output of about seven hundred males and virgin queens. One Arkansas nest released 3,168 sexuals on a single day (Lofgren et al. 1975). Sometimes both sexes leave the nest simultaneously, but the males often fly a little earlier than the females, and on at least some occasions a nest may liberate only one sex or the other in a given flight. The males and virgin queens participating in the nuptials can be produced by colonies that are less than six months old. Even sterile males take wing (Vinson 1986; Hung et al. 1974).

There is no shortage of information on the timing of RIFA mating flights. In the United States these typically occur from spring to fall, though winter flights are common in more southerly areas of the country, and the insect flies throughout much of the year in its Brazilian homeland (Wojcik

1986). The peak period for both Texas and northern Florida is April through August (Vinson and Sorensen 1986). Farther north, Arkansas has its peak in June (Roe 1974). I observed a January nuptial flight in Austin, Texas, along the curb of a busy street. It was 4:00 P.M., partly cloudy, with the temperature in the low seventies, and there was little wind. Workers patrolled the sidewalk, where some could be seen carrying motionless males in their jaws. Both sexes were visible on the mound but only the males were taking off.

Just as the flight season varies with geography, so does the daily window of departure. In the United States this is typically between late morning and late afternoon. In Brazil the time interval is of similar length but begins earlier in the day (Wojcik 1986). Both imports, the RIFA and the BIFA, tend to fly earlier in the afternoon than either the tropical fire ant or the southern fire ant that is native to the United States (Ross et al. 1987b).

It is more difficult to generalize about the required meteorological conditions. Favorable conditions include a 77–95°F temperature, 60–80 percent relative humidity, and recent rainfall (Bhatkar 1990), although the temperature can be as low as 68°F. Tuning the nuptial flight to a period just after a rain is adaptive because the queen finds it easier to dig her little nest if the soil is moist and if the rain is no longer falling.

Both winged forms, known as alates, can be stimulated to fly in captivity. They will not mate under these conditions, perhaps requiring the lower air pressure of higher altitudes (Rhoades 1977). Outdoors, they can be successfully stimulated to at least fly under conditions somewhere between those of the laboratory and those of nature; colonies cultured in buckets of soil will send up their alates under otherwise normal circumstances if water is poured into the container (Milio et al. 1988). This ruse also stimulates flight and presumably mating in wild colonies.

Both sexes mate only once (Ball and Vinson 1983; Vinson 1997), but because the vast majority of males in polygyne nests are sterile for some reason, virgin queens of this social type must often rely on finding mates of the monogyne type, where sterility is not so common (Ross 1992). Brother-sister mating is a possibility in polygyne nests (Fletcher 1983; Ross and Shoemaker 1997; Ross et al. 1999), though deemed unlikely (Ross 1993).

Mated queens prefer to land near reflective surfaces. This adaptation increases the chance of settling near water (Bhatkar 1990). Queens may fly as far as twelve miles from their birth nests in search of a suitable site to begin a nest of their own (Vinson and Sorensen 1986). Both in the air and on the ground the RIFA queen is under strong pressure to escape from predators, and she is quick to exploit cracks or crevices in the soil. This saves the time and energy that would otherwise be expended upon the excavation of a nest opening (Tschinkel 1998b).

Several monogyne-type queens (queens raised in a monogyne colony) sometimes cooperate temporarily in the construction of a nest. This behavior is known as "pleometrosis." Sooner or later one prevails over the others, though this might not happen until a few or even all of the queens have raised a first brood of workers. It is not exactly clear what makes for a winning queen when the fights finally break out. Sometimes the winner appears to be the egg-layer that has produced the most offspring, even though workers usually do not take part in the fight (Bernasconi et al. 1997). On other occasions it appears that the heaviest queen wins (Bernasconi and Keller 1996; Balas and Adams 1996a). There is indeed a positive correlation between the head size of queens in founding groups and their survival in the conflicts that follow (Bernasconi and Keller 1998). Conflicts between the queens of a pleometrotic colony sometimes arise before the first workers mature (Bernasconi and Keller 1999).

One study found that workers killing some queens but not others do so largely on the basis of the queen's physical condition, and not so much on the basis of their relationship to her. The queens picked out for attack tended to be those that had been isolated from the other ants as well as those that had been kept at high temperatures (Adams and Balas 1999).

Monogyne-type queens have yet another strategy at their disposal when it comes to occupying a nest in which to lay their eggs. Those with unusually low energy reserves sometimes act as social parasites by joining established monogyne colonies that have lost their own egg-layer. They run the risk of conflict with resident virgins, which might also attempt to replace their former queen (Tschinkel 1996).

Perhaps only one of every thousand mated queens survives the rigors of the swarming season (see chapter 12) and goes on to found a successful nest after shedding her wings (figs. 3.13, 3.14). Once in place she can lay her own weight in eggs every day (Tschinkel 1986). As noted earlier, some of the nutrients for this and for feeding the resulting first brood are produced when her flight muscles break down, though the queen carries stored food in her digestive tract when she leaves her birth nest and embarks upon the nuptial flight. The blood of newly mated queens contains a factor that induces this flight-muscle breakdown, an example of programmed cell death or "apoptosis" (Davis et al. 1989).

Egg production begins in March along the Gulf Coast of the United States (Markin and Dillier 1971). Newly laid eggs are pearly white and sticky enough to be transported in clumps (Vinson 1997). There are about

Fig. 3.13. A RIFA nest queen, wingless and mated.

Fig. 3.14. The wing scars of a RIFA queen (arrow).

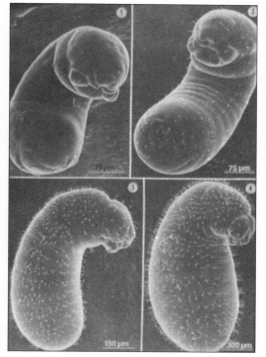

Fig. 3.15. RIFA larvae (scanning electron micrographs): first instar, *top left*; second instar, *top right*; third instar, *bottom left*; fourth instar, *bottom right*. Reprinted from Vinson and Sorensen 1986. By permission of the senior author and Texas Department of Agriculture.

fifteen eggs in the first batch, the larvae within hatching in just over a week (fig. 3.15) (Vinson and Sorensen 1986), and trophic eggs are not yet among them (Glancey and Fletcher 1980). The type of egg laid (trophic vs. embryonated) is determined by a combination of nutritional state and juvenile hormone level. High levels of both components produce viable, embryonated eggs, the kind from which larvae can hatch (Voss 1981). The queen's ovary contains eight to ninety ovarioles, and a given ovariole contains only one mature egg cell at a given time (Hermann and Blum 1965). These must have a supply of juvenile hormone if they are to continue development (Barker 1979). Virgin queens occasionally lay eggs before their flight from the birth nest (Fletcher and Blum 1983b).

One social form of the RIFA, the polygyne type, sometimes has tens of thousands of egg-laying queens (both mated and unmated) functioning simultaneously, and even the monogyne type can have backups both mated and unmated to step in should the single laying queen perish (Tschinkel 1986). Older queens tend to be the heaviest and can accordingly lay more eggs than younger queens, often about three thousand per day. A "physogastric" queen is one so full of eggs that her abdomen is visibly swollen (fig. 3.8). The monogyne type is typically physogastric. The polygyne type (fig. 3.9) usually is not (Porter 1992). Each queen of the polygyne society lays fewer eggs than the single mated queen of the monogyne colony, and a polygyne colony also produces fewer sexuals overall (Vargo 1990), though it tends to produce more workers than the monogyne colony does. As previously noted, established queens require the presence of the oldest larval stage to maintain peak egg production. This also requires a temperature range of 68–93°F (Williams 1990; Glancey et al. 1973a). The optimal temperature for colony growth can be designated more precisely as 90°F (Porter and Tschinkel 1993). Each egg weighs about 0.0051 mg and is up to 0.22 mm in diameter. A queen weighing roughly 20 mg and able to lay her own weight in eggs every day (a realistic figure) would therefore lay approximately five thousand eggs in that short period of time.

In the warmer regions of the RIFA's range within the United States, brood are produced year-round. May is a peak month (Lofgren et al. 1975). The viability of eggs laid by mated polygyne queens under laboratory conditions is nearly 100 percent, ten times that of eggs laid by unmated queens. Viability in the wild is generally lower than this. Nonviable eggs are cannibalized (Vargo and Ross 1989).

The reproductive success of a polygyne queen is tied to her genetic constitution. Queens with a particular genetic makeup are executed before they have a chance to lay eggs. Strangely enough, these are the individuals with the greatest reproductive potential (Keller and Ross 1993a; DeHeer et al. 1999; Goodisman et al. 1999). The selective value of this culling behavior might be to maximize the number of queens for purposes such as replacement or defense, because higher numbers of queens are tolerated by workers if their individual fecundities are low. The same or perhaps a different gene allows workers that bear it to recognize queens that do not, and this identifies the queens that must be killed. Because of their role in singling out individuals with particular genetic traits, the products of such genes are known as "green-beards" (they make the bearer conspicuous to others). The signal in this case appears to be an odor (Keller and Ross 1998; Anonymous 1998). Biologists predicted the existence of green-beards for decades, and it was female red imported fire ants that provided the first example. Social species with recognition marks of this kind are good candidates for speciation because their populations are that much more likely to become reproductively isolated from one another based on the presence or absence of the signal(s) (Wright 1949). This is cause for concern when seen among wide-ranging pests that are difficult enough to understand and control as it is.

The RIFA queen can live and lay eggs for more than seven years (Vinson 1997; Tschinkel 1998a)—a considerable life span for an individual insect—and the colony's ability to replace its queen or queens makes the society itself seem potentially immortal (Tschinkel 1993a). On the other hand, the short-lived fire ant workers pose no direct reproductive threat because they are females without ovaries, or at best with only a rudimentary apparatus. They cannot produce eggs of any kind, either embryonated or trophic (Voss et al. 1988). An early report of egg-laying workers (George 1958) is probably erroneous.

It may be shocking to learn of artificial insemination of a pest species because the practice is usually associated with increasing the population of endangered species or with conventional animal and plant husbandry. Nevertheless, it has been accomplished in the case of the RIFA despite difficulties predicted in an early study of the queen's reproductive tract for any such attempts (Hermann and Blum 1965). Forced copulation was achieved first (Cupp et al. 1973), followed one decade later by a true artificial insemination (Ball et al. 1983). The protocol for forced mating is remarkable. First, a male is decapitated and impaled. Then he is presented with an anesthetized female. The headless male begins mating on contact. The entire process requires about thirty seconds. For a detailed description of the male reproductive system, see Hung and Vinson (1975).

Males (fig. 3.16) begin producing sperm while they are still pupae. Their

Fig. 3.16. A RIFA male.

Fig. 3.17. A RIFA sperm cell. 1 μ = 10⁻⁶ meter. Reprinted from Thompson and Blum 1967. Copyright 1967 by the Entomological Society of America.

testes degenerate when they become adults (Glancey et al. 1976a), and the sperm must then be stored in other structures until the mating flight. The sperm cell itself (fig. 3.17) is about 70 micrometers long (Thompson and Blum 1967). Approximately seven million of these are received by the RIFA queen during copulation, the vast majority of the total supply carried by the male (Tschinkel 1987; Glancey and Lofgren 1985). She stores the sperm in a structure called the spermatheca. This reservoir is drawn upon during the years of egg laying that follow the mating flight. The RIFA queen is said to use her sperm more efficiently than honey bee queens use theirs. About three sperm are used up in one way or another for every worker produced by the colony (Tschinkel and Porter 1988). Indeed, some are likely to be defective. Pathological sperm with two tails have been photographed through the microscope (Thompson and Blum 1967). It appears that some males with twice as many genes as normal males are able to mate successfully even though these have been assumed to be sterile (Krieger et al. 1999).

The red imported fire ant is not limited to sexual reproduction. The species also has two, perhaps three, forms of asexual reproduction: (1) unfertilized eggs that develop into males (though males can develop from fertilized eggs); (2) polygyne nests that bud off daughter colonies in a manner like that of a budding yeast cell, when queens simply leave with a contingent of workers (Porter and Savignano 1990); and (3) virgin queens that are said to be capable of producing workers (Tschinkel and Howard 1978). Furthermore, colonies that lose large numbers of workers continue to produce the sexual forms (Cassill and Tschinkel 1999c).

It is now possible to culture fire ant ovaries in the laboratory for a period of at least eight months. This organ could be useful when studying the effects of potential biocontrol viruses (Kral et al. 1986).

Development

The RIFA queen loses half her weight while caring for the first brood (O'Neal and Markin 1975a; Toom et al. 1976b). She begins by applying venom to the surface of her freshly laid eggs, and by licking them too, presumably applying antibiotics in the process (O'Neal and Markin 1973). The egg stage lasts five to eight days but varies with caste and sex. Hatching is followed by a series of four larval stages called instars, followed by a pupal stage and finally by the adult stage. Ant larvae are also known as grubs. Between instars the grub sheds its skin by muscular contractions that split the exoskeleton down the back, allowing the creature to work itself free of the old shell. Workers typically assist the juveniles at such moments (O'Neal and Markin 1973), though the youngest larvae can go it alone.

Nurse workers, like the queen herself, apply venom to the larval brood under their care (Obin and Vander Meer 1985). The youngest of these are stored among the eggs in the egg pile (Markin et al. 1972), where a sticky coating keeps them together as a group and therefore safe from the dangers of isolation. As they grow older they grow hairier too. The hairs interlock and provide a second level of adhesion. Prior to entering the pupal stage the larva defecates for the first time, expelling the pellet of waste material (meconium) that has accumulated from the time of the grub's first meal. Workers help out but are not absolutely necessary (O'Neal and Markin 1973; Petralia and Vinson 1979).

When the juvenile passes into the pupa stage it is usually removed from among the remaining larvae and stored with other pupae. All juvenile stages are moved about within the nest by workers that seek out humidities and soil temperatures promoting optimal development (Potts et al. 1984; Francke and Cokendolpher 1986). Indeed, these are said to be the prime functions of the famous fire ant mound. Larval tissues break down during the pupal stage and reorganize radically to form the adult. The exit from the pupal skin by the newly formed adult is called eclosion. Workers must help remove this last of the shed skins if the young ant is to survive the rite of passage. The old skin is then eaten by nestmates (Lamon and Topoff 1985). Recently eclosed adults are called callows. They are soft and light in color, becoming darker and harder in a day or two until they assume the familiar form seen above ground (fig. 3.18).

A new colony's first workers, called minims, are smaller than those of later generations, and they require a total development time of eighteen to twenty-one days (O'Neal and Markin 1975a). Their small size is dictated not by genes but by the queen's nurture (Vinson 1986). They weigh only one-tenth as much as an average worker (about 0.2 mg vs. 2.0 mg), and are less than 3 mm in length (Vargo 1988a). At the other end of the scale is the major worker of later generations. These giants can be twenty times as heavy as minors and reach lengths of 5 mm (Tschinkel 1988b). Minors fall

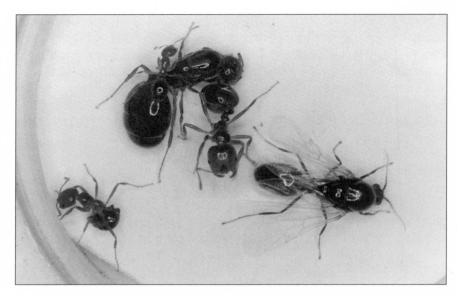

Fig. 3.18. The castes and sexes of the RIFA. A minor worker rides a queen while a major worker and the winged male stand to their right. At lower left is a media worker.

between these extremes, as do the larger medias. A typical minor is about 3 mm in length (Vinson 1997). Using the minor worker as an example, the time spent in each developmental stage is as follows: five days in the egg, eleven days as a larva, seven days as a pupa, and a few weeks to a few months as an adult. Total time from egg to adult is therefore approximately three weeks (Porter 1988). Majors and sexuals require more time than this. For the majors it is four weeks, for the sexuals five weeks (O'Neal and Markin 1975a).

With the exception of the minim class, workers, whether minor, media, or major, change behavioral roles as they age. First they act as nurses that care for queen and brood. Then they become "reserves," which continue caring for the juveniles while broadening their role to receive food from incoming foragers. The final role is the most dangerous of all. Now the worker no longer merely intercepts foragers but becomes one itself. The insect will likely meet its end outside the nest while searching for food or while returning home from the hunt. These behavioral changes have been documented by observing banded workers. Each was tagged with a tiny ring around one leg, much like a banded pigeon (Anonymous 1978).

Though the minims do not progress through these changes, they do have a peculiarity of their own. They engage in "brood-raiding." This begins when a party leaves its own nest and invades another, where the minims attempt to capture that colony's juvenile stages. These are not eaten. They are carried home and raised as additions to the raiders' worker force, a form of slave raiding similar to that practiced by the sickle-jawed red Amazon ants of the genus *Polyergus*. However, the capture of slaves by fire ants is different because it is a temporary practice in the early life of the colony and because the slaves and masters are members of the same species. Back-and-forth raiding often continues for an entire month as members of the raided nest attempt to recoup their losses (Tschinkel 1992b). This just happens to be the maximum lifespan of a minim.

Major workers can live much longer, for more than half a year (Vinson and Sorensen 1986). Yet the oldest colonies tend to have more minor workers than majors (Wood and Tschinkel 1981). Perhaps this is an adaptation to maximize the aggressive defense of the nest. Minor workers are more prone to sting.

RIFA development occasionally goes awry. Low humidity in particular seems to be one cause of deformed legs and antennae. Sexual abnormalities include three known gynandromorphs (part male, part queen; Roe 1974; Hung et al. 1975); an intercaste (part worker, part queen; Glancey 1986b); and deformed individuals of both sexes (Morrill 1974a). Wingless sexuals attempt to fly from the mound during the nuptial flight (fig. 3.12). There could be no better testament to the fire ant's overwhelming instinct to reproduce.

CHAPTER 4

The Black Imported Fire Ant
(*Solenopsis richteri*)

That the variety *richteri* has been introduced into
the United States is a fact which may in the future
attract the attention of economic entomologists. . . .
The area occupied at present is small, not extending
more than six or seven miles from Mobile, but there is
no reason why the insect should not spread widely.

—W. S. Creighton (1930)

THE black imported fire ant reached the south-eastern shore of the United States at the end of the First World War, preceding the arrival of its more famous cousin the red imported fire ant by two decades or perhaps a little more. William Steel Creighton's concern was realized shortly thereafter when the first accidental import began fanning out in all landward directions. Chemical analysis of its glandular products indicated the BIFA's point of origin as about sixty miles north of Buenos Aires, Argentina, near the Uruguay border (Vander Meer and Lofgren 1990). Some specialists believe the insect arrived in the United States with a shipment of South American fruit (George 1958).

The red imported fire ant has taken over much of the range of its unwelcome predecessor. This action pushed the BIFA to the northeastern corner of the total imported fire ant range as it exists within the United States in the year 2000 (fig. 4.1). Buren (1972) suggested that those interested in BIFA biology should visit that reduced stronghold before the RIFA, in collaboration with humanity, managed to

Fig. 4.1. The natural range (South America) and accidental distribution (North America) of the black imported fire ant.

eradicate the invader altogether. Yet fire ants seldom go quietly. In 1997 the BIFA was resisting eradication attempts imposed by our own species shortly after its discovery within the city limits of Memphis, Tennessee, 330 miles north of its original port of entry at Mobile, Alabama (Jones et al. 1997). Buren et al. (1974) predicted an expansion into Tennessee more than twenty years before it occurred, just as they predicted a future invasion of Kentucky.

The biology of the two imported fire ant species is quite similar, though much less has been written about the BIFA than its more famous relative. The struggle between these two species and their hybrid is treated in chapter 8.

Nesting Sites

In the United States the black imported fire ant prefers the open areas of pastures, cultivated fields, and lawns. For example, its nests were found on the lawns of Mobile, Alabama, where it first came ashore (Creighton 1930). Colonies tend to move to drier sites as they grow older and more populous (Green 1952). The grassy Argentine pampas is the prime habitat of the BIFA in its South American homeland. Moisture and altitude do not seem to be very limiting in that part of the world, the species being found in dry and wet areas at elevations of up to twelve thousand feet. Pastures in the vicinity of Buenos Aires support mound densities of sixty per acre, and this increases to one hundred mounds per acre near the border with Uruguay (Hays 1958). In southern Buenos Aires Province the BIFA lives in seasonally waterlogged grassland (Cox et al. 1992). It is readily collected along roadsides near the city of Buenos Aires (Briano and Williams 1997).

The Nest

In the United States, BIFA mounds resemble those of the RIFA but are sometimes larger and covered with a thatching of pine needles or other vegetation (Creighton 1930; Wilson and Eads 1949; Wilson and Brown 1958). They rise to three feet in height, extend to three feet in width, and lie thirty to forty feet from one another in prime habitat. Damaged nests are patched up with plant debris (Green 1952). Giant mounds three feet high and eight feet wide are formed from what appears to be a temporary fusion of colonies during times of bad weather and/or reduced food supply. Giant mounds of a very different origin occur in South America, as discussed later. The North American giant colonies are thought to disperse into smaller units when conditions improve, and they also split or "fission" if disturbed. Such large nests are probably of the polygyne type (Green 1962). Several years before Green's report, Favorite (1958) published observations of IFA colonies that appeared to have more than one queen. This is perhaps the earliest record of polygyny among the imported fire ants.

Rains trigger mound-building activity (Rhoades and Davis 1967). Colonies sometimes build several mounds in one day, and they move back and forth between them (Green 1952). The juvenile stages are kept in a "brood nest" near the top of the mound during wet weather and moved down to ground level or below the soil surface when the nest dries out or when conditions become extreme in some other way. BIFA outbreaks are in fact correlated with periods of high rainfall (Green 1962), for the founding queen must have moist soil to excavate her incipient nest successfully. Her new home lies within an inch of the soil surface (Lofgren et al. 1975), and is thus shallower than that prepared by the newly mated RIFA queen.

The largest fire ant mounds of all occur in South America where polygyny is common and may be the rule rather than the exception (Trager 1991; Briano et al. 1995c). Like their RIFA relatives, black imported fire ants construct subterranean foraging tunnels that connect the nest with the outside world. When the ants colonize high ground their tunneling and digging activities cause the formation of large earthen structures known as Mima mounds that reach heights of ten feet and widths of eighty feet (Cox et al. 1992). Some believe that centuries of insect labor are required to build each huge edifice. The origin of Mima mounds in South America was a mystery until the BIFA was offered as an explanation. The name Mima is actually of North American origin, for similar mounds dot the Mima Prairie of western Washington State, where they are thought to be the work of pocket gophers. More conventional Argentine BIFA colonies live in mounds as voluminous as 16 gallons. The average mound has a height of eight inches and a width of two feet.

Argentine BIFA colonies change their nesting sites frequently, often moving more than forty feet from the previous site. Rain is at least one stimulus for emigration (Briano et al. 1995b).

Nest Population, Foraging Behavior, Diet, and Feeding Behavior

The two imported fire ants have similar colony populations, foraging behaviors, diets, and feeding behaviors. For example, insects (at least one hundred species) are high on the BIFA diet, as are the oilier types of seeds (Hays 1958). Preferred insects include long-horned grasshoppers, cucumber beetles, various ground beetles, and spittle bugs. Spiders are favored among the other arthropods. There is a lesser fondness for stink bugs, ants, and adult house flies. The BIFA is not as keen on sucrose as the RIFA is (Ricks and Vinson 1970), nor does there seem to be a replete subcaste of workers specializing in the storage of food within their bodies for long periods of time (Ricks and Vinson 1972a), though the RIFA is said to maintain such specialists within the nest. Some insects are captured but not killed. These are kept alive, tended, and "milked" for their excretions. The BIFA builds soil shelters over these animals, and mealybugs in particular are actually housed within the nest itself. On one occasion they were seen huddled together inside a tunnel (Green 1952).

Optimum foraging conditions include an air temperature of between 70 and 85°F and a soil temperature less than 95° F (Rhoades and Davis 1967). The BIFA practices a division of labor while hunting for certain prey items. When a forager captures a larva of the pestiferous face fly *(Musca autumnalis)*, the ant stings the maggot and leaves it behind for nestmates that arrive later and carry the prey back to the mound (Combs 1982).

Communication

The Dufour's gland chemistry of the BIFA is different from that of the closely related RIFA (Vander Meer 1986a), as is the chemistry of its exoskeleton (Nelson et al. 1980). Some of these outermost molecules play a role in nestmate recognition and others probably afford protection from desiccation (Brill and Bertsch 1985). Cuticular hydrocarbons vary significantly even within a single worker subcaste of a single colony (Brill and Bertsch 1990).

There is a chemical necrophoric signal that compels workers to transport dead nestmates to the trash pile (Talice et al. 1978), and workers stridulate when alarmed (Hickling 1998). An interesting comparison has been made between the anatomy of the black imported fire ant and the synthetic diodes used in electronic circuits. The living ant's sensory antenna and the lifeless circuit component both contain small amounts of certain chemical substances known as trace elements (Levy et al. 1979). In diodes at least, these cause electric currents to flow in one direction only.

Reproduction

BIFA nuptial flights occur at temperatures as low as 70°F (Lofgren et al. 1975). This is quite close to the minimum acceptable temperature for the

RIFA. There is evidence that the black imported fire ant might have existed for a brief period in Florida, where mating flights occurred at air temperatures of between 75 and 90°F (with soil temperature higher than 65°F), usually in the afternoon, and in every month except January. Cloud cover was not important but humidity was always high. Wind was found to be an important factor in the dispersal of the sexuals when the vast majority of new nests were discovered downwind of swarming colonies (Rhoades and Davis 1967). It is possible, however, that these Florida data apply to the RIFA instead. The two were not distinguished as different species until 1972. In Uruguay, nuptial flights occur from January to mid-April (San Martin 1971).

Colonies in the United States mature in approximately two years, with the seasonal egg production beginning around March. During this annual cycle sexual brood are produced before worker brood. Production of both classes comes to an end with the onset of winter (Green 1952).

In subequatorial Uruguay the BIFA has peak periods of egg production from the end of January to March (the summer cycle) and from mid-July to mid-September (the winter cycle). Only workers develop from the summer eggs, whereas all castes and sexes develop from winter eggs (San Martin 1971) (figs. 4.2, 4.3, 4.4, 4.5).

Fig. 4.2. A BIFA winged queen collected by E. O. Wilson in the early days of fire ant research.

Fig. 4.3. A BIFA male.

Fig. 4.4. A South American BIFA nest queen, a larva, and a parasitic nematode worm shown as it would appear leaving the body of an infected, unmated, winged queen. Modified from San Martin 1971. By permission of Academic Press.

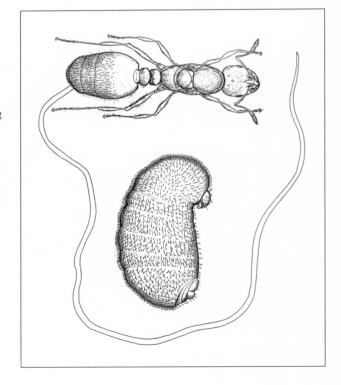

Fig. 4.5. A BIFA worker seen head-on.

Development

BIFA development is similar to that of the RIFA. Winged forms in Florida nests (if these were not the RIFA) began appearing when the colonies were about four months old (Rhoades and Davis 1967). In Uruguay, winged sexuals can be found in the nest year-round (San Martin 1971).

CHAPTER 5

The Tropical Fire Ant
(Solenopsis geminata)

It is difficult to say whether this ant is more
granivorous than entomophagous, for it attacks
and eats almost everything that comes in its way.

—*William Morton Wheeler* (1910)

F IRE ant study began in 1804 when J. C. Fabricius
reported the original collection locality of the tropical
fire ant as "habitat in America meridionali." Yet in
time this New World native became the most widely
traveled fire ant in the world. Commerce has accidentally introduced the TFA to new cities and shores
in North America, South America, Africa, Australia,
Asia, and the isles of Oceania (fig. 5.1). Stowaways
were discovered on one occasion in a shipment of orchids traveling from Honduras to New Zealand (Keall
1980). And in Canada, where the species cannot survive out of doors, these ants were discovered in an
enclosed tropical display that had been in place for
two and a half years (Ayre 1977). African Equatorial
Guinea immortalized the TFA's globe-trotting prow-
ess on a postage stamp. Only two of the seven continents have so far proven immune to invasion: the
cool, high latitudes of Europe and Antarctica are perhaps too forbidding for even the hardiest of colonial
fire ants.

Because of its accidental transportation with
shipping commerce, the TFA repeatedly deals out to

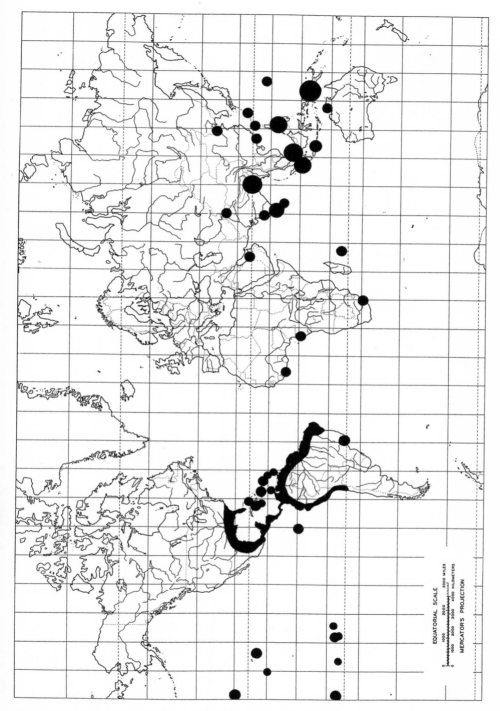

Fig. 5.1. The natural range and accidental distribution of the tropical fire ant. Prepared using blank map no. 1M, *Goode's Series of Base Maps*, ed. Henry M. Leppard. Copyright 1939. By permission of the University of Chicago.

native ants what it must itself absorb (as a possible native) from the RIFA where the two meet in the southern United States. The New World's lower latitudes, those closer to the equator, are a different matter altogether. Here, in the year 2000, there are as yet no red imported fire ants and the TFA remains "in possession of a large portion of the soil of the American tropics" (Wheeler 1910).

Texas State Geologist S. B. Buckley (1867) was perhaps the first writer to put in print the fire ant's most famous attribute when he described the Texas TFA as "active and warlike." Farther east and nearly a century later, Travis (1941) found that human breath alone was enough to stir up a mound.

Nesting Sites

The TFA is adept at colonizing disturbed areas (Risch 1981), and has been described as a pioneer species that invades such habitats with exceptional success (Perfecto 1991). This much it has in common with the RIFA. Yet it has an even broader tolerance for nesting sites. It is more common in orchards and woods (Essig 1926; Wilson and Brown 1958), though it is also at home in the open areas preferred by the imported fire ants and the species that are clearly native to the United States. This tolerance allows the TFA to occupy sand, heavy clay, swampy areas, and dry and low elevations (Travis 1941; Moody et al. 1981), cultivated fields (Whitcomb et al. 1972; Way et al. 1998), sites beneath water drip lines (Muniappan and Marutani 1992), edges of roads and trails, and loamy soil along streams. Nests can be found under stones and even beneath piles of dried cow dung (Wheeler 1910).

The TFA is persisting in Florida in habitats where the RIFA does not penetrate so well. These include sandy areas (Buren et al. 1974), well-drained woods (McInnes and Tschinkel 1995), and the dry uplands of long-leaf pine forests (Tschinkel 1988a). Nests are more common in open fields and in stumps in wooded areas than in the extreme of the deepest forest (Creighton 1950). When this species does colonize woodland, it prefers firelanes, scrubby areas, sandy soil beneath litter, and the roots of plants such as the palmetto. Sometimes a log harbors part of a tropical fire ant nest, the remainder being constructed in the soil just below (Van Pelt 1958; pers. obs.).

Generally speaking, the TFA prefers high humidity and mild winters (Snelling 1963), and it was historically more common in the southeastern

United States than in the Southwest. Nevertheless, it dwells on the eastern edge of West Texas at altitudes below twenty-six hundred feet, where most nests are constructed on ground that is both level and in the open. Some colonies in this area nest under rocks, while others choose shelter inside trees or at their bases (Moody and Francke 1982). Reports of the TFA in states farther west are disputed for lack of confirmation in the ensuing decades. These reports include those of Cole (1934) for southern Arizona and for sandy soil along the Colorado River near Needles, California. Perhaps the species in question was the southern fire ant.

In southwestern Mexico the TFA apparently avoids the forest but chooses cultivated areas and those in early second growth. It prefers to build its nest near its favored seeds (Carroll and Risch 1984). Workers have been collected inside caves in southern Mexico, and their nests have indeed been encountered at cave entrances (Reddell 1981), but there is no report of a nest located within a cave. In Central America the tropical fire ant occurs from the lowlands to mid-elevations (Perfecto 1994). On Costa Rican coffee farms it prefers open areas to shaded areas (Perfecto and Vander Meer 1996). Wherever it goes in this region its nesting site must be warm and dry (Perfecto and Snelling 1995).

On the Caribbean island of St. Vincent, the ant was, and perhaps still is, common in the open below altitudes of fifteen hundred feet. Forel (1893) reported finding nests along the shore, under stones, and in houses. This report appears to be the first publication dealing with the biology of the tropical fire ant. In Cuba the TFA builds its nest along the borders and footpaths of sugarcane plantations (Fontenla Rizo 1993; Fontenla Rizo and Hernandez 1993). In Puerto Rican pineapple plantations, in the early part of the twentieth century at least, nests were usually associated with roots, but they occurred higher up too, in the axils of leaves, where the worker ants brought soil from below (Wolcott 1933). On this same island the ant occurs at elevations as high as three thousand feet (Smith 1936b). On Brazilian cocoa plantations the TFA is sometimes the dominant ant in the leaf litter (Delabie and Fowler 1995; Fowler and Delabie 1995).

In Hawaii the TFA is usually found nesting beneath rocks or in open areas, where it heaps up soil but does not build a true mound. It is common in the drier regions and at low elevations (Huddleston and Fluker 1968). In pineapple fields it is more common along paths than among the plants themselves (Phillips 1934). Nests on the Philippines Islands are built in the dikes of rice paddies (Sison 1938; Way et al. 1998).

In India the TFA builds its nest in open fields in humid areas and is common on plains (Veeresh 1990a), along banks of waterways, and in red, sandy loam (Murthy 1959). Colonies nesting in the irrigated areas of Bangladesh have been seen floating as living rafts in the midst of floods (Way et al. 1998). In India too, the tropical fire ant is not averse to making its home within human habitations (Lakshmikantha et al. 1996).

There is general agreement that a dark form of the TFA is prone to occupy woods whereas a lighter form is more common in the open (Hölldobler and Wilson 1990). All of the tropical fire ants photographed for this book were collected in a sandy Central Texas semiarid forest of loblolly pines and oaks. Under bright microscopic illumination the major workers appear red enough, but in the field they appear to be much darker.

The Nest

Nests constructed in the open are surmounted by numerous craters and entrances (fig. 5.2). They are shallow and contain seed granaries (Wheeler 1910). In the southeastern United States there can be long periods (up to eight months) when no mound or superstructure is visible at the surface due to colony inactivity and to gradual erosion by the elements. When mounds are present they are typically irregular in shape but sometimes

Fig. 5.2. A tropical fire ant nest.

contain more than four gallons of soil. Entrances are irregularly placed and are plugged with soil and plant matter during times of drought. Storage and refuse chambers are maintained inside. The shallow lateral tunnels can extend more than one hundred feet in any direction but are limited to the upper three inches of soil. Vertical tunnels often exceed six feet in depth and have short lateral branches of their own. Emigrations from one nesting site to another occur in these tunnels, where the action is largely underground and unseen. When trails are formed above ground they are often roofed over with soil pellets, creating a structure resembling those built by certain termites and army ants. Colony emigrations are unpredictable and the tendency to make a move varies from nest to nest. One of these moved 117 feet, all but seven feet of the journey entirely underground (Travis 1938, 1939, 1941, 1943).

TFA mounds are not as striking on the outside as those of the two imported fire ants, but they are riddled with underground galleries, a feature that may prohibit the species from moving into higher latitudes where cold air would permeate the nest (Francke et al. 1986). Nest craters are sometimes two feet wide and one foot high, and the number of entrances in a single mound can exceed twenty (Van Pelt 1958). Mounds are generally not dome shaped but can be as big as a bushel basket (Hung et al. 1977). Yet in Puerto Rico, a survey of TFA mounds discovered none more than six inches in height (Pimentel 1955).

Hawaiian nest depths can reach at least three feet. Heavy rains on the islands do great damage to nests and cause the ants to congregate in the top few inches while those trapped underground perish. Many of the trapped and dying ants are virgin queens, their wet wings working against them by sticking to the soil, making it impossible to climb to safety. Colonies in the area use an open tunnel or trench when they emigrate (Phillips 1934).

Nest density varies greatly and depends upon the number of queens in the colonies. In some areas of the United States there are usually no more than ten nests per acre, but in Florida the density reaches eighty (McInnes and Tschinkel 1995). Using a linear measure in place of an area measure, they exist at about eight nests per mile along transects through their favored Florida habitats (Tschinkel 1988a).

In Mexico, densities of more than a thousand mounds per acre have been recorded for multiple-queen (polygynous) colonies (MacKay et al. 1990). This is fifty times the density of single-queen colonies in the same area. Philippine rice fields also appear to support polygyne societies (Way et al. 1998).

Nest densities in India can exceed fifteen hundred per acre, perhaps the highest counts on record. These too may be polygyne populations (Veeresh 1990a). Indian nests are usually no deeper than three feet (Murthy 1959) but can extend to a depth of six feet. They have up to sixteen entrances, and the shape of the superstructure can be described as something between a crater and a mound. Nest building reaches its peak during the cool periods of the rainy season (Veeresh 1990a). The propensity of the tropical fire ant to emigrate from one location to another makes long-term study of this species difficult (Lakshmikantha et al. 1996).

Nest Population

There are surprisingly few head counts of the denizens within the tropical fire ant nest. Strangely enough, these come from the Old World, not from the insect's New World place of origin. The census ranges from lows of 4,130 to 11,137 in India (Veeresh 1990a) up to 100,000 in Philippine rice fields, nearly an order of magnitude higher than the Indian counts (Way et al. 1998). New World estimates run from ten to twelve thousand ants per nest (Forel 1893) to hundreds of thousands of ants per nest (Perfecto 1994).

Foraging Behavior

The tropical fire ant has a typical form of chemical mass recruitment. It secretes different amounts of trail pheromone depending upon the distance from the food to the nest and the quantity and quality of food discovered (Jaffe et al. 1985). This generalization conflicts with an earlier report that the continuity and intensity of the recruitment trail does depend upon food quality, distance from the nest, and the starvation status of the colony, but not upon quantity (Hangartner 1969a). In any event, the chemical is laid down from the tip of the sting as it touches the ground. The extruded sting, the hairs at the tip of the abdomen, and even the feet are all used to apply the chemical to the substrate (Wilson 1971).

Researchers have reported that the TFA will follow the trail pheromone of its close relative the southern fire ant, although neither of these species will follow the trails of the two imported ants (Barlin et al. 1976). Contrary reports claim that the trail substances of the other fire ant species are not followed by the TFA (Hölldobler and Wilson 1990).

Using the tropical fire ant as a model organism, Taylor (1977, 1978) explored technical aspects of foraging theory in general. He found the recruitment rate to be positively correlated with the amount of food discovered but inversely related to its distance from the nest; note that this last relationship is the opposite of findings (Horton et al. 1975) for the introduced RIFA. Larger foragers tend to carry larger food items (Wilson 1978).

Rising temperatures pose a threat to foragers working outside the nest. At 113°F, half of the exposed insects are dead within an hour (Perfecto and Snelling 1995). Major workers survive these stresses longer than minors, and the TFA as a species is more resistant to desiccation than were the other fire ants tested—GFA, RIFA, SFA (Braulick et al. 1988). In the southeastern United States foragers sometimes get a reprieve from excessive heat when they forage in the kitchens of human habitations (Travis 1941). In the same area Travis observed foragers covering moist food with soil prior to feeding upon it. He also saw them tending aphids and stroking them for their honeydew excretions (Travis 1941).

In corn and bean plots in Mexico the red and the black forms of the TFA dominate or displace other ants, both below and above ground, including in the trees. Subterranean foraging is the norm when temperatures exceed 97°F (Bhatkar 1982). In fact, TFA foraging trails are often entirely underground, channeling through the soil for a distance of many yards (Perfecto and Vander Meer 1996), though sometimes they are only partially covered or are entirely in the open (Perfecto 1994). In Costa Rica these protected trails allow the fire ant to forage at higher temperatures than competing ants can tolerate (Perfecto and Snelling 1995).

In the forests of Costa Rica the TFA raids the nest burrows of the sand wasp *Stictia maculata.* The wasp counters with an "ant-clearing behavior" in which it carries the intruders away in its jaws before dropping them some distance from its nest. One wonders why the wasp does not simply bite its enemy in half at the narrow waist. There must be an even more passive defense within the wasp's burrow, for ants that get past the protective mother fail in their mission. Perhaps the underground nest architecture prevents the forager from reaching the brood (Matthews et al. 1981). Not so fortunate is the mason wasp *Pterocheilus texanus.* The fire ant enters the burrow and preys upon this wasp's eggs and the caterpillar provisions intended for the larvae that might have hatched from those eggs (Grissell 1975).

In Central Texas the plant *Wedelia hispida* uses fire ants to disperse its seeds. The seeds have oil-rich appendages called "elaiosomes" that the insects eat after they collect the seed and take it back to the nest (Nesom 1981). The discarded seeds germinate at a distance from the parent plant, thus perhaps avoiding competition with others of their own species. The plant's strategy is called myrmecochory. The arrowroot plant *Calathea mi-*

Fig. 5.3. The seed of the arrowroot plant *Calathea microcephala,* showing its aril appendage. Reprinted from Horvitz 1981. Copyright 1981, Springer Verlag. By permission of the author and publisher.

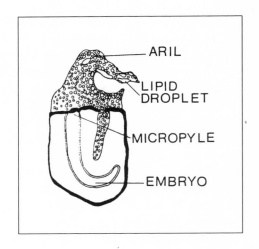

crocephala (fig. 5.3) of tropical Mexico has similar success (Horvitz 1981). But the ploy does not always work. The TFA takes the elaiosomes of the related arrowroot *C. ovandensis,* leaving its seeds behind, still attached to the plant and undispersed (Horvitz and Schmeske 1986). The ants build soil tunnels over these seeds while they do their work. At least one violet species is able to save its seeds from fire ant predation with an elaiosome (Beattie and Lyons 1975). In the Dominican Republic the TFA disperses seeds of the pope's head cactus *Melocactus communis* in a similar fashion (Howard and Zanoni 1989).

In the Galápagos Archipelago the tropical fire ant forages around the clock (Meier 1994). In Hawaii, it is active even during the hottest part of the day. A colony tolerated one month of 95°F temperatures in an artificial nest, though they were unusually aggressive during this tribulation. The fire ant's natural enemy *Pheidole megacephala,* another widely traveled ant species, lasted only four days under identical conditions (Phillips 1934). When rice fields are flooded the TFA alters its strategy to suit the occasion. It leaves the soil and begins foraging across the canopy of plants. Given the nature of a chemical trail, it is noteworthy that TFA workers forage across moist mud that would seem to weaken the signal (Way et al. 1998).

In India, optimal foraging conditions lie between 77 and 91°F (Veeresh 1990a), but the prime temperature is 78°F, with a critical thermal maximum at about 122°F and a critical thermal minimum at about 36°F (George and Narendran 1987). At these extremes the ants can no longer move and they face certain death unless the temperature moderates. Indian minors are said to remain in the nest while the medias and majors forage, these latter two subcastes hiding when they are disturbed while searching for food (Veeresh 1990a). This subcaste role characterization conflicts with reports from the New World, where minors are known to forage.

Prey are often killed and butchered outside the nest. When collecting screwworm maggots the foragers first sting the larva to death (Lindquist 1942). The tropical bont tick *Amblyomma variegatum* is processed in a stereotyped procedure that is also utilized by the RIFA. One group of ants amputates the legs, chews a hole through the body, and removes its contents, while a second group begins burying the carcass by removing soil from beneath it. This behavior was observed in Guadeloupe, French West Indies (Barre et al. 1991), and may be linked to repellent chemicals the tick possesses.

The tropical fire ant deals with competing ants at a food source by recruiting help and by fighting the other insects, unless these happen to be foragers of the red imported fire ant. In that case the TFA sometimes appeases the RIFA by regurgitating food to it (Hölldobler and Wilson 1990).

Diet

The economically important foods of the tropical fire ant are described in chapter 13. All fire ants are presumably omnivorous in the sense that they feed upon animals, plants, even bacteria and fungi. And they eat them alive or dead. In this way they are more omnivorous than our own species, for we generally shrink from eating the living. Some interesting dietary items that do not have a clear economic impact are used here to illustrate the breadth of the TFA diet.

In Central Texas, seeds are the most commonly collected solid foods. Springtails, a type of very small arthropod, are the most commonly collected animal food. However, most foragers return home with liquid food, carried inside the crop, a condition that can be discerned by close observation of the abdomen. This is sometimes so swollen that it assumes a "striped" appearance from dilation of the body segments. The RIFA forages in a similar manner. Chemical analysis suggests that these liquids are obtained from bugs living on roots (Tennant and Porter 1991).

In Mexico some researchers say the TFA is more predaceous, with little attention to seeds (Butler et al. 1979). Yet the ants do collect seeds of the plant genus *Malachra*, a member of the cotton family (Carroll and Risch 1984). In Florida they collect seeds of carpet grass and alyceclover, a hay and pasture crop (Van Pelt 1958).

On the island of Guam the brush-footed butterfly *Hypolimnas anomala* attempts to guard its eggs from TFA foragers by straddling the eggs and beating its wings together (Nafus and Schreiner 1988). Even prodding with a finger will not drive this dedicated parent from its eggs. The butterfly's tactic repels some predators but not the fire ant, which proceeds to carry off whole clutches.

Feeding Behavior

It is not widely known that adult fire ants feed primarily upon liquids. Travis (1942) realized this and concluded that insoluble poisons were not good choices for those interested in controlling the fire ant because foragers simply sucked liquid from the test baits and left the rest uneaten. Even when the ants were consuming seeds, the liquid portion was imbibed and the solid remainder was discarded (Travis 1941). Adults and larvae eat a seed appendage known as the aril after workers remove it from the seed (Horvitz 1981). The teeth of the major workers eventually wear away from the abrasion caused by these and other seed-processing activities (Trager 1991). Rejected remains are tossed aside in waste dumps or kitchen middens outside the nest (Travis 1941).

As in monogyne nests, trophallaxis (regurgitational exchange of liquids) also occurs within polygyne nests, even though genetic relationships are not as close as those within monogyne nests (Adams et al. 1976a; Goodisman and Ross 1998). Workers from different colonies exchange food in this manner, the larger workers receiving more than the smaller ones (Bhatkar 1979).

I cultured two tropical fire ant colonies while writing this book. On two occasions I fed the larger colony with a species of common brown stink bug. It has an unpleasant defensive odor easily detectable by humans. I thought they might reject it altogether but was amused by the results. The workers transported the entire bug into the chamber of the queen and brood, where I assumed they would butcher it. Later that day I found that the odorous bug remained in place though the entire colony had evacuated its chamber. I attributed this response to the odor and assumed that I had been right about the bug's inedibility. But the next day its remains were back outside and the ants were once again in their chamber. The bug had been dismembered and eaten overnight. The second bug was treated differently, as if the ants had learned from the first experience. It was carried into the chamber, placed less than an inch from the brood, and cut to pieces on the spot. The strong defensive odor of the stink bug did not deter the ants from eating it.

Travis (1942) was surprised to find that the tropical fire ant starved to death within ten days when deprived of food. In line with this is the finding by Sidhu et al. (1979) that its glycogen (animal starch) energy reserves are lower than those of several other closely related insects that were also tested.

Communication

TFA communication via the chemical trail has been treated under "Foraging Behavior." These pheromones are secreted by the Dufour's gland (Barlin et al. 1976), which contains an alkene chemical (Attygalle and Morgan 1983). In one of the first studies on the subject, E. O. Wilson (1962) reported that the Dufour's gland secretion of a TFA worker does not provoke a response from the RIFA, though it does attract the TFA's nestmates. The TFA secretion was noted to attract its closer relative, the SFA, and the RIFA secretion did have a slight, unreciprocated attraction for the tropical fire ant. However, some researchers believe that early comparisons underestimated the response of the various fire ant species to the secretions of others (Lofgren et al. 1975).

The TFA marks its territory with the contents of a very different secretory structure, the metapleural gland of the anterior abdomen. Its colony-specific substance is applied to newly discovered turf whether or not food is present. This can be described as a "land-rush," though its effect, and hence the claim itself, dissipates in less than one day. Pheromones important for the recognition of one colony member by another have been found in the head and thorax but not in the gaster. Cuticular hydrocarbons of the exoskeleton are part of this identification process. Indeed, the hydrocarbons of the tropical fire ant differ from those of the closely related southern fire ant. A complex mixture of this class of molecules is secreted by the postpharyngeal gland of the head. Yet the cocktail mixed by the gland varies even among members of the same colony (Jaffe and Puche 1984; Jaffe 1986; Vander Meer 1986b).

An unidentified substance on the TFA exoskeleton decreases the viability of narcissus pollen. This may explain why ants are not pollinators, though they would appear to be ideal candidates because they are dominant arthropods and because pollination behavior is so widespread among their wasp and bee relations (Hull and Beattie 1988).

Like the RIFA, the TFA has a queen recognition pheromone. Workers will gather at a spot on blotter paper where their own queen was previously confined. The signal persists for three days after she is removed (Jouvenaz et al. 1974). These workers will not respond to the queen recognition pheromone of the RIFA, whether this is obtained naturally or synthesized in the laboratory (Glancey et al. 1984a).

Aggregation is stimulated by the presence of carbon dioxide (Hölldobler and Wilson 1990). Workers chew through any negotiable obstacle to get to a source of the gas. The adaptive value of their response might be the rescue of nestmates trapped by cave-ins or an attraction to brood piles that require tending (Hangartner 1969b). Similarly, the RIFA is attracted to the dry ice (carbon dioxide) of tick traps placed in the field by people studying these parasitic arachnids (Teel et al. 1998).

Certain trace elements are more concentrated in tropical fire ant adults than in the juvenile stages. The significance of this fact is unclear, but only the adults have conspicuous antennae. Antennae are organic detectors, which may utilize trace-element doping, as do diode-type electronic devices that cause electric currents to flow in one direction only (Levy et al. 1979).

Reproduction

The nuptial flight time of the tropical fire ant differs somewhat from that of the RIFA. The TFA commonly flies late on the day of a rain (at dusk) whereas the RIFA usually waits until the day after and then flies in the late morning to afternoon, according to a review by Trager (1991). Yet in Florida, Travis (1941) found that TFA nuptial flights began in late spring and occurred in late afternoon on days following a rain, and he discovered that each nest had several flights per season. Even sprinkling the nest with water can stimulate a flight if conditions are otherwise favorable.

The nuptials of east-central Texas typically occur in late afternoon from May through July (Hung et al. 1977), though I have seen the tropical fire ant flying near Austin as late as December. Smith (1928) observed Mississippi flights on a warm late afternoon in early July, several days after a rain, when the sky was clear, and when the ground had dried considerably. Workers fanned out around the nest while the sexuals poured forth (figs. 5.4, 5.5). The winged reproductives commonly climb into the vegetation surrounding the nest before takeoff. They reenter the nest if the wind picks up or if the temperature drops (Bhatkar 1990).

On July 4, 1999, I witnessed TFA nuptial flight activities going on after dark, when the only light shining on the nest was a streetlight on the University of Texas campus. Dozens of winged females were visible at any one

Fig. 5.4. A TFA major worker, winged queen, and male.

Fig. 5.5. A TFA male.

time, with hundreds to thousands of workers, both majors and minors, in attendance. Not a single male was in sight, and not even the queens were seen to fly though many were climbing to the tips of the grass blades surrounding the nest. It had last rained only an hour or so before, and the dark sky was cloudy.

Generally, TFA flights in the United States span the period from late May until December, with a midsummer peak (Van Pelt 1958; McInnes and Tschinkel 1995). On one fall evening, queens flew to my ultraviolet light in the piney woods of Central Texas. This appears to be the first record of such behavior.

In India, flights occur from March to November (Veeresh 1990a). Yet Phillips (1934), studying this well-known pest in Hawaii, neither saw nor heard of any TFA mating flights. The earliest record of an attempted flight is of an aborted one on the Caribbean island of St. Vincent. That colony was infesting a home. Workers dragged the winged sexuals toward a closed window, which put a stop to their efforts (Forel 1893).

Travis (1941) observed virgin queens flying off with workers still attached to their bodies. The females often climbed into the vegetation before taking flight, though the males commonly flew from the mound itself.

In the United States, multiple-queen colonies (the polygyne social type) have been discovered in Florida and Texas (Banks et al. 1973d; Hung et al. 1977; Lanza et al. 1993; pers. obs.). These are known elsewhere in both the New and the Old World. Polygyne nests have from two to ninety queens, with about thirty being a typical number. Their societies do not produce as many sexuals as monogyne societies, and they are not as populous. Part of this discrepancy is explained by the fact that many of the polygyne queens are not mated. They lay nonviable eggs or eggs that develop into males (unfertilized eggs). On the other hand, thirty-one functional queens were discovered in a single Florida nest. All of these produced workers, so it seems likely that all of them were mated—a process that apparently does not occur in the nest (Adams et al. 1976a). Like RIFA polygyne colonies, those of the TFA can have more than one mound (Vargo 1993).

In Veracruz, Mexico, both social types occur. Polygyne colonies in the area were found to have up to sixteen queens per nest. Like the RIFA polygyne societies, these have smaller workers and higher nest densities than the monogyne type. The workers are also lighter in color than monogyne workers (MacKay et al. 1990).

With the tropical fire ant there is another dimension beyond the two social types known as monogyne and polygyne. There are also two different sizes of queen. These are the large "macrogyne" and the smaller "microgyne" produced by monogyne nests. And their behavior differs too, for their nuptial flights are taken at different times of the year. Macros fly in spring and summer whereas micros fly in the fall. Macros begin their nests alone whereas microgynes join colonies that are already established. It is not clear how the little queen is accepted—every microgyne actually observed landing on an established colony was killed by resident workers (McInnes and Tschinkel 1995). There is no mention in the literature of TFA pleometrosis, a temporary condition formed in some incipient RIFA nests when several queens cooperate in nest founding until the first brood appears. Nevertheless, on several occasions in Central Texas I discovered small groups of up to three winged queens beneath stones.

In Florida at least, each TFA queen seems to mate only once, and in monogyne colonies no virgin queens have been observed to lay eggs (Ross et al. 1988). In one of the earliest and most intriguing studies of the consequences of queen removal from each of several nests, juveniles continued to appear for at least one year (Travis 1938). These could have been overlooked cases of polygyny, with one mated queen or more still present and with both male and female brood still in production. Or they might have been colonies with virgin queens beginning to lay male eggs after the supposedly single mated queen was removed. Unfortunately, the report does not specify the sex of these broods.

Tropical fire ant queens do not seem to produce the diploid variety of the male sex, though the RIFA can (Vargo 1993). Diploid males have twice as many gene-bearing chromosomes as the more common haploid variety of male ant. Nor are the winged TFA virgin queens likely to shed their wings and begin laying eggs when the mated mother queen is removed from her nest. The tendency to do so seems to be unique to one or a very few fire ant species and perhaps evolved when recently mated queens attempted to usurp the reproductive role after joining established colonies (Tschinkel 1998a).

The breakdown of the mated queen's flight muscles as she begins caring for her brood is triggered or at least accompanied by an elevation of calcium ions (Jones et al. 1982). Mating and wing removal normally precede this atrophy in nature, but neither is necessary for the initiation of the process. This was shown when hemolymph (blood) from newly mated winged queens was injected into unmated winged queens, causing their flight muscles to begin degeneration (Davis et al. 1989).

TFA queens possess approximately one hundred ovarioles (Vargo 1993)

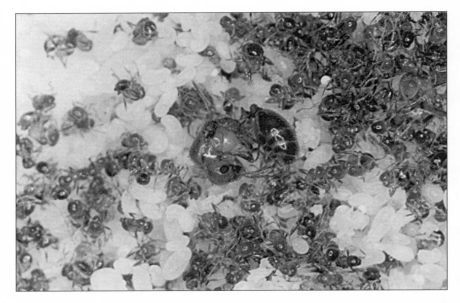

Fig. 5.6. Chilled to inactivity, this TFA queen is surrounded by her workers and brood.

and can lay up to 1,123 eggs per day, with the greatest activity in spring (Travis 1941) (fig. 5.6). They showed no humidity preferences when confined in artificial nests (Phillips 1934). Winged virgins lay few eggs, and all of those observed by Travis (1941) were nonviable. In that early report the author concluded that each colony harbored only one functional queen, and nearly sixty years later, colony budding or fission like that practiced by the polygyne RIFA remains unknown for the TFA. Nor has anyone reported the longevity of the egg layers themselves.

Small tropical fire ant colonies deprived of their queen for weeks will often accept a RIFA queen and even her brood (Wilson 1951). The converse offer is not accepted. Red imported fire ants always kill the proffered TFA queen (Jouvenaz et al. 1974).

Development

Total development time for the TFA shows surprising geographical variation if the reports in the literature are accurate. In the United States, total time of development for all castes is about three to four weeks (Vargo 1993). In India the egg stage (fig. 5.7) is said to last two weeks, the larval stage (figs. 5.8, 5.9, 5.10) six weeks, and the pupal stage (figs. 5.11, 5.12) al-

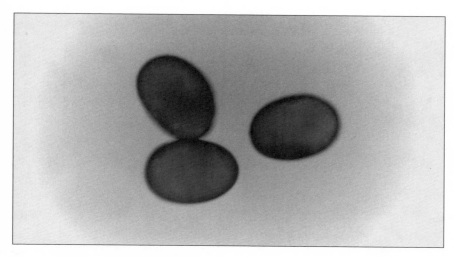

Fig. 5.7. TFA eggs at high magnification.

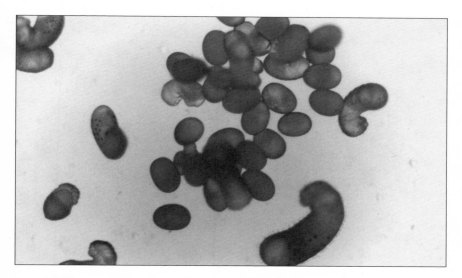

Fig. 5.8. TFA eggs and larvae in various stages of development.

most two weeks (Veeresh 1990a). In Hawaii the egg stage was found to be about seventeen days, the larval period twenty-four days, and the pupal stage nineteen days. Wheeler and Wheeler (1955) reported that the transition from egg to adult requires about two months. These authors found that newly hatched larvae are about 0.63 mm in length, and that those

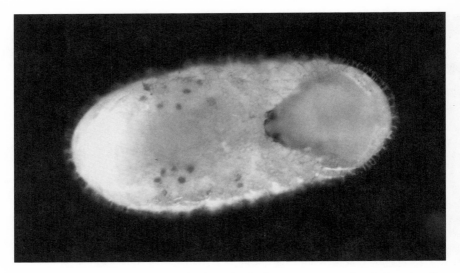

Fig. 5.9. A TFA larva lying on its back in the feeding position, its head closest to the camera.

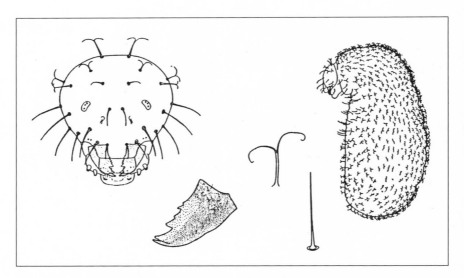

Fig. 5.10. A TFA larva: head, mandible, two body hairs at high magnification, and the entire larva. Reprinted from Wheeler and Wheeler 1955. By permission of *American Midland Naturalist*, published by the University of Notre Dame.

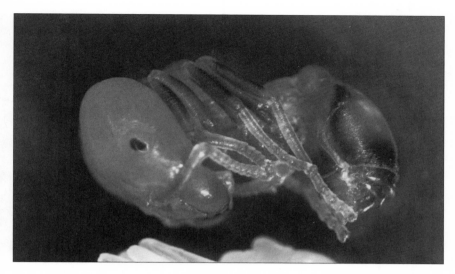

Fig. 5.11. A TFA major worker pupa in an advanced stage of development. Young pupae are white *(bottom)*.

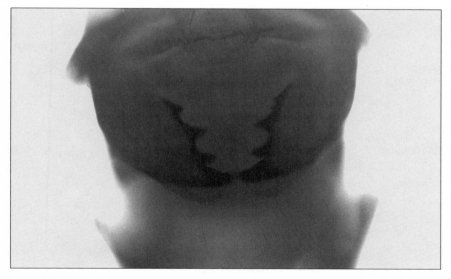

Fig. 5.12. The developing jaws of a TFA media worker pupa, showing an anomaly. There are four teeth on one mandible and five on the other.

developing into minor worker larvae will grow to about 2.6 mm, whereas those developing into major worker larvae will grow to about 5.2 mm. A rudimentary third eye is sometimes present in major workers (Snelling 1963).

The mean weight of the hefty TFA major worker is twice that of the RIFA major, at about 63 mg. TFA minors weigh roughly 4 mg (Munroe et al. 1996) or down to as little as a mere 0.38 mg, according to Wilson (1976). These small workers care for the brood (Wilson 1978), which are most abundant in summer (Van Pelt 1958). Brood chambers are moved about within the nest to track mound areas warmed by the sun (Perfecto and Snelling 1995; Perfecto and Vander Meer 1996). When brood are present the TFA prefers near−100 percent humidity over lesser values (Potts et al. 1984). Tropical fire ant colonies become mature in one to two years (Wilson and Taylor 1967).

CHAPTER 6

Fire Ants Native to the United States

Of all the native ant pests in California,
this is probably the most important.

—*A. Mallis, on the southern fire ant* (1941)

The Southern Fire Ant
(Solenopsis xyloni)

THE most northerly fire ant in the world is known as the southern fire ant (fig. 6.1). This name is not as far off the mark as it seems, in that the ant was discovered in the southern part of its U.S. range and at a time when little was known about either the existence or the distribution of fire ants in general. The SFA became known to science before the other two species that are clearly U.S. natives because its wider geographical range includes the more heavily populated southeastern states that saw earlier Euroamerican colonization and because of its greater economic importance. Henry C. McCook was the Philadelphia minister who achieved the distinction of discovering this ant during his study of cotton-field insects (McCook 1879). For this reason the SFA made its first appearance in the literature as a beneficial predator of destructive caterpillars. This is also the first report on the biology of any fire ant. A Texas state geologist who had an interest in ants might have beaten McCook to the punch by twelve years if he had been more precise in his published descriptions

Fig. 6.1. The range of the southern fire ant.

of "Atta brazoensis" and "Myrmica sabeana" (Buckley 1867). It is not clear what insects these really were.

The southern fire ant has been eliminated over much of its range by the two imported species. It is now rare or even absent along the Gulf Coast (Trager 1991). Other common names for the SFA include California fire ant and cotton-ant.

Nesting Sites. Southern fire ants build their nests in dry deserts, grass-lands, arroyos, in sandy areas along streambeds, and at the bases of vegetation and trees. Like their close relatives they can nest in the open or under cover, such as beneath stones (Wheeler 1915; Wisdom and Whitford 1981; Creighton 1930). Even soil described as "hard ground" is not off limits (Essig 1926; pers. obs.). Yet they often choose moist, sandy, shaded areas (Creighton 1950) and disturbed habitats (Hooper and Rust 1997). This species was probably one of the unidentified New Mexican fire ants that took advantage of a disturbance caused by grazing cattle—they utilized the newly available cow pats as cover for nesting sites, and thereby increased in abundance while a formerly dominant species declined (Nash et al. 1998).

The SFA is more prone than the RIFA to nest within artificial structures (Wilson and Eads 1949). For example, in California, the southern fire ant colonizes commercial buildings and homes, using kitchens, wall spaces, and areas near basement furnaces, where its nests can be unusually large (Mallis 1938, 1941; Knight and Rust 1990). Nests are common along sidewalks, on lawns, in cracks and crevices of concrete, and beneath logs, cow chips, and even carcasses. Old bones buried by dogs are said to be favorite nesting places. In California's wilder habitats this fire ant occurs in sand dunes, in creosote bush–palo verde habitats, in cholla cactus–palo verde habitats (Wheeler and Wheeler 1973), and even in the extreme heat of Death Valley, at elevations ranging from −160 feet to 4,500 feet (Wheeler and Wheeler 1986). E. O. Essig (1926) reported the presence of the SFA in strawberry fields. In nearby Nevada the species was found only in the hot desert areas in the southern part of the state. One nest was in a pile of discarded seed chaff near a colony of harvester ants (Wheeler and Wheeler 1986).

A survey of the ants of western Texas found the SFA at altitudes ranging from just over three hundred feet to almost three thousand, where it prefers clay and sandy loam over more purely sandy soil. Most nests were found in the open, but some occurred under boards, rocks, and cow dung (Moody and Francke 1982). Along the coast of Texas in the early part of the century the SFA was reported to nest in telephone company electrical boxes

(Eagleson 1940). It is possible that these were tropical fire ants, which were often confused with southern fire ants in the early literature. In Louisiana the SFA was found in the shade beneath trees where it had been driven from the sun by red imported fire ants (Baroni Urbani and Kannowski 1974).

Like the TFA, the SFA exists as a dark, blackish variety and as a light, reddish variety. The dark phase prefers more humid habitats and the light phase prefers the desert (Trager 1991).

The Nest. None of the three fire ant species clearly native to the United States builds a mound as large as those of the imported species. Yet conspicuous crater-type superstructures are common when southern fire ants nest in open areas. These are irregular in shape and can be several feet wide, with a height of an inch or so. Vinson (1997) described the southern fire ant's mound as flatter than that of the RIFA, and my own limited experience in West Texas supports that generalization.

Sometimes the superstructure is a crater several inches wide with a single small entrance or an irregular sandy mound thrown up at the base of a plant. The largest example on record appears to have been a structure six feet wide with thirty-six craters on top, each about an inch in width (Wheeler and Wheeler 1973). Sometimes the nests are marked by little more than a hole or a few cracks in the ground. When nesting beneath a stone the ants often heap soil to one side, but of course one does not expect to see any mound at all in this situation.

SFA mounds have a porous texture and have been described as "sponge-like" (Mallis 1938, 1941), though Francke et al. (1986) found the internal anatomy less gallery-riddled than in those of the TFA and the imported species. The insect sometimes changes the location of its nest entrance (Zalom and Bentley 1985).

Wray (1962) discovered hundreds of mounds up to ten inches in height along a railroad track in North Carolina. Other nests were located beneath rocks. It is tempting to suggest that the big mounds were actually those of RIFA colonies. In fact, Francke et al. (1983) were quick to point out the great anatomical similarity between the two ant species.

Nest Population. The literature contains no census, exact or approximate, of a southern fire ant nest. Wheeler (1915) and Cole (1934) simply describe the colonies as "populous."

Foraging Behavior. In New Mexico the southern fire ant forages on fruiting yucca stalks (Van Zee et al. 1997). In Georgia it patrols corn (Barber 1933), and in Baja California it collects nectar from barrel cacti in the central desert region (Blom and Clark 1980). Foragers in southern California are active year-round, though they remain in the nest during the hot-test hours in summer. They are attracted to lights at night, where they prey upon other insects with a similar habit. Foraging is more constant from sheltered nests than from nests in open areas (Mallis 1938), and activity is greatest in the morning and just before sunset (Zalom and Bentley 1985). Other investigators found the SFA foraging mostly at night, beginning a few hours before sunset (Hooper and Rust 1997). In the Mojave Desert, for-aging occurs when surface soil temperatures are between 70 and 109°F (Bernstein 1979). The workers are said to move slowly in their search for food. They once entered a home and foraged for cookies in a desk drawer (Wheeler and Wheeler 1973).

Along the coast of Texas (before the SFA was extirpated by the invading RIFA), foraging activity appears to have been greatest during the months from May to October (Eagleson 1940). Once again, this may be a mis-identification of the tropical fire ant. Both species, and all other fire ants oc-curring in Texas, die within hours when exposed to a temperature of 100°F (when the humidity is zero percent). Though it is a native of hot climes and deserts, one study found that the SFA does not survive heat stress as well as the RIFA (Braulick et al. 1988). On the other hand, Munroe et al. (1996) re-ported that the SFA does indeed resist desiccation better than the RIFA.

Southern fire ants are group foragers (Davidson 1977), meaning that they commonly form long files as they leave the nest to retrieve food for the colony.

Diet and Feeding Behavior. Like all U.S. fire ants, the SFA has a broad and opportunistic diet. For example, it is a dominant omnivore in New Mex-ico grasslands (Wisdom and Whitford 1981). Specific examples of dietary items that make the southern fire ant economically important are covered in chapter 13. The literature offers nothing on the feeding behavior of this species.

Seeds are sometimes stored in the nest (Wheeler and Wheeler 1986), and in New Mexico these comprise 25 percent of the ant's diet (Whitford 1978). Experiments designed to identify the best baits for use with poisons found a combination of freeze-dried egg and anchovy to be most satisfac-tory foods (Hooper and Rust 1997).

Communication. Little research has been done on the means of com-munication between southern fire ants. The cuticular hydrocarbons of the SFA are said to be "normal" and can be used to identify the species (Vander Meer 1986b). These compounds are probably useful in nature for nestmate recognition.

Reproduction. The California swarming season lasts from May through September. Flights are likely to occur on warm evenings following a period of several cool days (Mallis 1938). In summer these nuptial flights peak around 6:00 P.M. when temperatures are near 86°F. The sexuals (figs. 6.2, 6.3) were observed taking off from shaded areas (McCluskey and Mc-Cluskey 1984).

Fig. 6.2. A SFA winged queen.

Fig. 6.3. A SFA male.

Arkansas flights have been reported to occur in late afternoon from 3:30 to 5:30 P.M., reaching their peak in June. About one half hour before the flight, workers patrolled the nest area and prepared exit holes for the males and winged virgin queens. A single nest produced 3,754 alates during one season—less than half the number produced by the most prolific RIFA nest in the same area. Each colony tended to specialize in the production of one sex or the other, and the overall sex ratio for a given population of nests was about 2:1, female to male (Roe 1974).

The first southern fire ant nest known to be polygynous was found in Texas. That colony had at least twelve queens (Summerlin 1976). Polygyne nests are now known from California, where Hooper and Rust (1997) found this to be the only social condition of the species at their field site.

Development. SFA workers show no preference for particular humidities except when tending brood. At these moments they prefer very high humidity indeed (Potts et al. 1984). This seems to be generally true of fire ants. And SFA brood-tending workers also prefer higher temperatures than do the other U.S. fire ants (Cokendolpher and Francke 1985).

The Golden Fire Ant *(Solenopsis aurea)*

This attractive insect is also known as the desert fire ant. Of the six fire ant species found in the United States, only *Solenopsis amblychila*, lacking even a common name, has been studied less than the GFA. In a sense they have been studied together because until fairly recently, *S. amblychila* was not recognized as a separate species. The most striking aspect of both insects is the golden color of the smallest workers.

Nesting Sites. The golden fire ant was discovered by William Morton Wheeler in Austin, Texas, but is now less common there than it once was. The red imported fire ant is partly responsible for this development. GFA colonies are found beneath stones (Wheeler 1906; Francke et al. 1986), beneath dung and logs, and in open areas (Creighton 1930; Moody et al. 1981; Moody and Francke 1982). Creighton (1950) generalized that golden fire ant nests are usually built in the open, in dry, coarse, gravelly soil. Yet Wheeler (1908a) found them always nesting beneath stones.

On a coarser geographical scale (fig. 6.4), the GFA lives in deserts, in the mountains of southern California (Snelling 1963), and in arid western Texas at elevations from just over 325 feet to a little over one mile, where it nests in all kinds of soil, though the preference is for sand and sandy loam (Moody and Francke 1982). Altitude does not seem to be an important factor (Moody et al. 1981).

Fig. 6.4. The range of the golden fire ant.

The Nest. I happened upon a true mound of the golden fire ant in the middle of RIFA country, on the University of Texas campus where Wheeler worked one hundred years before. It was on a lawn in a heavily trafficked and RIFA-infested area. At the time I did not realize that a simple photograph and description of the small nest would have been worth publishing. In fact, I assumed it was just another RIFA nest until I examined members of all sexes and castes under a microscope. The literature supports the generalization that GFA mounds, when present at all, are insignificant structures (Creighton 1930; Francke et al. 1986; Braulick et al. 1988). The internal anatomy of the nest is unknown.

Nest Population. The literature provides no census of a golden fire ant nest. Wheeler simply described the colonies as small.

Foraging Behavior, Diet, and Feeding Behavior. Being a fire ant, the GFA is omnivorous (Whitford 1978). Yet what little is known about its foraging behavior is strikingly different from the foraging behavior of the other U.S. fire ants. The GFA is more strongly committed to nocturnal hunting (Wheeler 1906; pers. obs.), and its small eyes are certainly suggestive of that fact. In Wheeler's words, "It appears to be nocturnal or hypogaeic, unlike the typical *geminata*, which is found abroad at all hours of the day."

Creighton (1930) supported Wheeler's generalization. Workers were rarely seen outside the nest during the day. Several foragers demonstrated this propensity while carrying a beetle home to the nest one morning. When the sun rose high in the sky they dropped the food and hid beneath stones. And when a covered nest was exposed to light, the workers disappeared inside. Red imported fire ants greet disturbance by moving in the opposite direction.

I once saw workers long after dark, running down the trunk of an oak tree on the University of Texas campus in Austin. Their great speed, density, and fervor suggested a colony emigration rather than a foraging party. I also caught a winged queen after dark in the same area. It had been attracted to an incandescent light on the side of a building. I have not found the sexuals (figs. 6.5, 6.6) of any other fire ant at such lights, though TFA queens flew to my ultraviolet light in the piney woods of Central Texas. I am unaware of any previous records of fire ants being attracted to lights at night.

When temperatures rise above 107°F, at least half of the exposed workers die after one hour (Francke et al. 1985). Surprisingly, in those experiments the desert fire ant did not tolerate experimental heat stress as well as

Fig. 6.5. The castes and sexes of
the golden fire ant. *From top:*
winged queen, male, major
worker, minor worker.

Fig. 6.6. A GFA male.

the RIFA, though the RIFA did not come to the United States from any desert. Its larger size may be responsible for its greater survival in these tests. Another surprise was the GFA's preferred temperatures. It preferred *lower* temperatures than did all other fire ants tested (Cokendolpher and Francke 1985), and it did not survive desiccation as well as the tropical fire ant (Braulick et al. 1988). There does not seem to be much difference among the U.S. fire ants regarding the other extreme of freezing tolerance (Francke et al. 1986). All in all, calling this species the desert fire ant is not as useful as one might imagine.

Communication, Reproduction, and Development. The literature contains no reports on GFA communication and reproduction. Cokendolpher and Francke (1983) discovered a gynandromorph (part male, part queen) in western Texas (fig. 6.7). As is true for every fire ant species tested, brood-tending GFA workers seek out high humidity for the soft-bodied juvenile stages.

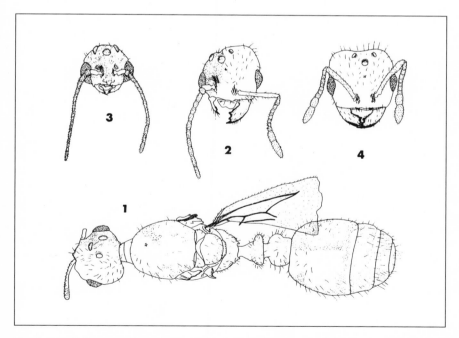

Fig. 6.7. A GFA gynandromorph. Head of normal male *(top left),* head of gynandro-morph *(top center),* head of normal queen *(top right),* and dorsal view of gynandromorph *(bottom).* Reprinted from Cokendolpher and Francke 1983. By permission of New York Entomological Society.

Fig. 6.8. The range of *Solenopsis amblychila*.

Fig. 6.9. A *Solenopsis amblychila* winged queen.

Fig. 6.10. A *Solenopsis amblychila* male *(bottom)*, with major worker *(center)*, and media worker *(top)*.

Solenopsis amblychila

This fire ant has no common name. It also could be called golden, were that not already taken by its closest relative, *Solenopsis aurea*. The lack of a common name is understandable to the extent that this insect has often been considered a mere subspecies of the GFA. It is the least known of all fire ants native to the United States (figs. 6.8, 6.9, 6.10).

William Morton Wheeler discovered *S. amblychila* nesting in populous colonies under large stones at high elevations in the Huachuca Mountains of southern Arizona. He also had samples from Guadalajara, Mexico. Considering the supposedly small colonies of its relative the golden fire ant, I was surprised to read that *S. amblychila* has populous colonies (Wheeler 1915). The true variation in colony size has yet to be assessed for either species.

Creighton (1950) reports this insect as nesting in open, gravelly areas, with no mound. According to Trager (1991), *Solenopsis amblychila* nests at higher elevations than the GFA.

CHAPTER **7**   Fire Ants Endemic
to South America

We found some colonies with more than a
million ants inside. I've been studying fire ants
for 17 years, and I've never seen anything like it.

—*D. F. Williams, on a South American fire ant,*
  perhaps the formiga rúiva (Adams 1994)

LITTLE is known about the fire ant species that
do not occur within the borders of the United States.
Unfortunately, this number comprises roughly two
thirds of the world's fire ant species. All are found in
South America and nowhere else. Furthermore, their
taxonomy (identification by scientific name) has been
highly unstable over the years, making it risky to
match early natural history notes with the species
names that are recognized today. I have drawn upon
the excellent review by Trager (1991) unless otherwise noted. (Two *Solenopsis* species that may or may
not be fire ants are mentioned in appendix 1 but
are not treated here.) The RIFA, BIFA, and TFA are
South American natives that are not confined to that
continent. Each has a chapter of its own.

Solenopsis bruesi Creighton

This Peruvian species occurs in sandy deserts
and in cities.

Solenopsis daguerrei (Santschi)

Solenopsis daguerrei of Argentina, Brazil, and Uruguay is a social para-site. In other words it has no worker caste and must make its living in the nests of other fire ants, usually existing among its hosts in a polygyne con-dition. These host species include *S. macdonaghi, S. saevissima,* the RIFA, and the BIFA (Briano et al. 1997). Details on the biology of Daguerre's fire ant can be found in chapter 12. It will no longer be endemic to South Amer-ica if it becomes established in the United States for biocontrol against the RIFA.

Solenopsis electra Forel

A species known from Argentina, Bolivia, and Paraguay, this ant builds cryptic nests in the well-drained soils of dry lowlands and in rocky areas of the Andean foothills.

Solenopsis gayi (Spinola)

Found at low elevations in Chile, Peru, and Colombia, *S. gayi* is the smallest of the South American fire ants. It is known to be a group forager in northern Chile, where it collects seeds of the plantain *Plantago hispidula* and the filaree *Erodium cicutarium* (Medel and Fuentes 1995). Perhaps it is South America's harvester fire ant, as the TFA is a harvester of more cos-mopolitan distribution.

Solenopsis interrupta Santschi

Solenopsis interrupta dwells in the deserts of northern Argentina and in the Andean foothills of Bolivia. It seems to have polygyne societies in addi-tion to the presumably primitive monogyne type.

Solenopsis macdonaghi Santschi

This floodplain species has been collected in Argentina, Bolivia, Para-guay, and Uruguay. Bruch (1926b) discovered a new species of histerid bee-tle that was living in a nest of these ants beneath a stone.

Solenopsis megergates Trager

A native of Brazil, *S. megergates* has the largest workers of any fire ant species.

Solenopsis pusillignis Trager

This ant is a small species with a correspondingly mild sting. It lives in the cerrado (savanna region) of Brazil.

Solenopsis pythia Santschi

Solenopsis pythia may be a social parasite living in the nests of other fire ants. It occurs in Argentina and Brazil.

Solenopsis quinquecuspis Forel

A resident of Argentina, Brazil, and Uruguay, *S. quinquecuspis* has polygyne colonies in addition to the primitive monogyne society.

Solenopsis saevissima (Smith)

This species is known in Brazil as the *formiga rúiva* (red ant). Gonçalves (1940) was among the first to publish on the biology, pest status, and chemical control of a South American fire ant, writing about this pest when the RIFA was just beginning its invasion of the United States. The fire ant mound photos in that publication are the earliest of which I am aware. The formiga rúiva makes its nest in sandy soil and avoids clay. The resulting mounds could pass for those of the RIFA and BIFA, complete with their honeycombed interiors.

Solenopsis saevissima is a pest in citrus groves. It builds its nest at the base of a tree and gnaws at flowers, new leaves, and even the bark in the proximity of the mound. Again on the negative side, it tends and protects the scale insect *Pseudococcus comstocki,* which is also a pest in these same orchards. The tiny bug attacks leaves, branches, and roots. The ants carry female scales into the nest and even allow them to enter the mound without escort. Eventually the bugs are carried outside and placed on the roots of the host plant. Creoline emulsion and cyanide salts were prescribed to kill the ants. The formiga rúiva is also a formidable pest of *Solanum gilo,* a member of the potato family that is cultivated for its edible fruit (Picanco et al. 1997).

Fifty-three years after the pioneering paper of Gonçalves, what appeared to be *Solenopsis saevissima* flared up spectacularly in the town of Envira, Brazil. Some nests were ten feet long and contained over a million ants, which were even more aggressive than the RIFA in the United States (Adams 1994). Habitat disturbance was perhaps one factor in this development. Habitats are disturbed whenever rain forest is cleared away, and fire ants are excellent recolonizers of the resulting ecological vacuum. The problem was exacerbated when use of DDT was discontinued; it probably controlled fire ants while killing its principal target, the malaria mosquito.

Though the RIFA has not made it west across the sea to the Galápagos Islands, *Solenopsis saevissima* has. This species and the tropical fire ant are considered threats to the endemic diversity of the archipelago (Peck et al. 1998).

On the beneficial side, *Solenopsis saevissima* is also a predator of the pest weevil *Rhigopsidius tucumanus*, which attacks potatoes in South America (de Manero Estela and Vilte 1982).

The socially parasitic fire ant, *Solenopsis daguerrei*, invades the nests of several fire ant species in South America. The formiga rúiva is one of these (Pesquero et al. 1998). Other natural enemies of this ant include certain tiny flies of the family Phoridae, and some of these parasitoids are currently being used for biocontrol of the RIFA in the United States. Phorids are commonly known as humpbacked flies or scuttle flies. *Solenopsis saevissima* is said to be attacked by more phorids than any other fire ant known to date, though the conclusion could be due to sampling bias. Part of the fly's life cycle is spent inside the adult ant's head (see chapter 12). Other phorid species live inside the nest as "houseguests" (Disney 1994).

Apodicrania termophila is a phorid fly said to attack certain South American fire ants (Wojcik 1990), though it is not clear if *S. saevissima* is one of them. If so, it would be unusual because this fly is also reported to live part of its life as a parasite of the fire ant *larva* and to spend another part of its life being tended by the fire ants. I could find no confirmation of fire ant hosts for this fly in the standard reference on phorids (Disney 1994).

Solenopsis weyrauchi Trager

This fire ant is a Peruvian native restricted to the high altitude grasslands of the Andes Mountains (over 14,000 feet).

In conclusion, it is clear that almost nothing is known about the vast majority of fire ant species. Research opportunities in South America are wide open.

CHAPTER 8

The Origin and Evolution of Fire Ants

Of course a progressive advance may eventually
come to a dead end, as has happened with the insects,
when all the biological possibilities inherent in
the type of organization have been exploited.

—*Julian Huxley* (1943)

JULIAN HUXLEY gave the Modern Evolutionary Synthesis its name. In his book (1943) he suggested that the evolution of the insects had come to an end. Nevertheless, it is a mistake to count insects out of the evolutionary game. They are tens of millions of species strong, they are incredibly diverse, they continue to mutate, and their environment is always changing. Huxley scored one of his many successes several pages later by gazing far enough into the future to visualize cloning. It is too early to know if he was correct in his vision of a cloned human race with a caste system like that of the ants. William Morton Wheeler seemed to share Huxley's conviction that the evolution of ants stopped or at least stalled millions of years ago (Wheeler 1928). But in reality, ants and all other insects continue to evolve, as the fire ants are doing at this very moment. We see it in the polygyne social form, in hybrids between the U.S. natives, and in hybrids between the two imported species (fig. 8.1).

The story began at least thirty million years ago in South America where the first fire ant came onto

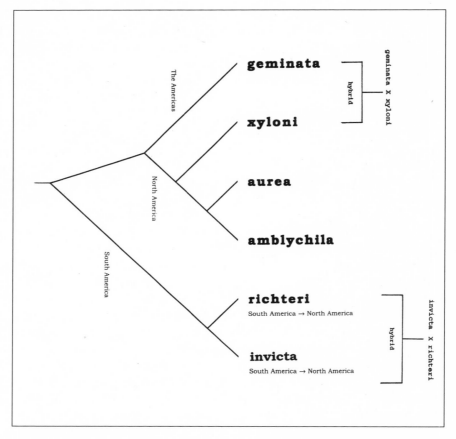

Fig. 8.1. Genetic relatedness among the U.S. fire ants when considered alone. The family tree would look very different if it included all of the South American species, but this problem has not been solved.

the scene (Wilson 1986); pieces of Dominican amber twenty-five million years old contain a typical fire ant worker and its thief ant relatives. This was probably a tropical species, though the modern RIFA and BIFA are better described as creatures of the temperate zone (Hays 1959), a fact which goes a long way toward explaining their success in the United States. The closest relative of the fire ant genus *Solenopsis* also arose in the neotropics, where it remains to this day. Little-known *Oxyepoecus* is a genus of eleven species that inhabit leaf litter and the nests of other ants (Bolton 1987). They have no common name and no impact on humans.

The most successful of the modern fire ants display the hallmarks of highly derived or "advanced" species. These include large colonies, deep nests, and extensive trail systems. Although the evolutionary tree has not been explicitly worked out in this case, the phylogeny of the harvester ants, also arising in the New World tropics, supports that contention entirely if the general trends in the two groups have been roughly parallel (Taber 1998). Sometimes the evolutionary success of a group can be linked to a very specific characteristic or feature. The unusual alkaloid venom of the fire ants may have a great deal to do with their success (Wilson 1986). Its effect on our own species when used in defense of the colony gave these insects their common name. The venom has a second defensive function that is not widely known. Workers apply it within the nest as a microbe-killing fumigant (Escoubas and Blum 1990). Yet the venom's original adaptive value might have been offensive in nature. The insects also use it to subdue their prey (Vinson 1997).

Hypotheses have been offered to explain the adaptive value of the subterranean foraging tunnels that fan out in all directions from the fire ant mound. These tunnels protect workers from excessive heat, and perhaps that was their original function. Or perhaps the underground refuges evolved as a defense against attacks by the deadly phorid flies that plague workers outside the nest (Porter et al. 1995c) (see chapter 12). The adaptive value of the mound itself is treated in chapter 3. It can be thought of as an incubator for developing brood.

There are surprisingly few fire ant species, given the individual successes of some of their number and the apparent age of the group as a whole. A satisfactory solution to this puzzle must await the reconstruction of a more complete evolutionary tree than that of fig 8.1. Such an analysis would ideally but unrealistically include the roughly 150 thief ant species that round out the genus *Solenopsis*. Three possibilities come to mind: (1) the thief ants and fire ants are sister groups and are therefore of an equal age, (2) the fire ants arose from within the family of thief ants, or (3) the thief ants arose from within the family of fire ants. If fire ants do indeed comprise a monophyletic or complete family group (see glossary), then the third alternative is ruled out. All in all the second possibility seems most likely. In this case the fire ant lineage evolved from some thief ant ancestor, perhaps as the result of an adaptive radiation linked to an increase in body size over the smaller primitive condition.

The successful ongoing hybridization between the distantly related RIFA and BIFA in the United States could be explained by evolution so rapid that barriers against such matings have lagged behind the evolution of other structures and behaviors (Maynard Smith and Száthmary 1995). The

BIFA is actually more closely related to *Solenopsis quinquecuspis,* and the RIFA's closest relative has not been determined. Similarities among fire ants are certainly conducive to hybridization when considered at the level of chromosome number. For example, the females of South American *S. saevissima* and those of all U.S. species that have been karyotyped display a diploid number of thirty-two (Crozier 1970; Glancey et al. 1976c; Taber and Cokendolpher 1988; Goni et al. 1983).

Heterozygosity is one measure of genetic variation and is therefore an indicator of evolutionary potential. The greater the heterozygosity, the more likely it is that the species in question can adapt to a sudden change in its environment. Regarding the potential for future evolution of the RIFA and BIFA populations on U.S. soil, Ross and Trager (1990) discovered that these colonists are not significantly less heterozygous than the South American populations from which they came. This is unexpected because the colonization of the north was accomplished recently and by only a few individuals that presumably brought with them only a small portion of the total genetic diversity possessed by the species. Perhaps the explosive proliferation and range expansion of these disturbed-habitat specialists compensated for any variation that might have been left behind in the large South American gene pool.

In some respects the genetic structure of fire ant populations fits predictions. Because the tropical fire ant has been a U.S. resident longer than either import, its genetic diversity in this part of the world is expected to be higher than that of either the U.S. RIFA or the U.S. BIFA. This has been confirmed. And although the BIFA arrived shortly before the RIFA, its range has been greatly diminished since the latter came ashore, and its genetic diversity would be expected to have been lowered as a consequence. This too has been demonstrated (Ross et al. 1987b).

An evolutionary paradox posed by ants in general has been addressed with the RIFA and a few other species serving as model organisms. The paradox is the existence of a sterile worker caste. Charles Darwin was aware of this fact and was unsure how to explain it with his new hypothesis. How could natural selection possibly favor the loss of an ability to lay eggs? He soon got onto the right track (Darwin 1859, pp. 237–42), but it was the modern theory of "kin selection" that finally gave us answers in the form of measurable quantities. The idea was put forward that worker ants, in the simplest scenario, are more closely related to their sisters (75%) than they would be to any theoretical offspring they might have had (50%), though for similar reasons they are rather distantly related to their brothers (25%). It would then be better in a genetic sense to raise sisters (including the reproductive future queens of the queen's brood) instead of daughters, even if the workers in question *could* reproduce on their own. Presumably it was selection and not willpower that acted on this genetic peculiarity until the workers lost the ability to reproduce altogether. The RIFA has confirmed one prediction of this theory—colonies do produce approximately three times as many sexual females as males (Vargo 1996).

The Red Imported Fire Ant

The ultimate origin of the RIFA itself is unclear, and there is little on record even in the way of speculation. Allen et al. (1974) suggested that this fire ant is a rather recently evolved species that made its first appearance when rain forest began shrinking near the Pantanal region along the Brazil/Paraguay border. Habitat alterations subsequently triggered the origin of the insect. Today this historically important region is a cattle ranching area sparsely populated by humans.

However the species came onto the scene in South America, the total amount of genetic variation possessed by the homeland population is roughly equal to the amount of variation possessed by the descendants of the North American colonists, as mentioned earlier. An even greater surprise was the later discovery that the mitochondrial DNA within a single South American RIFA population showed more variation than one normally sees when comparing different *species* of ants (Ross et al. 1997). Its variability could be explained if it has occupied the area in question for a very long time, allowing large numbers of mutations to accumulate. With its substantial intraspecific diversity it is no surprise to find that the RIFA is not an inbreeding species (Ross et al. 1987b). All in all it appears that the RIFA possesses an abundance of the raw material needed for future evolution.

Pleometrosis. The origin of cooperative nest founding from the primitive condition of a single founder is as unclear as the origin of the RIFA itself. In fact, the RIFA and perhaps the TFA appear to be the only fire ants that engage in this collectivist behavior, known to myrmecologists as pleometrosis. It is easy to enumerate certain adaptive advantages of pleometrosis. Cooperating queens do tend to be more robust in terms of survival ability than those that begin their nests alone (Tschinkel and Howard 1983; Tschinkel 1998b). Indeed, a group of three RIFA queens is better able to hold off attacking tropical fire ant workers than a queen on her own, though when as many as four queens are present the competition among them can overwhelm the advantages of mutual defense (Jerome et al. 1998). Perhaps these associations have something to do with the fact that mated queens typically devote their sting apparatus to brood care instead of using it as a weapon (though virgin queens do sometimes sting objects that disturb the nest). A second and equally obvious advantage of pleometrosis is the (albeit temporary) presence of at least twice as many egg layers as in a colony begun by a single queen. Vargo (1988a) identified a third advantage that seems related to the second. Sexuals are produced earlier in a colony's life when it is founded by pleometrosis. Those who rate the RIFA as a pest would prefer that a fourth possibility never materializes. What if the sterile female caste reversed its evolution and began adding eggs to the pile by the tens of thousands? Unmated workers of a Japanese ant do precisely this. In fact, evolution did away with their queen altogether (Hölldobler and Wilson 1990). A disadvantage of pleometrosis, to some queens at least, is the fact that all but one of the initially cooperating foundresses will perish soon after the first brood appears.

The Two Social Forms of the RIFA: Monogyne and Polygyne. Monogyne colonies are those relatively mature nests with a single functional queen. They are typically begun by a single queen or by a few queens, but only one survives the battles that break out soon after the first workers appear. The more complex polygyne society arose from such a monogyne condition, perhaps on several or even numerous occasions. It differs from monogyne colonies because mature nests have more than one queen whether or not the colony arose from a single founder, from pleometrosis, or from a pre-existing polygyne nest.

Polygyne colonies thus have at least two functional queens and sometimes as many as twenty thousand. Some are mated and some are not. In this case the society's egg layers are able to coexist on an essentially permanent basis despite their lack of relatedness (Goodisman and Ross 1998, 1999). It is notable that they seem to represent a random sample from the queens of the surrounding area. The origin of sociality itself presents an evolutionary question because insect societies contain individuals that work but do not transmit their genes to offspring. Polygyny adds a second level to the problem because we must explain how groups of unrelated social insect queens form associations in which the reproductive success of some egg layers is presumably lower than the success they would have on their own (Ross 1989).

The use of marked and released individuals shows that polygyne-type queens (those raised in polygyne society) can be adopted by colonies not originally their own (Glancey and Lofgren 1988) or by their birth colonies (Porter 1991). Polygyne societies are known to accept foreign queens of the monogyne type (those raised in a monogyne society) as well as those of the polygyne type, and monogyne colonies sometimes accept polygyne queens (Ross et al. 1987b). The single exception from among the four possible scenarios is the monogyne/monogyne combination. Monogyne societies kill encroaching monogyne-type queens. Young polygyne-type queens do have lower energy reserves than monogyne queens. This could be the driving force behind their attempt to take an easy way out by joining an established nest (Keller and Ross 1993b). Perhaps the association arises again and again when swarms of recently mated queens saturate available nesting sites and begin entering mounds in such great numbers that resident workers are unable to kill or expel them (Porter et al. 1988; Morel et al. 1990; Tschinkel 1998a).

The polygyne condition is considered a greater threat to native ecosystems than the monogyne type and may owe its origin to habitat disturbances caused by humans (Ross and Fletcher 1985a). The condition presents a problem for pest control because there are more queens to kill (sometimes tens of thousands), and because polygyne colonies are more resistant to the popular Amdro bait than are monogyne colonies (Glancey et al. 1990). Polygyny may also represent a step in the direction of a new species.

Polygyny was first reported by Glancey et al. (1973c) for a U.S. colony harboring twenty queens. This was followed by the discovery of a single supercolony with at least thirty-six mounds and over three thousand queens (Glancey et al. 1975) and one with more than twenty thousand queens (Glancey et al. 1976c). However, polygyny may have been stumbled upon earlier by Favorite (1958), and then by Rhoades and Davis (1967), who found that marked ants of one colony were accepted readily by the ants of "other colonies." The insects were from northwestern Florida (near Mobile, Alabama), and because this date is an early one in the history of fire ant research and both species may have occupied the location, it is not clear whether these were RIFA or BIFA nests.

There are profound physical and behavioral differences between the members of the two RIFA societies. Characteristics of the polygyne form include: (1) two or more mated, egg-laying queens, (2) functional virgin queens in the nest that lay eggs developing into males, (3) small workers, (4) less aggressive workers, (5) higher mound density, (6) high frequency of sterile males, (7) queens that are individually less prolific than monogyne queens, (8) queens lighter in weight than monogyne queens, and

(9) lighter-colored workers (Vinson and Ellison 1996). Polygyne nests sometimes contain no workers large enough to be described as majors (Trager 1991), and they can grow to become "supercolonies" with many mounds, though these are not necessarily larger than monogyne mounds (Porter et al. 1991). One can see how these differences might well point toward the evolution of a new fire ant species. The polygyne type is spreading in the Central Texas area and is encroaching on ground held by the monogyne type (Greenberg and Vinson 1986). Yet they are not expanding rapidly in the southeastern United States. It appears that early fears of explosive polygyne expansion were premature (Porter 1993).

As stated earlier, polygyne red imported fire ants are said to be a greater threat to native ecosystems than the monogyne type. For example, an advance across the grounds of a Central Texas biological field station was accomplished primarily by budding, something that a monogyne society cannot do. Budding occurs whenever a queen leaves the nest with a following of workers. Nuptial flights, the only mode of colony reproduction practiced by the primitive monogyne type, were often unsuccessful in the area (Porter and Savignano 1990). A single polygyne mound can bud into eight in less than half a year (Vargo and Porter 1989). The consequences of this Texas advance are described in detail in chapter 13.

What might be a second type of polygyne colony was also discovered in Texas. The three queens were physogastric and heavy, conditions normally associated with the monogyne type. Even more surprising was an egg-laying rate exceeding that of monogyne queens. Two of these polygyne queens were executed by their own workers when isolated from the brood (Vinson and Ellison 1996).

Perhaps the origin and proliferation of the polygyne colony in the United States is due to escape from natural enemies that suppress it back home in Brazil, where mounds are smaller, colonies are less common, and the native ants are more diverse (Porter et al. 1992). Indeed, no polygynous colonies were known in South America in the early days of fire ant research (Wojcik 1986; Fowler et al. 1990), though multiple-queen colonies are now known to exist on both continents (Trager 1991; Tschinkel 1998a). The RIFA queens of South American nests are fewer and are close relatives, not essentially unrelated like those of U.S. polygyne nests.

Although the RIFA polygyne type has been thought by some to be a species in the making, early biochemical studies showed no real differences between the two social forms. This work did find differences between the BIFA and each of the RIFA social types, and it showed the TFA to be even more different from either form (Ross et al. 1987b). A chemical difference between the Texas monogyne and polygyne types was eventually discovered (Greenberg et al. 1990).

Gene flow between Georgia polygyne and monogyne colonies has been detected, so that there is no longer any reason to believe that these forms are on their way to becoming separate species in the United States (Ross and Shoemaker 1993). In fact, quite a few ant species maintain both social forms without displaying evidence of incipient speciation as a result (Ward 1989). Schmidt (1995) speculated that the differences between South American RIFAs and the populations expanding in the United States might someday culminate in the evolution of two different species and that, whether we manage to control them or not, "at least the little creatures may teach us some things about evolution." Greenberg et al. (1992) echoed the sentiment: "The mystery concerning the nature and origin of the polygyne fire ant continues."

Whether monogyne or polygyne, the RIFA society has the potential to grow to enormous size. Kaspari and Vargo (1995) identified a selective agent that might be driving the evolution of large colonies—seasonal famine. The larger the colony, the greater the ability to store energy for long periods of time. If this is true, one could apply a variation of Bergmann's rule to the RIFA, as the original version is applied to backboned animals. According to that dictum, animals in cool climates tend to have larger bodies than animals in warm climates because a larger body has a smaller surface area per unit volume and will not lose heat as readily as a smaller body. Selection will of course act on such differences in body size depending upon the environmental conditions at hand. The huge RIFA colony of the cooler temperate zone, much more populous than its relative in the warmer tropics, can then be seen as a "superorganism" that survives famine by virtue of its greater size. In this case it is not the individual that evolves in magnitude but the society as a whole.

Hybridization with the Black Imported Fire Ant. Hybridization between the RIFA and BIFA on U.S. soil (Lofgren et al. 1975) was not reported until the process had been a going concern for probably thirty years or more, and it was ongoing at the time of this writing (Goodisman et al. 1998). Hybrids have intermediate-type alkaloid venoms, intermediate hydrocarbons, intermediate Dufour's gland chemistry, and intermediate climatic niches. Some hybrids are of the polygyne social type. The offspring of these RIFA x BIFA unions are fertile, and that fact led some to believe that the two imports are merely variants of a single species after all (see Vinson 1986). This view is not generally accepted today.

It is often found that hybrids are superior in some ways to both parental species, a condition known variously as hybrid superiority or hybrid vigor. An increase in genetic variation is considered an indication of the phenomenon, and although this increase is apparent in the case of the RIFA x BIFA hybrid (Obin and Vander Meer 1989b), the supposed superiority over the parental types does not seem to hold because hybrid fire ants which resemble a given parent more than the other are inferior in competition with that same parent (Shoemaker et al. 1996). Yet the hybrid *is* encroaching upon the BIFA's range and may eliminate the original import with the help of the red imported fire ant. In fact, the range of the hybrid now exceeds that of the BIFA (compare figs. 14.3 and 4.1). This trend would seem to conflict with the generalization (Ridley 1996) that hybrids are inferior to the parental types that surround them, and with the generalization that hybrids more like one parent than the other suffer in competition with that parent.

The two bona fide species are no longer in direct confrontation as they were in the past, due to the hybrid-zone buffer in between (Vander Meer and Lofgren 1989), and it is the hybrid that now faces the RIFA. Hybridization is sometimes said to be unknown in South America (Ross and Robertson 1990), but it does occur to some extent (Ross and Trager 1990). The possibility of natural hybridization was raised shortly before its existence was confirmed when Cupp et al. (1973) performed a successful cross between the RIFA and BIFA in the laboratory, via artificial insemination, as well as a cross between the BIFA and the hybrid (i.e., a backcross). To this day there is no evidence of hybridization between the RIFA and any of the native fire ants, including the possibly native TFA.

The Black Imported Fire Ant

Polygyny occurs in South American populations of the black imported fire ant and in populations of its closest relative, *Solenopsis quinquecuspis* (Ross and Trager 1990). Evidence suggests that polygyny also exists in U.S. populations of the BIFA (Green 1962).

The Tropical Fire Ant

E. O. Wilson (1978) concluded that the TFA, with its big-headed major worker, is more highly evolved in this regard than the RIFA. The derived or "advanced" condition of polygyny in some populations but not in others (Banks et al. 1973d) is something the two species do have in common, though it presumably evolved separately in the two lineages. Yet another highly derived condition is the existence of two tropical fire ant queen types that differ in both size and behavior. These are the microgyne and the macrogyne, and they are apparently associated with the monogyne condition. Here we may be witnessing a step in the evolution of social parasitism in which a workerless species evolves while living in the nest of a different ant, which retains the sterile working caste. The newly mated TFA microgyne does seek out established colonies (McInnes and Tschinkel 1995). She is sometimes adopted by them, and once accepted, she presumably produces workers of her own. The queens of the two socially parasitic harvester ant species (Taber 1998), like the TFA microgyne, are smaller than the host queen. But among the harvester ants the process has run its course in one sense and the worker caste has been entirely lost, as it has in Daguerre's fire ant *(Solenopsis daguerrei)* of South America. This species harms its fire ant hosts and is being considered for the biocontrol of the red imported fire ant in the southern United States. Perhaps a native North American socially parasitic species is already on the rise in the form of the TFA microgyne.

There is no evidence of hybridization between the TFA and the RIFA. However, the TFA does hybridize with the SFA. All of the hybrids are female, as expected (fertilized eggs of ants are almost always female). More surprising is the observation that paternal alleles, those from the TFA fathers, are repressed in these offspring (Hung 1985). The hybrids are thought to be less fit than either parent species (Hung and Vinson 1977; Ross 1988a).

The TFA has greater genetic diversity than any of the other U.S. fire ant species examined (Ross et al. 1987b). This is expected because it has been in the United States much longer than the imported species and its global range is much greater than that of the native species. One manifestation of its genetic variation is the existence of two color forms that are correlated with different habitats. These are the dark and the red forms. No one has suggested that the two are different species, as was eventually found to be the case for the imported ants ("dark" = BIFA, "light" = RIFA).

The Southern Fire Ant

An interesting feature of the southern fire ant in California is its red and black coloration, a combination exhibited by many desert insects. It may be a warning or aposematic coloration that evolved as a defense (Wheeler and Wheeler 1973), much like the red and black bands of certain mutillid wasps ("cow killers") and the red bodies and black wings of various paper wasps. All of these back up the warning with painful stings. The southern fire ant exists in both monogyne and polygyne form (Summerlin 1976).

From the summary in this chapter, it is clear that little work has been done to reconstruct the patterns and processes of fire ant evolution. The patterns will remain a mystery until genes, anatomy, and behavior are known well enough to work out a complete family tree. Light can be shed upon the processes that produced this pattern by studying the natural distributions of the species and by investigating the origins of pleometrosis and of multiple-queen colonies.

CHAPTER 9

Nest Symbiants of Fire Ants

The beetles are often carried about by
the ants in their jaws and permitted to ride
for hours at a time on their backs.

—*William Morton Wheeler* (1910)

ANT nests routinely house creatures that have relationships with their hosts varying from hostility to peaceful coexistence and even mutual aid. Despite myriads of aggressive workers, fire ants are no exception to the rule. Their houseguests are more formally known as symbionts or myrmecophiles. The nature of most of these associations is poorly known, so that our knowledge is usually limited to records of the guest's existence and little more. Yet harmful symbionts are prime candidates for biocontrol (see chapter 12), especially when used together and in conjunction with other enemies of the fire ant (Wojcik 1990).

Symbionts of the Red Imported Fire Ant

The pioneer paper on red imported fire ant myrmecophiles is that of Collins and Markin (1971), who reported fifty-two arthropod species from RIFA nests. Among these were springtails, a wide variety of rove beetles, some scarab beetles, and tiny uropodid mites, which attach to the female fire ants but never to the males. Perhaps this is a consequence of the fact that

Fig. 9.1. A thysanuran (silverfish) taken from a RIFA nest.

males die outside the nest after the mating flight and would be dead-ends for any creature that rode them into the sky. The authors believed that many of the arthropods mentioned in their paper were accidentals, not true myrmecophiles, and it is impossible in some cases to determine which of the two fire ant species was under investigation (Buren's landmark paper would not appear until the following year). I refer the reader to Collins and Markin for further details.

In Texas RIFA nests the symbionts include silverfishes (fig. 9.1) such as one or more species of the genus *Grassiella,* the seed bugs *Cnemodus mavortius* and *Pachybrachius bilobatus,* the crickets *Myrmecophila nebrascensis* (fig. 9.2) and *Anurogryllus muticus,* a ground beetle (*Discoderus* sp.), a darkling beetle (*Blapstinus* sp.), the scarab beetles *Rhyssemus neglectus* and *Myrmecaphodius excavaticollis,* and yet another scarab beetle of unknown genus and species (Neece and Bartell 1981; Summerlin 1978). All of these guests are insects.

In the southeastern United States the millipede *Calytodesmus schubarti* (a scavenger sometimes eaten by the ants) lives in the RIFA nest, as does the cricket *Myrmecophila pergandei.* The tiny crickets of this genus lick the exoskeletons of their hosts until they are eventually caught and killed. Found in RIFA nests of the United States and elsewhere in the New World are the scarab beetles *Rhyssemus neglectus* and *Martinezia dutertrei,* and the rove beetle *Myrmecosaurus ferrugineus* (Wojcik 1990) (fig. 9.3). Two previously unknown mite species, *Oplitis carteretensis* and *O. communis,* were retrieved

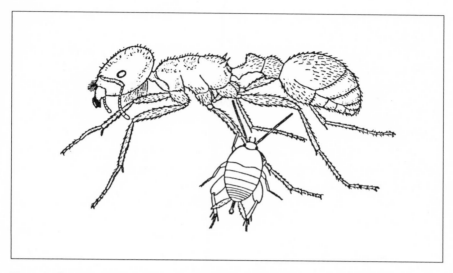

Fig. 9.2. The tiny cricket *Myrmecophila nebrascensis* feeding upon the secretions of a harvester ant. Reprinted from Wheeler 1900. By permission of Cambridge Entomological Club.

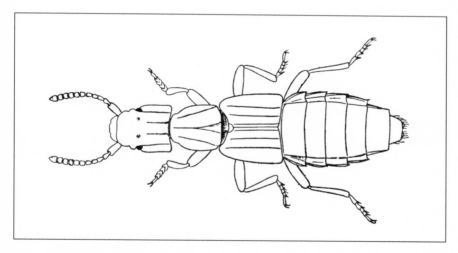

Fig. 9.3. The houseguest beetle *Myrmecosaurus ferrugineus.* Reprinted from C. Bruch. 1932. Algunos estafilinidos de Misiones (Coleoptera). *Physis* 11: 1–8. By permission of Asociación Argentina de Ciencias Naturales.

from South Carolina RIFA nests (Hunter and Farrier 1976a), and *O. virgilinus* was found in Florida nests (Hunter and Farrier 1976b). *Oplitis moseri* is a symbiont sometimes eaten by the host ants when food is scarce (O'Neal and Markin 1973).

RIFA workers feed the rove beetle *Myrmecosaurus ferrugineus* by trophallaxis when it begs for food. This guest was probably introduced into the United States with its hosts (Frank 1977), and the highly evolved association has little or no potential for biocontrol (Wojcik 1980). On the other hand, *Martinezia dutertrei* takes food from adult RIFAs, eats their larvae, eats dead ants, and scavenges booty brought into the nest by foragers (Wojcik et al. 1991).

Nymphs of the planthopper bug *Oliarus vicarius* were found in abandoned galleries in Georgia RIFA mounds. They survived and emerged as adults (Sheppard et al. 1979). Termites and various ant species are also known to occupy abandoned fire ant mounds (Trager 1991). In Central Texas I found a scorpion and a moth cocoon in the empty galleries of a single mound, as well as another ant species that moved in after the fire ants left their nest.

South American nest symbionts of the RIFA (excluding certain species already listed) include leaf beetle larvae, scarab beetles, hister beetles, silverfishes (at least some of which eat the ants' brood), and millipedes (Wojcik 1986).

Symbionts of the Black Imported Fire Ant

One of the strangest symbionts is a metalmark butterfly that spends much of its juvenile life inside the mound of the black imported fire ant in South America. In Santa Fe Province, Argentina, these caterpillars of *Hamearis epulus signatus* leave the nest at night to feed on the leguminous host plant *Vicia graminea*, a type of vetch. During the day when the caterpillar is within the nest, the ants feed on a greenish secretion from a pair of small tubular organs on the creature's eleventh body segment. The butterfly also pupates unmolested because it has similar organs in that otherwise helpless stage of development (Bruch 1926a). More striking still is a report that the caterpillar feeds upon its hosts in addition to the plants growing outside the nest. Pieces of ant larvae were found in its gut (Wojcik 1990). The same report mentions a wingless and still unidentified phorid fly seen running about inside BIFA nests in Argentina.

BIFA colonies can survive floods and disperse to safer ground by forming a floating ball with all stages of development protected inside. Even the nest symbionts are carried along. One colony floating down the Passa-Tres

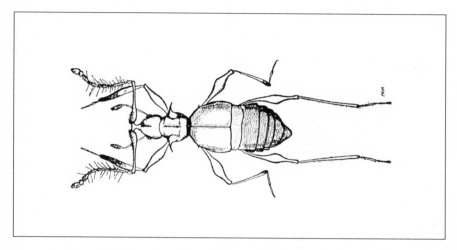

Fig. 9.4. The houseguest beetle *Metopioxys gallardoi.* Reprinted from San Martin 1968.

River of Brazil contained more than four hundred *Neoblissus* seed bugs in various developmental stages, eighteen *Myrmecosaurus gallardoi* rove beetles, numerous mites, three proctotrupid wasps of an undetermined species, and five beetles of a species new to science. The beetle was named *Myrmecochara tricuspidis* (Reichensperger 1927).

South American BIFA nests contain millipedes; the short-winged mold beetles *Metopioxys gallardoi* (fig. 9.4), which rides about on its hosts, and *Fustiger elegans,* which has been seen with its jaws filled with BIFA eggs; the scarab beetle *Martinezia dutertrei;* the lace bug *Anommatocoris coleopteratus;* the seed bug *Neoblissus parasitaster;* and a few unidentified wingless phorid flies. More than five hundred *Fustiger elegans* beetles were found in a single BIFA colony, where they secreted a substance attractive to the ants.

The bug *Neoblissus parasitaster* (also known as *Blissus parasigaster*) can occur in the thousands in a single BIFA nest. It is not known what this symbiont eats, but it might be feeding on plant roots. The creature was found in every one of the examined Argentine colonies, where it might be playing a role in the life cycle of the fire ant's microscopic enemy *Thelohania solenopsae* (Briano et al. 1995c). Resident workers aid *N. parasitaster* during its development (Wojcik 1990).

Rove beetle myrmecophiles of the BIFA include *Myrmecosaurus ferrugineus, M. gallardoi,* an unidentified species of *Myrmecosaurus, Dinusella convexicollis, D. santschii, D. solenopsidis,* and *Dinardopsis solenopsidicola* (Kistner 1982). *Dinardopsis plaumanni* (fig. 9.5) was found in a Brazilian fire ant nest that might have belonged to the BIFA (Reichensperger 1935). Black im-

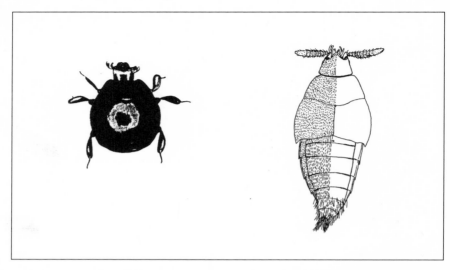

Fig. 9.5. The houseguest beetles *Hippeutister solenopsidis (left)* and *Dinardopsis plaumanni (right)*. Reprinted from Reichensperger 1935.

ported fire ants apparently lick secretions from their mold beetle guest *Metopioxys gallardoi* (San Martin 1968).

The scarab beetle *Myrmecaphodius excavaticollis* lives in BIFA nests in both hemispheres, where it acquires the host's surface chemicals and resists their attacks with its armor. When the chemicals are removed and the beetle is added to fire ant nests, it must fend them off with the armor alone until it reacquires chemical protection (Vander Meer and Wojcik 1982). The flight time of *Myrmecaphodius* is nearly synchronized with the nuptial flights of its host (Wojcik et al. 1978). *Gymnolaelaps shealsi* is a mite that lives inside Mississippi BIFA nests (Hunter and Costa 1971).

The darkling beetle *Poecilocrypticus formicophilus* (fig. 9.6) is a South American species somehow introduced into the southern United States. In South America it lives inside the BIFA nest. It is not known from any fire ant nest in the United States (Steiner 1982), though it is sometimes common in debris just outside RIFA mounds (Steiner, pers. comm.). The ants and the beetles do not seem to interact in any way. What might be the larva of *Poecilocrypticus* has been found living in soil just outside the mound. One hour after receiving this e-mail message from Dr. Steiner, I picked through a RIFA colony that I had frozen for just such purposes months before, and discovered the remains of what appears to be one of these beetles (fig. 9.7). It could have been a symbiont, or it could have been prey that was dragged inside. The fire ant nest was collected in Bastrop, Texas.

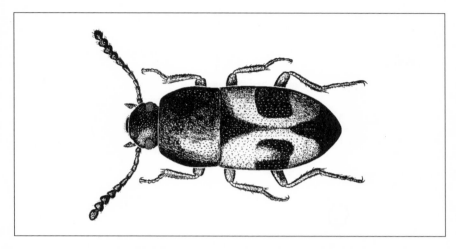

Fig. 9.6. The beetle *Poecilocrypticus formicophilus*. Reprinted from Steiner 1982. By permission of the author.

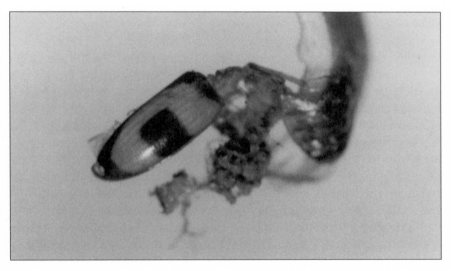

Fig. 9.7. Remains tentatively identified as those of the beetle *Poecilocrypticus formicophilus*, recovered from a red imported fire ant nest in Texas.

Symbionts of the Tropical Fire Ant

In Costa Rica a new genus and species of hister beetle, *Hippeutister solenopsidis*, was discovered inside TFA nests (fig. 9.5). These tiny houseguests ride about on the backs of their major worker hosts (Reichensperger 1935). Other coleopterous nest symbionts of the TFA include the rove beetles *Eu-*

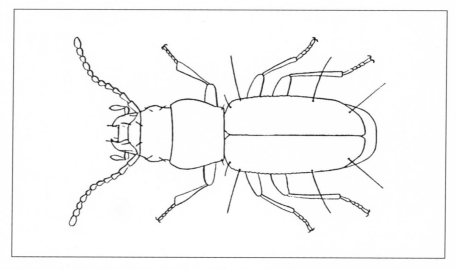

Fig. 9.8. The blind houseguest beetle *Anillus affabilis.* Reprinted from Brues 1902. Copyright 1902, Ginn & Company, Publishers. By permission of University of Chicago, current publisher.

thorax pictipennis, Apocellus schmidtii, and an *Oxypoda* species (Kistner 1982; Reichensperger 1935; Wojcik 1990), the blind ground beetle *Anillus affabilis* (fig. 9.8) (Brues 1902), and the scarab *Martinezia dutertrei,* which scavenges and obtains food from the living ants (Wojcik et al. 1991). *Oxypoda* appeases TFA workers by presenting secretions from the tip of its abdomen. The rove beetle *Paederus littoreus* usually occupies abandoned mounds instead (Travis 1941).

In Mexico the silverfish *Grassiella praestans* is a TFA symbiont (Wojcik 1990). An unidentified species of this same genus lives in Texas nests (Neece and Bartell 1982). Houseguests of the southeastern United States include the millipede *Calytodesmus schubarti,* which scavenges in TFA nests until it is killed by the fire ants, and a cricket, perhaps *Myrmecophila pergandei.* In Hawaiian colonies the cricket species is *M. quadrispina* (Zimmerman 1948). Crickets of this genus are known to lick the bodies of their hosts.

True bugs appear to be common TFA symbionts. In the southeastern United States a mealybug feeds upon broom-sedge roots within the nest (Travis 1941), and in Texas there is the seed bug *Atrazonotus umbrosus* (fig. 9.9) (Neece and Bartell 1982). The TFA is reported to house a scale insect that is attacked by a fly (Chauvin 1970).

A new genus of phorid fly was discovered inside Texas TFA nests. The female of *Commoptera solenopsidis* (fig. 9.10) has such rudimentary wings

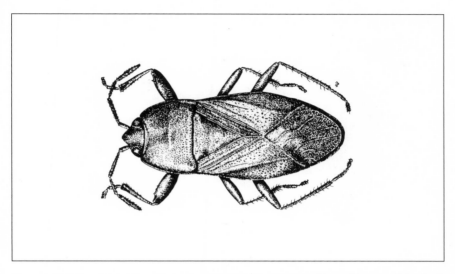

Fig. 9.9. The houseguest bug *Atrazonotus umbrosus.* Reprinted from Slater and Ashlock 1966. By permission of Entomological Society of Washington.

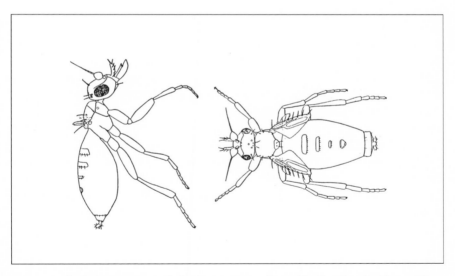

Fig. 9.10. The houseguest scuttle fly *Commoptera solenopsidis.* Reprinted with modification from Brues 1901. Copyright 1901, Ginn & Company, Publishers. By permission of the University of Chicago, current publisher.

Fig. 9.11. A phorid fly with useless wings, found running across the forest floor with its army ant hosts.

that she cannot fly (Brues 1901), an evolutionary development perhaps explained by her habit of running about inside the confining tunnels of the fire ant mound. It is not hard to believe that large wings are a liability in this environment (fig. 9.11). Other female phorids living within the nest are *Apterophora attophila, Placophorina obtecta, Puliciphora incerta,* and *Zikania schmidti* (Disney 1994). The males of these species are presumably winged and visit the nest to mate with the females.

The tropical fire ant sometimes plays host to its thief ant relatives. Both host and guest are members of the genus *Solenopsis.* The most famous thief ant is *Solenopsis molesta,* occurring in TFA nests of the southeastern United States (Travis 1941).

Symbiotic mites include *Oplitis arborcavi* and *O. communis* of the southeastern United States (Hunter and Farrier 1976a, 1976b), and an unidentified mite from the same area that rides about on the adult ants, tapping them with its legs and bobbing up and down as it goes. It feeds from both ends of the host (Travis 1941).

Symbionts of the Southern Fire Ant

In New Mexico, mealybugs *(Phenacoccus solenopsis)* have been found in SFA nests (Essig 1926). Numerous colorful rove beetles were seen as they exited colonies in California (Mallis 1938). Likewise, Texas colonies house a rove beetle of the genus *Apocellus*, the darkling beetles *Araeoschizus decipiens* and *Conibius* sp., the silverfishes *Grassiella* sp., *Mirolepisma* sp., and *Prolepismina* sp., the tiny cricket *Myrmecophila nebrascensis*, a cixiid bug of the genus *Bothriocera* (Neece and Bartell 1982), the scarab beetles *Myrmecaphodius excavaticollis* and *Rhyssemus neglectus*, and an unidentified darkling beetle of the genus *Blapstinus* (Summerlin 1978). Neece and Bartell (1981) also reported an unidentified species of darkling beetle from Texas. The scarab beetles *Euparia castanea* and *Martinezia dutertrei* live in SFA nests in the southeastern United States (Wojcik 1990).

A new species of mite *(Oplitis exopodi)* was discovered in North Carolina SFA nests (Hunter and Farrier 1976a). In Texas, symbiotic mites include an unidentified *Holostaspis* species and a specimen not even identified to the genus level (Neece and Bartell 1982).

Symbionts of the Golden Fire Ant

Nests in western Texas have yielded as houseguests an unidentified false darkling beetle (family Melandryidae), silverfishes (*Grassiella* sp., *Prolepismina* sp.), and a mite (*Parasitus* sp.) (Neece and Bartell 1982).

Symbionts of *Solenopsis amblychila*

This little-known fire ant surely harbors other creatures within its nest, but no symbionts have been reported in the literature.

CHAPTER 10 Medical Importance
of Fire Ants

Unlike many insect pests that are either
an urban, agricultural, or medical problem,
the imported fire ant is one of the only pest
species that is a problem in all of these areas.

—*S. B. Vinson* (1997)

The Red Imported Fire Ant

THE fire ant's sting (not its bite) provokes a painful burning sensation, which earned these insects their common name (figs. 1.1, 1.2, 1.3). But pain seldom spells the end of an encounter with an imported fire ant. A white pustule usually forms within twenty-four hours (figs. 1.4, 1.5, 1.6). That response alone is considered sufficient to diagnose the cause when the assailant itself is not available for inspection. In severe cases with multiple stings, the condition resembles smallpox. Some people never react to fire ant stings with pustules, and at the opposite end of the sensitivity spectrum are those few who react with pustules to every fire ant sting, including those inflicted by species native to the United States.

Rarer and much deadlier than a skin reaction is allergy-induced anaphylactic shock, discussed in more detail later. Whether it is fatal or merely annoying, the RIFA's attack remains the most common cause of insect venom allergy in the southeastern United States. Its allergenic proteins are among the most potent known (Hoffman 1993). There is a good side to the killing power of the RIFA's alkaloid venom.

Its antibiotic properties sterilize the developing pustule so that secondary infections of the wound are rare unless the pustule breaks open (Adams 1986). But should they arise, these secondary infections can be fatal. There is even speculation that fire ant stings can kill in a direct sense because of the inherent toxicity of the venom (Prahlow and Barnard 1998). And, strange as it may seem, fire ants are capable of triggering grand mal seizure (Candiotti and Lamas 1993). This rare response is more commonly associated with epilepsy.

Caro et al. (1957) were among the first to deal comprehensively with the medical importance of fire ants. Their paper includes a drawing of the sting apparatus (fig. 10.1), photomicrographs of developing pustules in the skin, and one of the first descriptions of the results of a stinging episode. When a human is stung several times a flare quickly appears around the wound and can grow to a width of two inches. A wheal follows. Small bumps appear in an hour and a half, followed by the characteristic fire ant pustule(s) within twenty-four hours. Pustules remain for a few days to more than one week and when they eventually rupture they leave a crust and sometimes a scar. Dermatitis occasionally develops when the lower extremities are stung. These local reactions are unpleasant and unusual as insect stings go, but the greatest threat is to sensitive or allergic

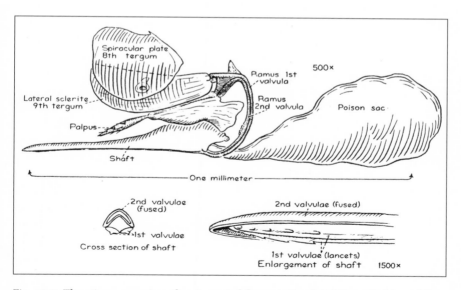

Fig. 10.1. The sting apparatus of an imported fire ant. Reprinted from *Archives of Dermatology* 75, p. 477, 1957. Copyright 1957, American Medical Association.

people. They can die from anaphylactic shock. Symptoms can include fever, headache, dizziness, nausea, vomiting, perspiration, loss of consciousness, coughing, hoarseness, reduced heart rate, hives, a swollen larynx, and low blood pressure (Prahlow and Barnard 1998). In one case the victim died from a heart attack within an hour of being stung. Epinephrine and the antihistamine Benadryl are commonly prescribed. Stricken individuals occasionally compare the aftermath of a stinging episode to an alcoholic hangover.

Massive sting episodes can require skin grafts or even limb amputations (Lofgren 1986c). Caro and colleagues described several multiple-sting cases, including an alcoholic who fell asleep on a mound and a woman who was massively stung while pinned between a car and a stop sign following an accident. Under such circumstances, and especially when the victim is fatally injured, fire ants sometimes *feed* upon humans too (Prahlow and Barnard 1998; see their fig. 5).

The mass retaliation suffered by those who disturb the nest makes these encounters all the more dangerous and painful. Individual RIFA workers often have no opportunity to sting more than once, but a single attacker can raise a line or even a circle of pustules if it is allowed to move unmolested across the victim's skin, stinging repeatedly (Vinson 1997). A single jab can last for almost half a minute (Prahlow and Barnard 1998). Nevertheless, humans and guinea pigs find the pain mild compared to that of harvester ants and paper wasps (Hunt and Hermann 1973).

In 1985 about forty million people in the United States were living inside the range of the red imported fire ant. Roughly fourteen million of these were being stung at least once per year. Perhaps six out of a thousand suffer anaphylaxis, meaning that more than eighty thousand people per year require medical attention. And about one fourth of those in the exposed population develop sensitivity to RIFA venom after one stinging episode or more. The number of deaths per year has been estimated at one hundred but is probably underestimated because the possibility of fire ant attack is rarely investigated when the cause of death is unknown. Emergency room physicians in infested areas now check between the toes and elsewhere on the legs when patients present with anaphylaxis, because the sting victims themselves are not always aware of what has happened to them. Prahlow and Barnard (1998) offered six steps toward the diagnosis of death by fire ant sting: (1) direct knowledge of an attack, (2) history of hypersensitivity to fire ant stings, (3) evidence of anaphylaxis, (4) elevated blood-tryptase (an enzyme), (5) elevated venom-specific IgE antibody levels, and (6) no other explanation for the death at hand.

The most common problems for allergy sufferers are hives and swollen blood vessels. Respiratory distress is the least common complaint but is also the most dangerous (Adams 1986; deShazo et al. 1990; Hoffman 1993; Stimac and Alves 1994; Prahlow and Barnard 1998). Fatal reactions are becoming more common, especially in Florida and Texas (Hoffman 1995), though the reasons for the observed increases are not known. The increase in indoor attacks could be a consequence of the expanding range of the polygyne social type and of a decrease in the chemical residues from effective but long-banned insecticides (Drees 1995). "It is quite possible that with the increased density of the ants and increased competition for food sources, the ants may more frequently move into inhabited buildings and become even more aggressive than previously noted" (deShazo and Banks 1994). Occasionally people feel the need to move away from these infested areas because of allergic family members who risk death from a single additional encounter (Yoffe 1988). Skin tests can reveal this hypersensitivity and the need for therapy (Rhoades et al. 1975). Therapy includes injections with an extract of the fire ant that does not cause an allergic response. By this means one can build up a resistance over time.

Economics can be a factor even when the next episode threatens to be fatal. One allergic high school football player bent upon obtaining a college scholarship refused to stop playing on an infested field and instead opted for an untested rush-procedure therapy. The rush immunotherapy (RIT) proved successful, and although the patient was indeed stung again during practice, the consequences were limited to pustules rather than the life-threatening anaphylaxis experienced only weeks before. This new method used a whole-body extract ("fire ant mix") prepared from the RIFA and the BIFA and injected subcutaneously over a period of months. Fire ant mix is a product of Bayer Pharmaceutical Division of Spokane, Washington (Duplantier and Barnard 1998).

Another life-threatening case included itching, burning, hives, labored breathing, chest pain, dizziness, and shock with its attendant low blood pressure and unconsciousness. Intravenous epinephrine and steroids were administered to the victim. Occasionally patients require oxygen treatment. The bite that anchors the ant and allows it to sting from the other end may introduce its own allergen(s), but this possibility has been entirely overlooked (Rhoades et al. 1975).

One physician's survey discovered eighty-four deaths from anaphylactic shock following fire ant stings. Most were in Florida and Texas. These included an infant falling into a mound, an individual who refused immunotherapy, and one person who was in the middle of a course of immunotherapy (Rhoades et al. 1989). A survey of RIFA victims living in Georgia reported mostly mild reactions (87 percent of the cases). Only 1 percent reported severe reaction (Adams and Lofgren 1981). A second study in the same state found that almost half of all arthropod attacks at Fort Stewart were due to the red imported fire ant (Adams and Lofgren 1982). In a small and intriguing survey of suburban residents of New Orleans, more than half said they had been stung by the RIFA during the year of the survey. Most of them had an usually large lesion associated with the usual pustule, a response that had never been reported before (deShazo et al. 1984) or since, as far as I can tell. It raises the possibility of a RIFA variant with a unique venom chemistry.

At least five cases of lethal or life-threatening response to indoor multiple fire ant stings were on record at the time of this writing. These involved the elderly and an infant. One elderly person was stung repeatedly while lying in a motel bed. Stroke and death followed within one month. A second individual was stung a thousand times but survived. A third victim survived after enduring *ten thousand* stings. The fourth case was an infant in a crib, who responded to multiple stings by going into a coma. The child survived with neurological damage. The fifth case was a bedridden nursing home resident. After the fatal attack an ant colony (presumably that of the RIFA) was discovered in the home. "Food particles" reported from a victim's bed might have been the brood carried by an emigrating fire ant colony. Cases like these have resulted in lawsuits against nursing homes (Adams 1986).

An immediate treatment for fire ant stings is a solution of 50 percent bleach and 50 percent water applied to the wound area (Vinson and Sorensen 1986). Stings can also be treated with a paste of meat tenderizer and water. Enzymes in the tenderizer might break down some of the harmful proteins in the venom. Nonprescription cortisone cream relieves the itching. Prevention is obviously better than treatment. If the ants cannot be entirely avoided, they can be discouraged from climbing up a leg to begin with by applying talcum powder to the clothing about the ankles (Sorensen and Trostle 1986). Talc is slippery and can foul the insect's appendages. The Watson Clinic recommends leaving the pustules alone to avoid secondary infection. Sometimes the reaction in a stung extremity includes swelling serious enough to require prescription medicine (Roth 1998). Oral antihistamines relieve itching, while oral steroids in conjunction with antihistamines may be required in severe cases. Antibiotics are unnecessary because the blister is sterile.

The California Department of Food and Agriculture was facing a RIFA invasion in late 1998, and it gave the following caution to citizens who were about to confront an unfamiliar enemy. First, if an extremity is stung, it should be elevated and ice should be applied to the wound. Then, if blisters should form, clean the area with soap and water without breaking the blisters in the process.

As early as 1971 about ten patients per year were seen, each of whom carried the marks of thousands of stings and a story with one other element in common (Smith and Smith 1971). The victims were all alcoholics who had spent a night on a fire ant mound in a drunken stupor. One unfortunate with more than five thousand stings was treated with zinc oxide lotion and hydrocortisone, though the authors of this report believed that no contemporary treatment was satisfactory—the zinc and cortisone did more to calm the patient than to repair the damage. Smith and Smith concluded that "after a night on the town, one should make an all-out effort to return home for the fire ant is quite reluctant to share his bed with strangers."

I have been much luckier in my own experiences with red imported fire ants. Though I have been stung hundreds of times I am not allergic. I almost never react with a pustule, and when these do develop they are quite small and easily overlooked. The pain is noticeably worse than that inflicted by the tropical fire ant, which I find little more than a nuisance even when I am excavating the nest.

Sometimes the mound and its occupants get involved in politics. A display of bravado backfired on a former Texas government official when he chose to place his hand on a fire ant nest to show his determination to overcome the pest. His constituents interpreted the move as a lack of common sense, especially when he winced in pain and slapped his arm free of the stinging ants in full view of television cameras. A participant in a fire ant television special avoided this gaffe while appearing to repeat it. The appendage was a realistic artificial arm that cost three thousand dollars to make and use. Its hand writhed in agony under the direction of a pumping device (Conniff 1997).

Fire ants cause philosophical problems as well as political fiascos. For example, coroners are physicians who certify the cause of death when our fellow humans expire. Some of these medical examiners believe that death by anaphylaxis following a stinging episode should be certified as a natural cause, because the underlying problem lay within the decedent's own immune system. Others would rule the deaths accidental because fire ants are part of the environment and because chance plays a role in determining whether insect and human will collide (Prahlow and Barnard 1998).

The Chemistry and Anatomy behind the RIFA's Medical Importance. The chemical composition of fire ant venom is very different from that of most other insects. It is about 95 percent alkaloid with only a small amount of protein. Most venoms have no alkaloid and rather more protein. The alkaloid causes the sterile pustules and the protein is responsible for the allergic reactions. A bee sting injects fifty thousand times as much protein with results that are not necessarily more life-threatening than the consequences of a single fire ant sting (Adams 1986).

Fire ant alkaloids were first isolated and named "solenopsins" by MacConnell and Blum (1970), who noted that such chemicals are more typical of plants than animals. The particular alkaloid type shared by fire ants in general is the class known as "2,6-dialkylpiperidine" (MacConnell et al. 1976). These natural chemicals are able to penetrate insect exoskeletons and kill as efficiently as some commercial poisons. The triumph of the imported fire ant over native species may be due in part to the greater ability of their venoms to penetrate the bodies of their foes. When injected into mammals, these venoms cause cell death and red blood cell rupture, and they act as herbicides, fungicides, and bactericides (Sinski et al. 1959; Brand et al. 1972; Escoubas and Blum 1990). These latter properties can be helpful around and inside the nest by keeping it free of microbes that could infect the colony. Gram-positive bacteria species are more susceptible to the antibiotic power than gram-negative bacteria (Jouvenaz et al. 1972). Fire ant alkaloids block neuromuscular transmission in frogs by decreasing sensitivity to the neurotransmitter acetylcholine (Yeh et al. 1975), and the primary venom alkaloid inhibits respiratory rate in the mitochondria that provide energy for cells (Cheng et al. 1977). The popular fire ant bait Amdro hits back by disabling the *ant's* mitochondria.

RIFA venom contains five alkaloids. They have been synthesized in the laboratory and are believed to be unique among animals, though the scientists who broke that ground did not realize that proteins are present too (MacConnell et al. 1971). The chemical structure of the solenopsins, the alkaloid venom components of both RIFA workers and RIFA gynes, has been worked out (Leclercq et al. 1994, 1996). They bear a similarity to the hemlock alkaloid coniine, which uses acetate as building blocks, but Leclercq and colleagues did not yet understand how fire ants make their alkaloids.

Some of the unpleasant effects of allergies, including breathing difficulties, are caused by the body's response to the chemical known as histamine. Yet the RIFA venom itself has no histamine. Its alkaloids cause release of the chemical from the cells of its mammalian victims, as well as causing aggregation of white blood cells and platelets. The workers of the various fire ant species differ noticeably in their alkaloid complements, and even those of the first brood (the minims) differ from those of later workers. On the other hand, the queens of the various species are similar with respect to their own alkaloid complements (Vander Meer 1986b). The venoms of the RIFA and BIFA are more similar to each other than either type is to the venoms of native fire ants (MacConnell et al. 1976), and a RIFA worker's venom is four times as potent as that of a TFA worker (Read et al. 1978; Javors et al. 1993).

RIFA venom contains four allergenic proteins in addition to at least five alkaloids (Lofgren and Adams 1982; Hoffman 1987; Smith and Hoffman 1992). The proteins are designated by a species abbreviation and Roman numerals. For example, Sol i III denotes the third protein allergen of *Solenopsis invicta,* and Sol r II denotes the second protein allergen of *S. richteri.*

Sol i I cross-reacts with allergens from bee and wasp venoms, so that a person already sensitive to these last two can have an allergic reaction at first exposure to the RIFA (Hoffman et al. 1988b). The Sol i III allergen is also similar to certain wasp antigens but different enough from the Sol r III allergen to be distinguished from it with standard tests using antibodies that bind to such proteins (Hoffman et al. 1991). When the DNA sequence of Sol i II was cloned it was found to have no significant similarity to any other DNA sequence on record (Schmidt et al. 1993). The protein product specified by that DNA was successfully produced in bacterial cells as a consequence of these cloning efforts (Schmidt et al. 1996). The amino acids of three of the four identified allergenic proteins have also been sequenced (Hoffman et al. 1988a). Sol i II is a phospholipase unlike any other known protein, and Sol i IV is unusual too.

The ant injects its protein/alkaloid concoction through a barbed stinger that bears a "dorsal fin" (Callahan et al. 1959), imagery calling to mind a shark attack in miniature (see fig. 10.1). There is no mention in the literature of autotomy, though this is common for insects with barbed stings that become snagged in the skin of the victim (e.g., honey bees and various harvester ants). Autotomy is the loss of an appendage and is often a defensive adaptation, such as the sacrifice of a lizard's tail in the jaws of a predator. The lizard runs off while the predator is distracted by a still-moving but expendable body part. Yet an insect losing its stinger will die as surely as it would have died if it had been eaten instead. Natural selection favors individual sacrifices if egg-laying relatives in the mound or hive are saved from further attack. Red imported fire ants are not required to make this sacrifice.

The first report of immunotherapy for IFA-sensitive individuals was published in 1973, and the subject has been controversial ever since. A common treatment consists of subcutaneous injections of fire ant wholebody extract. Doses gradually increase until a steady maintenance dose is reached (deShazo et al. 1990). Paull and colleagues (1983) reported that both RIFA venom and commercially available whole-body extracts of the ant contain allergens and that skin tests and "radioallergosorbent" testing, or RAST, can be used to diagnose allergy to the fire ant. This method uses radioactive antibodies that bind to other fire ant–specific antibodies produced by sensitive subjects (Brady and Turk 1999). Butcher and colleagues (Butcher and Reed 1988a, b; Butcher et al. 1988a) found that RIFA whole-body extract was the only material actually being used to diagnose and treat RIFA-sensitive individuals. Unlike the venom, this extract has at least twenty-nine antigens, though not all of the venom antigens are present. This is obviously a potential problem because the attacking ant injects venom, not whole-body extract. The authors concluded that it might be wiser to use venom (though this was harder to obtain) for treatment of sensitivity than the usual whole-body extract. In addition, the lack of standardized extracts produced variable results.

Support for the venom view was provided by Butcher and coworkers (1988b)—RAST testing showed RIFA venom a better indicator of allergy than whole-body extract (in this case the patients were already known to be allergic). Additional support came from Bahna and colleagues (1988), and especially from Stafford and colleagues (1989, 1990, 1992), who determined that whole-body extract was no better for treatment than a placebo. Regarding the process of testing for sensitivity to fire ant proteins, they found that whole-body extract skin testing, venom skin testing, and venom RAST were more effective than whole-body extract RAST. Again, skin testing with IFA venom appeared to be safe, and was better for diagnosis of allergy than whole-body extract (Robinson et al. 1992). The evidence seemed to be accumulating in favor of using venom for both allergy detection and treatment of hypersensitivity.

Nevertheless, Freeman and colleagues (1992) found that RIFA whole-body extract immunotherapy *is* effective in decreasing the incidence of anaphylaxis following subsequent sting attacks. And according to Tracy and coworkers (1995), when an imported fire ant–specific IgE antibody is produced by the victim in response to a stinging episode, whole-body extract skin testing is better able to detect the antibody than is the venom RAST method. Unfortunately for one allergic woman killed when fire ants stung her arm, the antibodies in her blood were not discovered by a simple skin-test but by a postmortem scrutiny (Prahlow and Barnard 1998). Perhaps the situation was best summed up by Hoffman (1995), who found that immunotherapy with whole-body extract had been tried with variable success for over two decades. If skin testing for fire ant sensitization is not feasible, yet another test requires blood serum instead. This fluorescent enzyme immunoassay uses whole-body extract with success (Feger et al. 1995).

Individuals known to be unsensitized (according to the skin test) because of no prior stings by the RIFA showed conversion to sensitization (once more via skin test) when stung while living in a RIFA-infested habitat (Tracy et al. 1995).

The four major allergenic RIFA proteins responsible for allergic responses in human sting victims are similar enough in amino acid sequence to certain wasp venoms to support the long-suggested evolutionary relationship between wasps and ants (Hoffman 1995).

The Black Imported Fire Ant

As noted, the venoms of the two imported fire ant species are more similar to one another than to any of the native species' venoms, but some of the alkaloids of the BIFA seem to be more powerful than those of the RIFA. They are certainly more deadly to termites when applied topically (Brand et al. 1972; Escoubas and Blum 1990). And as is the case for the RIFA, worker venom alkaloids differ from those of their queen. There is also variation within the worker caste itself (Brand et al. 1973).

BIFA venom contains at least three allergenic proteins (the RIFA has four). These are Sol r I, II, and III. It is the RIFA's Sol i IV that has no counterpart in the BIFA venom (Hoffman 1995). The hybrid RIFA x BIFA venom contains all four RIFA proteins. As a result, RIFA immunotherapy should be useful for treating problems caused by both imported species and by their hybrid (Hoffman et al. 1990). The venoms of native fire ants are also generally cross-reactive with those of the imports (Hoffman 1997).

The Tropical Fire Ant

There is not as much literature on the medical importance of the TFA as one might expect. This would probably be true even if the two imported species had never arrived in the United States. Although the RIFA and BIFA eclipsed the other U.S. fire ants before the surge of scientific publications began in the late twentieth century, the TFA and the natives seem never to have had much medical impact. Yet the first historical account of fire ant problems does point to the TFA as culprit. As reported in an eighteenth-century manuscript, the trouble occurred in the Caribbean in the 1500s, and we must remember that the identification of the culprit as the TFA is an educated guess. There are no voucher specimens surviving from that time.

In this case the tropical fire ant was accused of consuming enough vegetation on certain islands to cause famine, and prayers were uttered to Saint Saturnine in hopes that intercession would put an end to the plagues (Reaumur 1926). The resulting truce between ant and human was broken two hundred years later when sugar plantations were hit hard (ca. 1750), and cattle were blinded by the insects unless a circle of tar was painted around their eyes. Children's eyes were also favorite targets for attack, and people were stung in bed as they slept. These horrors generated the earliest chemical attempts at fire ant control, in which arsenic and corrosive sublimate (mercuric chloride) were tried without success. Nature solved the problem with a timely hurricane.

Risch and Carroll (1982b) report that Mexicans do not fear the sting of the TFA as much as people north of the border fear the RIFA sting, but I find that completely understandable—the RIFA sting is worse. Yet Mexican coffee farmers do see the TFA as a pest in their fields, where the problem is the sting, not destruction of their crop (Nestel and Dickschen 1990). Asian tobacco field laborers suffer the same agonies (Hill 1987).

There are no reliable reports of human deaths caused by TFA stings, and only a few cases of anaphylactic shock are on record (Helmly 1970; Hoffman 1997). The three reported victims were living on the Pacific islands of Hawaii, Guam, and Okinawa. As a result of the earliest incident, in Hawaii, Helmly suggested that sensitive persons carry antihistamines and adrenaline when frequenting TFA habitats. Trade names for such kits include EpiPen and AnaKit (California Department of Food and Agriculture 1998). Hoffman (1995) concluded that the TFA sting is not a significant medical problem and that a pustule reaction is rare. More typical effects of the venom include pain, itching, and wheals (Hung et al. 1977; Read et al. 1978). Members of a fire ant population in South America that have been tentatively identified as tropical fire ants are said to raise pustules like those of the two U.S. imports. This might be a previously unrecognized species instead (Trager 1991).

We now know that the venom of the TFA causes certain rat cells to release histamine, a reaction that in humans causes pain and a skin reaction. The alkaloids are responsible for its release (Lind 1982). Phospholipase and hyaluronidase proteins are present in addition to the famous fire ant alkaloids (Baer et al. 1979), but no histamine has been detected. Phospholipase destroys cell membranes and hyaluronidase causes tissues to break down. This in turn allows the venom to spread.

There is variation within the species for the relative amounts of alkaloid in TFA venom. It differs between workers and queens and even within the worker caste. Major workers carry 0.06 microliters of venom whereas minor workers carry one third that amount (Brand et al. 1973). TFA alkaloids are similar to those of the SFA and less like those of the RIFA and BIFA (Brand et al. 1972). The two types in question are members of the solenopsin-A group (Leclercq et al. 1994), and they have been synthesized in the laboratory (Ryckman and Stevens 1987).

Fire ants are not known to transmit disease. A single report suggests that they are capable of doing so (Griffitts 1942). In Puerto Rico the dysentery-causing bacterium *Shigella flexneri* was discovered on the bodies of TFA foragers when the pathogen grew in tiny pathways left by the ants as they walked across a culture dish in a laboratory.

The Southern Fire Ant

A sting from the southern fire ant can probably sensitize a person to stings of the imported species (Hoffman et al. 1990). The pain is not as intense and pustules are seldom produced. This is true of all native fire ants (Snelling 1963; Vinson 1997). Wheeler and Wheeler (1973) described the minor worker's sting as slightly bothersome for fifteen minutes but hardly noticeable thereafter. Some people are more vulnerable than others. There is at least one record of an infant fatality and one of life-threatening anaphylaxis in an adult. Other sting victims mentioned in the early literature include newborn, freshly oiled babies, children attacked while playing, and sleeping persons who were driven from their beds. One child stung on the foot developed hives, coughing, and itching but no pustules. Minor workers are reported to be more prone to sting humans than are majors, and they seek out the softer skin of the hand when doing so. A few victims suffer from the effects for hours; others hardly notice it for more than thirty seconds. That the sting when used against humans is defensive rather than offensive is supported by the observation that the tendency to sting apparently decreases as one moves farther from the nest (Mallis 1938; Wheeler and Wheeler 1973; Lockey 1974; Hoffman 1997).

An early study of SFA venom chemistry found antifungal, antibacterial, hemolytic, and insecticidal properties much like those of RIFA venom. The stings of both species produce a flare and a wheal. If and when pustules follow SFA attack, they are tiny (Blum et al. 1961). Southern fire ant venom seems to be unique for its unsaturated piperidine alkaloid (Stimac and Alves 1994).

The Golden Fire Ant

The golden fire ant has a very limited attack record. One woman was stung in her home in Corona, California, and suffered an allergic response as a result. This included hives and swelling but no pustules like those inflicted by the imported species (Ellis et al. 1992). These authors also reported great cross-reactivity among fire ant venoms. The sting of the GFA, like that of the SFA, is not as painful as the sting of the tropical fire ant and the imported fire ants (Snelling 1963).

Golden fire ants have a unique venom chemistry that differs in alkaloid composition from those of the more commonly encountered species (Blum et al. 1973). Its chemical composition resembles that of the TFA and SFA more than it resembles those of the imports. The biosynthesis of GFA venom appears to be of a primitive kind, and its dominant venom alkaloid is of the 2,6-dialkylpiperidine class (MacConnell et al. 1976).

No medical importance has been reported for the sixth fire ant species occurring in the United States, *Solenopsis amblychila*, and as should be clear from the foregoing, much remains to be learned about fire ant venom. These problems are compounded by the fact that it is not always clear which IFA species was being studied in the early work on the subject. Blum and colleagues (1958) published the first analysis and noted that fire ant chemistry was unlike that of any known insect venom. They knew it to be proteolytic (able to break proteins apart) but did not realize that this unusual material was rich in alkaloids. It was as toxic as DDT to flies, weevils, and mites. It had antibiotic activity against the bacterium genus *Streptococcus*, possibly accounting for the sterile condition of pustules. These authors raised an intriguing possibility that has no published follow-up: "The chemical composition of fire ant venom and the effect of it on malignant cells are being studied" (Blum et al. 1958). Findings in this regard could change our view of the insects overnight if their venom proved to cure any form of cancer.

As nasty as fire ant stings are, it may be some consolation to know that they cannot compare with the dreaded *tucandeira* ant *(Paraponera clavata)* of the RIFA's Brazilian homeland. A botanist described his own encounter: "I was in agonies, and had much to do to keep from throwing myself on the ground and rolling about as I had seen the Indians do. . . . I can only liken the pain to that of a hundred thousand nettle stings . . . with difficulty I repressed a strong inclination to vomit" (Patton and Evans 1929). Because of the shooting pain, this insect is known to its victims as the bullet ant.

CHAPTER II

Chemical Control
and the Pesticide Issue

With the loss of Mirex, the hopes for an
eradication program also failed.

—*S. B. Vinson and A. A. Sorensen* (1986)

A The Red Imported Fire Ant

As this chapter will show, every attempt to eradicate red imported fire ants from the United States with pesticides and other chemicals has been controversial, arguably more harmful than the insect itself, and ultimately unsuccessful. A host of early failures gradually persuaded government officials and applied entomologists that the invader was here to stay and that damage control was their only hope. The chlorinated hydrocarbons heptachlor and mirex figured largely in these early battles against the RIFA. They are no longer used. Chlorinated hydrocarbons in general act as contact poisons (meaning that they enter the insect through the exoskeleton) and as stomach poisons taken through the mouth as the insects feed. They tend to have great residual killing power in the environment, their effects lasting for days, weeks, or even years after application. This very feature causes environmental concerns whether or not chlorinated hydrocarbons defeat the pest in question.

Heptachlor was used in the 1950s and 1960s, before its successor mirex, but was soon abandoned because of excessive impact upon nontargeted animals and crops. It acted primarily as a contact insecticide and was never used in the form of bait. Mirex, on the other hand, began making its mark in 1961 when it was first used in bait form against the RIFA. It acts as a stomach poison. Bait was produced by mixing the mirex toxicant (poison) with soybean oil and corncob grits. Soybean oil served as both attractant and solvent. Corncob grits were chosen as the vehicle or carrier. At first there were few objections to the use of mirex. It seemed that wildlife was not being harmed, and the bait did not stay on the ground long because the ants collected it and took the poison home to the nest.

The picture was not so rosy a few years later. By the 1970s it appeared that mirex was accumulating in nontarget organisms after all, and it was not biodegrading rapidly enough to satisfy its critics. Allied Chemical stopped making the product and government agencies agreed to cancel its registrations as an insecticide. The use of mirex in the United States ground to a near halt between 1977 and mid-1978, though an exception was made for Harvester Bait 300. An Environmental Defense Fund (EDF) letter dated March 1979 (vol. 10, no. 2) reported the findings of Canadian scientists that ferriamicide, a fire ant pesticide containing both mirex and Kepone, was a potential health threat. This was relevant even at this late date because the Environmental Protection Agency (EPA) had approved trials with ferriamicide the previous year, though by the date of the letter the product had not actually been used. In the event, ferriamicide was not approved for general use (Collins 1992). The EDF condemned mirex as a cause of cancer, birth defects, and nerve damage in experimental animals and was behind the efforts to cancel its registration. Yet the related compounds DDT, aldrin, and dieldrin are reported to inhibit tumor formation (Alley 1973).

A suitable substitute for mirex has been sought ever since its demise (Lofgren 1986a). The search is fraught with complications requiring a considerable knowledge of insect life history. For example, baits are not effective against newly mated queens because they do not forage for food. An important paper in the history of toxicant selection is that of Stringer and colleagues (1964), setting forth standards that a good candidate must meet. Some poisons were found unsuitable for use against the RIFA because the ants detect them and move the nest away from danger. The remainder of this chapter reviews the stormy history of the attempt to control fire ants with heptachlor, mirex, and other chemicals.

Many insecticides were tested in Alabama in the early years of the war on the red imported fire ant. This, after all, was the first of many southern states to confront the invader (Hays and Arant 1960). DDT was among the prospects, but Kepone, similar to mirex, was even more effective. The peanut butter bait used in these trials was carried back to the nest by foragers and placed in storage cells within the mounds. In a related experiment seventy cattle ate large amounts of Kepone with no ill effects. Nevertheless, Kepone was eventually deemed too dangerous for mammals. Heptachlor took center stage.

Heptachlor was broadcast into the environment from both ground and air. Appraisals of its effectiveness varied considerably. It was found to be completely effective against the fire ant in one early study (Lofgren et al. 1961a) but not in others (Bartlett and Lofgren 1961; Lofgren et al. 1961b). Its long-term effects on the environment were unclear at first. When the RIFA was eradicated from one test plot, various species used as ecological indicators rebounded from the poison's effects within a single year. Interestingly, Rhoades (1962) also concluded that "imported fire ants appeared to have very little effect upon the other species studied." The lack of long-term chemical effects on nontarget wildlife and the supposedly benign effect of the RIFA itself would both be challenged by contrary findings. These included a 1958 request by an Alabama senator and a congressman for a moratorium on heptachlor use (Collins 1992).

Other early trials ranked the related chlorinated hydrocarbons aldrin, dieldrin, and chlordane behind heptachlor in descending order of effectiveness (Banks et al. 1964). Chlordane gave residual protection in the field for years (Lofgren et al. 1964a), and both this and heptachlor were so repellent to worker ants as to reduce their foraging activities (Lofgren and Stringer 1964). All four pesticides provided good control for as long as five years after application because their residues remained in the soil. This property became a bone of contention between those who wished to continue their use and those who wished to put an end to it.

Blake and coworkers (1959) observed that fire ants returned in greater numbers than ever when the soil residues disappeared. They were among the first to discover the RIFA's supreme ability to dominate disturbed habitats. How does this come about? The chemicals kill off native ants as well as the imports, and because the fire ants happen to be better at colonizing ecological vacuums than are natives, they rebound in force while the others are permanently eradicated from the area. Another problem with these early attempts at control was the tendency of fire ant colonies to fission (split) during treatment (Banks et al. 1966). This *increases* the number of mounds and suggests to today's specialists that the colonies were of the polygyne type. Lofgren and colleagues (1965) found that heptachlor treatments remained effective against the fire ant when application was reduced to one fourth the standard rate—to only half a pound per acre.

The fire ant control program of the U.S. Department of Agriculture (USDA) came under fire in the years 1958–60. During this period the National Audubon Society complained that native wildlife was being harmed (Anonymous 1959). At about the same time, the Southeastern Association of Game and Fish Commissioners (1958) concluded that insecticide broadcasts should be discontinued until more was known about their effects. Glasgow (1959) wrote: "Because of the conflicting evidence released to the press, and because of unethical actions, Entomologists as well as game biologists are losing the faith and respect of the people." This paper denied as mere rumor a claim that fire ants were wiping out muskrats in a Louisiana parish.

When heptachlor was sprayed from aircraft in an early attempt to control fire ants in Texas, its effect upon fishes became a target of study. The imagery of Boudreaux and his coworkers (1958) is that of a world turned upside down: "On occasion, gizzard shad, black bullheads, and sunfishes were seen fighting to get out onto the banks. This appeared to be the ultimate aim of the affected . . . to get out of the water." It is hard to imagine wildlife more desperate than this. The authors concluded that "an ill-supervised fire ant control program could result in at least temporary poor fishing and in the local extermination of some species throughout the Gulf Coast states." But it has long been known that the ants can be just as hard on individual fishes as are the chemicals used to fight the ants. As recently as June 3, 1998, local television news in Austin, Texas, reported that more than twenty-two thousand rainbow trout and sunfish were killed when they ate fire ants that had fallen into a Guadalupe River fishery near the town of Sattler. Some fishes consumed as many as five hundred winged ants descending from their nuptial flights (Texas Parks and Wildlife Department 1998; *Miami Herald* 1998). Yet these are not members of the stinging worker caste. Because males cannot sting and because queens rarely do, the deaths may have been due to toxins released during digestion (Contreras and Labay 1999).

The problem had been occurring for several years in a row, and the U.S. Army Corps of Engineers began weighing the benefits of an increased water release from a nearby dam. The resulting tide would carry the ants away before the fish had a chance to eat them.

Early methods of insecticide packaging and dispersal called for the dissolution of heptachlor (or dieldrin) in heavy naphtha, followed by absorption into clay pellets. The pellets were then scattered over the area to be treated. Wildlife groups were concerned that birds might feed upon the pellets because of their resemblance to seeds. After treatment of one Alabama RIFA infestation, "fencerows reeked with the smell of dead animals" (George 1958).

An unusual type of bird census taken on Georgia lands following hepta-chlor and dieldrin treatments produced disturbing results. The investigator listened for the calls of male bobwhite quail and found that on a thousand acres of treated land, about four calls were heard, compared to twenty-seven calls on the same area of untreated land (Rosene 1958). Baker (1958) reported that every quail of thirteen coveys died following treatment of an area with these same pesticides.

A Texas survey following a heptachlor application at two pounds per acre found dead mammals, fishes, amphibians, and a variety of dead inver-tebrates. Lay (1958) wrote: "The present so-called 'eradication' program is in fact a spot control program. Until more facts are available, I question the wisdom of the program." The same treatment in Louisiana reduced the red-winged blackbird population in one area from 135 to zero in two months. A similar fate befell the local meadowlarks. Earthworms, an important food for many birds, were contaminated with the poison (Glasgow 1958). In a different part of Louisiana autopsies found lethal concentrations of hepta-chlor in the birds themselves (Newsom 1958). Concern obviously escalated when a modified form of heptachlor was discovered in both meat and milk (Collins 1992).

According to George (1958), the goal of the USDA's Plant Pest Control Division was to "perfect a wall of insecticide around the peripheral and sec-ondary infestations of the ant to prevent further spread. . . . Hopefully, a quarter of a century and 125 million dollars from now, the present infested area (not allowing for new areas or natural die-offs) will have been treated once and the ant will have been eradicated." An entomologist of the 1950s likewise predicted that "in two years, Georgia will, from a practical stand-point, be free of imported fire ants" (Anonymous 1959). We will never know if heptachlor and its allies would eventually have wiped the RIFA from the map of the United States. Judgment errors were committed on both sides of the long-standing pesticide controversy. Some critics of these chemicals claimed that fire ants did not harm crops (Anonymous 1959). In this they were clearly wrong.

An early study of the effects of heptachlor on Texas wildlife provides a useful transition to the subject of mirex. On this occasion, the Texas Game and Fish Commission discovered a heavy toll of birds, mammals, fishes, and untargeted insects (Lay 1958a, b). Kepone is similar to mirex and was some-times found to be a better toxicant than heptachlor, though at other times it was not effective. Breakfast cereal turned out to be a fine attractant or bait to lure the ants to the poison (Lofgren et al. 1961b). Kepone was thus briefly entertained after the demise of heptachlor before yielding place to the most famous bait product of all. The new toxin itself was first known by Allied Chemical Company's code designation GC-1283 (Lofgren 1962). Another name is Dechlorane. But this compound is best known by its common name of mirex. The substance is a white crystalline solid that decomposes at 485°C. Like DDT, mirex is a chlorinated hydrocarbon, but it is much more persistent. The boxlike chemical structure explains part of its stability (Anonymous 1978).

Mirex was not devised with fire ants in mind. It was originally marketed as a rodenticide and as a smoke-generating compound and has been widely used in plastics as a flame retardant. The chemical was first prepared in 1946, first put to use in 1954, and first used against fire ants in 1961 (Alley 1973; Davidson and Stone 1989). In 1962, mirex finally replaced heptachlor as the toxicant of choice. It differs in chemical structure from heptachlor, and it differs in its mode of application because it was dispensed as a bait. Mirex bait consists of soybean oil (the attractant), corncob grits (the carrier or vehicle), and the poison itself (the mirex toxicant).

World War II B-17 and B-26 bombers were soon outfitted to broadcast mirex from the air. Guidance was first achieved with helium balloons, then with electronic signals from the target area (Lofgren et al. 1964c; Lofgren et al. 1975; Copeland 1997). The standard preparation was settled upon during the trials of 1960–61 as 1 percent mirex, 85 percent corncob grits carrier, and 14 percent soybean oil attractant (Lofgren et al. 1963; Banks et al. 1973b, c). Standard application at the time was about 1.25 pounds of mirex per acre (Wojcik et al. 1975). Banks and colleagues (1973c) found that the bait could hold more oil and required less mirex when it was surrounded by a latex coat. This preparation truly became a worthy adversary of the red imported fire ant. From 1958, at the beginning of the eradication program, to 1977, over 3,200 alternative baits received consideration. Only mirex was developed commercially during that period, topping a list of 402 toxic baits actually tested for effectiveness (Levy et al. 1974a).

Control of fire ants by ant bait requires a poison acting slowly enough to allow the foragers which collect it to supply the bait to the colony before dying themselves. The queen or queens must perish if the nest is to perish (Lofgren 1986b). Mirex had this property and was especially suitable because it did not repel the ants as they foraged. The magnitude of its power was driven home by an aerial broadcast in the environs of Savannah, Georgia. A search of the area afterward turned up only one surviving colony. This nest was located inside a commercial building where the ants were able to feed upon insects out of range of the bait (Banks et al. 1973a). In a sense, the sole survivors rode out the attack in a bomb shelter.

Fire ants stored mirex bait in large quantities in their mounds. They drank the oil and discarded the grits outside on the rubbish heap. Within two days of treatment, piles of dead ants also began showing up in the trash. The smallest workers died first, followed by the brood and the queen. Major workers and winged sexuals were the last to expire. Entire colonies were exterminated within a single week. Sometimes the insects avoided this fate by abandoning their mound (Lofgren et al. 1963). Other studies found that one month or more was required for effective destruction of the colony (Banks et al. 1971). Later advances in bait dispersal included microencapsulation, in which the bait was contained and protected in gelatin or plastic capsules about the size of an ant's head (Markin and Hill 1971).

The "weediness" of the RIFA—its ability to occupy disturbed habitats—enabled the species to rebound from single mirex treatments as it had from heptachlor. An application at one Louisiana site eradicated the fire ant from the area, but within a year the infestation was restored by fresh invasions (Markin et al. 1974a, b). And though mirex was effective against the RIFA in sugarcane fields, the ants later reinfested the area until they were present in greater numbers than ever (Adams et al. 1981).

Questions began to arise about the effect of mirex on nontarget organisms and on the environment in general. Its residues were detected in the bodies of annelid worms (lugworms) living in coastal waters. The worms ate less and were less active when mirex was present (Schoor and Newman 1976). Along the coast of South Carolina, animals were checked for mirex residues two years after its aerial application on nearby soil. Some fishes tested positive for its presence but most animal samples were negative. No mirex was found in the bottom sediment (Borthwick et al. 1974). On land, mirex residues were detected in nontarget ants after aerial application. Just over one year later, the RIFA reinfested that same area in levels exceeding those before treatment (Summerlin et al. 1977a).

A different study found that residue accumulation within insect tissues peaked and then declined greatly, all within one year of the treatment of the area. Other invertebrates were much less affected. Among the vertebrates, birds and the fat tissues of mammals had the highest levels. Kendall and coworkers (1977) reported mirex from the tissues of bobwhite quail. Nevertheless, within two years of its application, mirex residues in exposed animals were low or had dropped to zero (Wheeler et al. 1977).

Other reports from the peer-reviewed scientific literature of that time can help us form our own opinions about the costs and benefits of mirex. For example, researchers in one study found the toxicant in the tissues of a wide variety of animals, both terrestrial and aquatic, but could find no mass mortalities to associate with it (Borthwick et al. 1973). In an examination of beef cattle from areas treated with mirex and DDT, mirex was found in most fat samples and DDT was found in all of them (Ford et al. 1973). Residues were detected in the feces, milk, and tissues of a Jersey cow during a feeding program that included radioactively labeled mirex. Even so, residues were not detectable in brain or muscle four weeks after that feeding program was terminated (Dorough and Ivie 1974).

Samples were collected from invertebrate animals for one year following a single aerial application of mirex. Residues were detected in carnivores and omnivorous scavengers but were essentially absent from the tissues of herbivores. Levels fell off gradually during the course of study (Markin et al. 1974a, b). Honey bee populations were not affected by aerial application (Glancey et al. 1970b). Soil samples and vegetation became the subjects of a different study that followed a single aerial broadcast of mirex. This analysis did find residue in pond sediment and in plant tissues (Spence and Markin 1974). According to Kaiser (1978), mirex contaminated the biota of Lake Ontario. It could not have been used against fire ants in this case.

Alley (1973) reviewed the situation and concluded that the less-publicized use of mirex in polymers as a fire retardant could introduce more toxin into the environment than its use as a pesticide. It is indeed toxic to crayfishes, crabs, and shrimps but its toxicity to birds is low. Crabs pick up the bait and eat it underwater, just as the fire ant does on land. The listing of mirex as a potential carcinogen followed claims that it induced tumors in test animals. It must be remembered that commercial use of mirex would never approach the levels experienced by these experimental subjects. Alley wrote: "There have been no reports, in spite of the widespread application of this pesticide of any harmful effects in the field to wildlife when normal application rates were employed." The author recalled the Mrak report of 1969, which categorized mirex and three other hydrocarbon pesticides as potential causes of tumors. Yet those same three toxins inhibited tumors, according to other data. Alley concluded that the cautious use of mirex bait was the only available hope for real control of the fire ant. Heptachlor did the job faster and was cheaper, but its harmful effects are clearly greater than those of mirex.

According to the authors of a second review, mirex was first used as a pesticide as early as 1959 (Waters et al. 1977). They reported that mirex is highly persistent in the environment, causes liver damage and perhaps hepatomas in mice, and crosses the rat's placental barrier so that offspring are smaller in size and have cataracts.

Sittig (1991) characterized mirex at length. It is reported to be an animal carcinogen, though it has not been linked to cancer among humans. And no cases of toxicity to humans following the ingestion of mirex are known. It does require a shipping label of "Keep Away from Food." It is moderately toxic to rats and causes cataracts, cancer, and birth defects in mice as well as rats, but "Whether it does so in humans is not known." At this point it is worth a reminder that the original plans for mirex called for its use as a rodenticide. Sittig's *Handbook* also lists aldrin, chlordane, DDT, dieldrin, toxaphene, and heptachlor as carcinogens. The appearance of testosterone on the list reminds the reader that even chemicals necessary for the survival of our own species can be hazardous in excess.

Mirex was widely used in the United States from 1965 to 1978 (Markin 1981). The EPA canceled its registration in 1971, allowing some continued use until June 30, 1978, and Allied Chemical announced in 1976 that it would stop producing mirex due to pressures from those who saw the chemical as a danger to the environment. The factory and the rights were sold to the state of Mississippi for one dollar (Davidson and Stone 1989). Mirex remains in use outside the United States (Williams 1986a), and its production was continued by Union Carbide.

Various chemical substitutes have been considered since the loss of mirex. These include (1) other delayed-action chemicals applied in bait form, (2) insect growth regulators, or IGRs, (3) inhibitors that prevent the queen from laying eggs, (4) inhibitors that prevent the insect's protective enzymes from detoxifying pesticides, and (5) a variety of more conventional chemicals (Lofgren 1986b). Another possibility is chemical inhibition of the enzymes that fourth instar larvae use to digest their food (Whitworth et al. 1998). In fact, the RIFA's own chemistry could be turned against it if the trail pheromone proves useful in control. When added to soybean-oil bait, the pheromone makes the bait more attractive to the RIFA than is soybean oil alone (Vander Meer et al. 1982b). One of the queen pheromones could be used to shut down the production of sexuals (acting in a way opposite to that of the IGRs, which are discussed later). A different queen pheromone could incite workers to execute their own egg layer(s). Nestmate recognition chemicals, perhaps the hydrocarbons of the exoskeleton, would make symbiotic enemies more acceptable to naturally hostile ants, which would otherwise kill them (Vander Meer 1996).

In 1978, when the use of mirex against fire ants finally came to an end in the United States, one amidinohydrazone chemical became a promising candidate for control of the red imported fire ant (Davidson and Stone 1989; Williams et al. 1980a). The toxicant in bait form was actually carried by a treated colony to a new nesting site, where the ants proceeded to die off until the entire colony was extinct (Manley 1981). Compound AC-217, 300, as it was then known, was more effective against queens than against workers in early field trials (Banks et al. 1981). D. P. Harlan and colleagues (1981) rang in one of the most popular successors to mirex with the following words: "A conditional registration has been granted to the American Cyanamid Co. by the EPA for a bait formulation containing AC-217, 300 under the trade name Amdro®." It gave 73 percent control when four tablespoons were used against each mound (Manley 1982).

The active ingredient of Amdro is hydramethylnon, not a chlorinated hydrocarbon but a fluorinated hydrocarbon. It is a flammable yellow to orange solid that kills the ant by inhibiting the function of its electron transport chain (Hollingshaus 1987), as does cyanide when ingested by humans. In other words, it prevents the conversion of the ant's food into energy (Drees et al. 1996), and it does this without posing a residue problem (Worthing and Hance 1991). Amdro retained the soybean oil attractant of mirex but replaced the corncob grits carrier or vehicle with "pregel defatted grits" (Banks 1990). But one weakness common to Amdro, mirex, and all nonspecific bait poisons is the eradication of native species that forage in a manner similar to the fire ants. Not only do these suffer directly, but the resulting empty ecological niche is eventually filled by the return of the RIFA. Thus the problem can be made worse than ever. Attractants that are especially stimulating to the RIFA might someday alleviate this problem. For example, RIFA foragers are especially drawn to a substance present in okra flowers. If they arrive at the bait and dominate it well before the other ants arrive, and if the native ants are not as attracted to okra in the first place as they are to the traditional soybean oil, then fewer natives will be killed by the toxin (Williams 1986a). Efforts were also under way in 1999 to develop a mechanical solution to the problem: bait stations that would admit the RIFA while keeping native ants out.

Others found that Amdro did not have an effect on nontargeted ants after all and that there was no broadcast residue even on the day following its application. Multiple treatments became necessary because newly mated queens are not discouraged from settling in baited areas (Apperson et al. 1984a). Best results are obtained when the product is applied in the spring of the year (Collins et al. 1992).

There is agreement that Amdro does not work as well as mirex. On the other hand, it is considered less toxic to mammals (and does not cause deformities), it degrades rapidly, it is only slightly soluble in water (Davidson and Stone 1989), and it has a 95 percent kill rate (Anonymous 1978). Amdro is not labeled for use inside homes (Sorensen and Trostle 1986). Although less toxic to mammals according to some reports, hydramethylnon is considered moderately toxic to humans when accidentally consumed and slightly toxic when making contact with the skin. It is toxic to fish, unlikely to contaminate groundwater, and it breaks down quickly. Hydramethylnon does not accumulate in living plants, and it decomposes more rapidly when exposed to light than when held in the dark. Its manufacturer at the time of writing was American Cyanamid Company of Wayne, New Jersey (Vander Meer et al. 1982c; Mallipudi et al. 1986; Extoxnet 1993). Siege is a product very similar to Amdro (Vinson, pers. comm.)

Insect growth regulators (IGRs) have been turned against the red imported fire ant. They were already being evaluated when mirex was on its way out (Vinson et al. 1974). Not as fast acting as typical toxicants, this class of chemicals mimics the natural action of the insect's own hormones and causes the colony to die off when it produces too many sexuals and not enough workers. Methoprene and hydroprene are two examples. Their precise mode of action is unknown but they do not kill the queen, at least not directly. Insect growth regulators do not leave residues in the environment (Banks 1986a).

Juvenile hormones are IGRs that can deform pupae, deform adults, stop larval metamorphosis, sterilize the queen temporarily, and/or shift production away from workers toward sexuals (Lofgren et al. 1975). Two of these, the juvenile hormone analogues ZR-515 and ZR-512, prevent fire ants from pupating (Cupps and O'Neal 1973).

Well-known IGR products include Logic (fenoxycarb) and Pro-Drone, which is no longer used (Banks 1990). Logic was granted registration by the EPA in 1985 (Glancey 1986b). Exposure to it can sterilize developing RIFA queens and stunt their growth (Glancey et al. 1989a), though the sterilization caused by egg resorption is reversible (Glancey and Banks 1988). And fenoxycarb-treated queens are less able than untreated queens to prevent other queens from removing their wings (Obin et al. 1988). This could be useful in control because if virgin queens do remove their wings (one step toward egg-laying), they will be unable to participate in a mating flight and will probably be limited to the production of male offspring, which are commonly sterile in polygyne colonies anyway.

Fenoxycarb treatment of RIFA larvae causes them to grow larger than usual (Wheeler 1990), and it has more impact on the RIFA than on native ants (Jones et al. 1997). In one southeastern Arkansas study, native ants increased on fenoxycarb-treated plots while decreasing on hydramethylnon-treated plots. Ants of the subfamily that includes fire ants were particularly susceptible to hydramethylnon and were practically eradicated, with the exception of the fire ant itself (Zakharov and Thompson 1998a). Other studies of fenoxycarb's effects on nontarget ants showed that their populations do decline but rebound later (Williams 1986b), and nontarget organisms in general are at minimal risk (Ferguson et al. 1996). At least one Internet web page linked fenoxycarb to cancer. The validity of that claim is unclear.

Both Logic and Award (which also contains fenoxycarb) prevent worker development but act slowly (Drees et al. 1996). The fastest kills are achieved when Logic is applied in the spring of the year (Collins et al. 1992). Award was being tested for use on commercial turfgrass at the time of this writing (Gorsuch and McWhorter 1997a). Teflubenzuron is yet another chemical with IGR activity. Used in bait form it slows or halts the synthesis of chitin, one of the materials comprising the insect exoskeleton. Juvenile stages are thus prevented from molting to the next developmental stage. In this manner teflubenzuron destroys the colony by halting the production of workers (Williams et al. 1997). The IGR pyriproxyfen was found to be as effective as Logic against the RIFA (Banks and Lofgren 1991).

Pro-Drone (Stauffer MV-678) was an IGR that was effective against the RIFA when applied in a cow pasture (Lemke and Kissam 1988), but it gave unsteady results elsewhere. In fact, in one area there were no effects on any ants. In another locality the RIFA was significantly reduced. Pro-Drone caused deformation and death of larvae as well as a shift away from worker production to sexual production (Phillips and Thorvilson 1986). This was the first aerially applied IGR registered for use against the RIFA (Phillips et al. 1985), but it was too slow acting to satisfy most homeowners (Lemke and Kissam 1987).

In general, IGRs strongly affect juvenile development and survival. Workers cannibalize pupae and there is a decline in the production of eggs and larvae. Sexual pupae tend to increase in numbers but even these become deformed and are finally destroyed by the workers. Ants that do survive to become workers lose legs and antennae to attacking nestmates. High IGR levels are thus capable of destroying the entire colony (Vinson and Robeau 1974). When IGRs are applied topically to the queen, they cause her egg production to decline. The fact that treated queens sometimes eat their own eggs suggests that these chemicals also inhibit maternal instinct (Glancey et al. 1990). Colonies deprived of their queen and fed with IGR show an increase in intercastes, majors, and gynes (Robeau and Vinson 1976). Though some natural juvenile hormones cause premature wing removal when applied to virgin queens, the treatment does not affect males (Kearney et al. 1977).

Avermectins are contact insecticides that attack the insect's nervous system. They are natural products obtained from the soil bacterium *Strep-*

tomyces avermitilis and are combined to make "abamectin." This active ingredient of Affirm bait inhibits queen reproduction when fed to the RIFA colony, though colony death is slow (Lofgren and Williams 1982). It causes permanent damage to the queen's ovaries so that she is sterile or reduced in fecundity (Glancey et al. 1982). Affirm gave results as good as or better than those with Amdro (Greenblatt et al. 1986). In tests of its efficacy avermectin killed workers and usually the queen, but what were thought to be the virgin queens of the colony produced larvae that developed into more virgin queens. These were presumably mated queens after all (Mispagel 1986). Studies of the effects of Affirm on nontarget ants showed that they do suffer but rebound later (Williams 1986b). One or more avermectins comprise the active ingredient of Ascend as well as of Raid Fire Ant Killer, an outdoor granular oil bait.

Malathion and carbaryl drenches are effective against RIFA colonies and are better than aerial sprays where the human population is dense because the toxins are poured directly onto the mound (Morrill 1976a). Malathion is an organophosphorus insecticide. Carbaryl is a methyl carbamate. Both kill the ant by inhibiting an enzyme necessary for the proper function of its nervous system. This is a common mode of attack among contact insecticides (those which do not have to be ingested to be effective). Diazinon and chlorpyrifos drenches (both are organophosphorus compounds) disabled RIFA colonies so thoroughly that less than 10 percent of them were able to muster a worker retaliation when the mounds were disturbed the following day (Morrill 1977c). Like their chemical relative malathion, these toxins attack the nervous system. Diazinon sprays reduce RIFA foraging and even the mounds themselves to a useful extent (Sheppard 1982). Chlorpyrifos (e.g., Triumph 1G, Dursban) is also used to treat nursery stock (Collins 1986). This agent is moderately toxic to humans but is not known to cause deformities. Like the active ingredient of Amdro, it is poisonous to fishes though unlikely to contaminate groundwater. Unlike hydramethylnon, however, it can accumulate in plant tissues.

One comparison of drench efficacy found that Dursban killed about 80 percent of the treated colonies whereas Orthene 75S (acephate, also a variety of organophosporus compound) killed only about 11 percent (Collins and Callcott 1995). But a different study praised acephate as an effective choice (Williams and Lofgren 1983). When using these drenches against a nest, one should sneak up on the mound without causing the ground to vibrate with heavy footfalls. Otherwise the queen might be hustled into the safety of the depths (Sorensen and Trostle 1986).

Vander Meer and coworkers (1986) found that less than 1 percent of seventy-five hundred screened chemicals have the delayed killing power needed to wipe out a colony after the worker brings bait home from the field. Products in various form that Francke (1983) tested and found effective were Amdro, Bant (phenylenediamine), Dursban (chlorpyrifos), Ficam (bendiocarb, similar to carbaryl), Knox-Out (diazinon), Sevin RP-2, and Sevin SL (both carbaryls). Bushwhacker is a product that combines boric acid with a bait (Yoffe 1988). Boric acid is a slow-acting poison that begins working after the insect eats it. More than four thousand such chemicals have been tested for use against the RIFA since mirex was discontinued in 1977 (Banks 1990).

Some agents are little known, under evaluation, or not readily available to the public. For example, citrus peel oils are supposedly toxic to fire ants but have not been officially endorsed (Anonymous 1997e). Sulfluramid is an effective organofluorine compound (Banks 1990), and isofenphos (an organophosphorus compound) is reported to prevent reinfestation when the ants have been eradicated by some other means (Sorensen and Trostle 1986). Methylchloroform drench kills the mound occupants so quickly that their positions in the mound at the moment of treatment can be determined later (Pinson et al. 1980).

Pyrethroids are similar in structure to pyrethrins, which are botanical insecticides originally obtained from "the Dalmation insect flower" (Worthing and Hance 1991). The USDA approved the pyrethroids bifenthrin and tefluthrin for treating potted nursery plants against the RIFA before planting (Oi and Williams 1996), and the active ingredient of Bengal Fire Ant Killer (outdoor granules) is deltamethrin, another species of pyrethroid. A singular treatment against individual mounds uses the related compound resmethrin, injected at a temperature of 800°F (Thorvilson et al. 1989).

One of the more unusual products is Fire Ant Control, an EPA-registered combination of rotenone and deodorized liquid cow manure. Rotenone is a naturally occurring pesticide found in the roots of certain plants. The cow manure serves two purposes. It masks the rotenone and aids in the regrowth of grass once the ants are eliminated from their unsightly mound.

Perhaps the simplest of all recourses is a natural drench using three gallons of 194°F water (not quite boiling), poured slowly onto the RIFA mound. This is a useful home remedy and often kills the colony (Tschinkel and Howard 1980). It is best to use hot water on sunny mornings when the ants are clustered in the mound for warmth of a very different kind. Soaps and wood ashes soaked into the mounds may have some effectiveness by removing protective layers of the ant's waxy exoskeleton (Drees et al. 1996). Leaded gasoline is effective against RIFA mounds but is illegal to use in this manner. Some people believe epsom salts and Clorox bleach to be effective

(Lemke and Kissam 1987), but grits sprinkled on the ground will not cause the ants eating them to explode (as some think). The grits supposedly swell up inside the ant's digestive tract. However, because fire ants mainly imbibe liquids from their food and thereby consume only the smallest of microscopic particles, the grits are unable to enter the body in a suitable form for explosive expansion (Sorensen and Trostle 1986).

Diatomaceous earth scrapes away the protective outer layer of the exoskeleton so that the ant is more likely to dry out or desiccate (Drees et al. 1996). Perhaps the metallic element zinc could be used in some way to control fire ants. When flue dust containing zinc was applied to land as a nutrient source for plants, the fire ants seemed to avoid the metal—it was found in only low levels in the mounds (Davis-Carter and Sheppard 1993). On the other hand, the RIFA is more tolerant of high ozone levels than mammalian species like ourselves (Levy et al. 1974b).

Three treatment methods using a variety of popular chemicals were endorsed by the Texas Agricultural Extension Service (TAES) in the late 1990s. Program 1 (the "Two-Step Method") is intended for large areas and requires as the first step the broadcast of bait once or twice a year by handheld device or from car or airplane. The period from late summer to early fall is recommended because rain-free periods are more predictable at this time of year and because rain interferes with the bait's effect. Midmornings or late afternoons in particular are recommended so that neither dew nor excessive heat will compromise the bait's efficiency. Furthermore, treatments should be applied between 65 and 95°F. When the ants are of the polygyne variety, the treatment might have to be 35 to 40 meters in width (Martin et al. 1998).

Hydramethylnon bait is said to require about one month to achieve maximum effect, fenoxycarb about six times as long. The second step is treatment of individual mounds in difficult areas and in those that escaped the effects of broadcast. Baits, drenches, injections, granules, and hot water are used in step two.

Program 2 is intended for small areas and consists of the second step of Program 1. Program 3 is the all-out eradication effort that requires a contact insecticide applied every month or two whether or not bait was used previously.

From this short summary of a vast literature, it is easy to see that a chemical war is being waged against the red imported fire ant. E. O. Wilson described that conflict as "the Vietnam of entomology" (Conniff 1990). Yet the alternatives seem little better than surrender. These include mechanical and electrical devices marketed by overly optimistic entrepreneurs. One of these inventions was a tractor of the riding lawnmower variety that churned the mound into a wet slurry. When the slurry dries it hardens and entombs the ants trapped within. Another device was a small windmill that drove a wheel across a track, crushing any ant that attempted to cross the barrier. Most products invented to electrocute ants, cause vibrations in the mound, or send microwaves into the mound are not recommended by the Texas Agricultural Experiment Station (TAES).

The Black Imported Fire Ant

The first coordinated efforts aimed at controlling the BIFA used calcium cyanide dust (Lofgren 1986c). An early study reported that the BIFA is harder to control with chlorinated hydrocarbons than its cousin the RIFA (Rhoades and Davis 1967). Chlordane is one of these. It causes the ants to leave the mound, exiting underground and out of sight. Methyl bromide fumigation was not as effective. It provoked a singular behavior: some ants left the nest while others remained inside and bored ventilation holes through the mound surface. The colony returned at a later date (Green 1952).

Mirex was broadcast aerially in northeastern Mississippi to control the BIFA. The treatment did not harm honey bees, for no mirex was found in the hives and bee populations were not reduced (Glancey et al. 1970b).

Chlorpyrifos has been tried in combination with piperonyl butoxide. Chlorpyrifos is absorbed across the insect's exoskeleton and is metabolized within. Piperonyl butoxide slows down that metabolism and is thereby useful because this allows the poison more time for distribution among nestmates (Chambers et al. 1983). Presumably this distribution is via trophallaxis.

The BIFA can be killed by photoxidation after it consumes a dye called rose bengal. The effectiveness depends upon the concentration of the dye and the intensity of the light (Broome et al. 1975). Light can play a similar role in the efficacy of a bait called phloxin B. This kills in two ways, one way requiring light and the other not (David and Heitz 1978).

The Tropical Fire Ant

Some of the first studies using bait toxicants to attempt fire ant control were done by Travis (1939, 1942, 1943), using the metallic element thallium in a syrup base and the tropical fire ant as its target. Thallium acetate and thallium sulfate were tried, along with many other poisons including arsenic, lead, mercury, and rotenone. Most of these would not even be considered in a modern political climate. Of the thallium preparations, the acetate form was effective whereas the sulfate form was accepted by the ants in early spring but not in late summer. Travis learned that fire ants suck liquid from baits instead of eating solid particles. He therefore concluded that insoluble toxins, those that would not be imbibed with liquid, would be ineffective in baits. During the trials the TFA often took baits into the nest, only to carry them out again later. The rejected poison was then covered with soil. Sometimes poisons simply provoked the ants to move to a new location (Wolcott 1933).

In Florida in 1962, the TFA coexisted with the RIFA somewhat more extensively than it does today. Mirex controlled the tropical fire ant even better than it controlled the imported fire ant. When the amount of bait was limited, the workers appeared to feed the queen before feeding any other colony members (Bartlett and Lofgren 1964). In southern Mexico, mirex in combination with corn grits and vegetable oil was still being used long after its ban from the United States (Risch and Carroll 1982a, b), though these authors deemed it unwise. Even before mirex was banned in the United States, some writers concluded that its use against the tropical fire ant would only cause the RIFA to step into the vacuum left by the other's demise (Bartlett and Lofgren 1964; Summerlin et al. 1977a). A more serious problem would then replace a lesser one.

Amdro with its hydramethylnon active ingredient is one of the most popular modern poisons. Williams and colleagues (1990) looked for alternative ways of dispensing the toxin and found that fly pupae treated with hydramethylnon were avidly collected by tropical fire ants. This new carrier or vehicle worked well but was not as cost-effective as the standard corn-grit preparation.

Past attempts at chemical control of the TFA include use of dieldrin, gamma-BHC, and diazinon (Hill 1975; Muniappan and Marutani 1992), heptachlor, chlordane, and aldrex (Murthy 1959), and carbolic acid and aldrin (Wolcott 1933, 1951). The early and seminal papers of Travis list many others. Conspicuous on those lists are cyanide and sodium fluoride.

An unusual solution, which cannot be classified as either chemical control or biocontrol, was that advocated by Ordelheide (1929). When standard methods failed, tobacco seedbeds were physically protected from TFA depredation by a covering called "klamboe." It resembles cheesecloth.

The Southern Fire Ant

Early in the twentieth century, arsenical baits and syrups were used unsuccessfully against the southern fire ant in California. Thallium sulfate worked but is dangerous to humans and could not be used by private citizens. A mixture of carbon disulfide and carbon tetrachloride was both successful and readily available. First, owners of infested homes were encouraged to poke around with a screwdriver to locate the ants by stirring them up. A bag was used to cover the fumes when the mixture was applied indoors. Ants in closets were driven out with a mixture of ethylene dichloride and carbon tetrachloride, held in a saucer. An unusual approach called for a bellows to force lime dust into the ventilators of the house (Mallis 1938).

One Mississippi program designed to wipe out the Argentine ant (not a fire ant, but one of its enemies) used "Government Formula Argentine Ant Poison," a compound containing arsenic. This succeeded against its target in the city of Columbus but not against the southern fire ant, which then became the worst ant pest in town (Haug 1934).

Mirex was able to eradicate the SFA from a Louisiana habitat, though the absence of the RIFA was only temporary (Markin et al. 1974a, b). California almond growers handle their own southern fire ant problems with diazinon (Zalom and Bentley 1985). Elsewhere in the state exterminators use that same toxicant, but also cypermethrin, bendiocarb, hydramethylnon, boric acid, and chlorpyrifos, under their various trade names (Knight and Rust 1990).

One fact is easily overlooked in this controversy over the chemical control of fire ants. Heptachlor and the other chlorinated hydrocarbons saved the lives of many people who were allergic to fire ant venom or would have become allergic after being stung. Part of this was made possible by soil residues from banned chemicals that kept fire ant complaints at a low ebb from the 1960s until the late 1970s (Lofgren and Adams 1982; Adams 1986). The toxins did this work unseen and perhaps unappreciated.

In the last sentences of *Silent Spring* Rachel Carson (1962) had no kind words for the attempts to control insect pests with chlorinated hydrocarbons: "The concepts and practices of applied entomology for the most part date from that stone age of science. It is our alarming misfortune that so primitive a science has armed itself with the most modern and terrible weapons, and that in turning them against the insects it has also turned them against the earth." Beatty (1973) realized that the author of *Silent Spring* was prone to speak in hyperbole but agreed that "We can all be hopeful, as was Rachel Carson, that biological control is just around the corner." That possibility is the subject of the next chapter.

CHAPTER 12

Enemies and
Biocontrol of Fire Ants

The need for effective weapons against a
menace as serious as the fire ants is too urgent
to brook uncompromising obstruction.

—*Philadelphia Inquirer, November 30, 1958*

IF fire ants are perceived as pests, and if chemical
control is not the answer, then perhaps biocontrol
is. Biocontrol is defined as the management (if not
elimination) of one living thing by another, or by a
collection of living things. E. O. Wilson (1958) and
C. M. Tarzwell (1958) were among the first to suggest
that biocontrol might be necessary to control the imported fire ants. This approach will probably be less
effective than chemical control and likely will require
a host of enemies chipping away at the fire ants simultaneously if it is to have any measurable impact.
Even those scientists engaged in biocontrol research
are pessimistic about its effectiveness. Larry Gilbert
(1996) reminded us that biocontrol has never been
effective against a pestiferous ant. In any event, the
search for the best biocontrol agent requires a complete survey of fire ant enemies, both large and small.
And that is the purpose of this chapter.

The survey begins with the fire ant's worst enemies, and it should not be surprising to find that these
are other ants. That is the way of competition: the
more alike two creatures are, the greater the chance

that they will compete for similar resources. E. O. Wilson elaborated: "It is entirely possible that *Solenopsis invicta* is kept within its present relatively modest range and low population densities in Brazil and Argentina by pressure from *Pheidole* and other ant enemies that have adapted to its presence during thousands of years of coevolution" (Conniff 1990). Drees and colleagues (1996) agreed that the best biological control program is the preservation of native ants that are able to compete with the RIFA.

South American ant exports are indeed a noxious group. They include some of the RIFA's worst enemies, and the Argentine ant *Linepithema humile* is high on the list. It arrived in the United States before either of the IFAs, and it has been fighting both ever since. Following the customs of human nature, the Argentines prefer to call this pest the Brazilian ant. It was already pushing a truly Argentine ant (the BIFA) out of the Mobile, Alabama, area when a truly Brazilian ant (the RIFA) entered that port city. Yet Wilson and Eads (1949) found that only five red imported fire ants were sufficient to destroy several hundred Argentine ants and their queen. Oddly enough, the distribution of the Argentine ant in the United States in 1936 was almost identical to the distribution of the RIFA in the United States today (1999), including the California infestations so widely disjunct from the main infestations in the southeastern part of the country (M. R. Smith's map in Elton 1958).

Enemies of the Red Imported Fire Ant

RIFA enemies lurk within their own ranks in the form of territorial foragers, sterile males, pleometrotic queens, brood-raiding minims, and workers that kill foundresses before they have a chance to establish their own colony. Release of sterilized males (made so by X-radiation) was effective against the screwworm menace but does not seem a realistic solution to the RIFA problem (Lofgren et al. 1975). This is true even though naturally sterile males are already in abundant supply among wild polygynous colonies. However, the queen mates only once and union with a sterile male would remove her from the reproductive game.

Besides territorial combat among workers of competing RIFA colonies (Wilson et al. 1971), there is much brood raiding between young colonies during the lifetime of the first workers, the cohort known as minims (see chapter 3). And RIFA foragers sometimes kill newly mated queens that happen to land in their territory. Queen execution by a squad of workers begins when they grasp and tug at her appendages until she is spread-eagled between them. Then they bite her to pieces (Stamps and Vinson 1991).

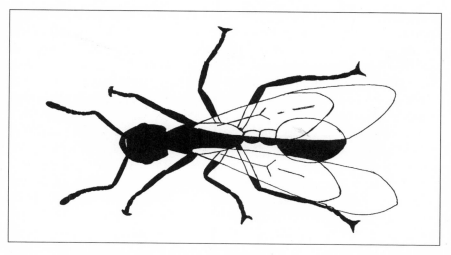

Fig. 12.1. Daguerre's fire ant (queen). The actual color is yellow to reddish brown. Modified from Santschi 1930. By permission of Sociedad Entomológica Argentina.

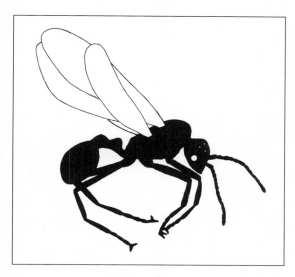

Fig. 12.2. Daguerre's fire ant (male). The actual color is brown. Modified from Santschi 1930. By permission of the Sociedad Entomológica Argentina.

Solenopsis daguerrei is an unusual South American fire ant that lives in the nests of other fire ants (figs. 12.1, 12.2). The species has queens and males but no worker caste, and is called a "social parasite" because it must live off the efforts of its host colony. There is some interest in using this species to control both the RIFA and the BIFA. In South America *S. daguerrei* also parasitizes *S. saevissima* and *S. macdonaghi* (Calcaterra et al. 1999). At one time Daguerre's fire ant was thought to behead the host queen (from the outside, not from the inside as the internally parasitic phorid flies do), but now it appears that no royal heads roll (Briano et al. 1997; Williams 1980). The parasite simply clings with jaws and legs to the host queen while receiving food from host workers. Parasite matings occur in the host nest and the young queen flies off to infect a colony of her own.

Southern fire ants *(S. xyloni)* prey upon RIFA queens (Nichols and Sites 1991), as do tropical fire ants *(S. geminata)*. Thief ants (fig. 1.14), also members of the genus *Solenopsis*, are enemies of fire ants in general (MacKay and Vinson 1989a). They have a broad and natural distribution in the United States. One of the better-known species is *S. molesta.*

The ant *Dorymyrmex insanus* kills newly mated queens while these search for a nesting site. This species destroys 97 percent of the would-be founders landing in its territory. The RIFA queen runs, hides, stands still, and shakes but these seemingly feeble defenses are not enough to save her (Nickerson et al. 1975; Roe 1974). *Dorymyrmex flavopectus* kills males after the nuptial flight, and *Lasius neoniger* kills some virgin queens before they leave the ground and others when they return (Whitcomb et al. 1973). Death of a male after the nuptial flight is of no consequence because it would soon die anyway, but the ant genus *Dorymyrmex* does contain at least the two above-mentioned formidable enemies of the RIFA, and it is therefore surprising that a third species, *D. pyramicus*, is allowed to nest at the edge of the fire ant mound (Wilson et al. 1971).

Harvester ants kill RIFA queens too. The Texas harvester *(Pogonomyrmex barbatus)*, Comanche harvester *(P. comanche,* fig. 12.3), Florida harvester *(P. badius)*, and tiny *Ephebomyrmex imberbiculus* are enemies living in the southern United States whereas *E. naegelii* displaces or destroys young RIFA colonies in the Brazilian homeland (Fowler 1993; Stimac and Alves 1994; pers. obs.). In the laboratory I have seen the relatively huge harvesters snip fire ants in half at the waist. Afterward they rub their jaws against the bottom of the tray as though the swift execution were a distasteful process.

The little black ant *Monomorium minimum* (fig. 12.4) sometimes drives RIFA foragers from baits in the field, even when these are placed directly on the fire ants' mound. It sprays venom into the air by lifting and vibrating the abdomen (Baroni Urbani and Kannowski 1974). The fire ant does the same—not surprising since these two species are closely related. Newly mated queens fall prey to the little black ant (Nichols and Sites 1991), and sometimes entire small colonies are wiped out (Vinson, pers. comm.).

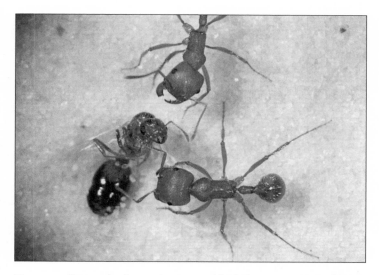

Fig. 12.3. Comanche harvester ants with their prey, a winged RIFA queen captured after a nuptial flight.

Fig. 12.4. The little black ant *Monomorium minimum.*

A Brazilian study discovered that the RIFA was not the dominant ant in the area at hand, this status being achieved by a *Pheidole* or a *Dorymyrmex* (Fowler et al. 1990). In the United States both genera are also major opponents of the RIFA but the fire ant somehow manages to come out on top (Stimac and Alves 1994). Ants superior to the RIFA in defensive combat

Fig. 12.5. A fire ant's natural enemy: a *Pheidole dentata* major worker.

Fig. 12.6. The blind army ant *Labidus coecus.*

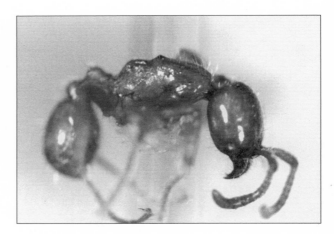

tend to be woodland species (e.g., *Pheidole dentata*) whereas those inferior tend to live in open areas, as the RIFA does (Bhatkar 1988).

Pheidole dentata (fig. 12.5) can be an even match for the RIFA when the two meet up in the southern United States (Jones and Phillips 1987). Sometimes the entire fire ant colony is destroyed (Vinson, pers. comm.). This suggests the possibility of seeding *P. dentata* in or near fire ant habitats. Exposed RIFA queens are killed by the broadly predatory army ant *Labidus coecus* (Nichols and Sites 1989, 1991) (fig. 12.6), and *Paratrechina arenivaga* is yet another ant enemy that fire ants must deal with (Stimac and Alves 1994).

Fig. 12.7. An *Aphaenogaster* ant.

Red imported fire ants are clearly overmatched when pitted against *Aphaenogaster occidentalis,* an ant that is not currently within the RIFA's range (fig. 12.7). Fire ants start the fight but their stings cannot penetrate the other's armor. *Aphaenogaster* applies its own venom to the fire ant's exoskeleton and the result is paralysis and death (Jones and Phillips 1989).

In North Carolina the RIFA has encroached upon the range of the pavement ant *Tetramorium caespitum.* When the colonies of the two species are brought into contact under laboratory conditions, the pavement ant attacks in mobs and destroys the fire ant nest. RIFA guards dispense venom into the air by flagging their gaster but the pavement ants shrug off the effects and pluck their enemies out of the nest, dismembering them with biting jaws. Still, the pavement ant's sting was not as effective in these fights as the sting of the RIFA (King and Phillips 1992).

Workers of the ant *Lasius neoniger* battle the RIFA in both field and lab. *Lasius* slides the antenna of the RIFA through its own mandibles and sprays formic acid onto the fire ant's face, perhaps marking it for execution by nestmates. *Lasius* can kill two or three RIFAs this way before succumbing to the venom of its opponents. The overwhelming numbers of the fire ant colony eventually carry the day. Bhatkar and his colleagues (1972) described a laboratory battle between the native and the import. The fire ants built a barrier from the bodies of the dead and began pushing it forward until they entered the *Lasius* colony, crossing a landscape of corpses in the process. The *Lasius* defenders built their own barrier of soil and wood fragments. RIFAs

Fig. 12.8. An *Orasema* wasp. Reprinted from Wheeler 1910.

breached the barrier while *Lasius* moved queen, sexuals, and brood deeper into the nest for protection. Fire ants followed aggressively, killing all guards and finally the queen and the other sexuals, which offered little resistance. The decapitated body of the queen was taken back to the fire ant nest and eaten. When the war was over the fire ants moved into the *Lasius* nest.

Fire ants have plenty of enemies on more distant branches of the insect evolutionary tree. Wasps, for example. A Brazilian eucharitid wasp of the genus *Orasema* (fig. 12.8) has a larval stage that lives as a parasite on RIFA pupae. The juvenile wasp acquires the fire ant odor and is treated like a member of the colony (Vander Meer et al. 1989a).

The tiger beetle *Cicindella punctulata* (fig. 12.9) preys upon the RIFA outside the nest (Stimac and Alves 1994), whereas the nest-dwelling scarab beetles *Euparia castanea* and *Martinezia dutertrei* eat RIFA larvae where hordes of tending fire ants would seem to make such a feat impossible (Wojcik et al. 1991). Secretions of several beetle larvae are fire ant repellents. Larvae of the ground beetle genus *Pseudomorpha* (fig. 12.10) release these chemicals from mushroom-shaped hairs on the head and thorax (Erwin 1981). The leaf beetle *Gastrophysa cyanea* secretes a material from glands that are extruded when the grub is attacked. One component of this repellent is called "chrysomelidial" because it is produced by a chrysomelid (a leaf beetle). The red clover thrips releases a defensive secretion from its anus, repelling the RIFA. This contains a substance known as "mellein"

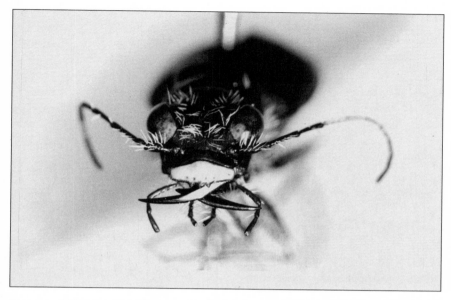

Fig. 12.9. A tiger beetle. Its large, sickle-like jaws are used to kill its prey, which includes fire ants.

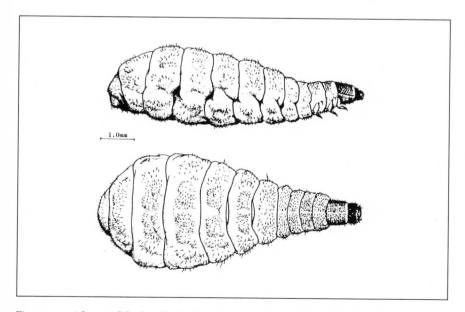

Fig. 12.10. A larva of the beetle *Pseudomorpha*. Reprinted from Erwin 1981.

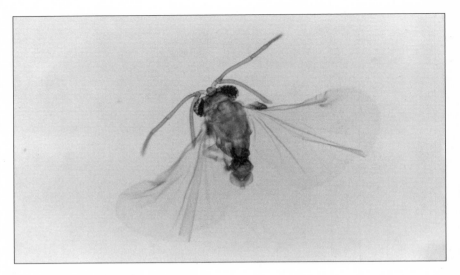

Fig. 12.11. An adult male strepsipteran.

(Blum et al. 1992). Gypsy moth caterpillars secrete from dorsal abdominal glands a substance that deters RIFAs from feeding but does not really repel them (Aldrich et al. 1997). Naphthalene, the chemical used as moth balls to prevent moths from damaging clothes, has been detected in the termite *Coptotermes formosanus.* This paralyzes the RIFA at levels tolerated by the wood chewer (Chen et al. 1998).

An unexpected enemy of the RIFA was discovered in the United States, but its extensive New World distribution (in many areas where the RIFA does not live) shows that it is not specific to the fire ant. This insect may have added the RIFA to its list of hosts only recently. It is a member of the strange insect order Strepsiptera, the closest relatives of the beetles or perhaps true beetles after all. These "twisted-wing" insects (fig. 12.11) are so unusual in appearance that some entomologists have argued for a closer relationship to flies than to beetles. The species attacking the RIFA is *Caenocholax fenyesi.* Early juvenile stages (fig. 12.12) of both sexes live outside their host but they soon seek it out and become internal parasites. Only the male is known to parasitize the RIFA, and it is the grublike larval stage of the ant that is attacked. The female parasitizes the restless bush cricket *Hapithus agitator.* These tiny invaders can be seen protruding from between the body segments of their hosts. A successful female will spend the remainder of her life inside the cricket with only enough of herself protruding through the host's surface to allow mating with the male. The male flies to

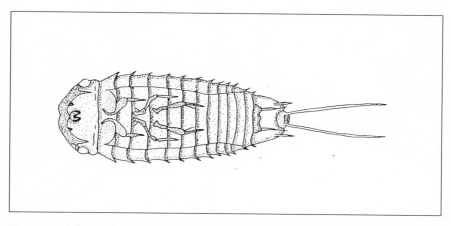

Fig. 12.12. A larva of the strepsipteran *Caenocholax fenyesi*. Reprinted from Cook 1996. By permission of the author.

her after leaving the ant in which he developed. He has about an hour to do this before dying. The ant dies too, shortly after the parasite flies from its body. *Caenocholax fenyesi* prefers intermediate-size workers when using this caste as a host. It uses the sexuals too. Parasitized worker ants eventually leave the colony and climb objects when the enemy within is ready to make its exit. The position assumed is similar to the defensive gaster-flagging posture. About 1 percent of the ants in an infected colony harbor the tiny killer (Cook 1996; Cook et al. 1997).

Four Brazilian phorid fly species were imported into Texas in the 1990s for laboratory tests as potential biocontrol agents of the red imported fire ant. As juveniles they are all internal parasites of fire ants and are invariably lethal to their hosts. The four in question attack workers. These are *Pseudacteon litoralis* (fig. 12.13), *P. wasmanni*, *P. tricuspis*, and *P. curvatus*. The latter species also attacks the tropical fire ant (Gilbert and Morrison 1997). Most specialists believe that the fly's egg is always injected into the thorax of the host, where the ant tries in vain to remove it. A striking discovery is the fact that flies developing in larger workers tend to become females (Morrison et al. 1999a), which are larger than the males of the species. It appears that the environment determines the sex of this parasite. One Brazilian species, *Pseudacteon solenopsidis*, is striking for a different reason—it flies *backward* while pursuing its host (Orr et al. 1997). *Pseudacteon obtusus* also attacks RIFA workers (Williams and Banks 1987), and yet another species is said to attack the winged queen, though this latter claim has been disputed.

Flying phorids zoom about and oviposit on RIFA workers with such

Fig. 12.13. The phorid fly *Pseudacteon litoralis* (female). Its small size is evident here, for it is glued to the shaft of an insect pin.

force that the impact knocks the ant onto its side. Those stricken soon regain their feet, run off a little way, and then stop. Some RIFA workers do not run away when the scuttle flies show up but make a stand, defending food items outside the nest while the flies go about their lethal work. Nevertheless, foraging typically decreases by 80 percent even though the flies manage to kill very few ants per colony. Their appearance alone is enough to reduce greatly the activities of workers outside the nest. The ants sometimes manage to kill their fast-darting tormentors, which are thought to have evolved from a scavenger ancestor into parasitoids that are attracted to disturbances of the mound (Porter et al. 1995c; Williams 1980). Eighteen phorid species were known to attack fire ants at the time of this writing. More will probably be added to the list as research continues.

Pseudacteon tricuspis provides an example of the life cycle of these parasitoids. From the egg injected into the ant's thorax, the larval fly hatches, moves into the ant's head, and begins feeding upon brains, glands, and everything else until the victim's head falls off, presumably from the action of a dissolving chemical. The decapitated body remains twitching on its feet for some time while the empty "skull" becomes a pupal case for the parasite inside (fig. 12.14). Shed skins from earlier stages can be seen floating in the blood within the ant's body. Total development time from egg to adult is

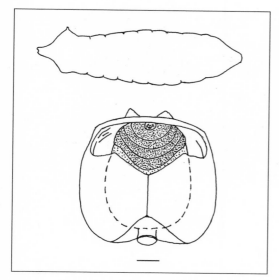

Fig. 12.14. A phorid fly larva *(top)* and a pupa (stippled) occupying the mouth cavity of a fire ant, which the larva decapitated while still inside (ventral view). Scale bar = 0.2 mm. Reprinted from Porter et al. 1995b. Copyright 1995, Entomological Society of America.

about forty days. The strange caplike pupal case suggests a long association between the two species, for it precisely fits the opening of the ant's mouth. The ant's jaws are removed by the parasite before pupation and the empty spaces left behind are filled by the parasite's projecting breathing tubes. Developing flies that fail to remove both jaws die in the pupal stage more often than those that manage to remove both obstructions (Porter et al. 1995b, 1997a, b).

South American phorids are being raised in greenhouses prior to their release as adults in the United States. *Pseudacteon tricuspis* was the first of these introductions to take wing, at Brackenridge Field Laboratory, in Austin, Texas, in December 1995. Other Texas releases followed, including *P. litoralis* (fig. 12.13), and there were Florida releases in July of 1997 and December of 1998. Some early Texas efforts were compromised by droughts, though release sites in Austin and Laredo were still being monitored in 1999. The Florida flies were a going concern at the time of this writing (L. Gilbert, pers. comm.). Host-choice tests suggest that the flies will accept nothing but fire ants (Porter et al. 1995a). In other words, if the introduced insects do broaden their host spectrum, native fire ants will be their most likely victims.

When phorid flies become locally abundant they might allow "bubbles" of native ants to surface here and there across the RIFA's range in the United States, adding competition to parasite pressure. The polygyne social type's great colony density will work against it for a change because it will be that

Fig. 12.15. The green darner dragonfly *Anax junius*, head-on.

much more apparent to the enemies that hunt them down (Gilbert 1996). Indeed, the fact that fire ant densities in the United States are about five to seven times as high as those in South America suggests that something is keeping them under control on the other side of the equator. Perhaps the phorid flies are major players.

Many arthropods already in place in the United States kill red imported fire ants when the opportunity arises. An unidentified silverfish species living inside the nest eats the RIFA's brood (Wojcik 1990). Sexuals are devoured during the nuptial flight by the dragonflies *Pachydiplax longipennis* (the blue dasher), *Tramea carolina, Somatochlora provocans,* and *Anax junius* (the green darner, fig. 12.15) and immediately after the flight by the striped earwig *(Labidura riparia)* and various wolf spiders (Stimac and Alves 1994).

The ant-lion *Brachynemurus nebulosus* lies beneath the sand and pulls passing RIFAs under, biting them with venomous jaws before eating them as prey (Bahls and Deyrup 1988). RIFA workers sometimes lock their own formidable jaws onto those of their foe and die in place (fig. 12.16), so that the dead fire ant kills its enemy when the latter eventually expires from starvation (Lucas and Brockmann 1981).

Dragonflies, particularly the huge green darner mentioned earlier, were the most effective predators of flying sexuals during mating flights in Arkansas. Other predators in that state include a variety of spiders, the Carolina mantis, and a robber fly (Roe 1974). Dragonflies catch the sexuals in flight and eat only the abdomens, so that large numbers of queens lose their egg-laying organs in midair and drop to the ground, where they soon die (Vinson 1997).

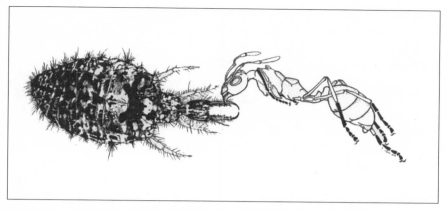

Fig. 12.16. An ant-lion and a fire ant locked in mutual destruction. Reprinted from Lucas and Brockmann 1981. By permission of Kansas Entomological Society.

Fig. 12.17. A female black widow and her egg sac.

Spiders, mites, and ticks round out the list of the RIFA's known arthropod enemies. The striped lynx spider *Oxyopes salticus* preys upon the RIFA in Texas cotton fields (Nyffeler et al. 1987). Black widows in these same fields can sometimes rely upon the RIFA for 75 percent of their prey (fig. 12.17). All castes and sexes have been found in the webs (Nyffeler et al. 1988). The black and yellow garden spider *Argiope aurantia* catches and eats RIFA sexuals that take wing for the nuptial flight (Lockley 1995a). Several other species, including a spitting spider of the genus *Scytodes*, prey upon red imported fire ants (Mackay and Vinson 1989b).

The straw-itch or fire mite *Pyemotes tritici* feeds on RIFA larvae, pupae, and queens, but field trials of its biocontrol potential were disappointing, to say the least. The mite proved ineffective against its intended target while sending the researchers themselves to the hospital with a severe rash (Sorensen and Trostle 1986; Thorvilson et al. 1986, 1987). Bruce and LeCato (1980) provide a photo of this mite attached to a RIFA pupa, the parasite distended with the host's body fluids. Queen fire ants occasionally harbor massive infestations of an unknown species of mite. Perhaps these are members of the genus *Mesostigmata* (Vinson and Ellison 1996). Winged queens are sometimes so encumbered with the tiny arachnids that they are unable to fly (Markin et al. 1971).

Another mite that has attracted attention as a possible enemy is *Tyrophagus putrescentiae*, which eats RIFA eggs under laboratory conditions. These predators were collected from the mound itself (Bass and Hays 1976b). The American dog tick *Dermacentor variabilis* is a large mite that repels the RIFA with a defensive secretion containing squalene (Yoder 1995). Experiments showed that RIFA larvae are not suitable intermediate hosts for the tapeworm *Moniezia expansa*, a species already known to use mites in that capacity. Workers did feed worm proglottids (egg-bearing structures) to fourth instar larvae, but the worm's eggs were passed out with the meconium. This tapeworm was therefore deemed unsuitable as a biocontrol agent (Fritz 1985).

Though tapeworms have so far failed, a different worm phylum holds great promise for RIFA biocontrol. These are the nematodes or "roundworms." *Tetradonema solenopsis* was first discovered in Brazil, where it lives as an internal parasite of the RIFA (fig. 12.18). It kills every infected ant and attacks one fourth of all individuals in a colony. All stages of both sexes live in the gaster of adult fire ants (Nickle and Jouvenaz 1987).

Control of the RIFA in South Carolina has been attempted with the nematode *Steinernema riobravis* (Gorsuch and McWhorter 1997b). The closely related nematode *S. carpocapsae* infects and kills RIFA sexuals and brood but does not infect the worker caste. When these worms were released into a colony, workers attempted to remove them from their own bodies and from the bodies of their nestmates. Some workers did perish, though this was attributed to exhaustion from efforts to fend off the small but highly energetic parasites that are able to jump a distance equal to nine

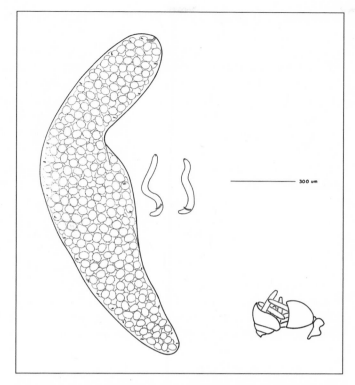

Fig. 12.18. The parasitic nematode *Tetradonema solenopsis:* egg-filled female *(left)*, two males *(center)*, and several worms inside a dissected fire ant abdomen *(right)*. By agreement with the *Journal of Nematology*.

times their own body length (Campbell and Kaya 1999). Biocontrol with *S. carpocapsae* is problematic because the ants leave their nest (and the worms) behind when it is treated. Other nematode biocontrol candidates have received consideration (Drees et al. 1992c; Lofgren et al. 1975).

The red imported fire ant in the United States has many vertebrate enemies beyond the humans who are seeking to eradicate them. Among the many birds known to eat RIFA sexuals at the time of the nuptial flight are eastern bobwhites, chimney swifts, and eastern kingbirds (Vinson and Sorensen 1986; Stimac and Alves 1994). The RIFA is a major prey item of the Florida swallow-tailed kite (Lee and Clark 1993). No one seems to know if the horned lizard *Phrynosoma cornutum* is feeding upon the RIFA that is displacing its natural harvester ant prey (Donaldson et al. 1994). At least one mammal, the armadillo, occasionally eats fire ants (Drees et al. 1996), but I could find no records of South American anteaters doing the same.

Microorganisms may offer the greatest hope for successful biocontrol. These include the kingdoms of the bacteria, fungi, and protozoa as well as the enigmatic microsporidians. It is not clear which kingdom of life the latter microbes belong to. A search for parasites of the RIFA in the southeastern United States turned up one particular microsporidian species in one out of 1007 colonies, a type normally associated with the tropical fire ant. Some colonies were infected with yeasts (Jouvenaz et al. 1977). At the other extreme of the RIFA's range, an extensive survey of ants in western Texas found next to nothing in the way of native microorganisms that might be used for biocontrol (Beckham et al. 1982). One *Pseudomonas* bacterium isolated from dead Mississippi ants did kill every larva that fed upon it in the lab (Lofgren et al. 1975). Nevertheless, the literature clearly reflects a common belief that successful microscopic biocontrol agents must be found in the South American homeland.

One of the most promising candidates is the fungus genus *Beauveria* (fig. 12.19) (Lofgren et al. 1975). These fungi can apparently penetrate the adult exoskeleton through the tarsal joints of the legs, and both adults and

Fig. 12.19. The fungus *Beauveria bassiana* growing on a cicada.

larvae can be infected orally. The food filter of the major workers does not give them complete protection from the spores, perhaps because the largest workers may have openings in their filters that are large enough to admit the parasite. Dead ants are carried to the trash pile before the developing fungus produces another round of infective spores (Siebeneicher et al. 1992). *Beauveria* in South America infects up to 90 percent of the nests in a given area and 70 percent of the individuals inside them. When *Beauveria bassiana* was used against Florida RIFAs it caused a reduction in foraging while other ant species increased their activity outside the nest (Oi et al. 1994). Tests show that it is more effective to inject a powder containing spores than simply to mix them into the nest because the presence of soil hinders the mixing process (Stimac et al. 1993; Pereira and Stimac 1992). Private sector help will probably be needed if progress is to be made in this line of research (Stimac and Alves 1994).

A second fungus known to infect the RIFA in South America is *Metarhizium anisopliae* (fig. 12.20). *Aspergillus flavus* has been tried in the lab (Allen and Buren 1974; Lofgren et al. 1975), and other fungi that attack the

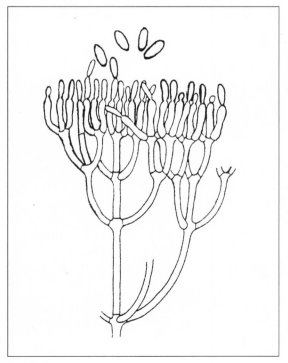

Fig. 12.20. The parasitic fungus *Metarhizium anisopliae* and its spores. Reprinted from Carmichael et al. 1980. By permission of the authors.

RIFA include the genera *Hirsutella, Candida, Paecilomyces* (Stimac and Alves 1994), and *Conidiobolus* (Sánchez-Peña and Thorvilson 1992). *Conidiobolus* killed larvae very effectively whereas *Metarhizium* killed exposed queens.

A black "yeast" fungus *Myrmecomyces annellisae* occurs in the blood of U.S. RIFAs. It seems to make the ants succumb more readily to stress. This might be the only microorganism imported into the United States with the fire ants that is a specific enemy of the insect (Jouvenaz and Kimbrough 1991; Briano et al. 1995d). As usual the RIFA fights back. Its venom alkaloids inhibit the growth of *Beauveria bassiana, Metarhizium anisopliae,* and *Paecilomyces fumosoroseus* (Storey et al. 1991).

The microsporidian *Thelohania solenopsae* infects the RIFA in its Brazilian homeland (Allen and Buren 1974; Knell et al. 1977); decades after its initial discovery in South America, it was discovered infecting the imported ant in Florida, Mississippi, and Texas (Williams et al. 1998). This parasite attacks fat bodies in general as well as the queen's ovaries, and its victims tremble from the effects. Early attempts to transmit the disease in the lab failed. Infected colonies collected by Williams and his coworkers suffered a loss of brood and the loss of at least some queens. Lab and field colonies were successfully infected when brood carrying the parasite were added to the nests, though the mechanism remained unknown (Williams et al. 1999). If such a natural enemy could force a pest species to stop producing males, it could be a valuable weapon against that pest because reproduction would stop if the enemy became sufficiently widespread. *Thelohania hereditaria* does have this effect on the females of its crustacean host (Maynard Smith and Szathmáry 1995), though *T. solenopsae* has not been reported to do the same when infecting fire ant queens.

Also a microsporidian, *Vairimorpha invictae* infects the RIFA in Brazil, where it is present in about 2 percent of wild colonies. Attempts to transmit the parasite under laboratory conditions were unsuccessful (Jouvenaz and Ellis 1986). *Burenella dimorpha* is a microsporidian parasite of the TFA that can be orally transmitted to the RIFA (Jouvenaz and Hazard 1978).

According to Jouvenaz (1986, 1990), microbiological control must somehow overcome: (1) the care given to queens by workers, (2) the low susceptibility of the queen, whose gut is almost free of microbes, (3) the filter protecting the ants' digestive tract, and (4) the fire ants' own biocontrol— workers fumigate the nest with their venom.

The bacterium *Bacillus thuringiensis* is a biocontrol agent successfully employed against many insects, but the feeding filter of the red imported fire ant does prevent entry in this case (Jouvenaz et al. 1996). A very different approach was tried with the bacterium *Pseudomonas syringae.* Topical mist

Fig. 12.21. A legume of the genus *Sesbania,* this species is commonly known as rattlepod or rattlebush.

applications raised the freezing point of RIFA workers above that of un-treated workers. This could raise the mortality of fire ants too, making them more susceptible to freezing during the winter (Landry and Phillips 1996). Other potential "formicides" or "myrmecocides" include four more proto-zoa, a virus, and a fungus discovered in the United States (Jouvenaz 1986).

Even the plant kingdom holds possibilities for biocontrol. *Sesbania* is a legume used in pecan orchards to improve soil nitrogen (fig. 12.21). It is so repellent to the RIFA that foragers will not collect honeydew from the aphids that live off the plant by sucking its sap. *Sesbania* extracts were found to be lethal to fire ants (Kaakeh and Dutcher 1992), though the tropical fire ant and the harvester ants (Taber 1998) do collect and presumably eat the seeds of rattlepod species. These seeds contain a toxin of the saponin class and have caused the death of children and livestock.

We have seen that biocontrol has not yet solved the problem of the RIFA, but consider the following pair of facts and then imagine how much worse the problem might be if the insect had no enemies at all. First, nearly 99 percent of newly mated queens are killed by enemies under natural con-ditions before they can establish a nest. Second, in one particular case, of one hundred queens actually observed above ground, only five managed to elude their predators (Whitcomb et al. 1973). Will biocontrol eventually succeed where poisons have failed? Oliver (1997) answered the question in a poem inspired by the RIFA:

> *And they call her Queen Invicta*
> *Fire Ant Invincible*
> *Nothing here could stop her*
> *Predator or chemical*

Enemies of the Black Imported Fire Ant

The socially parasitic fire ant *Solenopsis daguerrei* (figs. 12.1, 12.2) was discovered as a new species when it was collected from BIFA mounds in South America (Santschi 1930). Daguerre's fire ant is unusual in having no worker caste. Carlos Bruch studied its biology in artificial nests and believed that its queen decapitated the BIFA queen. Such behavior is known for some ant species, but decapitation in this particular case has been disputed (Wojcik 1990). The current view is that the parasite queens cling to the host's body and steal her food. Up to ten parasites will cling to a single BIFA queen. Their young are more attractive to BIFA workers than the BIFA's own juvenile stages. A single nest can contain over three thousand parasites, and the colony infection rate in a given area is as high as 31 percent. Mound densities in infected regions are lower than densities where the parasite is not found, there are fewer queens per colony, and there is a decline in the production of BIFA workers (Calcaterra et al. 1999). Wojcik (1990) was optimistic about the potential of Daguerre's fire ant: "This species of parasite is a prime candidate for biological control of fire ants in the United States."

The "Argentine ant" *(Linepithema humile)* was one of the BIFA's early enemies in the United States. Perhaps both of these introduced species hail from the same part of the world (Lofgren 1986a) or even from the same country.

Five phorid fly species are known to attack the BIFA in South America. Generally, if not always, they feed as larvae inside the host ant's head until the head falls off, as discussed earlier for RIFA enemies. These five are *Apocephalus normenti, Pseudacteon curvatus, P. litoralis* (fig. 12.13), *P. obtusus,* and *P. tricuspis* (Disney 1994). *Pseudacteon tricuspis* also attacks U.S. RIFA x BIFA hybrids under laboratory conditions (Porter et al. 1997). In Argentina, these flies cause a reduction in foraging and their presence inhibits large workers from leaving the protection of the nest (Folgarait and Gilbert

1999). Hays (1958) was among the first to mention the phorid fly as a parasite of the black imported fire ant.

The fungi *Beauveria bassiana* (fig. 12.19), *Metarhizium anisopliae* (fig. 12.20), and *Aspergillus flavus* are pathogenic to the BIFA (Lofgren et al. 1975). Larval stages can be orally infected with *Beauveria* spores. They germinate in the gut within three days and the growing fungal filaments soon penetrate the wall of the digestive tract. Gut contents leak into the body cavity through the resulting puncture. Infections are usually fatal (Broome et al. 1976). *Myrmecomyces annellisae,* also a fungus, infects the BIFA in South America (Briano et al. 1995d).

The microsporidian *Thelohania solenopsae* infects the BIFA under natural conditions in Argentina. It is the commonest enemy in the mounds and probably has a significant effect on fire ant populations. For example, infected colonies are smaller than uninfected colonies (Briano et al. 1995a, 1995c), and they do not live as long either. Mortality of afflicted individuals is 92 percent. The organism is transmitted to the next generation in the queen's eggs (Briano et al. 1996). Briano and Williams (1997), suggested considering *Thelohania* for introduction, but it was soon discovered that the pathogen was *already* occupying RIFA nests within the United States (Williams et al. 1998). A related microsporidian enemy of the BIFA in South America is *Vairimorpha invictae* (Briano et al. 1995d).

Hays (1958) knew that an *Orasema* wasp (fig. 12.8) uses the BIFA as a host in South America, but he concluded that "these parasites would probably be of little value in a biological control program in the United States." A pathogenic nematode was found in a Mississippi BIFA nest (Lofgren et al. 1975), but nothing seems to have come of it with respect to control of the black imported fire ant.

Enemies of the Tropical Fire Ant

The enemies of the TFA are legion. Yet there is no current interest in biocontrolling this or any other native fire ant species in the United States. All biocontrol efforts are focused on the two imported species that have become worse pests than the TFA while replacing the same. In fact, the tropical fire ant is hardly ever spoken of as a pest in the United States today. It does remain a problem in cultivated regions of southern Mexico and Central America where the RIFA has yet to penetrate, and where an unusual and indirect form of biocontrol has been suggested to replace chemical control. This approach requires the conservation of *habitats* favored by ants that compete with the TFA—shaded areas, for example (Perfecto 1994).

Some biocontrol agents could be worse than the original problem. For example, *Pheidole megacephala* was observed in the act of replacing TFA populations in Hawaii, but this introduced species was already considered a worse pest than the introduced fire ant. TFA corpses were seen in heaps both inside and outside the *Pheidole* nests. In single combat the TFA managed to crush the head or abdomen of its foe, but when greatly outnumbered the fire ant was spread-eagled and torn apart in procrustean fashion (Phillips 1934).

The same *Pheidole* species reached a standoff with the TFA in the early part of the twentieth century on one of two islands east of Puerto Rico (Wheeler 1910). The TFA dark form dominated the island of Culebra, whereas nearby Culebrita was held by *Pheidole.* Each prevented invasions by the other after wiping out the native ant fauna of their respective stronghold, and they were still at odds when the RIFA arrived on Puerto Rico itself (Levins and Heatwole 1973).

Pheidole dentata is common in the forests of the southern United States, where it does more than just compete with the TFA for food (Wilson 1975; pers. obs.) This natural enemy has evolved a special response to the presence of fire ants. *Pheidole dentata* major workers (fig. 12.22) are recruited by their smaller nestmates to intercept and kill TFA scouts before the scouts can return to their own nest and lead an army to destroy the *Pheidole.* If any scouts escape, the *Pheidole* abandon their nest before the fire ants can arrive in force. One cannot help but compare these behaviors with those of human armies. The reaction of *Pheidole* to the TFA is based upon the fire ant's exoskeleton odor and its venom odor (Wilson 1976). *Pheidole oxyops* majors are specialized to kill fire ants in the same way (Fowler 1984).

Pheidole dentata's close relative *P. morrisii* is another TFA enemy. This species organizes "regal raids" against newly mated TFA queens that have just begun their nests and are yet on their own. Raiding columns behave differently from those recruiting to a food source. They are faster, their ranks are more tightly closed, and a greater sense of urgency is apparent. Up to a thousand workers are recruited to destroy the fire ant queen. Even callow majors join up, individuals too young and soft-bodied to leave the nest under most conditions. Carlin (1988) writes: "The destination consisted of a hole or crevice in the soil and once at the site, a number of majors circled about opening and closing their mandibles slowly. The other ants crowded downward into the opening and after 2 to 10 minutes, they reemerged pulling out a queen ant which was being attacked on all quarters. The queen was killed in short time." The tropical fire ant reciprocates by raiding *established* nests of *Pheidole morrisii.* Majors and minors were killed

Fig. 12.22. Fire ants (light) and *Pheidole dentata* (black), locked in mortal combat. Reprinted from Wilson 1976, fig. 1. Copyright 1976, Springer Verlag. By permission of the author and publisher.

at one targeted nest, but they were not taken home to feed the fire ant colony.

A related South American enemy is *Pheidole radoszkowskii.* It is better at finding food than the TFA but not as good at guarding it once that food is found. Nevertheless, the TFA has been described as a poor competitor in the presence of other ants (Perfecto 1994; Perfecto and Vander Meer 1996; Perfecto and Snelling 1995). In Colombia, the crazy ant *Paratrechina fulva* eats TFA brood (Zenner de Polania and Bolaños 1985).

Labidus coecus (fig. 12.6) is an army ant that attacks the TFA in Costa Rica in spectacular fashion. One embattled fire ant colony under observation was small, the other large, and when one of these was excavated, thousands of fighting ants were seen in a conflict that normally occurs underground and out of sight. Here we have native vs. native. TFA majors brought dead army ants out of the depths, yet they and their small colony were eventually wiped out. If the underground trails of the TFA do serve as protection against phorid fly attack, the branching arteries could be back-firing in the case of the army ant. This subterranean hunter probably follows the natural subway system into the fire ant nest (Perfecto 1992).

The Argentine ant *Linepithema humile* exterminates the TFA wherever they meet (Patton 1931). When they do battle in Hawaii it is import vs. import (Fluker and Beardsley 1970). Two ant species of the genus *Prenolepis* are also lethal enemies of the TFA in Hawaii (Phillips 1934). In Florida, the introduced ant *Tapinoma melanocephalum* stops TFA workers from recruiting their nestmates by biting them and by daubing a secretion from the pygidial gland (Tomalski et al. 1987).

The lion ant *Dorymyrmex pyramicus* harasses TFA colonies in the southeastern United States. Each fire ant raises its gaster and waves it, with a droplet of venom visible at the tip of the stinger. If the lion ant contacts the venom it runs away and rubs its body against the ground. The only ant that regularly subdued the TFA in that area at that time (1941) was *Camponotus floridanus*, a veritable monster, which simply bites the fire ant into pieces. The army ant *Neivamyrmex nigrescens* (fig. 12.23) was seen destroying two TFA colonies (Travis 1941).

The little black ant *Monomorium minimum* (fig. 12.4) prevents the TFA from collecting seed elaiosomes by getting there first and by swarming over the seed appendage in great numbers (Nesom 1981).

Fig. 12.23. A queen army ant *Neivamyrmex nigrescens* and one of her workers.

The ongoing decimation of the tropical fire ant by its cousin the RIFA was witnessed on a small scale on the grounds of a Texas biological field laboratory (Porter et al. 1988). Bhatkar (1988) got an even closer look when a passageway was opened between lab colonies of these archenemies. Individual responses depended upon caste and subcastes. For example, the curved seed-milling mouthparts of the TFA majors are not adapted for grasping the bodies of their opponents, and as a result these majors were at a disadvantage in combat (fig. 12.24). Their large size also worked against

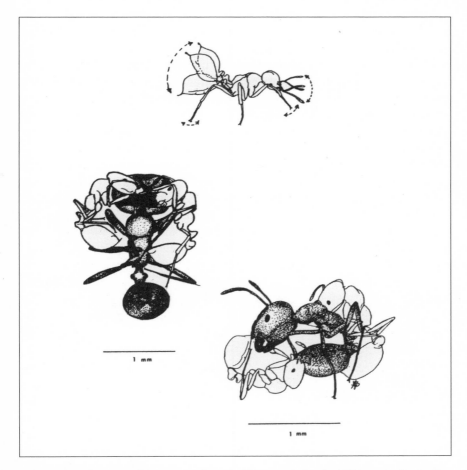

Fig. 12.24. Red imported fire ants and tropical fire ants in battle. RIFA gaster-flexing behavior *(top)*, RIFA minors (light) biting and stinging a dark TFA major *(center and bottom)*. Reprinted from Bhatkar 1988. By permission of Brill Academic Publishers.

them. Each species used its venom against the other, applying the lethal substance externally (to the surface of the exoskeleton), and internally by the familiar stinging behavior. RIFA venom is the more potent of the two. TFA workers die within six to twenty minutes while RIFA workers cling to life for thirty to fifty minutes. The smooth, slick exoskeleton of fire ants makes it difficult to pierce without having a stinger slide off to one side in a glancing blow. This smooth exterior is illustrated by figure 3.18, where it shines under illumination from a circular overhead lamp. The TFA managed to plug the connection between the lab colonies until the RIFA penetrated that barrier by using a particle of quartz as a shovel. Thus one can argue that this lowly insect is a tool-using animal. Eventually the TFA queen was reached, killed, dismembered, and carted away for food. Her brood were eaten too. The conquered nest was used briefly for food storage and eventually abandoned. In nature such battles have been discovered underground. Bhatkar speculates that the RIFA might expand by such means into the neotropics until it eventually dominates every nesting site suitable to itself. The dark and red varieties of the TFA war against each other too.

The RIFA long ago pushed the tropical fire ant out of Florida soybean fields (Whitcomb et al. 1972), and a similar fate has befallen the native in Alabama (Glancey et al. 1976b) and South Carolina (Bass and Hays 1976a). When competing for food with the TFA, RIFA foragers raise their gasters and secrete a droplet of venom, which adheres to the tip of the sting. As the abdomen vibrates, the venom is dispersed as an aerosol. This flagging behavior and the advance of the RIFA with open jaws causes the TFA to supplicate with regurgitated food (Hölldobler and Wilson 1990). Note that the RIFA uses its venom in almost every imaginable way. It is injected, applied topically, and sprayed as a mist. Painting extracts of RIFA queens onto TFA workers temporarily protects them from harm (Glancey 1986).

Certain phorid flies might be ranked as the most horrible enemies of the TFA. They dart in long enough to lay an egg on a worker and then fly off (Coquillett 1907). A larva hatches from the egg, enters the ant's head, and eats the entire contents before emerging as an adult. Species attacking the TFA are all members of the genus *Pseudacteon: P. antiguensis, P. arcuatus, P. bifidus, P. browni, P. crawfordi* (fig. 12.25), *P. grandis, P. longicauda, P. solenopsidis,* and *P. wasmanni,* (Gilbert and Morrison 1997; Morrison and Gilbert 1998; Morrison et al. 1999b; Brown and Morrison 1999). Laboratory tests suggest that *P. tricuspis* (Porter and Alonso 1999) and *P. curvatus,* well-known enemies of the RIFA, will also attack the tropical fire ant. The small size of both the fly and its egg combined with the speed of its attack make it

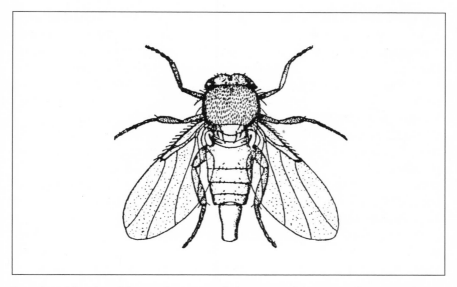

Fig. 12.25. The phorid fly *Pseudacteon crawfordi*. Reprinted from Coquillett 1907. By permission of Entomological Society of Canada.

difficult to see what is going on, but it appears that *P. crawfordi* (for example) lays its egg on a very specific part of the ant's body—in a groove or suture on the thorax, not on the head as widely assumed, and it rides on its victim's back while doing so. The largest workers tend to be favored targets. A fire ant's defense consists of a slow rotation and an upward pointing of the sting and mandibles, so that the ant assumes a C shape directed at its enemy. The effect on exposed foragers is magnified beyond the immediate effects a colony would suffer if a few workers were simply parasitized without disturbing the rest. Foraging practically comes to an end while the agitated ants attempt to escape. Some phorid flies benefit fire ants because they harass one of the TFA's natural enemies, *Pheidole dentata,* until the victim no longer defends food from encroachment by the TFA.

There is some controversy over the potential efficacy of phorid flies in the biocontrol of fire ants (Feener and Brown 1992). Williams and colleagues (1973) were among the first to raise the possibility. They wrote of *Pseudacteon* phorids visiting Brazilian fire ant nests: "They may possibly be used in programs aimed at manipulating populations of other species in the *S. saevissima* complex such as *S. invicta* Buren and *S. richteri* (Forel)."

According to Smith (1928), the small number of organisms known to parasitize ants might be explained by the seclusion of their nests, their agility, and the grooming behavior of ants in general. Phorid flies may be the worst of their enemies. In Mississippi, Smith saw *Pseudacteon crawfordi* attacking numerous TFA workers that erupted from a nest to guard sexuals leaving on a nuptial flight. The sexuals were never attacked. It was the workers that were knocked off their feet by the fly's ovipositing strike. The fire ants responded by lunging with open jaws.

The TFA may be exacting some measure of indirect revenge against the RIFA, for it could be the original U.S. host of the parasitic strepsipteran *Caenocholax fenyesi* (fig. 12.12), a tiny insect now attacking the RIFA in the southern United States (Cook 1996). If this scenario is correct, then the parasite has very recently broadened its host spectrum in a way that could take some pressure off the tropical fire ant.

A houseguest beetle, the scarab *Myrmecaphodius excavaticollis*, lives in the TFA nest, where it eats fire ant larvae. All beetle stages—eggs, larvae, pupae, and adults—live in this seemingly hostile enemy camp. It is not clear how the soft eggs, larvae, and pupae escape destruction. Presumably they are camouflaged by assuming the odor of their hosts. This scarab also lives with imported fire ants and was introduced into the United States with them (Vander Meer and Wojcik 1982; Wojcik et al. 1977). The scarab beetle *Euparia castanea* eats TFA brood in the nest and is groomed by workers. It is expected to disappear as the imported fire ants displace the native species (Kistner 1982).

One of the most interesting enemies of the TFA is an assassin bug. *Acanthaspis concinnula* of Ceylon attacks and kills the introduced fire ant while wearing a disguise. With the empty husks of previous victims sticking to its back, it stabs the ant with its beak, injects venom, sucks it dry, and adds the remains to the rest. This "aggressive mimicry" has two benefits—camouflage from its own predators and the attraction of more fire ants to eat (Kistner 1982).

A houseguest that may also be an enemy is the lygaeid bug *Neoblissus parasitaster* of Brazil. If so, its attack is probably indirect, for it has been suggested that it feeds upon stored seeds in the nest (Miller 1971). Direct indeed are the blind soldiers of the subterranean termites *Reticulitermes flavipes* and *R. virginicus*, which lunge at the TFA with snapping jaws (Zalkow et al. 1981).

One of the first reports of a parasitic nematode infecting fire ants was made by Mitchell and Jouvenaz (1985). The worms were 3 mm long and were found inside the abdomens of tropical fire ants in Florida. This or another nematode species was later discovered in major workers and sexuals, also in Florida. Uncoiled from the gaster of its host, the worm is 16 mm long, several times the length of the ant. It escapes by boring out through the body wall, killing its host in the process (see fig. 4.4). Of the several TFA female sexual forms that are currently known, only the macrogyne type is infected. Infected sexuals do not participate in nuptial flights (McInnes and Tschinkel 1996).

At least a few birds and a few mammals are enemies of the tropical fire ant. Quail eat the insects (which themselves eat quail hatchlings), while sparrows and cotton rats go for the seeds stored inside the mound (Travis 1941).

Microscopic enemies include at least one virus or virus-like particle, four microsporidia, and a protozoan. The best-known fire ant microsporidian is *Burenella dimorpha,* host-specific for the TFA under natural conditions. Only the larva is susceptible to infection. This occurs when the adults feed them with spore-infected food. The effects are seen shortly thereafter, in the pupal stage, when the brain shrinks and the eyes become deformed. After the pupa dies it is cannibalized and the infection is spread to more larvae as workers feed them. Why don't the adults succumb? Once again, the filter in the mouth region may be saving them. This sieve is fine enough to screen out the spores of the pathogen (Jouvenaz 1986). Another microsporidian parasite is *Vairimorpha "undeeni"* from Florida (Stimac and Alves 1994).

The parasitic protozoan is *Mattesia geminata.* Again, the pupa of the ant reveals the progress of disease. It turns black and dies without fail. The mode of transmission is unknown (Jouvenaz 1986; Jouvenaz and Anthony 1979).

Consideration might be given to natural substances known to repel the tropical fire ant. These include extracts of first instar larvae of the root-stalk borer weevil *Diaprepes abbreviatus* (Pavis et al. 1992); secretions of the youngest nymphs of the southern green stink bug *Nezara viridula* (Pavis et al. 1994b); and chemicals produced by the tropical bont tick *Amblyomma variegatum* (Pavis et al. 1994a). There are complications that could affect the efficacy of such repellents against fire ants. For example, the TFA is known to prey upon the eggs of the stink bug, the RIFA prefers the young to the adults (Krispyn and Todd 1982), and the TFA preys readily upon engorged adult bont ticks (Barre et al. 1991).

Caterpillars of two Venezuelan brush-footed butterflies *(Dione junio* and *Abananote hylonome)* also secrete chemicals that repel the TFA (Osborn and

Jaffe 1998). The presence of oleic acid in the secretions is notable because this chemical is present in dead ants of various species, and it causes nestmates to carry them to the trash heap. Even when the fire ants killed caterpillars in the experiments, they did not carry them back to the nest for food. They covered them with soil, a behavior reminiscent of the treatment meted out by fire ants to the carcasses of ticks they have eviscerated. Hybrid fire ants have enemies too. The TFA x SFA hybrid is parasitized by a eucharitid wasp of the genus *Orasema* (Heraty 1994).

Controlled burning may seem like a good form of control, but long ago it caused increases in the abundance of the TFA in the southeastern United States (Travis 1941). One must remember that fire ants are specialists at occupying disturbed habitats. The insect is probably not common enough now to be affected in this way. Modern controlled burning is likely to favor the advance of the RIFA instead.

Enemies of the Southern Fire Ant

Perhaps the earliest example of fire ant biocontrol was the use of horned lizards against an unidentified "small red ant" that destroyed the bark of orange trees in North Cucamonga, California (Turner 1891). The vertebrate was apparently successful in its endeavor. The Texas horned lizard *Phrynosoma cornutum* preys upon *Solenopsis* species in the Chihuahuan desert (Blackshear and Richerson 1999), but these were not identified to species and it is unclear whether the ants in question were southern fire ants, golden fire ants, *S. amblychila*, thief ants, or some combination thereof.

Once again, the greatest enemy of an ant seems to be other ants. The RIFA is extirpating the SFA wherever the two come into contact (Wilson and Brown 1958), and the native fire ant can no longer be found in much of its extensive former range. Even before this conflict began the TFA was possibly doing the same to the SFA along the Gulf Coast (Vinson 1997). Likewise the Argentine ant *Linepithema humile* has been eliminating the SFA in parts of the southeastern United States (Wilson and Eads 1949) and at the other end of the latter's range, in California (Mallis 1938).

Pheidole militicida, like *P. dentata*, specializes in recruiting its major workers to attack fire ants. Both species are enemies of the SFA (Feener 1986; Wilson 1976). Nevertheless, the southern fire ant was successful against *Pheidole hyatti* when this species invaded houses already occupied by the fire ant (Mallis 1938).

The small and very distantly related ant *Forelius mccooki* responds to the SFA's presence by secreting the alarm pheromone 2-heptanone from its gaster. The spray repels the fire ant, which responds by raising its gaster to the "flag" position (apparently dispersing venom) and by a behavior that suggests the ant is trying to bury itself in the soil (Scheffrahn et al. 1984).

In the grasslands of the southwestern United States the army ant *Neivamyrmex harrisii* specializes on the SFA as a prey item, though a closely related army ant will not touch it (Mirenda et al. 1980).

The ant *Forelius pruinosus* of southern California apparently kills and eats the southern fire ant. Its refuse piles become stacked with SFA corpses (Wheeler and Wheeler 1973).

Likewise the little black ant *Monomorium minimum* (fig. 12.4) battles the SFA over baits in the field, but the latter is often able to crush the head of the smaller species between its jaws (Baroni Urbani and Kannowski 1974).

Sometimes the southern fire ant takes the offensive on a massive scale. It has been seen raiding the nests of *Pheidole gilvescens*, the California harvester ant *Pogonomyrmex californicus*, the rough harvester ant *P. rugosus*, and *Messor pergandei* (Wheeler and Wheeler 1986).

Like the RIFA, BIFA, and TFA, the SFA falls prey to parasitic phorid flies. These are *Pseudacteon crawfordi* (fig. 12.25) of Texas and Arizona and *P. curriei*, which supposedly lives in British Columbia (Essig 1926; Feener 1987a), though modern data do not show any fire ants living in Canada. Other phorid enemies are *P. spatulatus* and *Apocephalus coquilleti* (Disney 1994).

One lethal microsporidian enemy of the TFA, *Burenella dimorpha*, has been transmitted to the SFA (Jouvenaz and Hazard 1978).

Enemies of the Golden Fire Ant

The golden fire ant falls prey to a spider of the genus *Euryopis* in the Sonoran desert. When the insect is caught in the arachnid's silk, it releases an alarm pheromone that can work against its nestmates when these arrive to help but end up as additional prey instead. However, the summons occasionally drives the spider away for a little while. The ants do not free entangled nestmates, so the spider will eventually dine on at least the original intruder (Sullender 1998). Presumably the golden fire ant has many enemies yet to be discovered.

Jouvenaz (1990) suggested that a wide variety of less familiar biocontrol candidates be considered for use against troublesome fire ants. Among the bacteria are *Bacillus sphaericus*, *Serratia marcescens*, *Pseudomonas aeruginosa*, *P. chlororaphis*, and a few others that attack honey bees. Rounding out the list are the microsporidian *Nosema*, the nematode *Heterorhabditis helio-thidis*, various baculoviruses, and a honey bee virus. Jouvenaz believes that fungal biocontrol candidates might do more damage if they were geneti-cally engineered to do so. It should be noted that of the bacteria listed, *Ser-ratia* and *Pseudomonas* are known to infect humans. The microsporidian genus infects some mammals. These problems must be considered when se-lecting biocontrol agents to be used in the vicinity of our own species.

Virus-like particles were found in the fat tissues of an undescribed Brazilian fire ant (Avery et al. 1977), and Fincher and Lund (1967) noticed that fungi collected from an imported fire ant nest killed the colony mem-bers if they were confined in a container.

An interesting foe of South American fire ants is the paper wasp *Polybia occidentalis*. It defends its nest against attack by hovering above the intruder and fanning its wings hard enough to bend the ant's antennae backward (fig. 12.26). Sometimes the fire ants retreat from the blast (Jeanne 1991).

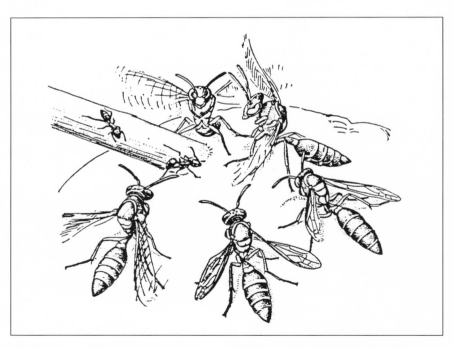

Fig. 12.26. South American paper wasps *(Polybia occidentalis)* defending their nest against fire ants by fanning the invaders with their wings. Reprinted from Jeanne 1991. Copyright 1991, Cornell University. Used by permission of Cornell University Press.

Biocontrol, like chemical control, should be pursued with caution. A case in point is provided by the eucharitid wasps, which count enemies of the fire ant among their number. One species of this family did so much damage to banana plants in the nonparasitic part of its life cycle that its host ants became targets of elimination in an effort to destroy the troublesome wasp (Wojcik 1990).

CHAPTER 13

Fire Ants Pro and Con

I followed after the living thing,

I went upon the broadest and narrowest paths

that I might know its nature.

—*Friedrich Nietzsche,* Also Sprach Zarathustra (1883)

THE fire ant has an image as a nuisance at best, a killer at worst, and as a pest with an impact somewhere in between. Few people see it through neutral eyes, and perhaps fewer still appreciate the red imported species in particular as a beneficial accident of introduction. In this chapter I review the harm done by fire ants but also explore their lesser known positive side, to see whether on balance they are indeed a curse—or perhaps a blessing in disguise. Some evolutionists and even a few ecologists seem to believe that the introduction of an exotic is good for all but the invader's closest competitors because the presence of an additional species increases biodiversity (Mayr 1963; Elton 1958). This view is definitely opposed to the mainstream opinion. However, the issue has never been properly addressed in the case of the fire ants.

Neither the golden fire ant nor *Solenopsis amblychila* is regarded as a pest (Stimac and Alves 1994), nor are there reports of any beneficial behaviors; the literature (and therefore this review) is focused on the other four species occurring in the United States.

The Red Imported Fire Ant as a Crop Pest

There is a great deal of agreement that the red imported fire ant is a pest (Vinson 1997). The Southern Association of Commissioners of Agriculture made this designation official as early as 1957 (Lofgren 1986a), and Florida citrus growers concur with that evaluation. Irrigated groves sometimes harbor more than 225 colonies per acre. During cold weather the ants move their nests to the bases of young trees and kill them by girdling the bark. They prune stems, devour fruits, and protect other insects that damage the same trees (Adams 1986; Knapp et al. 1996), and the insects pack soil into the wounds they feed upon (Lofgren 1986c). This is a source of infectious disease for the plants. When citrus orchards are not chemically treated against the RIFA, tree mortality can be seven times as high as the level in treated orchards. Some growers describe the red imported fire ant as the worst problem of all, followed by spider mites (Childers 1994). Others rank it the second worst of the insect pests (Banks et al. 1991).

The RIFA eats soybeans and damages harvesting machinery with its rigid mounds. The problem is exacerbated by the fact that soybeans must be harvested close to ground level (Lofgren and Adams 1982). North Carolina fields average as many as fifty-seven mounds per acre, and combine operators are forced to raise the machine's header bar to avoid the obstructions. The consequence is a loss of about one bushel per acre (Adams et al. 1977). Soybean yield in RIFA-infested fields is significantly lower than in RIFA-free fields (Adams et al. 1976b), with infested fields yielding up to 512 pounds per acre fewer soybeans. The ants feed upon the roots of the older plants and consume the young plants entirely (Adams et al. 1983). Similar damage is inflicted upon the roots of rabbiteye blueberry. Roots are exposed and destroyed, fruits are eaten, and humans who attempt to harvest the crop by hand are stung (Smith and Lockley 1993).

Much of the damage to soybeans, corn, and okra goes unnoticed by the farmer because the RIFA feeds upon the roots underground and does the injury out of sight (Stimac and Alves 1994). A second form of hidden damage is the destruction of planted seeds. Fire ants can consume most of the planted sorghum seed in a field (Vinson 1997), and wheat seeds in particular should be treated with insecticide before planting to avoid fire ant predation (Morrison et al. 1997a). They should also be as dry as possible—moist seeds can be twenty times as likely to sustain feeding damage as seeds that are kept dry (Morrison et al. 1999c).

In northeastern Florida the RIFA damaged up to 26 percent of Sebago and Russett potatoes, and caused up to a 30 percent loss in the process, a level described as serious (Adams 1986; Adams et al. 1988). In Georgia pecan orchards the ant protects mealybug pests (Tedders et al. 1990; Dutcher et al. 1999), which presumably reciprocate by supplying the excretion known as honeydew. Elsewhere it carries starving corn leaf aphids to fresh food plants, the tiny plant louse sometimes riding on the back of its guardian. This aphid is a major corn pest. If and when it is parasitized by a wasp, the RIFA detects the problem and carries the aphid into the mound, where it is presumably killed (Vinson and Scarborough 1991).

The RIFA as a Livestock and Wildlife Pest

The red imported fire ant causes annual losses to the Texas cattle industry of between 67 million and 255 million dollars. This includes direct losses of calves in the field and indirect losses when cattle are tormented but not killed. Research was under way in 1999 to determine if different cattle breeds respond in different ways to fire ant stings and if some livestock feeds attract fire ants more than others.

The pygmy mouse, the smallest rodent in North America, avoids infested areas when choosing its own nesting site. Other, larger rodents are not so wary (Lechner and Ribble 1996). In the Florida Keys the RIFA kills young rabbits, rats, and mice (Detroit Free Press 1997). It is a problem for trappers because the ants mutilate and kill animals that are caught in cages (Mitchell et al. 1996). In northeastern Texas, fewer small mammals were found in traps in areas where the RIFA was abundant than in areas where it was not. The cotton rat *(Sigmodon hispidus)* was an exception. Fire ant abundance did not affect its capture rate, and when adult rats and their young were stung there was no mortality. Adults even feed on the fire ants (cotton rats excavate TFA mounds for the stored seeds). The South American ancestry of the cotton rat may explain its startling ability to deal with an insect accidentally imported from the same continent (Ferris et al. 1998). Deer mice alter their behavior in the presence of the RIFA, harvesting seeds more efficiently than they otherwise would (Holtcamp et al. 1997).

Fire ants kill squirrels and perhaps white-tailed deer (Allen et al. 1994). Fawns are certainly more common where pesticides have been used to control the RIFA than on nearby lands where the pest persists. The young deer are probably injured and even killed on occasion (Allen et al. 1997a). Fawns make themselves vulnerable by freezing in the presence of danger (Yoffe 1988). This adaptation probably evolved in response to pressures from large mammalian predators that detect the motion of potential prey, but it becomes a no-win situation when the fawn is faced with a new predator that is only able to attack if the deer stands still. Fire ants accumulate around watering holes during times of drought to the point of preventing such large animals from using it (Vinson 1997), and mammals as substantial as young cattle are vulnerable to attack (Lofgren et al. 1975).

Red imported fire ants kill wood ducks, roseate spoonbills, barn swallows, Mississippi kites, black-bellied whistling ducks (Adams 1986), cliff swallows, Attwater's prairie chickens, northern bobwhites, scissor-tailed flycatchers, nighthawks, ground-doves, eastern meadowlarks, terns, giant egrets, quail (Allen et al. 1994), and nestlings of the crested caracara in South Texas (Dickinson 1995). When a caracara chick was killed by fire ants the mother flew off with the body and dropped it one hundred yards from the nest (Dickinson and Arnold 1996). On another occasion, hatchling bluebirds were devoured in a synthetic box.

In just one minute, as few as fifty RIFA workers can sting a northern bobwhite chick with sufficient violence to affect the bird's chances of survival (Giuliano et al. 1996), and hatchling birds (should they survive for a sufficient time) react to these stings with a pustule, just as most humans do. If the prey dies, the insects make short work of it. A dead chick placed near a mound was reduced to skull and backbone in a mere twenty-four hours (Pedersen et al. 1996). The effects of the RIFA on quail populations have been debated. A comparison of Texas county records from before and after the ant's invasion suggests that northern bobwhite quail populations have been reduced (Allen et al. 1995). Elsewhere, despite early reports of quail deaths from IFA attack, George (1958) asserted that the birds were reaching record numbers in infested areas.

The RIFA has also been blamed for a decline of loggerhead shrikes, but other evidence questioned that finding. A resolution of the disagreement is considered important because if the ants are not to blame, the misguided use of pesticides *is* likely to cause a decline in the bird population (Yosef and Lohrer 1995). Birds classified as endangered species are that much closer to extinction when they nest on the ground in fire ant territory. The least tern suffered in this way on Mississippi beaches from the attacks of what was presumably the RIFA (Lockley 1995b), and on some islands in Galveston Bay, every hatchling colonial waterbird under observation was killed by foraging fire ants (Drees 1994). Domesticated and supposedly protected birds are not immune from attack. Fire ants invade poultry houses to prey upon other insects, causing the chicks to trample one another while trying to escape (Vinson and Sorensen 1986).

Nine reptile species have been decimated by the red imported fire ant in Alabama, where it made landfall in the early twentieth century (Stimac and Alves 1994). In the Marquesas Keys twenty-five miles from Key West, Florida, baby green sea turtles were killed and their eyes were eaten out of their heads (Anonymous 1997f). The RIFA has also been destroying sea turtles at Wassaw National Wildlife Refuge in Georgia (Moulis 1997). Hatching snapping turtles are destroyed (Conners 1998a), and in Florida the foraging ants swarm over hatchling alligators. Survivors have pustules like those formed when birds and humans are stung. The ants do not always wait until the victim hatches. They find and exploit shell weaknesses on the surface of alligator eggs, break inside, and eat the contents (Allen et al. 1997b) and do the same to snake eggs (Conners 1998b). Brazilian RIFAs destroy hatchling caimans, South American relatives of the alligator (Cintra 1985), and in North America they consume the eggs of whiptail lizards as well as hatchlings of the chicken turtle, box turtle, and gopher tortoise (Moulis 1997). The fire ant's damage to these and other reptiles ranges from direct predation to simple occupation of nesting sites and even to the ejection of female turtles engaged in the digging of nests (Whiting 1994). The gopher tortoise, the six-lined racerunner lizard, and the Texas horned lizard are affected in these ways (Allen et al. 1994). In fact, the insect seems to be partly responsible for the decline of horned lizards (Donaldson et al. 1994), although other factors could be insecticides and even malaria (*Dallas Morning News* 1999). In the 1960s the ornate box turtle was common in Central Texas. It is also tempting to blame the RIFA for the reptile's demise since that time, especially because the RIFA moved into the area soon after. This was also a period when housing subdivisions were blotting out the open fields where I routinely encountered the turtle as a boy. Probably both factors are to blame. The Texas Parks and Wildlife Department (Brochure W3000-021C) believes that the RIFA is one of several forces pushing the endangered Houston toad toward extinction.

Fishes sometimes die after eating workers and/or sexuals. Bluegills swallow whole masses when the insects are washed into the water by rains. They learn to stop eating the ants after a few stings, but if large numbers are eaten at once they have no time to learn and so die in distress (Green and Hutchins 1960). It is possible that the fish die from ingesting too much of the alkaloid solenopsin, whether or not the ants actually sting them. Floods sometimes wash entire colonies into the water, and swarms of winged sexuals land in the thousands on the surface after nuptial flights. In some Alabama ponds, the bluegills supposedly died when they ate these sexuals in large numbers. Crance (1964) looked into that claim and found distressed fishes, but recovery soon followed. I find this controversy interesting because males cannot sting, and the literature claims the queen does not, though she has a stinger. This suggests that distress upon eating a limited number of winged fire ants must be caused by something other than the usual injection of venom. Perhaps the toxin is effective in the fish's digestive tract even without stinging. Or perhaps the queen is not so reluctant to use her sting after all.

A Central Texas study found that the RIFA lowered the diversity of other ants (Hook and Porter 1990), though the red harvester might be able to coexist with the invader (Camilo and Phillips 1990). Earlier studies found no significant impact by the red imported fire ant upon the diversity of ants (Apperson and Powell 1984) or upon other species (Rhoades 1962). Yet the advance of the RIFA across a Texas biological field station resulted in a 70 percent loss of native ant species. A cricket, a roach, and a few other arthropods actually increased in abundance (Porter and Savignano 1990).

Carrion beetles are prevented from using mammal carcasses when the RIFA defends its newfound food from all competitors (Scott et al. 1987). It drastically and more directly reduces the abundance of other native arthropods that would also accelerate the natural decomposition and recycling of carcasses in the wild (Stoker et al. 1995). This activity can also interfere with the investigations of forensic entomologists (Wells and Greenberg 1994). For example, it is sometimes possible to determine time since death by the species of insects that are breeding in a corpse. Fire ants make this difficult or impossible when they eat the evidence. Similarly, dung-eating scarabs are killed off by the RIFA (Summerlin et al. 1984a).

The ant preys heavily upon juveniles of a beneficial wasp that attacks the harmful tobacco budworm (López 1982), and it kills hover fly larvae, ladybeetles, and lacewing larvae, all beneficial insects that prey upon cotton aphids (Vinson and Scarborough 1989). The RIFA is a major predator of some soil-nesting leafcutter bees (Williams et al. 1986), and its foragers are brazen enough to enter honey bee hives, where they pluck the larvae from their cells (Sorensen and Trostle 1986).

A study of monarch butterflies in Texas could not be completed because the ant apparently ate all the eggs and caterpillars (Calvert 1996), and it causes similar problems for mealworm breeders, who raise these beetle larvae for bait and for pet food. Fire ants got in the way of a Texas attempt to distribute oral rabies vaccines to coyotes in the form of bait (Farry et al. 1998). When the ants dominated the bait, the coyotes visited but they did not feed. The problem was so bad during summer months that the authors suggested concentrating or even limiting the distribution of bait to the winter season instead.

Though it remains to be seen if the RIFA can be biologically controlled, it is clear that this omnivorous creature can interfere with the biological control of other pests. A case in point is the attempted control of field bindweed *(Convolvulus arvensis)* by the imported moth caterpillar *Tyta luctosa*, which defoliates and kills the undesirable plant. Fire ants killed every caterpillar unless test plots were treated with insecticide beforehand (Ciomperlik et al. 1992).

Property Damage by the RIFA

Surfaced roadways are damaged when the ants dig beneath asphalt or concrete, causing potholes and erosion along the edges (fig. 13.1). A single colony can do 100 dollars worth of damage in this way. They also chew through the silicone sealant used to regulate highway surface expansion, causing losses totaling about three dollars per foot of sealant (Adams 1986). Foragers gnaw telephone cables and lighting cables until they short out (Lofgren et al. 1975), and they infest electrical junction boxes and damage air-conditioning units (Vinson and MacKay 1990). Air-conditioners and airport runway lights have been shut off in this manner (Lofgren 1986c). Concrete structures weaken and crack if fire ants build nests under them and then abandon their home. They gnaw at the outlets in drip irrigation lines (Vinson and Sorensen 1986), and they clog sprinkler tubing (Vinson

Fig. 13.1. A RIFA nest at the edge of an asphalt road.

1997). Sometimes laundry becomes infested due to droughts or floods that drive the ants into homes.

Texas pest control operators single out the RIFA as the most common pest ant. Their counterparts in peninsular Florida rank it as a major pest, though several other species are ranked just as high on the list (Klotz et al. 1995). Mounds can be a nuisance to golfers (Reagan 1986) and have actually provoked rule changes on Texas courses. If the ball lies too close to a mound it can be moved to a safer spot as long as it is no closer to the hole (Anonymous 1997c). Disgruntled patrons have sued infested golf courses (Copeland 1997).

Ervin and Tennant (1990) undertook a survey to determine if the RIFA deters visitors from Texas parks, where personnel tend to use chemical control in their fight to subdue the pest. These authors found that the RIFA had no significant effect on park use. However, a more recent opinion from a fire ant expert holds that park use is reduced (Vinson 1997).

The RIFA as a Beneficial Predator of Crop Pests

Juha Helenius (1998) presents a positive perspective on the fire ants in one chapter of a book on biocontrol. In this case, they are seen as potential *providers* of biocontrol. Ants in general are prepared for this assignment because they accept a variety of habitats, they attack in numbers via chemical recruitment, and those that store food continue to do so even when confronted with enormous numbers of economically important pests. Polygyny can actually work in the grower's favor because new colonies are easily established from mere fragments of other colonies. And fire ants, being dominant animals, are not easily displaced when chosen as biocontrol agents, though one must be careful not to destroy the nests by tilling the land.

Sugarcane growers benefit immensely from the red imported fire ant when it preys upon crop pests such as the sugarcane borer *(Diatraea saccharalis)*. Reagan et al. (1972) gave the following advice: "Because of their importance as predators of the sugarcane borer, the sugar industry should make every effort possible to maintain high levels of ant populations in fields."

The RIFA is beneficial in cotton, where it kills up to 85 percent of the boll weevil's larvae *(Anthonomus grandis)* and is often the beetle's major predator (Sterling 1978). The cotton fleahopper *(Pseudatomoscelis seriatus)* is the worst pest of Texas cotton, causing more damage than the more famous weevil. The RIFA kills this bug and the tobacco budworm *(Heliothis virescens)* in cotton fields, where the ant sometimes eats the moth's eggs before returning to the nest (Breene et al. 1989; McDaniel and Sterling 1979, 1982; McDaniel et al. 1981). The cotton leafworm *(Alabama argillacea)* is another pestiferous moth held in check by the fire ant (Gravena and Sterling 1983; Reagan 1986); recall that the SFA was discovered in the nineteenth century while performing this very service. The presence of only 0.06 foragers per cotton plant saves producers fifty-nine dollars per plant in lint that would otherwise be lost to boll weevils, bollworms, tobacco hornworms, and cotton fleahoppers (Brinkley et al. 1991). In East Texas cotton fields, the ant scavenges and reduces the numbers of harmful moths. Though the RIFA does tend the harmful cotton aphid *(Aphis gossypii)*, it can nevertheless be valuable for biocontrol (Sterling et al. 1979). Sterling (1978) echoed the sentiments of the sugarcane growers: "It is not inconceivable that were the ant not already here, serious consideration would be given to its importation into the U.S. for the biological control of the boll weevil."

The RIFA preys upon the velvetbean caterpillar *(Anticarsia gemmatalis)* in Louisiana and Florida soybean fields, where the ant accounts for up to 97 percent of predation on the pest (Lee et al. 1990, Buschman et al. 1977). It is a dominant predator of the eggs of the southern green stink bug *(Nezara viridula)* in Louisiana soybean fields (Nyffeler et al. 1987) and a destroyer of the soybean looper moth *(Pseudoplusia includens)* (Reagan 1986). This ant is the most important predator in Florida field crops (Whitcomb 1994), and its harmful effects on field laborers have been overstated (Sterling 1978).

In South Carolina the fire ant is an important predator of pupal pickleworms *(Diaphania nitidalis)* in cucumber fields (Elsey 1980), and it harvests the pupae of the cowpea curculio beetle *(Chalcodermus aeneus)* (Russell 1981). Foragers collect the striped earwig's eggs *(Labidura riparia)*, and the earwig itself becomes a pest when the RIFA is controlled with chemicals (Gross and Spink 1969).

RIFAs are major predators of fall armyworm caterpillars *(Spodoptera frugiperda)* in Georgia cornfields and in sweet sorghum fields (Pair and Gross 1989; Fuller et al. 1997). They also do away with the lesser cornstalk borer *(Elasmopalpus lignosellus)*, a pest of peanuts in the southeastern United States (Mack et al. 1988).

The list of crop and forest pests controlled by the RIFA goes on to include pecan weevil larvae *(Curculio caryae)* (Dutcher and Sheppard 1981), various aphids, Nantucket pine tip moth *(Rhyacionia frustrana)*, green cloverworm *(Plathypena scabra)*, the greenhouse whitefly *(Trialeurodes vaporariorum)*, rootstalk borer weevil larvae *(Diaprepes abbreviatus)*, springtails (Reagan 1986; Krispyn and Todd 1982), and the rice stink bug *(Oebalus pugnax)*. Regarding the toll the ants take upon stink bugs and their relatives, Miller (1971) wrote: "Ants, too, must be numbered among the foes from which even large and robust species with a relatively tough integument rarely escape alive; if they do, they will probably have been severely mutilated."

In greenhouse experiments the RIFA exterminated the pea aphid, did nearly the same to the larvae of the alfalfa weevil, removed thousands of whiteflies, and did all of this without harming the plants (Morrill 1977b, 1978).

The RIFA as a Beneficial Predator of Other Pests

Red imported fire ants help control insects and arachnids that plague livestock and humans. Flies suffer a terrible toll. For example, foragers found and destroyed 96 percent of the eggs of the fiercely biting mosquito *Psorophora columbiae* in both lab and field (Lee et al. 1994) and also destroyed eggs of the Asian tiger mosquito *(Aedes albopictus)* (Burnham et al. 1994). The tiger mosquito, like the fire ant, was accidentally imported into the United States, presumably inside rubber tires that retained rain water. Japan appears to be the source of the mosquito. It carries the viruses of dengue fever and eastern equine encephalitis. Tires imported from infested regions must now be cleaned, dried, and fumigated. The mosquito was first discovered in the United States in 1983, in Memphis, Tennessee. Victims of its bite describe the fly as a very tenacious pest (Taubes 1998).

In Florida the RIFA preys upon the larvae, pupae, and adults of the notorious horn fly *(Haematobia irritans)*. The horn fly (fig. 13.2) is the worst pest of cattle in the area, sucking their blood and causing more than sixty times as much damage as the RIFA (Hu and Frank 1996). It was introduced into the United States only a few decades before the fire ant. In Texas, the RIFA preys upon the stable fly *(Stomoxys calcitrans)* (Summerlin and Kunz 1978), and it is an important predator of house fly maggots and eggs in Florida poultry manure (Propp and Morgan 1985). Horse flies inflict painful bites upon livestock and humans. The fire ant kills their larvae (Reagan 1986).

The lone star tick *(Amblyomma americanum)* has declined in the wake of the RIFA's expansion. This arachnid is known to carry the causative agents of tularemia and Rocky Mountain spotted fever (Harris and Burns 1972; Schmidt and Roberts 1981). Yet the Gulf Coast tick *Amblyomma macu-*

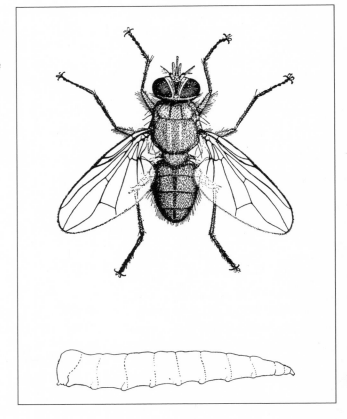

Fig. 13.2. The horn fly *Haematobia irritans.* Adult female *(top)*, larva *(bottom)*. Reprinted from Metcalf and Metcalf 1993. By permission of McGraw-Hill Book Company.

latum persists in the coastal prairies of Texas despite the long-term infestation of that region by the fire ant. In fact, this cattle pest was found to be the most abundant ectoparasite in the area (Teel et al. 1998).

Ants the world over favor termites as food, and the RIFA is no exception (Wilson and Oliver 1969).

Other Possible Benefits of the RIFA

RIFA mounds are higher in various elements than the soil nearby, and the activities of the insect may have some role in decomposing loblolly pine stumps (Lockaby and Adams 1985). Mound-building activity does reduce the acidity of the soil (Reagan 1986), and the presence of mounds along roadsides is due not just to the disturbed habitat but to the roadkills (Vinson and Sorensen 1986), which the ants help clean up. Queen RIFAs become an important food of Florida swallow-tailed kites when the nuptial flight is in full swing (Lee and Clark 1993).

All in all, the services provided by the red imported fire ant go a long way toward justifying its overall assessment as a nuisance instead of a genuine pest (Lofgren et al. 1975). Sometimes it is not clear if the fire ant is actually to blame for a perceived problem. For example, burying beetles are important scavengers of dead mammals, as is the RIFA, which competes with the beetle for these remains. It is tempting to blame the RIFA for the endangered status of one burying beetle species. However, most of the beetle's historical range lies well north of the fire ant. Its downfall in some areas has been linked variously to deforestation (Creighton and Schnell 1998) or a lack of suitable carrion (Amaral 1999). Perhaps the biggest price tag attached to the RIFA is the cost of the attempts to eradicate it (Stimac and Alves 1994).

The Black Imported Fire Ant

In the United States, BIFA mounds have a long history of damaging farm machinery (Green 1952) and of becoming a nuisance on lawns (Creighton 1930). Ferguson (1962) described some experiments undertaken to determine the impact of black imported fire ants on fish populations. The insects were thrown into ponds to see if fish would eat them and what would happen to any fishes that did. Bluegills fed on the ants for forty-five minutes. They were monitored while still in the pond for an entire week without discovering any harmful effects. Specimens were then caught and examined (including a turtle). Fire ants were present in their digestive tracts but had caused no apparent harm, with a single exception. Other studies have reported that fire ants injure and kill the fishes that eat them. In any event, the BIFA's total impact within the borders of the United States has been shrinking as fast as its range.

In São Paulo, Brazil, the BIFA is a potato pest. It eats tubers and branches. The severe damage features nearly circular holes cut into the potatoes (Boock and Lordello 1952). The ant is not considered a pest in Argentina, neither in fields nor among livestock (Hays 1958). Nevertheless, there appear to be no records of beneficial behavior.

The Tropical Fire Ant as a Crop Pest

The TFA is known as the seed-harvesting fire ant because of its special penchant for collecting seeds and then husking them prior to storage within the nest (Wheeler 1910). The earliest record of this seems to come from the Caribbean island of St. Vincent (Forel 1893), and it adds two more dimensions to a fire ant's destructive ability in the fields. First, the growers lose seeds from their crops. Second, they suffer the effects of noxious weeds that grow from seeds stored inside the mound and from those lying on the fire ants' refuse heap outside. The TFA deserves particular attention here because it collects eight times as many seeds as its more famous relative, the red imported fire ant (Tennant and Porter 1991).

The magnitude of the problem was illustrated by Perfecto (1994), who found that more than 90 percent of the tomato seeds were destroyed in a single planting season in Nicaragua. Corn suffered the same fate in southern Mexico (Perfecto 1994; Risch and Carroll 1982b). And in the moist lowlands of that country, the TFA was the only ant species observed in the act of collecting or storing seeds (Carroll and Risch 1984).

In Honduras the tropical fire ant is the major predator of sorghum seeds and seedlings (Trabanino et al. 1989). Strangely enough, seeds planted near the surface were safer than those planted at greater depths. Perhaps this is due to more intense foraging within the subterranean tunnels that fan out from the nest. In Mexico the presence of TFA foragers in the female flowers of the squash plant *Cucurbita moschata* prevents the bee *Peponapis* from doing its job as a specialist pollinator (Carroll and Risch 1983).

A compilation of tropical insect pests identified the tropical fire ant as a major enemy of seeds and seedlings in low latitudes. Its impact is felt by citrus, avocados, coffee, cocoa, and tobacco (Hill 1975), for it girdles bark, imbibes sap, and bites branches, shoots, buds, flowers, and fruits. Tobacco seedbeds are invaded in Java and Sumatra (Essig 1926; Laan 1952). Wheeler (1910) reported damage to strawberries and to gardens, where germinating seeds were toted off by foraging ants. It is noteworthy that the TFA is now common in the rice fields of the Old World but is not specifically reported as a pest of that crop's seeds (Way et al. 1998).

By the early part of the twentieth century the tropical fire ant was a pest of citrus in Puerto Rico. It consumed the tree's young twigs and built its nest at the base of the trunk (Essig 1926). Orange blossoms lost their nectar to foragers, and when the supply was exhausted the ants began attacking unopened flowers and fruits. Bark near the base of the tree was gnawed away beneath a covering of soil brought up from below (Wolcott 1933).

The Indian Ocean island of Mauritius was invaded no later than the year 1900 (Moutia and Mamet 1946), and the depletion of its seed beds and seedlings began shortly thereafter. On Guam, cabbage is particularly vulnerable after nursery seedlings have been transplanted to the field. The plants are girdled and killed (Muniappan and Marutani 1992). In southern India, sugarcane and eggplant ("brinjal") suffer depredation (Ayyar Rama-krishna 1963), as do cotton seedlings, hollyhock buds, crotons, and ailan-thus (Fletcher 1914), potato, hyacinth bean ("lablab"), cucumber, tomato, mango, papaya, sapota, okra, citrus, banana, and livestock, whether living or dead (Veeresh 1990a, 1990b). Potato and brinjal are especially suscep-tible to the tropical fire ant (Murthy 1959). It is noteworthy that both are members of the plant family Solanaceae. Eleven percent of the potatoes were damaged in one study area. This included the effects of girdling and gnawing (Lakshmikantha et al. 1996). Fire ants chew holes into the leaves of the Indian chickpea plant ("gram") (Nair 1975), and they damage the roots of the pigeon pea (Lateef and Reed 1990).

The TFA colonizes newly plowed fields in Nicaragua more rapidly than do nonharvesting ant species. The lack of food above ground at such times may explain the inability of potential competitors to keep up with an insect able to utilize seeds lingering in the disturbed soil. Perfecto (1991) found stored seeds in all six mounds excavated in one of these areas. Nevertheless, the fire ant does not store its seeds as long as desert-adapted harvester ants do, which is not surprising because food is much less available in harsh deserts. The TFA tracks its favorite seed sources by moving its nest until it is near those plants (Risch and Carroll 1986). Travis (1941) was able to locate colonies in the spring by the mere sight of grass sprouting from the mounds.

Phillips (1934) studied the tropical fire ant extensively in Hawaii. Seeds of the following plants were found in the upper part of the nest: amaranth, sow thistle, foxtail grass, crab grass, wiregrass, rattlepod, sorrel, purslane, and popola *(Solanum nodiflorum)*. A clump of twenty seeds provoked mass recruitment, and every mound of the hundreds examined contained seeds. The nest size itself spoke for the harvesting habit of *Solenopsis geminata.* The mound diameter was greatest where seeds were most abundant. The insect prefers grasses in Hawaii, though this is not always true elsewhere in the world. Plants grew from seeds removed from storage chambers within the mounds, showing that fire ants do not bite off the radicle to prevent germi-nation, as some harvester ants are said to do. At that time, only its natural enemy *Pheidole megacephala* prevented the TFA from becoming more of a problem in Hawaii. Phillips (1934) appreciated the preeminence of *Pheidole* on the archipelago: "A few hours' investigation of fire ant nests suffices to convey some indication of what work on the plantation would be like if it and not *Pheidole* were the dominant ant."

Many ants "tend" and stroke other insects, usually aphids (plant lice) or related bugs, consuming the excreted liquid waste or honeydew produced by these sap-sucking plant feeders, some of which vector plant diseases to their hosts. The association is often compared to that of a dairy farmer and his cows. The TFA is one of these ants. It builds earthen shelters over the scale insects it is tending (Phillips 1934). It nurtures and protects aphids and scale insects on the roots of grasses (Risch and Carroll 1982b; Larsen et al. 1991) and does the same for mealybugs on pineapples (Phillips 1934; Moutia and Mamet 1946; Reimer et al. 1990). In Puerto Rico the TFA carries living mealybugs about in its jaws (Wolcott 1933; Planck and Smith 1940), putting them on new leaves, even transporting them from plant to plant.

Smith (1942) placed the spoiled pineapples of New York markets at the end of a chain with three links. These were (1) mealybugs that pierce holes in the leaf while feeding, (2) ants that carry the bugs about, and (3) a fungus that invades the plants through the holes. Other bugs tended by the TFA include scale insects of coffee plants (Smith 1942), sugarcane mealybugs (Stahl and Scaramuzza 1929; Phillips 1934; Rao 1942), sugarcane aphids (Cleare 1928), ash tree mealybugs (Lobdell 1930), superb-milkweed aphids (Wheeler 1908d), and alfalfa treehoppers (Nickerson et al. 1977). This fire ant may be a custodian of the corn-leaf aphid, which is an occupant of the central leaf whorl and a major pest of corn (Risch and Carroll 1982a). The relationship is further suggested by the discovery that the ants remove parasite-infested aphids from their healthy "flock" (Carroll and Risch 1983). On Puerto Rican coffee plants the TFA visits the hemispherical scale for honeydew, which the ant obtains by stroking the scale insect with its antennae. Soil or cartonlike covers are erected over these bugs for protection. The ants were never observed to carry them about (Smith 1942). According to Chauvin (1970), the TFA shelters a scale insect within its nest. Something similar occurs in the relationship between this fire ant and a metalmark butterfly in Mexico. Here the ant visits the tentacular nectary organs of the caterpillar of *Eurybia elvina* (Horvitz et al. 1987) and builds soil shelters over the source of the secretion. Thus the caterpillar is sheltered not by the ants' home but by a tent erected in the field.

Risch and Carroll (1982a, b) concluded that although *S. geminata* has potential negative impacts in annual agroecosystems (it stings, eats corn seeds, and guards homopterans), its overall impact appears to be beneficial.

The TFA as a Pest of Livestock, Wildlife, and Home

Hatching quail chicks yet within their egg shells are killed by the TFA in the southeastern United States and consumed until only the harder parts of the skeleton remain. The intensity of the attack drives the mother bird from her nest (Travis 1938). Four young birds were observed to fall from a tree in Puerto Rico, only to be dispatched by foragers (Pimentel 1955). Like the RIFA, the TFA has a negative impact on reptiles. It kills hatchling loggerhead sea turtles on the beaches of Florida (Moulis 1997).

The tropical fire ant is a common household pest of India (Ayyar Ramakrishna 1963; Lakshmikantha et al. 1996), and according to Patton (1931), it once had a similar status in the United States. In India it is known as the "household red ant" because of its indoor nesting habit. In Hawaii it is also a common pest of buildings and playgrounds (Reimer et al. 1990), and the TFA was a house pest in Honolulu until the competing ant *Pheidole megacephala* drove it out (Phillips 1934). Travis (1941) reported the tropical fire ant entering houses in the southeastern United States while foraging. It can be a nuisance in Brazil too (Gilbert 1996).

Of the many ants introduced into the United Arab Emirates, the TFA (discovered in Dubai), is the worst. According to Collingwood and colleagues (1997), its attacks on cattle and horses in the United States indicate a risk to camels and race horses in the U.A.E.

Sometimes it is not clear if fire ants are doing harm or good. For example, on the island of Puerto Rico the Indian mongoose was released to control rats (as does the ant), though the mammal eventually became a pest itself. The TFA kills its young (Pimental 1955). Likewise, in Florida the fire ant kills nymphs of the predatory big-eyed bug *Geocoris punctipes* (Whitcomb et al. 1973), but the overall effect is hard to label as harmful or beneficial because the big-eyed bug eats a variety of insects.

Fear is inspired by the tropical fire ant whether this is deserved or not. In the words of Veeresh (1990a): "Having once tasted flesh, they attack even live animals. A farmer witnessed such behavior. After tasting meat left by the watch dogs, the ants attacked his poultry, forcing him to abandon the poultry house."

Property Damage by the TFA

Many ants damage fabrics and synthetics, even presumably inedible materials, and this is often unrelated to the need to build a nest. The tropical fire ant tunnels through fabric, plaster, shellac, and varnish (Travis 1938). Rubber surgical gloves are perforated in the same manner (Smith 1965). When the TFA made its way to South Africa it became notorious for damaging the PVC coatings of electric wires (Prins 1985). In India, stored silk cocoons are damaged until they become unusable, producing losses of up to 60 percent (Veeresh 1990a). Plastic irrigation tubes are chewed by major workers in Hawaii (majors are hardly restricted to seed milling, as has sometimes been claimed). The result is flooding of pineapple fields and uneven irrigation of sugarcane when the exit holes for the water are widened by the chewing ants (Chang and Ota 1976; Chang et al. 1980; Chang and Ota 1990). Mirex, Amdro, and other effective baits are not registered for use with these crops. Instead, modern tubes now have obstructions that prevent the large head of the probing major from reaching the tiny outlet hole. The fire ant was the worst offender of several species in the fields, and its gnaw marks are distinctive enough to identify it as the culprit.

The TFA as a Beneficial Predator of Crop and Lawn Pests

As early as 1907 this fire ant was known to be an enemy of the devastating cotton boll weevil, which had made its historic entrance into the United States from Mexico only a few years before (Mitchell and Pierce 1912; Smith 1924). It kills the beetle in the grub stage while it is feeding on the cotton flower.

All developmental stages of the chinch bug *Blissus insularis* are killed by the tropical fire ant in Florida. This bug happens to be the worst pest of St. Augustine grass in the region (Reinert 1978). Also consumed by the TFA in Florida are the eggs of the soybean-eating velvetbean moth *(Anticarsia gemmatalis)* (Buschman et al. 1977), cutworms and grasshoppers (Travis 1941), eggs of the soybean looper *(Chrysodeixus includens)* (Nickerson et al. 1977), and the New World corn earworm *(Heliothis zea)* (Whitcomb et al. 1972).

In southern Mexico the fire ant destroys two pestiferous caterpillars— the squash vine borer (*Melittia* sp.), and the pickleworm (*Diaphania* sp.)—as well as the corn weevil and other insects that damage squash and corn. The TFA acts as a beneficial seed predator where it collects, stores, and consumes the seeds of the weedy grass *Paspalum conjugatum,* a bane of farmers in tropical America (Risch and Carroll 1982a; Carroll and Risch 1984). In Nicaragua two corn pests fall prey—the fall armyworm *(Spodoptera frugiperda),* which eats seeds and defoliates plants, and a leafhopper *(Dalbulus maidis)* (Perfecto and Sediles 1992). Sugar water is being used to attract the TFA to corn fields in nearby Honduras, that it might prey upon the destructive armyworm. Fire ants were more abundant in treated fields than in the control fields that received pure water instead (Cañas and O'Neil 1998).

In Costa Rica, the TFA eats the eggs of rootworms. These are the grubs of leaf beetles that attack corn and cucurbits (Risch 1981). In Cuba, the cotton stainer bug *Dysdercus mimus* has been found dead in the jaws of TFA foragers (Myers 1927). In Guatemala and Hawaii, maggots and adults of the Mediterranean fruit fly *(Ceratitis capitata)* fall prey (Eskafi and Kolbe 1990; Wong and Wong 1988). This fly is a serious citrus pest and causes major concerns when it makes an appearance in the United States. Also in Hawaii the TFA preys upon Oriental fruit flies *(Dacus dorsalis)* (Wong and Wong 1988). Fly pupae in general make easy forage and are favored by the TFA (Williams et al. 1990).

It is not nearly that easy to get at the leaf beetle *Arthrochlamys plicata* (Wallace 1970). Its defense is not a chemical armor but the real thing. The creature builds a bullet-shaped case around itself, with an opening at the bottom where its legs can be seen as it walks about. The great resemblance between this case and the fecal pellets left behind by other insects gives it camouflage value too. When attacked by fire ants, the grub digs hooklike claws into the surface of the leaf it walks upon and presses the case opening against the leaf, so that all is sealed off from the fire ants. They cannot chew through it or sting through it and eventually must give up and find food elsewhere.

In Malaysia the TFA is the major predator of juvenile cabbage webworms *(Hellula undalis)* (Sivapragasam and Chua 1997). In Sumatra, eggs of the stink bug soybean pests *Nezara viridula* and *Piezodorus hybneri* are collected (Van den Berg et al. 1995), and in Philippine rice fields, the tropical fire ant kills and consumes the very injurious rice caseworm *(Paraponyx stagnalis)* (Sison 1938) as well as other serious pests, including flies, bugs, and the eggs and young of the golden snail *(Pomacea canaliculata)* (Way et al. 1998).

In India the ant preys upon lawn-chewing cutworms, and in the western part of the same country it takes juveniles of the sweet potato weevil *(Cylas formicarius)*, a serious pest of that crop (Teli and Salunkhe 1994). The preference of the TFA for virus-killed Old World corn earworms *(Helicoverpa armiger)* over living ones suggests that scavenging is sometimes favored over predation (Dhandapandi et al. 1994). This behavior could be beneficial if the virus is spread throughout the cotton fields when carcasses are dragged back to the nest.

The TFA as a Beneficial Predator of Other Pests

In Texas the tropical fire ant kills the deadly screwworm maggot *Cochliomyia hominivorax*, which harms and sometimes kills livestock (Lindquist

1942), though this service has been largely taken over by the RIFA. In Puerto Rico the TFA kills maggots of the disease-carrying house fly *(Musca domestica)*, the bothersome greenbottle fly (one or more species of *Phaenicia*), and a second screwworm species *(Cochliomyia macellaria)*. It kills young rats on the same island (Pimentel 1955).

On the Caribbean island of Guadeloupe the introduced tropical fire ant destroys the introduced tropical bont tick *Amblyomma variegatum.* This arachnid transmits microorganisms causing heartwater and dermatophilus in hoofed animals, and Senkobo disease specifically in cattle. The TFA attacks only blood-engorged ticks. Likewise the TFA kills the cattle tick *Boophilus microplus*, a transmitter of the agent of Texas cattle fever (Barre et al. 1991). The eight-legged pest causes severe losses in Mexico. Its gravid females are eaten by the TFA (Butler et al. 1979).

On isolated Christmas Island in the Pacific Ocean, the giant introduced African land snail *(Achatina fulica)* is killed and eaten by TFA foragers (Lake and O'Dowd 1991). This ravenous, prolific mollusc invaded the Pacific isles during World War II when the Japanese conquerors brought it along for food. The snail's threat remains alive today. According to Burch (1962), it was the worst molluscan challenge to native ecosystems of the United States at that time, and there is a more direct threat to humans, for the snail also harbors potentially deadly parasitic nematode worms (Pearse et al. 1987).

In India the TFA is part of a complex interaction involving predatory caterpillars and the scale insects *(Laccifer lacca)* that produce lac. People use lac to make shellac or varnish. The caterpillars are those of the noctuid moth *Eublemma amabilis* and the tineid moth *Pseudohypatopa pulvera,* very unusual species because they are as predatory as fire ants. They burrow through the resinous lac encrustation to feed upon the scale insects that secrete it. The fire ant performs a service by killing the caterpillars, but it also kills several life cycle stages of the scale. This harmful side effect was mitigated by painting molasses around the tree trunk or stem. The ants took the syrup instead of the insects (Glover 1930). Lac produced by female scales can be more than half an inch thick. The coated twigs are cut off, the lac material is melted and refined, and the resulting product is used to make shellac and varnish (Borror et al. 1989).

Other Possible Benefits of the TFA

Scavenging the remains of dead organisms is part of a natural recycling process that is surely of some benefit to humans and their property. A specific and lengthy list of scavenged remains is not necessary for such an opportunistic omnivore as the TFA, and the silence of the literature reflects this commonsense view. Suffice it to say that the tropical fire ant has been observed among the rotting fruits of abandoned orchards, at the bodies of beached marine mammals (Perfecto 1994), at the remains of dead molluscs (Wilson and Taylor 1967), in and around urban garbage cans (Pimentel 1955), and at the carcasses of terrestrial animals (Travis 1941). It is not hard to believe that fire ants play a large role in recycling the dead.

Porter (1992) found the TFA at 83 percent of those collection sites where the RIFA was absent but at only 70 percent of sites where the RIFA was abundant. There clearly is competition between the two species. The TFA's role as a competitor can be valuable if it slows down the expansion of red imported fire ants. For example, in Florida the RIFA failed to establish in one sugarcane field because of the TFA and because of native ants of the genus *Pheidole* (Adams et al. 1981). Yet such victories are not the rule. Here we also find an example of the relativity of pest assessment. Most people within the fire ant's range are happy to discover that something has slowed the RIFA down. The owners of these very sugarcane fields, however, probably have a different view: the RIFA destroys many pests of their crop and is a welcome invader.

Mention the medical importance of fire ants and the image of a stinging attack and the fear of anaphylactic shock come to mind. The balance may someday tip in the other direction. Research on the normal process of muscle atrophy in newly mated queens raises the possibility that this knowledge could be useful in the study of the human muscle degeneration characteristic of certain diseases (Davis et al. 1989). It is now known that an elevation of calcium ion concentration is associated with the normal breakdown of the queen's flight muscles (Jones et al. 1982).

The Southern Fire Ant as a Pest

The southern fire ant is the worst pest of harvested almonds in California orchards. It consumes the fruits while the almonds lie on the ground awaiting transport (Zalom and Bentley 1985; Bugg and Waddington 1993). In California and Arizona the SFA feeds upon the shoots of nursery trees and upon young orchard trees. The ants nest in strawberry patches, where they eat the fruit, and in Imperial Valley grapefruit orchards, where they remove bark from young plants. The edges of lemon leaves are nibbled away, potatoes are devoured, and the stems of this plant and of cabbage, sorghum, and passion vine are girdled (Essig 1926). Workers tunnel into the stalks of potatoes (Severin 1923) and are attracted to barley seed bait (Davidson 1977).

The SFA tends plant lice and scale insects in orchard and garden. It does harvest seeds to some extent, and foragers are attracted to stored fruit. When feeding on leaves they commonly strip off the outermost layer (Mallis 1938). Other plants suffering from SFA depredation include okra, pecans, althea, dahlia, and eggplant (Wheeler and Wheeler 1973). Even the grass of a homeowner's lawn is fair game (Mallis 1938).

Fire ants have a taste for hatchling birds, and the southern fire ant is no exception (Wheeler and Wheeler 1973). The endangered California least tern *(Sternus antillarum browni)* is one such victim. Its chicks are killed and the contents of its eggs are eaten. Hooper and Rust (1997) found no other ants at the study site in question.

When the southern fire ant builds its nests inside homes, it contributes to the formation of dry rot as workers pile soil on wooden beams. Outdoor concrete stairs are in danger of collapse when the soil beneath them is removed by nest-building activities, and mounds on the lawn are unsightly (Mallis 1938). Mallis, whose early papers remain the primary source on the biology of the SFA, believed it to be the most important native ant pest in California (Mallis 1941).

As regards property damage, this insect was apparently the culprit in the first reports of fire ant damage to commercial electrical circuitry. This happened to Southwestern Bell's property in Galveston, Texas, in the early part of the twentieth century. Workers chewed through wire insulation and caused short circuits as a result. They brought nesting material and food into the junction boxes until the equipment corroded from moisture. Electrical contacts became so fouled by dead ants that circuits could not close properly, and piles of dead ants accumulated when live ones were crushed by ringing telephone bells (Eagleson 1940). It is possible that the ants were misidentified and were actually tropical fire ants. The SFA also tunnels through linen and into boxes of silk hose (Mallis 1938).

The SFA as a Beneficial Predator of Pests

Henry C. McCook (1879) discovered the southern fire ant as a new species during a study of cotton pests, and in this way the SFA came onto the scientific scene as a beneficial predator, killing caterpillars of the destructive cotton leafworm *(Alabama argillacea)*. McCook was aware of the fire ant's tenaciousness from the beginning. The jaws of several workers remained fastened in death to one of his preserved caterpillar specimens.

Before the RIFA took over in coastal Georgia, the SFA helped control southern corn stalk borers *(Diatraea crambidoides)* (Barber 1933). This snout moth appeared to be rare in one area, represented by only a single caterpillar per several thousand corn stalks. But when the caterpillars were caged and watched, the southern fire ant entered the cages and killed the caterpillars. It had been responsible for holding the pest in check all along. The SFA seems to be quite good at this. In the case of the bordered patch butterfly *(Chlosyne lacinia)*, the caterpillars' combination of group defense and warning coloration is not enough to save them (Clark and Faeth 1997).

In the peanut fields of southern Texas, the SFA was found to be the only predator of the burrowing bug *Pangaeus bilineatus.* Adults and nymphs of this insect are pests of peanut pods (Smith and Pitts 1974).

In Texas the southern fire ant preys upon the blood-sucking chicken mite *Dermanyssus gallinae* (Wood 1917). Chicken mites cause dermatitis when they find their way onto human skin. The SFA gives further aid by killing house fly pupae in the poultry's manure (Mullens et al. 1986).

From the survey presented in this chapter it is clear that fire ants have a beneficial side that has been largely overlooked. It would be a mistake to brand them as noxious pests without giving proper regard to particular circumstances.

CHAPTER 14

Conclusion:
Prospects and Questions

No species of insect has disappeared from
the earth as a result of man's activities.

—*Clay Lyle, director of the Mississippi Agricultural
Experiment Station* (1952)

MANY animals have been driven to extinction
by human activity, but it is not certain that any insect pests are among that number. One possible exception is the Rocky Mountain plague grasshopper
Melanoplus spretus, known in the nineteenth century
as "the hateful locust." It is widely believed that the
last living specimen of what was once the worst agricultural pest in the western United States was collected in 1902, and it is also believed that humans did
indeed finish off a seemingly invincible native that
once darkened the sky with its swarms (details in
Lockwood and DeBrey 1990). But two qualifications
must be made. First, even in this case there appear
to be natural contributing factors. Second, an overlooked record of both sexes from Mexico suggests
that the species is not extinct after all (Rehn 1904).

For all we know, the introduced fire ants will
someday share the plague grasshopper's fate. The
worse of the two imports is widely considered to be
the red imported fire ant. Despite efforts to control
it, the species is actually expanding into the western United States and is expected to occupy the West

Coast and much of Mexico sooner or later. In the closing days of 1998, southern Californians were discovering a series of infestations that threatened to put down permanent roots. This event was predicted forty years earlier (Wilson 1959).

Prospects in the United States

The natural ranges and accidental distributions of the fire ants under discussion (as of 1999) were given in figures 3.1, 4.1, 5.1, 6.1, 6.4, and 6.8, with figure 14.3 showing hybrid distribution.

The Red Imported Fire Ant. For those who believe that an Act of Congress would be necessary to rid the United States of imported fire ants, I can say that it was tried without success in 1957. The Federal Imported Fire Ant Quarantine began the following year, and control programs have failed ever since. In 1967 the National Academy of Sciences announced that eradication was not feasible (Lofgren et al. 1975), and the original federal effort ended in 1978 (Copeland 1997). As Schmidt (1995) wrote: "Like many other stinging problems that politicians promise to quick-fix, the red-imported fire ant is here to stay."

In 1997, United States Senators Phil Gramm of Texas and Max Cleland of Georgia sponsored legislation (S 932) to increase the offensive against the RIFA, and the individual states are putting up their own fights. For example, in that same year the Texas legislature provided a total of five million dollars for the years 1998 through 1999 to the Texas Agricultural Experiment Station, these funds to be used against the RIFA by Texas A&M University, the University of Texas, Texas Tech University, and the Texas Department of Agriculture. This money represented the first two years of a six-year program known as the Texas Imported Fire Ant Research and Management Plan. At least thirty-five projects were funded for 1998 and 1999. Eradication is not expected, but the motto of the plan is: "Together we can lessen the sting of the fire ant problem" (Drees 1998). Part of that plan called for neighborhood volunteer efforts that sound rather optimistic, though members of one Austin neighborhood did appear on local television in 1998 claiming success in their cooperative efforts. It has been estimated that the RIFA causes more than three hundred million dollars worth of damage per year in Texas alone (California Department of Food and Agriculture 1998). Texas maintains a nine-member "Fire Ant Advisory Board" consisting of three high-ranking elected officials and six appointed members (Ramos 1998–99).

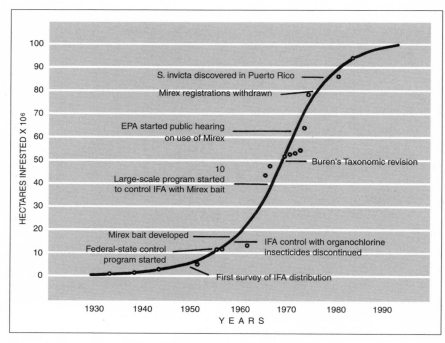

Fig. 14.1. The S-shaped growth curve showing IFA infestation over time as well as some important historical events. Reprinted from Lofgren 1986a.

In 1998 the Georgia House of Representatives introduced HR 842 to increase funds to fight the red imported fire ant, which was estimated to cause forty-six million dollars of damage in Georgia per year (Georgia House of Representatives 1998).

When the number of acres infested by U.S. imported fire ants is plotted against time, the resulting curve has an S shape (fig. 14.1). This phenomenon is familiar to ecologists. It shows an early, rapid growth followed by a gradual slowing to a maximum or plateau value as the species begins to realize its geographical limitations. Lofgren (1986a) estimated that the insects were occupying 250 million acres of U.S. soil at the time of that writing. He believed the West Coast to be in danger of infestation but thought the pests were indeed reaching their ecological limits in the Southeast. RIFA populations do seem to decrease in areas that have been infested for long periods of time (Reagan 1986). Nine years later, in 1995, the RIFA was occupying about 282 million acres in eleven states and Puerto Rico (Callcott and Collins 1996). By 1998 the estimate had reached 308 million acres

(Williams et al. 1999). Vinson (1997) estimated the area at 275 million acres in the southern United States alone. The eventual infestation could amount to one quarter of the land area of the United States (deShazo et al. 1990).

In the 1990s, the RIFA was accidentally transported to New Mexico, Arizona, and California in the far west (Jouvenaz 1990; Knight and Rust 1990; MacKay and Fagerlund 1997), and to Virginia and Maryland (including the Washington, D.C., area) in the northeast (Vander Meer 1996; Anonymous 1997d; California Department of Food and Agriculture 1998). There is one report of an infestation in Nebraska (Anonymous 1997d), and in 1998 the United States Department of Agriculture quarantined nine counties in Arkansas. The affected area included the state capital of Little Rock. By 1999, Puerto Rico and four southeastern states were entirely quarantined, and seven states were quarantined by county, but New Mexico, Arizona, and California had not yet made the list (Federal Code of Regulations, section 301).

Arid western Texas is proving an obstacle to the ant's progress, although advancing RIFA populations in that part of the state are more resistant to desiccation than their more easterly counterparts. This could be due to acclimatization or to natural selection. Whatever the cause, the species is adapting as it expands into drier areas (Phillips et al. 1996). Commercially transported nursery stock affords the ant a way of leapfrogging vast, inhospitable expanses that might otherwise prove impenetrable. San Angelo, Texas, was colonized from the east in this manner (Francke et al. 1983). For such reasons hay cannot be shipped from infested Texas counties to uninfested counties without approval from the Texas Department of Agriculture (Sorensen and Trostle 1986), nor can soil, plants with soil attached, grass sod, straw, logs, used soil-moving machinery, or anything else an inspector deems unsafe (Federal Code, section 301). Treatments of such materials typically cost between thirty and fifty dollars, and inspectors have the authority to destroy private property.

Brownsville, at the southern tip of Texas, has been infested since 1991 (Allen et al. 1993), and El Paso in the far west since at least 1989. Vinson and Sorensen (1986) predicted the El Paso invasion three years before the event. They saw the eventual western range as extending from the Big Bend area all the way up the West Coast to at least the Canadian border, with gaps here and there in the deserts. The Brownsville connection gave the RIFA a hold on the lower Rio Grande Valley, a mesic artery that bypasses the more arid stretches of western Texas and points the way to the West

Coast (Knight and Rust 1990). Laredo is on this path and is already infested. Northern Mexico is probably infested too, though I have seen no official record.

Before the slowdown of the species' continuous western front in the 1980s and 1990s, the pest was spreading through Texas at about thirty miles per year (Hung and Vinson 1978). These authors believed that the entire state would eventually be infested. A statistical model with predictions published in 1980 saw the RIFA expanding into eighteen additional Texas counties over the following decade (Pimm and Bartell 1980). A more recent computer simulation predicted that the RIFA will expand in Texas beyond previously suggested limits. This includes the counties lying on a curve extending from Central Texas through the Panhandle, all the way up to Oklahoma (Stoker et al. 1994). The authors had no idea what would stop the RIFA or when that might happen. The mathematical model used by Killion and Grant (1995) predicted a northern limit at the 0°F January isotherm (fig. 14.2), a line on a map indicating a position that is far enough north to commonly have a temperature that low in that winter month. Computer simulations of fire ant expansion sometimes generate thought-provoking results. For example, considering only the territorial, nonbudding, monogyne social type, Korzukhin and Porter (1994) predicted that populations in a newly infested area would be lower fifteen years after the event than they were after only four years of occupation. Why? One reason is the fact that founding queens do not have a chance to die of old age in only four years (they can live seven years or more).

With the exception of spotty infestations from nursery stock and the like, the western front of the RIFA remains in Texas at this writing. Its spread has clearly been slowed by its advance into that state, for it first arrived in 1953 in nursery stock (although it was eradicated), and the expanding front itself arrived three years later, in 1956 (Summerlin and Green 1977). The ant has not made it from one side of the state to the other though it has had more than four decades to do so. By the late 1990s, the Texas front was along a line connecting Val Verde County in the southwest to Clay County in the north. Still, several surrounded "island" counties in the extreme south had no records at the time, and there were isolated western and northern infestations beyond the main front. These included Odessa in Ector County and Sherman County on the Oklahoma border in the Texas Panhandle (Drees et al. 1996).

It appears that temperatures in the desert southwest need not prevent the RIFA from moving through that area (Braulick et al. 1988). The import tolerates heat about as well as the native fire ants already living in the

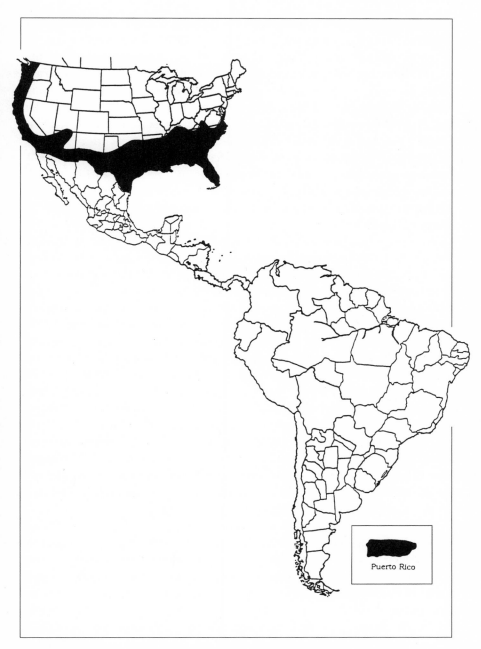

Fig. 14.2. The expected U.S. distribution of the red imported fire ant if its northward expansion reaches the 0°F January isotherm line.

Texas desert, and it is the only species of the group suspected of having an evaporative-cooling adaptation (Francke et al. 1985). Genetic variation for the ability to withstand desiccation in the lab was reported by Li and Heinz (1998). This suggests that some RIFA queens will be better able to penetrate the desert than others and raises the possibility of the evolution of a desert strain or strains. Nevertheless, during dry spells in Central Texas it can be difficult to find even a single mound. In the hot, dry summer of 1998, a San Antonio newspaper reported huge masses of fire ants in swimming pools. The combination of drought and the electrical devices associated with pools were thought to have lured them in. Perhaps one can generalize by saying that the northward spread of the RIFA will probably be limited by low temperatures, whereas its westward spread will be regulated by the presence or absence of sufficient water.

The people of the infested city of Marshall, Texas, put the best light on the situation and make a profit out of a problem. Their annual Fire Ant Festival takes place in the second week of October. It features a roundup, in which contestants kick a mound open and collect the angry ants in a bottle. Whoever collects the most ants wins. There is a fire ant–calling contest (with a 1998 prize of $150), a Miss Fire Ant contest, and a chili cookoff. One of the seasonings is never a guarded secret—a fire ant must be added to each pot. Meanwhile, several costumed fire ant mascots mingle with the crowd (Yoffe 1988; Conniff 1990). The 1988 festival featured a sculpture built from five thousand Amdro bottles (Anonymous 1988b). The Texas State Lottery cashes in too. It has a scratch-off game called Fire Ant Fever, which can pay up to twenty-five thousand dollars.

Arizona joined the ranks of the infested states when a large mound was discovered behind a greenhouse in the city of Mesa (Frank 1988). A horde of workers, hundreds of queens, and a contingent of males were present. Frank noted: "Little question should remain that RIFA can establish itself in the arid western U.S. under appropriate conditions."

Isolated New Mexican colonies were found in the ghost town of Steins (in the south near the border with Arizona) and near Albuquerque, where they arrived in 1994 or thereabouts. MacKay and Fagerlund (1997) concluded that the insect will "finally invade southern California, where it will probably become a major pest." In fact, Carpinteria in the Santa Barbara area had been hit almost a decade before those words were published. The ants were wiped out in time to prevent further spread (Knight and Rust 1990), but subsequent invasions included a date grove and almond groves where Texas beehives had been imported to aid in almond pollination (Les Greenberg, pers. comm.). In late 1998, infestations were discovered in several cities in Los Angeles, Orange, and Riverside counties. The ants were found in nurseries, on a sod farm, and along roadsides, including the first record of the RIFA in a residential area in California (California Department of Food and Agriculture 1998). Plans were being made to quarantine Orange County as early as January, 1999, with control by aerial applications of the insect growth regulator Award. The RIFA first began knocking on California's door in 1983 when it was intercepted at a border inspection station. The magnitude of the problem is indicated by the 108 interceptions made during 1997–98 alone.

On the eastern front, 1989 saw the invasion of Virginia. State inspectors now issue "stop sale notices" when they discover infested plants. The material must be treated or returned to its place of origin. Puerto Rico was penetrated much earlier, probably in or shortly before 1977, via oil refinery equipment (Vinson and Sorensen 1986).

The prediction of Vinson and Sorensen that the RIFA will reach the Canadian border may startle those who believe that cold will be the limiting factor in RIFA spread. Yet events have shown that the earlier projections of the northern limit were too conservative. One factor that is difficult to predict in simulations is the magnitude and direction of ongoing evolution. For example, the species could be evolving cold tolerance as it pushes the envelope of its range. Or global warming (if it truly is occurring) might allow the ant to push farther north than was originally expected (Vinson 1997). Reappraisals seem warranted (Stimac and Alves 1994) because the hybrid between the RIFA and BIFA is now found in northern areas of the southeast once thought too cold for any imported fire ants (fig. 14.3). It was also thought that the hybrid was an exceptional combination of genes conferring a greater cold tolerance than the RIFA parental species. Data now suggest that the RIFA's tolerance is at least equal to that of the hybrid (Diffie et al. 1997). Morrill (1977a) found the RIFA overwintering rather well near its northern limit in the Georgia Piedmont, even though the mounds froze hard enough to be lifted from the ground in a single piece. Female castes revived from subfreezing temperatures but the males seldom did (the air might have been at freezing temperature, but fire ants do not survive freezing of their tissues). The following year the same author saw the aftermath of a Georgia winter marked by record-breaking cold. Most RIFA colonies perished. Frozen ants were found in clumps inside the mounds. Surviving colonies tended to be those that happened to lie near some form of windbreak (Morrill et al. 1978).

Red imported fire ants can resist freezing until their temperature drops to 18°F, fourteen degrees below the normal freezing point of water. These

Fig. 14.3. The range of the RIFA x BIFA hybrid in the United States.

specimens were from Lubbock, Texas, the most northwesterly known infestation at the time and also one of the highest-altitude records (Taber et al. 1987). They were discovered in 1985, probably having entered on nursery stock, and were of the feared polygyne social type. Most of the colonies survived the cold Lubbock winters for several years until they were eradicated in 1990 by the combined use of several poisons (Thorvilson et al. 1992).

In sum, the prospect for eradicating the red imported fire ant seems bleak. C. S. Lofgren (1986a) concluded that "Their high reproductive capabilities, efficient foraging behavior, and ecological adaptability make it certain they will be here to perplex and harass us for years to come." As an intriguing example of the RIFA's unpredictable behavior, Agnew et al. (1982) noticed an increase in the ant's aggressiveness over the course of a single year in cotton fields. The reason was unclear.

When contemplating the long-term effect of the RIFA in the United States, we should remember the plague of tropical fire ants supposedly endured by Caribbean islanders hundreds of years ago. The region eventually recovered and talk of the TFA receded. Perhaps predators and competitors, combined with chemical control, will eventually force the red imported fire ant of the United States to share the fate of its Caribbean cousin. Or perhaps the hardy invader is here to stay.

The Black Imported Fire Ant. Regarding cold hardiness and the potential for northward expansion, it has long been known that the black imported fire ant produces glycerol, a form of antifreeze (Ricks and Vinson 1972a). In the United States this species does tend to be found north of the RIFA (fig. 4.1).

The homeland of the BIFA includes the South American pampas. Buren et al. (1974) posed a question. What would happen if the black imported fire ant reached the southern Great Plains of the United States, a vast habitat of grassland not too different from the insect's original home? The geographical leap could be made easily and immediately on a single shipment of infested nursery stock.

In the face of the combined onslaught of human control efforts and intrusions by the red imported fire ant and the hybrid between the two imports (fig. 14.3), the outlook for the BIFA in the eastern United States is bleak.

The Tropical Fire Ant. Prospects in the United States for this possibly native species are not good. The RIFA has been extirpating its rival in the

Southeast, except for forested pockets where the TFA clings to life. Elsewhere in the world this species is either expanding its range or holding its own (fig. 5.1). In Mesoamerica it remains a pest to some, and the species is commonly introduced by accident to new lands in both the New and Old Worlds.

The Southern Fire Ant, Golden Fire Ant, and Solenopsis amblychila. For the southern fire ant prospects are not good unless it can hold on in cooler, drier areas of its range. This seems unlikely because research has shown the RIFA to be more cold hardy, heat hardy, and desiccation resistant than was originally believed. The range of the southern fire ant will probably continue to contract.

The golden fire ant and its close relative *Solenopsis amblychila* face the same RIFA threat as the southern fire ant; their desert and semiarid habitats do not guarantee safety.

Some Open Questions

Question 1: What are the evolutionary relationships within the fire ant family tree? As famous as they are, and as troublesome as they can be, much remains to be discovered about the biology of fire ants. Edward O. Wilson (1986) wrote of the genus *Solenopsis* in general: "A substantial opportunity exists to address the Neotropical species as products of a major adaptive radiation, analyzing the entire assemblage with the aid of cladistic analysis and ecological theory." In other words, it would be helpful if we could work out the evolutionary relationships of the fire ants so that we can understand the evolution of their behaviors and the history of their dispersals. A few steps in this direction have been taken in the years since Wilson's comment, particularly the preliminary analyses of Ross and Trager (1990). Yet as of 1999 there was still no complete evolutionary tree for the fire ant clan, even though it consists of a mere eighteen to twenty species.

Question 2: How does the polygyne social type arise from the monogyne condition? Tschinkel (1998a) considered this question to be the "Holy Grail" of myrmecology.

Question 3: How often has the polygyne social type arisen?

Question 4: Is the U.S. RIFA polygyne type due to a second introduction, beyond that of an original monogyne invasion? The latter two questions arise in the work of Porter and colleagues (1988), Vinson (1997), and Tschinkel (1998a).

Question 5: What is the precise stimulus that initiates mating flights?

Question 6: How do the sexes locate each other hundreds of feet in the air?

Question 7: How are the different female castes and subcastes determined? An answer to this requires more study of nutrition and possibly genetics. Questions 5–7 were raised by Vander Meer (1996).

Question 8: Will species-specific biocontrol agents work against the RIFA x BIFA hybrid? Glancey and coworkers (1989b) called attention to this complication.

Question 9: How populous are native fire ant colonies compared to those of the imports? There does not seem to be a single head count or numerical estimation for any of the three clearly native species—the southern fire ant, golden fire ant, and *Solenopsis amblychila*. Colony size will be a factor in their ability to resist the RIFA.

Question 10 is better stated as a large and general problem to be solved. We know almost nothing about the biology of any of the three clearly native fire ant species. For example, the maps showing the geographic distributions of the GFA and SFA in the United States represent the historical and presumably maximum range of each species. Have the borders of these ranges actually retreated since the RIFA's arrival, and if so, what do they look like today? Do golden fire ants and *Solenopsis amblychila* have multiple queen colonies? Do they hybridize with one another? Does either species harbor a natural enemy, perhaps a nest symbiont, that could be turned against the red imported fire ant? Relatively simple natural history investigations could pay off with practical results. Amateur naturalists could make a big contribution here. The opportunity to learn is shrinking before the advance of the RIFA.

Fire Ant Species of the World

Fire Ants Found in the United States

Solenopsis amblychila Wheeler; range fig. 6.8
S. aurea Wheeler; range fig. 6.4
S. geminata (Fabricius); range fig. 5.1
S. richteri Forel; range fig. 4.1
S. invicta Buren (also known as *S. wagneri* Santschi); range fig. 3.1
S. xyloni McCook; range fig. 6.1
(RIFA x BIFA hybrid; range fig. 14.3)
(TFA x SFA hybrid; distribution uncertain, in at least some areas where the two
bona fide species overlap, e.g., Central Texas)

Fire Ants Endemic to South America

Solenopsis bruesi Creighton; Peru
S. daguerrei (Santschi); Brazil, Argentina, Uruguay
S. electra Forel; Bolivia, Argentina, perhaps introduced into Paraguay
S. gayi (Spinola); Chile, Peru, perhaps introduced into Colombia
S. interrupta Santschi; Argentina, Bolivia
S. macdonaghi Santschi; Uruguay, Argentina, Paraguay, introduced into Bolivia
S. megergates Trager; Brazil
S. pusillignis Trager; Brazil
S. pythia Santschi; Argentina, Brazil
S. quinquecuspis Forel; Argentina, Brazil, Uruguay
S. saevissima (Smith); Brazil, introduced into Ecuador (Galápagos Islands)
S. weyrauchi Trager; Peru

The name following each species is the last name of the individual who formally
described the species, making it known to science. If the species was not originally described as a member of the genus *Solenopsis*, the name of the individual
who described it under a different name appears in parentheses.

This list of the fire ant species of the world follows Trager (1991). Hybrids
are not recognized as distinct species.

Solenopsis hostilis (Borgmeier) of Brazil and *Solenopsis solenopsidis* (Kusne-
zov) of Argentina may be fire ants. They have not been studied well enough to
be sure. If so, the total number of bona fide species rises from eighteen to twenty.

The nest is usually available to anyone interested in identifying a fire ant species. This is fortunate because the major worker subcaste is the ideal choice for this purpose (Trager 1991), and majors can be obtained by breaking into the mound. The majors are the largest workers. All workers are wingless, and the only wingless adult that is not a worker is the queen (or queens, in a polygyne colony).

Queens are hard to confuse with workers. A queen has a very large gaster (the abdominal region behind the waist) and is the center of attention in a disturbance. It is best to have several major workers at hand so that identification does not rely on a single individual that might be unusual in some way. Minor workers of different species can look similar enough to cause confusion, so I do not provide a key for use with this small subcaste.

If minor workers, queens, or males must be identified, the keys provided by Hung and colleagues (1977) for Texas species can be helpful, but be warned that the black imported fire ant does not appear in those keys for the very good reason that it has never been found in Texas. Nor was *Solenopsis amblychila* recognized as different from the golden fire ant at that time. Snelling's keys (1963) can be useful too, though fire ant names have changed since then. There were no complete keys to the sexual forms at the time of this writing, and it is best to settle on major workers. The most obvious of the useful characteristics are head shape and color (Trager 1991).

The first task is to ensure that the specimen is a fire ant to begin with. Characteristics of fire ants include a two-segmented waist region, worker antennae with ten segments each (two of these forming a club at the tip—see figs. A2.1, A2.2); no spines on the propodeum, a region on the ant's back (Bolton 1987); and a long seta or hair arising from the middle of the anterior margin of the clypeus, a region just above the jaws (Bolton 1994). A mound and aggressive behavior are useful if present but are not as reliable as anatomical characters.

The next step is to determine if the species is a native or an import. Imported fire ants have a conspicuous median tooth on the front or anterior edge of the clypeus, flanked by a lateral tooth on each side, giving a total of three. The natives and the tropical fire ant lack the median tooth, and one species sometimes lacks even the lateral teeth (fig. A2.3). The following key was made possible by the work of Trager (1991). The range maps and photos elsewhere in the present volume should also be consulted when attempting identification.

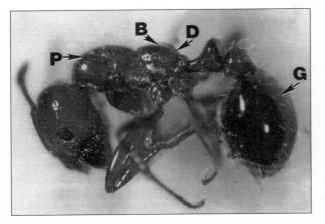

Fig. A2.1. A red imported fire ant worker, showing the pronotum (P), the basal face of the propodeum (B), the declivious face of the propodeum (D), and the gaster (G), which also shows the hairlike setae found on this surface and elsewhere on the exoskeleton. The mesonotum is the area just behind the pronotum.

Fig. A2.2. The two-segmented club of the fire ant worker's ten-segmented antenna, indicated by the arrow (TFA major worker).

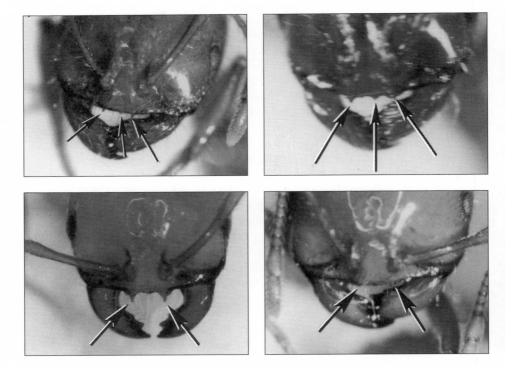

Fig. A2.3. The clypeal teeth (indicated by arrows) of imported fire ant major workers, *Solenopsis richteri (upper left)* and *S. invicta (upper right)*, compared to those of native fire ant major workers, *S. aurea (bottom left)* and *S. amblychila (bottom right).*

Fig. A2.4. RIFA major workers have a reddish spot in the area indicated by the arrow.

Fig. A2.5. BIFA major workers have a yellow spot in the area indicated by the arrow. These specimens were collected by W. F. Buren, author of the historic 1972 paper recognizing the existence of two imported fire ant species on U.S. soil.

Fig. A2.6. The head of a TFA major (arrow) compared to more typical fire ant heads, those of its nestmates: winged queens *(far left and bottom)* and male *(far right).*

Key to Major Workers of Imported Fire Ants*

1.   Head and first antenna segment reddish brown, spot on dorsum of first gaster segment (if present) not yellow but brownish red (fig. A2.4), dorsum of pronotum lacking a concavity . . . . *Solenopsis invicta* (red imported fire ant, also known as *S. wagneri*; southeastern United States to Central and southern Texas; Puerto Rico; occasional isolated infestations beyond the continuous range)

2.   Head and first antenna segment brownish black, dorsum of basal segment of gaster with a yellowish spot (fig. A2.5), middle of dorsum of pronotum with a concavity . . . . *Solenopsis richteri* (black imported fire ant; northern Alabama, northern Mississippi, western Tennessee)

Key to Major Workers of Native Fire Ants (Including the TFA)

1.   a. Head large, > 1.5 mm in width (fig. A2.6.) 2
    b. Head not large, ≤ 1.48 mm in width (fig. A2.6.) 3

2.   a. Dorsolateral junction of propodeum developed as a ridge along all or nearly all its length. . . . . *Solenopsis geminata* (Florida to western Texas)
    b. Ridge of propodeum more abbreviated than above, present only in the region of the junction between the basal and declivious faces . . . . *S. geminata* x *S. xyloni***

3.   a. Head and thorax red to dark brown, eye with 70–80 facets . . . . *Solenopsis xyloni* (southern United States, in an arc from the Carolinas to the area of Sacramento, California)
    b. Body golden or yellowish red, eye with 40–60 facets 4

4.   a. Clypeal teeth distinct (fig. A2.3), mesonotum with 18–30 erect setae . . . . *Solenopsis aurea* (from Central Texas to California, in deserts and semiarid regions of northern Mexico)
    b. Clypeal teeth indistinct or absent (fig. A2.3), mesonotum with 8–15 erect setae . . . . *Solenopsis amblychila* (southern Texas to California, in deserts and semiarid regions of northern Mexico)

---

*Hybrids of the two imported fire ant species are common between central Mississippi and western Georgia (Shoemaker et al. 1996). These have various combinations of the parental characters.

**The hybrid queen usually resembles the *S. xyloni* queen more than the *S. geminata* queen.

Preserving Fire Ants for Study

There are two ways to preserve ants for study and identification. The simplest and perhaps the best way is to place them in alcohol. This can be either 70 percent isopropyl alcohol or 80 percent ethyl alcohol. The isopropyl form (rubbing alcohol) is inexpensive and is as close as the nearest grocery store. Ethyl alcohol is the drinking variety. Professionals consider it a better choice than rubbing alcohol because the latter tends to make specimens brittle over time. However, most people do not have an 80 percent preparation at hand and it is not readily purchased. Either choice saves the specimens from breakage and from carpet beetles and other insects that would eat the dead fire ants if these were pinned in standard insect collection boxes without chemical protection. They can always be dried and "pointed" later if necessary (see procedure following). Pinned specimens must be stored in boxes with naphthalene, paradichlorobenzene, or some other chemical that will ward off the living insects that can destroy an entire collection in short order.

If the specimens must be preserved in a dry state, then they should be pointed. A specimen is pointed when it has been glued to the tip of a tiny piece of paper or cardstock that was first pierced by a standard insect pin (of size 2 or 3). Biological supply houses sell pins and special punches for cutting out these little points in a hurry. Otherwise, simply cut out a small isosceles triangle about one quarter inch in height from a piece of stiff card. Then pierce the triangle with the insect pin and run the triangle about two thirds of the way up the shaft. Now bend the tip down just a bit and apply to it a tiny amount of clear-drying, fast-drying glue. When the glue becomes tacky, hold the shaft of the pin in your hand and apply the triangle's tip to the right side of the ant, holding it there until the glue dries. For a similar but simpler approach, see figure A2.5.

The pin should also bear a label recording the collection locality, date, and collector's name. On this or on a second label, it is useful (though considered optional) to provide habitat information as well. The labels are pierced by the pin after the specimen has been pointed, the "required" label appearing higher on the shaft than any others. For example, a label accompanying a pointed red imported fire ant might bear the following information:

USA / Texas: Travis Co., Austin
VII–5–1995, Coll. S. W. Taber
In sandy field

Months are designated by Roman numerals to avoid confusing months and days, and it is best not to abbreviate the year by using only its last two digits; properly pointed and curated specimens will be available for study in collections hundreds of years after their collector is not. Professionals sometimes add latitude, longitude, and elevation to their data labels.

Glossary

alarm pheromone: A chemical that causes workers to gather in defense, whether this is for general defense of the nest or for defense of the sexuals preparing for the *nuptial flight*.

alate: A winged ant. These are (1) queens that have not yet removed their wings prior to egg laying, and (2) males.

alkaloid: A chemical usually associated with plants but also comprising part of the fire ant's *venom*. Alkaloids are responsible for the *pustule* produced by the *sting* of the imported fire ants.

alkene: A hydrocarbon of the *Dufour's gland* that is associated with the *recruitment pheromone*.

allergen: A molecule that causes an allergic reaction in at least some people.

anaphylactic shock: An extreme allergic reaction, which can lead to death by respiratory failure.

antihistamine: A drug that reduces swelling and inflammation.

aril: Part of a seed, in some cases particularly attractive to insects, which might consume it and disperse the seed in the process.

BIFA: The black imported fire ant, *Solenopsis richteri*.

brood-raiding: The removal of juvenile stages from a young nest by the workers of a different colony. It is a form of "slave driving" seen on a more regular basis among other species of ants.

callow: An adult that is temporarily soft and light-colored because it has just eclosed from the pupal stage.

caste: A subdivision of the female sex that reflects division of labor. Fire ants have two castes, the *worker* caste (carrying out all nonreproductive roles) and the *queen* caste (dedicated to reproduction).

chitin: A nitrogen-containing sugar, which comprises part of an insect's exoskeleton.

claustral founding: The manner of beginning a nest in which the queen seals herself off and produces a first brood using her own secretions as their source of nutrition.

crop: An abdominal organ that stores food.

cuticular hydrocarbons: Chemicals of the exoskeleton that vary both between and within nests and that identify individuals.

Dufour's gland: An abdominal gland that is the source of the *recruitment pheromone* and perhaps plays a role in brood collection, emigration, and aggregation.

eclosion: The transition from the completed pupal stage to the adult condition.

ecotype: A genetic variant associated with a particular environment.

elaiosome: An edible oil-rich seed appendage, which attracts insects that disperse the rest of the seed if the plant's strategy is effective.

endemic: Restricted to the area in question.

epinephrine: A hormone that stimulates heart beat and raises blood pressure. Also known as adrenaline.

farnesene: A hydrocarbon component of fire ant *recruitment pheromone.*

flare: A reddened area on the skin.

gallery: A tunnel in an ant nest.

gaster: The rounded back end of an ant, part of the abdomen. The gaster bears the sting at its tip.

GFA: The golden fire ant, *Solenopsis aurea.* Also known as the desert fire ant.

green-beard: An outward signal to nestmates that its bearer has a particular genetic constitution. Some green-beards are presumably odors.

gynandromorph: An individual with both male and female structures.

heptachlor: A chlorinated hydrocarbon used against the fire ants in early attempts at eradication. Its harmful environmental effects resulted in its own termination instead.

heterozygous: A term best described by example. A child who inherits the *allele* for blue eyes (assuming that only one gene is involved) from both parents is genetically uniform with respect to eye color and is said to be homozygous for the eye color gene. A child who inherits the allele for blue eyes from one parent and the allele for brown eyes from the other is less genetically uniform and is said to be heterozygous for the eye color gene.

homosesquiterpene: A hydrocarbon component of fire ant *recruitment pheromone.*

hydramethylnon: A popular fluorinated hydrocarbon *toxicant* in use against the fire ants.

hypersensitive: A condition in which one is prone to react in a dangerous manner to the presence of an *allergen.*

IFA: Imported fire ant. The earliest research was done without the knowledge that the United States was hosting two different species of imported fire ant. IFA is a useful term when dealing with the early publications, for it sometimes isn't clear which species is the subject of the report.

insect growth regulator (IGR): A chemical that affects the development of an insect.

instar: A stage in the growth and development of an insect. A fire ant *larva* passes through a total of four instars, shedding its skin between one instar and the next. The final juvenile instar is the *pupa*, followed by the adult stage.

intercaste: An individual with features of both the *worker* and *queen* castes.

juvenile hormone: A chemical that causes the retention of larval characteristics and inhibits metamorphosis to the adult stage.

lactones: Chemicals of the ester class that are components of the fire ant *queen recognition pheromone.*

larva: A stage of development in the metamorphosis of ants. It is the "grub" stage between egg and *pupa.*

major worker (major): The largest workers in the colony comprise the major worker *subcaste.*

male: A winged individual with no other function than to mate with the *queen.*

meconium: A mass of excretory material voided by the *larva* when it reaches the pupal stage.

media worker (media): a worker that is smaller than a *major worker* but larger than a *minor worker.*

metapleural gland: An abdominal gland, which in the tropical fire ant secretes a territorial *pheromone.*

midden: The colony's trash heap outside the nest. Also known as the kitchen midden.

minim: One of the workers developing from the queen's first brood. They are smaller than all workers of later broods, and their range of behaviors is different too.

minor worker (minor): The smallest workers in the colony comprise the minor worker subcaste (with the exception of the first-brood workers; see *minim*).

mirex: Perhaps the most effective of all poisons used against the fire ants. It is a chlorinated hydrocarbon, and its use in this manner (in the United States) was banned in the 1970s.

mitochondrial DNA: DNA contained not in the nucleus of the cell but in a compartment dedicated to the production of energy in the cell.

monogyne: A type of colony in which only one queen is laying eggs.

monophyletic: Referring to a group of species that contains an ancestor, all of its descendants, and nothing more. A monophyletic group is therefore a biologically "natural" family unit.

myrmecochory: The dispersal of seeds by ants.

myrmecologist: Someone who studies ants.

myrmecophile: An organism that spends at least part of its life cycle among a colony of ants.

nuptial flight: The mating flight of the fire ants, in which males and virgin queens leave the nest and take to the air in large numbers, to copulate on the wing.

parasitoid: A species that is parasitic in only part of its life cycle.

phagostimulant: A substance that stimulates feeding.

pheromone: A chemical or blend of chemicals used for communication within a species. Primer pheromones have a delayed effect, preparing an individual for a new behavior. Releaser pheromones are more direct in their action.

phorid: Any fly that is a member of the family Phoridae. Many phorids are enemies of fire ants. Also known as scuttle flies or humpbacked flies.

phylogeny: Another name for an evolutionary tree.

physogastric: Having an abdomen swollen with eggs.

pleometrosis: The establishment of a nest by two or more founding queens.

polycalic: Often considered synonymous with *polydomic.*

polydomic: A nest with more than one mound.

polygyne: A type of colony in which two or more egg-laying queens are present.

praesaepium: A "food basket" on the ventral surface of a larva. The fourth instar RIFA larva feeds upon solid food held in place by the praesaepium.

pupa: A stage of development in the metamorphosis of ants. The pupa is the stage just before the adult.

pustule: A blister commonly raised by the sting of the imported fire ants when mammals, birds, and reptiles are attacked.

pygidial gland: An abdominal gland that might play a role in *recruitment.*

queen: One of the two female castes characteristic of most ant species. The fire ant queen is the reproductive *caste.* Queens can be virgin or mated, and they can be winged or wingless. A synonym for queen is "gyne."

queen pheromone: Any of a number of chemicals or blends of chemicals that provides a signal from the queen to some other colony member. These can identify the queen to her nestmates, cause workers to channel larvae into more workers as opposed to queens, and prevent winged virgins from shedding their wings, thereby also inhibiting them from laying eggs.

queen recognition pheromone: A set of *lactones* known as invictolides that gives each queen her own unique aroma. It is produced by the venom gland and is attractive to her workers.

recruitment: The assembly of workers to a food source or in defense of colony or individual.

recruitment pheromone: A blend of hydrocarbons dispensed by the *Dufour's gland* to direct workers to some target, usually associated with a food source.

RIFA: The red imported fire ant, *Solenopsis invicta.* Also known as *S. wagneri.*

seta: A "hair" on the surface of the ant's body.

SFA: The southern fire ant, *Solenopsis xyloni.*

solenopsin: An alkaloid found in the *venom* of fire ants.

Solenopsis amblychila: This fire ant species has no common name; *amblychila* means "blunt lip," referring to a clypeus with reduced, blunted, toothlike projections. Sometimes these are absent entirely. This reduced condition is found mostly in major workers and queens of the species and is unusual for fire ants.

Solenopsis aurea: The golden or desert fire ant (GFA); *aurea* means "golden."

Solenopsis daguerrei: Daguerre's fire ant. The original collector was J. B. Daguerre.

Solenopsis geminata: The tropical fire ant (TFA); *geminata* refers to twinning of some sort, perhaps pointing to the existence of a distinct second class of workers, the big-headed majors, unlike those of any other U.S. species. Alternatively, it may refer to the pair of projecting clypeal teeth. The 1804 description by Fabricius gives no clue.

Solenopsis invicta: A more recent scientific name for the red imported fire ant than *Solenopsis wagneri; invicta* means "unconquered." It is both apt and euphonious.

Solenopsis richteri: The black imported fire ant (BIFA). The original collector was named Richter. Entomological custom allows the species to be known as Richter's fire ant.

Solenopsis saevissima: A well-known South American fire ant that has not been imported into the United States; *saevissima* means "the very cruel."

Solenopsis wagneri: The red imported fire ant (RIFA); named for its collector, E. R. Wagner. This name has historical priority over *S. invicta.* Entomological custom allows the RIFA to be known as Wagner's fire ant.

Solenopsis xyloni: The southern fire ant (SFA); *xyloni* perhaps refers to "cotton," for McCook described it during a study of cotton insects.

spermatheca: An organ in the queen's abdomen that stores the sperm of her mate.

squalene: A hydrocarbon found in shark oil and certain ticks. It has antibiotic properties.

sting: (1) the "stinger" through which the fire ant injects its *venom;* (2) the act of venom injection.

stridulation: The scraping together of abdominal plates to produce vibration and sound.

subcaste: The subdivisions of the worker caste. These are the *major* subcaste, the *minor* subcaste, and the *media* subcaste (though medias can be of various intermediate sizes.) The minims comprise an ephemeral subcaste. Workers age but do not grow and do not change from one subcaste to another.

swarming: The assembly of males and unmated queens for the nuptial flight.

symbiont: An organism that has some association with another organism not of its own species.

TFA: The tropical fire ant, *Solenopsis geminata.*

thief ants: *Solenopsis* species that are the closest relatives of the fire ants.

toxicant: A poison.

trail pheromone: See *recruitment pheromone.*

triolein: A chemical, perhaps a pheromone, present in fire ant sexual larvae and said to be attractive to workers.

trophallaxis: The movement of digestive-tract material from one individual to another or an exchange of such material. The transferred material enters the mouth but can exit the mouth or anus of the other individual.

trophic egg: An egg that is incapable of development and is used as food by larvae.

urticaria: Sometimes called hives, a rash suffered by those allergic to insect stings.

venom: The substance injected through the sting or stinger of the fire ant. Its alkaloids cause pustules and its proteins are responsible for allergic responses.

virgin queen: An unmated (and often winged) reproductive female.

wheal: A bump on the skin.

worker: One of the two female *castes* characteristic of most ant species. Fire ant workers are sterile whereas the queen, of course, is not.

Bibliography

Adams, C. T. 1986. Agricultural and medical impact of the imported fire ants. Pp. 48–57 in *Fire ants and leaf-cutting ants: Biology and management*, ed. C. S. Lofgren and R. K. Vander Meer. Westview studies in insect biology. Boulder, Colo.: Westview Press.

Adams, C. T., W. A. Banks, and C. S. Lofgren. 1988. Red imported fire ant (Hymenoptera: Formicidae): Correlation of ant density with damage to two cultivars of potatoes (*Solanum tuberosum* L.). *J. Econ. Entomol.* 81:905–909.

Adams, C. T., W. A. Banks, C. S. Lofgren, B. J. Smittle, and D. P. Harlan. 1983. Impact of the red imported fire ant, *Solenopsis invicta* (Hymenoptera: Formicidae), on the growth and yield of soybeans (*Glycine max*). *J. Econ. Entomol.* 76:1129–32.

Adams, C. T., W. A. Banks, and J. K. Plumley. 1976a. Polygyny in the tropical fire ant, *Solenopsis geminata* with notes on the imported fire ant, *Solenopsis invicta*. *Florida Entomol.* 59:411–15.

Adams, C. T., and C. S. Lofgren. 1981. Red imported fire ants (Hymenoptera: Formicidae): Frequency of sting attacks on residents of Sumter County, Georgia. *J. Med. Entomol.* 18:378–82.

———. 1982. Incidence of stings or bites of the red imported fire ant (Hymenoptera: Formicidae) and other arthropods among patients at Ft. Stewart, Georgia, USA. *J. Med. Entomol.* 19:366–70.

Adams, C. T., J. K. Plumley, W. A. Banks, and C. S. Lofgren. 1977. Impact of the red imported fire ant, *Solenopsis invicta* Buren (Hymenoptera: Formicidae), on harvest of soybeans in North Carolina. *J. Elisha Mitchell Sci. Soc.* 93:150–52.

Adams, C. T., J. K. Plumley, C. S. Lofgren, and W. A. Banks. 1976b. Economic importance of the red imported fire ant, *Solenopsis invicta* Buren: I. Preliminary investigations of impact on soybean harvest. *J. Georgia Entomol. Soc.* 11:165–69.

Adams, C. T., T. E. Summers, C. S. Lofgren, D. A. Focks, and J. C. Prewitt. 1981. Interrelationships of ants and the sugarcane borer in Florida sugarcane fields. *Environ. Entomol.* 10:415–18.

Adams, E. S., and M. T. Balas. 1999. Worker discrimination among queens in newly founded colonies of the fire ant *Solenopsis invicta*. *Behav. Ecol. Sociobiol.* 45:330–38.

Adams, E. S., and W. R. Tschinkel. 1995a. Effects of foundress number on brood raids and queen survival in the fire ant *Solenopsis invicta*. *Behav. Ecol. Sociobiol.* 37:233–42.

———. 1995b. Density-dependent competition in fire ants: Effects on colony survivorship and size variation. *J. Anim. Ecol.* 64:315–24.

Adams, S. 1994. Fighting the fire ant. *Agric. Res.* 42(1):4–9.

Adrouny, G. A., V. J. Derbes, and R. C. Jung. 1959. Isolation of a hemolytic component of fire ant venom. *Science* 130:449.

Agnew, C. W., and W. L. Sterling. 1981. Predation of boll weevils in partially-open cotton bolls by the red imported fire ant. *Southwest. Entomol.* 6:215–19.

———. 1982. Predation rates of the red imported fire ant (*Solenopsis invicta*) on eggs of the tobacco budworm (*Heliothis virescens*). *Prot. Ecol.* 4:151–58.

Agnew, C. W., W. L. Sterling, and D. A. Dean. 1982. Influence of cotton nectar on red imported fire ants and other predators. *Environ. Entomol.* 11:629–34.

Aldrich, J. R., P. W. Schaefer, J. E. Oliver, P. Puapoomchareon, C.-J. Lee, and R. K. Vander Meer. 1997. Biochemistry of the exocrine secretions from gypsy moth caterpillars (Lepidoptera: Lymantriidae). *Ann. Entomol. Soc. Amer.* 90:75–82.

Ali, A. D., W. H. Hudnall, and T. E. Reagan. 1986. Effects of soil types and cultural practices on the fire ant, *Solenopsis invicta,* in sugarcane. *Agric. Ecosyst. Environ.* 18:63–72.

Ali, A. D., T. E. Reagan, and J. L. Flynn. 1984. Influence of selected weedy and weed-free sugarcane habitats on diet composition and foraging activity of the imported fire ant (Hymenoptera: Formicidae). *Environ. Entomol.* 13:1037–41.

Ali, T. M. M. 1990. Role of ants in the pest management of finger millet (*Eleusine coracana* Gaertner). Pp. 93–94 in *Social Insects and the Environment,* ed. G. K. Veeresh, B. Mallik, and C. A. Viraklimath. New Delhi, India: Oxford and IBH.

Allen, C. R., S. Demarais, and R. S. Lutz. 1994. Red imported fire ant impact on wildlife: An overview. *Texas J. Sci.* 46:51–59.

———. 1997a. Effects of red imported fire ants on recruitment of white-tailed deer fawns. *J. Wildlife Man.* 61:911–16.

Allen, C. R., R. S. Lutz, and S. Demarais. 1995. Red imported fire ant impacts on northern bobwhite populations. *Ecol. Appl.* 5:632–38.

Allen, C. R., S. A. Phillips, Jr., and M. R. Trostle. 1993. Range expansion by the ecologically disruptive red imported fire ant into the Texas Rio Grande Valley. *Southwest. Nat.* 18:315–16.

Allen, C. R., K. G. Rice, D. P. Wojcik, and H. F. Percival. 1997b. Effect of red imported fire ant envenomization on neonatal American alligators. *J. Herpetology* 31:318–21.

Allen, G. E. and W. F. Buren. 1974. Microsporidian and fungal diseases of *Solenopsis invicta* Buren in Brazil. *J. New York Entomol. Soc.* 82:125–30.

Allen, G. E., W. F. Buren, R. N. Williams, M. de Menezes, and W. H. Whitcomb. 1974. The red imported fire ant, *Solenopsis invicta:* Distribution and habitat in Mato Grosso, Brazil. *Ann. Entomol. Soc. Amer.* 67:43–46.

Allen, G. E., and A. Silvera-Guido. 1974. Occurrence of Microsporida in *Solenopsis richteri* and *Solenopsis* spp. in Uruguay and Argentina. *Flor. Entomol.* 57:327–29.

Allen, R. H., Jr. 1958. History of the imported fire ant in the Southeast. Pp. 1–7 in *Proceedings symposium: The fire ant eradication program and how it affects wildlife.* Proc. Ann. Conf. Southeastern Assoc. Game and Fish Comm.

Alley, E. G. 1973. The use of mirex in control of the imported fire ant. *J. Environ. Quality* 2:52–61.

Alonso, L. E., and R. K. Vander Meer. 1997. Source of alate excitant pheromones in the red imported fire ant *Solenopsis invicta* (Hymenoptera: Formicidae). *J. Insect Behav.* 10:541–55.

Alvarez, F. M., R. K. Vander Meer, and C. S. Lofgren. 1987. Synthesis of homofarnesenes: Trail pheromone components of the fire ant, *Solenopsis invicta. Tetrahedron* 43:2897–2900.

Amaral, M. J. 1999. One zoo, two islands, and a beetle. *Endangered Species Bull.* 24(3):10–11.

Andersen, A. N. 1991. Seed harvesting by ants in Australia. Pp. 493–503 in *Ant-plant interactions,* ed. C. R. Huxley and D. F. Cutler. Oxford: Oxford University Press.

———. 1997. Functional groups and patterns of organization in North American ant communities: A comparison with Australia. *J. Biogeog.* 24:433–60.

Anderson, J. B., and R. K. Vander Meer. 1993. Magnetic orientation in the fire ant, *Solenopsis invicta. Naturwissenschaften* 80:568–70.

Anonymous. 1959. Pros and cons in the fire ant control program. *Agric. Chemicals* 14:46–47, 107–109.

———. 1978. *The imported fire ant program: A search for new control methods.* College Station: Texas Agricultural Experiment Station.

———. 1988a. Drought sends fire ants indoors. *Bryan-College Station Eagle,* September 13, 2A.

———. 1988b. Fire Ant Festival begins today with merchandise giveaway. *Bryan-College Station Eagle,* October 7.

———. 1997a. Fire ants attacked! *Detroit Free Press,* July 10 (downloaded from Internet).

———. 1997b. Japanese ant color image database. Mac2032.fujimi.hosei.ac.jp.

———. 1997c. When you meet this fellow on the course, be careful! Contact webmaster@ www.ldrs.com.

———. 1997d. Fire ant suppression and eradication program. Virginia Department of Agriculture and Consumer Services. Contact www.state.va.us/~vdacs/vdacs.htm.

———. 1997e. Fire ant control: Past, present and future. Contact deb mil@mail.utexas.edu.

———. 1997f. Fiery invaders. *Impact* magazine (University of Florida, Gainesville).

———. 1998. A green beard for red ants. *Bioscience* 48:880.

Appel, A. G. 1986. Smokybrown cockroaches, *Periplaneta fuliginosa* (Dictyoptera: Blattidae), displaced from their harborages by red imported fire ants, *Solenopsis invicta. Entomol. News* 97:61–62.

Appel, A. G., M. K. Miller, and T. P. Mack. 1991. Cutaneous water loss of several stages of the red imported fire ant, *Solenopsis invicta* (Buren). *Comp. Biochem. Physiol. A Comp. Physiol.* 98:281–83.

Apperson, C. S., R. B. Leidy, and E. E. Powell. 1984a. Effects of Amdro on the red imported fire ant [*Solenopsis invicta*] (Hymenoptera: Formicidae) and some nontarget ant species and persistence of Amdro on a pasture habitat in North Carolina. *J. Econ. Entomol.* 77:1012–18.

Apperson, C. S., and E. E. Powell. 1984. Foraging activity of ants (Hymenoptera: Formicidae) in a pasture inhabited by the red imported fire ant [*Solenopsis invicta*]. *Flor. Entomol.* 67:383–92.

Apperson, C. S., E. E. Powell, and M. Browne. 1984b. Efficacy of individual mound treatments of MK-936 and Amdro against the red imported fire ant [*Solenopsis invicta*] (Hymenoptera: Formicidae). *J. Georgia Entomol. Soc.* 19:508–16.

Arkansas Cooperative Extension Service. 1998. Commercial fish producers options. www.uaex.edu/natural/fire ant.

Aron, S., E. L. Vargo, and L. Passera. 1995. Primary and secondary sex ratios in monogyne colonies of the fire ant. *Animal Behav.* 49:749–57.

Attygalle, A. B., and E. David Morgan. 1983. Reaction gas chromatography without solvent for identification of nanogram quantities of natural products. *Anal. Chem.* 55:1379–84.

Avery, S. W., D. P. Jouvenaz, W. A. Banks, and D. W. Anthony. 1977. Virus-like particles in a fire ant, *Solenopsis* sp., (Hymenoptera: Formicidae) from Brazil. *Flor. Entomol.* 60:17–20.

Ayre, G. L. 1977. Exotic ants in Winnipeg. *Manitoba Entomol.* 11:41–44.

Ayyar Ramakrishna, T. V. 1963. *Handbook of economic entomology for south India.* Madras, India: Government of Madras.

Ba, A. S., and S. A. Phillips, Jr. 1995. Degradation of red imported fire ant (Hymenoptera: Formicidae) yolk spheres. *Flor. Entomol.* 78:463–66.

———. 1996. Yeast biota of the red imported fire ant. *Mycol. Res.* 100:240–51.

Baer, H., T.-Y. Liu, M. C. Anderson, M. Blum, W. H. Schmid, and F. J. James. 1979. Protein components of fire ant venom *(Solenopsis invicta). Toxicon* 17:397–405.

Bahls, P., and M. Deyrup. 1988. A habitual lurking predator of the Florida harvester ant. Pp. 547–51 in *Advances in myrmecology,* ed. J. C. Trager. New York: E. J. Brill.

Bahna, S. L., J. H. Strimas, M. A. Reed, and B. T. Butcher. 1988. Imported fire ant allergy in young children: Skin reactivity and serum IgE antibodies to venom and whole body extract. *J. Allergy Clin. Immunol.* 82:419–24.

Baker, M. F. 1958. Observations of effects of an application of heptachlor or dieldrin on wildlife. Pp. 18–21 in *Proceedings symposium: The fire ant eradication program and how it affects wildlife.* Proc. Ann. Conf. Southeastern Assoc. Game and Fish Comm.

Balas, M. T., and E. S. Adams. 1996a. The dissolution of cooperative groups: Mechanisms of queen mortality in incipient fire ant colonies. *Behav. Ecol. Sociobiol.* 38:391–99.

———. 1996b. Nestmate discrimination and competition in incipient colonies of fire ants. *Animal Behav.* 51:49–59.

———. 1997. Intraspecific usurpation of incipient fire ant colonies. *Behav. Ecol.* 8:99–103.

Ball, D. E., J. T. Mirenda, A. A. Sorensen, and S. B. Vinson. 1983. Instrumental insemination of the fire ant, *Solenopsis invicta. Entomol. Exp. Appl.* 33:195–202.

Ball, D. E., and S. B. Vinson. 1983. Mating in the fire ant, *Solenopsis invicta:* Evidence that alates mate only once. *J. Georgia Entomol. Soc.* 18:287–91.

———. 1984. Anatomy and histology of the male reproductive system of the fire ant, *Solenopsis invicta* Buren (Hymenoptera: Formicidae). *Int. J. Insect Morphol. Embryol.* 13:283–94.

Ball, D. E., H. J. Williams, and S. B. Vinson. 1984. Chemical analysis of the male aedeagal bladder in the fire ant, *Solenopsis invicta* Buren. *J. New York Entomol. Soc.* 92:365–70.

Banks, W. A. 1986a. Insect growth regulators for control of the imported fire ant. Pp. 387–98 in *Fire ants and leaf-cutting ants: Biology and management,* ed. C. S. Lofgren and R. K. Vander Meer. Westview studies in insect biology. Boulder, Colo.: Westview Press.

———. 1986b. Control of imported fire ants with new insect growth regulator and fluorocarbon baits. Pp. 76–82 in *Proceedings of the 1986 imported fire ant conference,* comp. M. E. Mispagel. Athens, Ga.: Texas Department of Agriculture and Veterinary Medical Experiment Station, University of Georgia.

———. 1990. Chemical control of the imported fire ants. Pp. 596–603 in *Applied myrmecology: A world perspective,* ed. R. K. Vander Meer, K. Jaffe, and A. Cedeno. Westview studies in insect biology. Boulder, Colo.: Westview Press.

Banks, W. A., C. T. Adams, and C. S. Lofgren. 1991. Damage to young citrus trees by the red imported fire ant (Hymenoptera: Formicidae). *J. Econ. Entomol.* 84:241–46.

Banks, W. A., H. L. Collins, D. F. Williams, C. E. Stringer, C. S. Lofgren, D. P. Harlan, and C. L. Mangum. 1981. Field trials with AC-217,300 a new amidinohydrazone bait toxicant for control of the red imported fire ant. *Southwest. Entomol.* 6:158–64.

Banks, W. A., B. M. Glancey, C. E. Stringer, D. P. Jouvenaz, C. S. Lofgren, and D. E. Weidhaas. 1973a. Imported fire ants: Eradication trials with mirex bait. *J. Econ. Entomol.* 66:785–89.

Banks, W. A., and D. P. Harlan. 1982. Tests with the insect growth regulator CIBA-GEIGY CGA-38531 against laboratory and field colonies of red imported fire ants *(Solenopsis invicta). J. Georgia Entomol. Soc.* 17:460–66.

Banks, W. A., D. P. Harlan, and C. F. Stringer. 1982. Effectiveness of emulsion and controlled-release granules of chlorpyrifos and isofenphos on red imported fire ants *(Solenopsis invicta)* in cultivated fields. *J. Georgia Entomol. Soc.* 17:259–65.

Banks, W. A., D. M. Hicks, J. K. Plumley, D. P. Jouvenaz, D. P. Wojcik, and C. S. Lofgren. 1976. Imported fire ants: 10-5, an alternate formulation of mirex bait. *J. Econ. Entomol.* 69:465–67.

Banks, W. A., D. P. Jouvenaz, C. S. Lofgren, and D. M. Hicks. 1973b. Evaluation of coatings for corncob grit–soybean oil bait used to control imported fire ants. *J. Econ. Entomol.* 66:241–44.

Banks, W. A., and C. S. Lofgren. 1991. Effectiveness of the insect growth regulator pyriproxyfen against the red imported fire ant (Hymenoptera: Formicidae). *J. Entomol. Sci.* 26:331–38.

Banks, W. A., C. S. Lofgren, D. P. Jouvenaz, D. P. Wojcik, and J. W. Summerlin. 1973c. An improved mirex bait formulation for control of imported fire ants. *Environ. Entomol.* 2:182–85.

Banks, W. A., C. S. Lofgren, and J. K. Plumley. 1978. Red imported fire ants: Effects of insect growth regulators on caste formation and colony growth and survival. *J. Econ. Entomol.* 71:75–78.

Banks, W. A., C. S. Lofgren, and C. E. Stringer, Jr. 1964. Laboratory evaluation of certain chlorinated hydrocarbon insecticides against the imported fire ant. *J. Econ. Entomol.* 57:298–99.

Banks, W. A., G. P. Markin, J. W. Summerlin, and C. S. Lofgren. 1972. Four mirex bait formulations for control of the red imported fire ant. *J. Econ. Entomol.* 65:1468–70.

Banks, W. A., J. K. Plumley, and D. M. Hicks. 1973d. Polygyny in a colony of the fire ant *Solenopsis geminata. Ann. Entomol. Soc. Amer.* 66:234–35.

Banks, W. A., C. E. Stringer, Jr., W. F. Barthel, and C. S. Lofgren. 1966. Control of imported fire ants with nonachlor. *J. Econ. Entomol.* 59:465–67.

Banks, W. A., C. E. Stringer, and N. W. Price. 1971. Effect of toxicant concentration and rate of application of mirex bait on control of the imported fire ant, *Solenopsis saevissima richteri* (Hymenoptera: Formicidae). *J. Georgia Entomol. Soc.* 6:205–207.

Banks, W. A., and D. F. Williams. 1989. Competitive displacement of *Paratrechina longicornis* (Latreille) (Hymenoptera: Formicidae) from baits by fire ants in Mato Grosso, Brazil. *J. Entomol. Sci.* 24:381–91.

Banks, W. A., D. F. Williams, and C. S. Lofgren. 1988. Effectiveness of fenoxycarb for control of red imported fire ants (Hymenoptera: Formicidae). *J. Econ. Entomol.* 81:83–87.

Barber, G. W. 1933. On the probable reason for the scarcity of the Southern corn stalk borer (*Diatraea crambidoides* Grote) in Southeastern Georgia. *J. Econ. Entomol.* 26:1174.

Barker, J. F. 1978. Neuroendocrine regulation of oocyte maturation in the imported fire ant *Solenopsis invicta. Gen. Comp. Endocr.* 35:234–37.

Barlin, M. R., M. S. Blum, and J. M. Brand. 1976. Fire ant trail pheromones: Analysis of species specificity after gas chromatographic fractionation. *J. Insect Physiol.* 22:839–44.

Baroni Urbani, C. 1995. Invasion and extinction in the West Indian ant fauna revised: The example of *Pheidole* (amber collection Stuttgart: Hymenoptera, Formicidae. VIII: Myrmicinae, partim). *Stuttgarter Beitr. Naturkunde* B, 222:1–29.

Baroni Urbani, C., and P. B. Kannowski. 1974. Patterns in the red imported fire ant settlement of a Louisiana pasture: Some demographic parameters, interspecific competition and food sharing. *Environ. Entomol.* 3:755–60.

Barré, N., H. Mauléon, G. E. Garris, and A. Kermarrec. 1991. Predators of the tick *Amblyomma variegatum* (Acari: Ixodidae) in Guadeloupe, French West Indies. *Exp. Appl. Acarol.* 12:163–70.

Bartlett, F. J., and C. S. Lofgren. 1961. Field studies with baits against *Solenopsis saevissima* v. *richteri*, the imported fire ant. *J. Econ. Entomol.* 54:70–73.

———. 1964. Control of a native fire ant, *Solenopsis geminata*, with mirex bait. *J. Econ. Entomol.* 57:602.

Bass, J. A., and S. B. Hays. 1976a. Geographic location and identification of fire ant species in South Carolina. *J. Georgia Entomol. Soc.* 11:34–36.

———. 1976b. Predation by the mite, *Tyrophagus putrescentiae* on eggs of the imported fire ant. *J. Georgia Entomol. Soc.* 11:16.

———. 1979. Nuptial flights of the imported fire ant in South Carolina. *J. Georgia Entomol. Soc.* 14:158–61.

Beattie, A. J., and N. Lyons. 1975. Seed dispersal in *Viola* (Violaceae): Adaptations and strategies. *Amer. J. Bot.* 62:714–22.

Beatty, R. G. 1973. *The DDT myth: Triumph of the amateurs.* New York: John Day Co.

Beckham, R. D., S. L. Bilimoria, and D. P. Bartell. 1982. A survey for microorganisms associated with ants in western Texas. *Southwest. Entomol.* 7:225–29.

Bernasconi, G., and L. Keller. 1996. Reproductive conflicts in cooperative associations of fire ant queens *(Solenopsis invicta). Proc. Royal Soc. London B,* 263:509–13.

———. 1998. Phenotype and individual investment in cooperative foundress associations of the fire ant, *Solenopsis invicta. Behav. Ecol.* 9:478–85.

———. 1999. Effect of queen phenotype and social environment on early queen mortality in incipient colonies of the fire ant, *Solenopsis invicta. Animal Behav.* 57:371–77.

Bernasconi, G., M. J. B. Krieger, and L. Keller. 1997. Unequal partitioning of reproduction and investment between cooperating queens in the fire ant, *Solenopsis invicta,* as revealed by microsatellites. *Proc. Royal Soc. London B,* 264:1331–36.

Bernstein, R. 1979. Schedules of foraging activity in species of ants. *J. Anim. Ecol.* 48:921–30.

Bessin, R. T., and T. E. Reagan. 1993. Cultivar resistance and arthropod predation of sugarcane borer (Lepidoptera: Pyralidae) affects incidence of deadhearts in Louisiana sugarcane. *J. Econ. Entomol.* 86:929–32.

Bhatkar, A. P. 1979. Trophallactic appeasement in ants from distant colonies. *Folia Entomol. Mex.* no. 41:135–43.

———. 1982. Manipulation of ants in Maya-type raised fields in Mexico. P. 65 in *The biology of social insects,* ed. M. D. Breed, C. D. Michener, and H. E. Evans. Boulder, Colo.: Westview Press.

———. 1985. Movement of marked ants between the fire ant colonies in a Texas pasture habitat. P. 16 in *Proceedings of the 1986 imported fire ant conference,* comp. M. E. Mispagel. Athens, Ga.: Texas Department of Agriculture and Veterinary Medical Experiment Station, University of Georgia.

———. 1988. Confrontation behavior between *Solenopsis invicta* and *S. geminata,* and competitiveness of certain Florida ant species against *S. invicta.* Pp. 445–64 in *Advances in myrmecology,* ed. J. C. Trager. New York: E. J. Brill.

———. 1990. Reproductive strategies of the fire ant. Pp. 138–49 in *Applied myrmecology: A world perspective,* ed. R. K. Vander Meer, K. Jaffe, and A. Cedeno. Westview studies in insect biology. Boulder, Colo.: Westview Press.

Bhatkar, A., W. H. Whitcomb, W. F. Buren, P. Callahan, and T. Carlysle. 1972. Confrontation behavior between *Lasius neoniger* (Hymenoptera: Formicidae) and the imported fire ant. *Environ. Entomol.* 1:274–79.

Bigley, W. S., and S. B. Vinson. 1975. Characterization of a brood pheromone isolated from the sexual brood of the imported fire ant, *Solenopsis invicta. Ann. Entomol. Soc. Amer.* 68:301–304.

———. 1979. Degradation of [^{14}C]methoprene in the imported fire ant, *Solenopsis invicta. Pestic. Biochem. Physiol.* 10:1–13.

Billen, J. 1990. A survey of the glandular system of fire ants. Pp. 85–94 in *Applied myrmecology: A world perspective,* ed. R. K. Vander Meer, K. Jaffe, and A. Cedeno. Westview studies in insect biology. Boulder, Colo.: Westview Press.

Blackshear, S. D., and J. V. Richerson. 1999. Ant diet of the Texas horned lizard *(Phrynosoma cornutum)* from the Chihuahuan Desert. *Texas J. Sci.* 51:147–52.

Blake, G. H., Jr., W. G. Eden, and K. L. Hays. 1959. Residual effectiveness of chlorinated hydrocarbons for control of the imported fire ant. *J. Econ. Entomol.* 52:1–3.

Blanchard, E. E. 1958. Un nuevo Eriosomátido argentino con clave de especies afines. *Acta Zool. Lilloana* 15:155–59.

Blom, P. E., and W. H. Clark. 1980. Observations of ants (Hymenoptera: Formicidae) visiting extrafloral nectaries of the barrel cactus, *Ferocactus gracilis* Gates (Cactaceae), in Baja California, Mexico. *Southwest. Nat.* 25:181–96.

Blum, M. S., J. M. Brand, R. M. Duffield, and R. R. Snelling. 1973. Chemistry of the venom of *Solenopsis aurea* (Hymenoptera: Formicidae). *Ann. Entomol. Soc. Amer.* 66:702–703.

Blum, M. S., R. Foottit, and H. M. Fales. 1992. Defensive chemistry and function of the anal exudate of the thrips *(Haplothrips leucanthemi). Comp. Pharmacol. Toxicol.* 102:209–11.

Blum, M. S., T. H. Jones, H. A. Lloyd, H. M. Lloyd, R. R. Snelling, Y. Lubin, and J. Torres. 1985. Poison gland products of *Solenopsis* and *Monomorium* species. *J. Entomol. Sci.* 20:254–57.

Blum, M. S., J. E. Roberts, Jr., and A. F. Novak. 1961. Chemical and biological characterization of venom of the ant *Solenopsis xyloni* McCook. *Psyche* 68:73–74.

Blum, M. S., J. R. Walker, P. S. Callahan, and A. F. Novak. 1958. Chemical, insecticidal, and antibiotic properties of fire ant venom. *Science* 128:306–307.

Blum, M. S., J. B. Wallace, R. M. Duffield, J. M. Brand, H. M. Fales, and E. A. Sokoloski. 1978. Chrysomelidial in the defensive secretion of the leaf beetle *Gastrophysa cyanea. J. Chem. Ecol.* 4:47–53.

Bohart, R. M., and A. S. Menke. 1976. *Sphecid wasps of the world.* Berkeley: University of California Press.

Bolton, B. 1987. A review of the *Solenopsis* genus-group and revision of Afrotropical *Monomorium* Mayr (Hymenoptera: Formicidae). *Bull. Brit. Mus. (Nat. Hist.) Entomol. Ser.* 54(3).

———. 1994. *Identification guide to the ant genera of the world.* Cambridge, Mass.: Harvard University Press.

———. 1995. *A new general catalogue of the ants of the world.* Cambridge, Mass.: Harvard University Press.

Boock, O. J., and L. G. E. Lordello. 1952. Formiga "lava-pé," praga da batatinha, *Solanum tuberosum* L *Rev. Agric.* (Piracicaba, Brasil) 27:377–79.

Bookhout, C. G. 1972. Effects of mirex on the larval development of two crabs. *Water Air Soil Pollut.* 1:165–80.

Borgmeier, T. 1926. Phorideos myrmecophilos da Argentina. *Boll. Mus. Nac.* (Rio de Janeiro) 2:1–33.

———. 1931. Sobre alguns Phorideos que parasitam a Sáuva e outras formigas cortadeiras (Diptera, Phoridae). *Arch. Inst. Biol. Defesa Agric. e Animal* 4:209–28.

Borror, D. J., C. A. Triplehorn, and N. F. Johnson. 1989. *An introduction to the study of insects.* 6th ed. Forth Worth, Tex.: Harcourt Brace Jovanovich College Publishers.

Borror, D. J., and R. E. White. 1970. *A field guide to the insects of America north of Mexico.* Boston: Houghton Mifflin.

Borthwick, P. W., G. H. Cook, and J. M. Patrick, Jr. 1974. Mirex residues in selected estuaries of South Carolina: June 1972. *Pestic. Monit. J.* 7:144–45.

Borthwick, P. W., T. W. Duke, A. J. Wilson, Jr., J. I. Lowe, J. M. Patrick, Jr., and J. C. Oberheu. 1973. Accumulation and movement of mirex in selected estuaries of South Carolina, 1969–71. *Pestic. Monit. J.* 7:6–26.

Boudreaux, J., K. Strawn, and G. Kallas. 1958. Fire ants, heptachlor, and fish kill. *Southwest. Nat.* 3:7–12.

Brand, J. M., M. S. Blum, and M. R. Berlin. 1973. Fire ant venoms: Intraspecific and interspecific variation among castes and individuals. *Toxicon* 11:325–31.

Brand, J. M., M. S. Blum, H. M. Fales, and J. G. MacConnell. 1972. Fire ant venoms: Comparative analyses of alkaloidal components. *Toxicon* 10:259–71.

Braulick, L. S., J. C. Cokendolpher, and W. P. Morrison. 1988. Effect of acute exposure to relative humidity and temperature on four species of fire ants (*Solenopsis:* Formicidae: Hymenoptera). *Tex. J. Sci.* 40:331–40.

Breene, R. G., W. L. Sterling, and D. A. Dean. 1988. Spider and ant predators of the cotton fleahopper on woolly cotton. *Southwest. Entomol.* 13:177–84.

———. 1989. Predators of the cotton fleahopper on cotton. *Southwest Ent.* 14:159–66.

Brenner, S. A., S. R. Lillibridge, D. Perrotta, and E. K. Noji. 1994. Fire-related mortality in floods: A newly discovered threat from fire ants. *Amer. Entomol.* 40:147.

Briano, J. A., L. A. Calcaterra, D. P. Wojcik, D. F. Williams, W. A. Banks, and R. S. Patterson. 1997. Abundance of the parasitic ant *Solenopsis daguerrei* (Hymenoptera: Formicidae) in South America, a potential candidate for the biological control of the red imported fire ant in the United States. *Environ. Entomol.* 26:1143–48.

Briano, J., D. Jouvenaz, D. Wojcik, H. Cordo, and R. Patterson. 1995d. Protozoan and fungal diseases in *Solenopsis richteri* and *S. quinquecuspis* (Hymenoptera: Formicidae) in Buenos Aires Province, Argentina. *Flor. Entomol.* 78:531–37.

Briano, J. A., R. S. Patterson, J. J. Becnel, and H. A. Cordo. 1996. The black imported fire ant, *Solenopsis richteri*, infected with *Thelohania solenopsae:* Intracolonial prevalence of infection and evidence for transovarial transmission. *J. Invert. Pathol.* 67:178–79.

Briano, J. A., R. S. Patterson, and H. A. Cordo. 1995a. Long-term studies of the black imported fire ant (Hymenoptera: Formicidae) infected with a microsporidium. *Environ. Entomol.* 24:1328–32.

———. 1995b. Colony movement of the black imported fire ant (Hymenoptera: Formicidae) in Argentina. *Environ. Entomol.* 24:1131–34.

———. 1995c. Relationship between colony size of *Solenopsis richteri* (Hymenoptera: Formicidae) and infection with *Thelohania solenopsae* (Microsporida: Thelohaniidae) in Argentina. *J. Econ. Entomol.* 88:1233–37.

Briano, J. A., and D. F. Williams. 1997. Effect of the microsporidium *Thelohania solenopsae* (Microsporida: Thelohaniidae) on the longevity and survival of *Solenopsis richteri* (Hymenoptera: Formicidae) in the laboratory. *Flor. Entomol.* 80:366–76.

Briggs, J. C. 1995. *Global biogeography.* New York: Elsevier.

Brill, J. H., and W. Bertsch. 1985. A novel micro-technique for the analysis of the cuticular hydrocarbons of insects. *Insect Biochem.* 15:49–53.

———. 1990. Comparison of cuticular hydrocarbon profiles of fire ants *Solenopsis richteri* from the same colony, using capillary column gas chromatography with pattern recognition. *J. Chromatogr.* 517:95–102.

Brinkley, C. K., R. T. Ervin, and W. L. Sterling. 1991. Potential beneficial impact of red imported fire ant to Texas cotton production. *Biol. Agric. Hortic.* 8:145–52.

Brody, R., and J. B. Turk. 1999. Allergic disorders. Pp. 174–80 in *Essentials of Otolaryngology,* ed. F. E. Lucente and G. Har-El. 4th ed. Philadelphia, Pa.: Lippincott Williams and Wilkins.

Broome, J. R., M. F. Callaham, A. L. Lewis, C. M. Ladner, and J. R. Heitz. 1975. The effects of rose bengal on the imported fire ant, *Solenopsis richteri* (Forel). *Comp. Biochem. Physiol. C Comp. Pharmacol.* 51:117–22.

Broome, J. R., P. P. Sikorowski, and B. R. Norment. 1976. A mechanism of pathogenicity of *Beauveria bassiana* on larvae of the imported fire ant, *Solenopsis richteri. J. Invert. Pathol.* 28:87–91.

Brown, B. V., and L. W. Morrison. 1999. New *Pseudacteon* (Diptera: Phoridae) from North America that parasitizes the native fire ant *Solenopsis geminata* (Hymenoptera: Formicidae). *Ann. Entomol. Soc. Amer.* 92:308–11.

Brown, W. L., Jr. 1988. Data on malpighian tubule numbers in ants (Hymenoptera: Formicidae). Pp. 17–27 in *Advances in myrmecology*, ed. J. C. Trager. New York: E. J. Brill.

Bruce, W. A., and G. L. Lecato. 1980. *Pyemotes tritici:* A potential new agent for biological control of the red imported fire ant, *Solenopsis invicta* (Acari: Pyemotidae). *Int. J. Acarol.* 6:271–74.

Bruch, C. 1926a. Orugas mirmecófilas de *Hameris epulus signatus* Stichel. *Rev. Soc. Entomol. Argentina* 1:2–9.

———. 1926b. Nuevos histéridos ecitófilos (Col.). *Rev. Museo La Plata* 29: 23, + 2 plates.

———. 1930. Notas preliminares acerca de *Labauchena daguerrei* Santschi. *Rev. Soc. Entomol. Argentina* 3:73–80.

Brues, C. T. 1901. Two new myrmecophilous genera of aberrant Phoridae from Texas. *Amer. Nat.* 35:337–56.

———. 1902. New and little-known guests of the Texan legionary ants. *Amer. Nat.* 36:365–78.

Buckley, S. B. 1867. Descriptions of new species of North American Formicidae. *Proc. Entomol. Soc. Phil.* 6:335–50.

Bugg, R. L., and C. Waddington. 1993. Managing cover crops to manage arthropod pests of orchards. Sustainable agriculture: University of California Sustainable Agriculture Research and Education Program. [Internet, 1997]

Burch, J. B. 1962. *How to know the eastern land snails.* Dubuque, Iowa: Wm. C. Brown Co.

Buren, W. F. 1972. Revisionary studies on the taxonomy of the imported fire ants. *J. Georgia Entomol. Soc.* 7:1–26.

———. 1983. Artificial faunal replacement for imported fire ant control. *Florida Entomol.* 66:93–100.

Buren, W. F., G. E. Allen, W. H. Whitcomb, F. E. Lennartz, and R. N. Williams. 1974. Zoogeography of the imported fire ants. *J. New York Entomol. Soc.* 82:113–24.

Burnham, K. D., R. S. Baldridge, R. E. Duhrkopf, and D. S. Vodopich. 1994. Laboratory study of predation by *Solenopsis invicta* (Hymenoptera: Formicidae) on eggs of *Aedes albopictus* (Diptera: Culicidae). *J. Med. Entomol.* 31:770–71.

Burns, E. C., and D. G. Melancon. 1977. Effect of imported fire ant (Hymenoptera: Formicidae) invasion on lone star tick (Acarina: Ixodidae) populations. *J. Med. Entomol.* 14:247–49.

Buschman, L. L., W. H. Whitcomb, R. C. Hemenway, D. L. Mays, N. Ru, N. C. Leppla, and B. J. Smittle. 1977. Predators of velvetbean caterpillar eggs in Florida soybeans. *Environ. Entomol.* 6:403–407.

Butcher, B. T., R. D. deShazo, A. A. Ortiz, and M. A. Reed. 1988a. RAST-inhibition studies of the imported fire ant *Solenopsis invicta* with whole body extracts and venom preparations. *J. Allergy Clin. Immunol.* 81:1096–1100.

———. 1988b. Superiority of *Solenopsis invicta* venom to whole-body extract in RAST for diagnosis of imported fire ant allergy. *Int. Arch. Allergy Appl. Immunol.* 85:458–61.

Butcher, B. T., and M. A. Reed. 1988a. Crossed immunoelectrophoretic studies of whole body extracts and venom from the imported fire ant *Solenopsis invicta*. *J. Allergy Clin. Immunol.* 81:33–40.

———. 1988b. Evaluation of commercial imported fire ant extracts by crossed immunoelectrophoresis and radioallergosorbent test. *J. Allergy Clin. Immunol.* 82:770–77.

Butler, J. F., M. L. Camino, and T. O. Perez. 1979. *Boophilus microplus* and the fire ant *Solenopsis geminata. Recent Advances in Acarology* 1:469–72.

Byron, D. W., and S. B. Hays. 1986. Occurrence and significance of multiple mound utilization by colonies of the red imported fire ant *[Solenopsis invicta]. J. Econ. Entomol.* 79:637–40.

Calabi, P., and S. D. Porter. 1989. Worker longevity in the fire ant *Solenopsis invicta:* Ergonomic considerations of correlations between temperature, size and metabolic rates. *J. Insect Physiol.* 35:643–50.

Calcaterra, L. A., J. A. Briano, and D. F. Williams. 1999. Field studies of the parasitic ant *Solenopsis daguerrei* (Hymenoptera: Formicidae) on fire ants in Argentina. *Environ. Entomol.* 28:88–95.

California Department of Food and Agriculture. 1998. News Releases. (1) Red imported fire ant infestation discovered in Orange County, (2) Red imported fire ant update. www.cdfa.ca.gov.

Callahan, P. S. 1971. Far infrared stimulation of insects with the Glagolewa-Arkadiewa "mass radiator." *Florida Entomol.* 54:201–204.

Callahan, P. S., M. S. Blum, and J. R. Walker. 1959. Morphology and histology of the poison glands and sting of the imported fire ant (*Solenopsis saevissima* v. *richteri* Forel). *Ann. Entomol. Soc. Amer.* 52:573–90.

Callcott, A. M. A., and H. L. Collins. 1996. Invasion and range expansion of imported fire ants (Hymenoptera: Formicidae) in North America from 1918–1995. *Florida Entomol.* 79:240–51.

Calvert, W. H. 1996. Fire ant predation on monarch larvae (Nymphalidae: Danainae) in a Central Texas prairie. *J. Lepid. Soc.* 50:149–51.

Camilo, G. R., and S. A. Philips, Jr. 1990. Evolution of ant communities in response to invasion by the fire ant *Solenopsis invicta*. Pp. 190–98 in *Applied myrmecology: A world perspective*, ed. R. K. Vander Meer, K. Jaffe, and A. Cedeno. Westview studies in insect biology. Boulder, Colo.: Westview Press.

Campbell, J. F., and H. K. Kaya. 1999. How and why a parasitic nematode jumps. *Nature* 397:485–86.

Cañas, L. A., and R. J. O'Neil. 1998. Application of sugar solutions to maize, and the impact of natural enemies on Fall Armyworm. *Int. J. Pest Manag.* 44:59–64.

Candiotti, K. A., and A. M. Lamas. 1993. Adverse neurologic reactions to the sting of the imported fire ant. *Int. Arch. Allergy Immunol.* 102:417–20.

Carlin, N. F. 1988. Species, kin and other forms of recognition in the brood discrimination behavior of ants. Pp. 267–95 in *Advances in myrmecology*, ed. J. C. Trager. New York: E. J. Brill.

Carmichael, J. W., W. B. Kendrick, I. L. Connors, and L. Sigler. 1980. *Genera of Hyphomycetes*. Edmonton: University of Alberta Press.

Caro, M. R., V. J. Derbes, and R. Jung. 1957. Skin responses to the sting of the imported fire ant (*Solenopsis saevissima*). *A.M.A. Archives of Dermatology* 75:475–88.

Carroll, C. R., and S. J. Risch. 1983. Tropical annual cropping systems: Ant ecology. *Environ. Man.* 7:51–57.

———. 1984. The dynamics of seed harvesting in early successional communities by a tropical ant, *Solenopsis geminata*. *Oecologia* 61:388–92.

Carson, R. 1962. *Silent spring*. Boston: Houghton Mifflin.

Cassill, D. L., and W. R. Tschinkel. 1995. Allocation of liquid food to larvae via trophallaxis in colonies of the fire ant, *Solenopsis invicta*. *Animal Behav.* 50:801–13.

———. 1996. A duration constant for worker-to-larva trophallaxis in fire ants. *Insectes Sociaux* 43:149–66.

———. 1999a. Task selection by workers of the fire ant *Solenopsis invicta*. *Behav. Ecol. Sociobiol.* 45:301–10.

———. 1999b. Regulation of diet in the fire ant, *Solenopsis invicta*. *J. Insect Behav.* 12:307–28.

———. 1999c. Effects of colony-level attributes on larval feeding in the fire ant, *Solenopsis invicta*. *Insectes Sociaux* 46:261–66.

Chambers, J. E., W. T. Redwood, and C. A. Trevathan. 1983. Disposition and metabolism of [14C] chlorpyrifos in the black imported fire ant, *Solenopsis richteri* Forel. *Pestic. Biochem. Physiol.* 19:115–21.

Chang, V. C. S., and A. K. Ota. 1976. Fire ant damage to polyethylene tubing used in drip irrigation systems. *J. Econ. Entomol.* 69:447–50.

———. 1990. Ant control in Hawaiian drip irrigation systems. Pp. 708–15 in *Applied myrmecology: A world perspective*, ed. R. K. Vander Meer, K. Jaffe, and A. Cedeno. Westview studies in insect biology. Boulder, Colo.: Westview Press.

Chang, V. C. S., A. K. Ota, and D. Sanders. 1980. Parallel ridge barrier to control ant damage to orifices of drip irrigation tubes. *J. Econ. Entomol.* 73:403–406.

Chauvin, R. 1970. *The world of ants: A science-fiction universe.* New York : Hill and Wang.

Chen, J., G. Henderson, C. C. Grimm, S. W. Lloyd, and R. A. Laine. 1998. Termites fumigate their nests with naphthalene. *Nature* 392:558–59.

Chen, Y. P., and S. B. Vinson. 1999. Queen attractiveness to workers in the polygynous form of the ant *Solenopsis invicta* (Hymenoptera: Formicidae). *Ann. Entomol. Soc. Am.* 92:578–86.

Cheng, E. Y., L. K. Cutkomp, and R. B. Koch. 1977. Effect of an imported fire ant venom component on respiration and oxidative phosphorylation of mitochondria. *Biochem. Pharmacol.* 26: 1179–80.

Cherix, D., and D. J. C. Fletcher. 1982. The eggs of founding queens of the imported fire ant. P. 249 in *The biology of social insects*, ed. M. D. Breed, C. D. Michener, and H. E. Evans. Boulder, Colo.: Westview Press.

Cherry, R. H., and G. S. Nuessly. 1992. Distribution and abundance of imported fire ants (Hymenoptera: Formicidae) in Florida sugarcane fields. *Environ. Entomol.* 21:767–70.

Childers, C. C. 1994. Biological control of phytophagous mites on Florida citrus utilizing predatory arthropods. Pp. 255–88 in *Pest management in the subtropics: Biological control—a Florida perspective*, ed. D. Rosen, F. D. Bennett, and J. L. Capinera. Andover, U.K.: Intercept Limited.

Choe, J. C. 1988. Worker reproduction and social evolution in ants (Hymenoptera: Formicidae). Pp. 163–87 in *Advances in myrmecology*, ed. J. C. Trager. New York: E. J. Brill.

Cintra, R. 1985. Birth of the young Paraguayan caiman *(Caiman yacare)* (Crocodylia: Alligatoridae) under seminatural conditions in the Brazilian swamp of Mato Grosso. *Pap. Avulsos Zool.* (Saõ Paulo) 36:91–101.

Ciomperlik, M. A., J. M. Chandler, and C. J. DeLoach. 1992. Predation by red imported fire ant on *Tyta luctosa*, released for control of field bindweed. *Southwest. Entomol.* 17:267–69.

Claborn, D. M., S. A. Phillips, Jr., and H. G. Thorvilson. 1988. Diel foraging activity of *Solenopsis invicta* and two native species of ants (Hymenoptera: Formicidae) in Texas. *Tex. J. Sci.* 40:93–99.

Clark, B. R., and S. H. Faeth. 1997. The consequences of larval aggregation in the butterfly *Chlosyne lacinia. Ecol. Entomol.* 22:408–15.

Clarke, S. R., and G. L. Debarr. 1996. Impacts of red imported fire ants (Hymenoptera: Formicidae) on striped pine scale (Homoptera: Coccidae) populations. *J. Entomol. Sci.* 31:229–39.

Cleare, L. D. 1928. Notes on an outbreak of yellow sugar-cane aphis. *Agric. J. British Guiana* 1: 149–54.

Cokendolpher, J. C., and O. F. Francke. 1983. Gynandromorphic desert fire ant, *Solenopsis aurea* Wheeler (Hymenoptera: Formicidae). *J. New York Entomol. Soc.* 91:242–45.

———. 1985. Temperature preferences of four species of fire ants (Hymenoptera: Formicidae: *Solenopsis*). *Psyche* 92:91–101.

Cokendolpher, J. C., and S. A. Phillips, Jr. 1990. Critical thermal limits and locomotor activity of the red imported fire ant (Hymenoptera: Formicidae). *Environ. Entomol.* 19:878–81.

Cole, A. C., Jr. 1934. An ecological study of the ants of the southern desert shrub region of the United States. *Ann. Entomol. Soc. Amer.* 34:388–405.

Collingwood, C. A., B. J. Tigar, and D. Agosti. 1997. Introduced ants in the United Arab Emirates. *J. Arid Environ.* 37:505–12.

Collins, H. 1986. Development of IFA quarantine treatments for nursery stock. Pp. 57–69 in *Proceedings of the 1986 imported fire ant conference,* comp. M. E. Mispagel. Athens, Ga.: Texas Department of Agriculture and Veterinary Medical Experiment Station, University of Georgia.

———. 1992. Control of imported fire ants: A review of current knowledge. USDA APHIS Tech. Bull. no. 1807.

Collins, H. L., and A. A. Callcott. 1995. Effectiveness of spot insecticide treatments for red imported fire ant (Hymenoptera: Formicidae) control. *J. Entomol. Sci.* 30:489–96.

Collins, H. L., A. Callcott, T. C. Lockley, and A. Ladner. 1992. Seasonal trends in effectiveness of hydramethylnon (Amdro) and fenoxycarb (Logic) for control of red imported fire ants (Hymenoptera: Formicidae). *J. Econ. Entomol.* 85:2131–37.

Collins, H. L., and G. P. Markin. 1971. Inquilines and other arthropods collected from nests of the imported fire ant, *Solenopsis saevissima richteri. Ann. Entomol. Soc. Amer.* 64:1376–80.

Combs, R. L., Jr. 1982. The black imported fire ant *(Solenopsis richteri)* a predator of the face fly *(Musca autumnalis)* in northeast Mississippi, USA. *J. Georgia Entomol. Soc.* 17:496–501.

Conners, J. S. 1998a. Testudines: *Chelydra serpentina* (Common Snapping Turtle). Predation. *Herp. Rev.* 29:235.

———. 1998b. Serpentes: *Opheodrys aestivus* (Rough Green Snake). Egg Predation. *Herp. Rev.* 29:243.

Conniff, R. 1990. You never know what the fire ant is going to do next. *Smithsonian,* July, 48–57.

———. 1997. How I stuck my "hand" in a fire ant mound for television and glory. *Smithsonian,* January, 108.

Contreras, C., and A. Labay. 1999. Rainbow trout kills induced by fire ant ingestion. *Texas J. Sci.* 51:199–200.

Cook, J. L. 1996. *A study of the relationship between* Caenocholax fenyesi Pierce *(Strepsiptera, Myrmecolacidae) and the red imported fire ant,* Solenopsis invicta Buren *(Hymenoptera, Formicidae).* Ph.D. dissertation, Texas A&M University, College Station.

Cook, J. L., J. S. Johnston, R. E. Gold, and S. B. Vinson. 1997. Distribution of *Caenocholax fenyesi* (Strepsiptera: Myrmecolacidae) and the habitats most likely to contain its stylopized host, *Solenopsis invicta* (Hymenoptera: Formicidae). *Environ. Entomol.* 26:1258–62.

Copeland, L. 1997. Fire ants fanning out north, west. *Seattle Times,* October 9.

Coquillett, D. W. 1907. A new phorid genus with horny ovipositor. *Can. Entomol.* 39:207–208.

Cox, G. W., J. N. Mills, and B. A. Ellis. 1992. Fire ants (Hymenoptera: Formicidae) as major agents of landscape development. *Environ. Entomol.* 21:281–86.

Crance, J. H. 1964. Fish kills in Alabama ponds after swarms of the imported fire ant. *Progressive Fish-culturist* 27:91–94.

Creighton, J. C., and G. D. Schnell. 1998. Short-term movement patterns of the endangered American burying beetle *Nicrophorus americanus. Biol. Conserv.* 86:281–87.

Creighton, W. S. 1930. The New World species of the genus *Solenopsis* (Hymenop. Formicidae). *Proc. Amer. Acad. Arts Sci.* 66:39–151.

———. 1950. *The ants of North America.* Bull. Mus. Comp. Zool. Harv. Coll., vol. 104.

Crespo, M. B., L. Serra, and A. Juan. 1998. *Solenopsis* (Lobeliaceae): A genus endemic in the Mediterranean region. *Plant Sys. Evol.* 210:211–29.

Crespo, M. B., L. Serra, and N. Turland. 1996. Lectotypification of four names in *Lobelia* (Lobeliaceae). *Taxon* 45:117–20.

Crozier, R. H. 1970. Karyotypes of twenty-one ant species (Hymenoptera: Formicidae), with reviews of the known ant karyotypes. *Can. J. Gen. Cytol.* 12:109–28.

Crozier, R. H., and P. Pamilo. 1996. *Evolution of social insect colonies.* Oxford: Oxford University Press.

Cupp, E. W., and J. O'Neal. 1973. The morphogenetic effects of two juvenile hormone analogues on larvae of imported fire ants. *Environ. Entomol.* 2:191–94.

Cupp, E. W., J. O'Neal, G. Kearney, and G. P. Markin. 1973. Forced copulation of imported fire ant reproductives. *Ann. Entomol. Soc. Amer.* 66:743–45.

Daehler, C. C., and D. R. Gordon. 1997. To introduce or not to introduce: Trade-offs of non-indigenous organisms. *TREE* 12:424–25.

Dallas Morning News. 1999. Scaling down: Malaria suspected in horned toads' decline.

Darwin, C. 1859. *On the origin of species by means of natural selection.* London, U.K.: John Murray (first edition facsimile, 1987, Birmingham, Ala.: Gryphon Editions, Inc.).

David, R. M., and J. R. Heitz. 1978. Toxicity of an imported fire ant bait based on phloxin B (D + C Red 27). *J. Agric. Food Chem.* 26:99–101.

Davidson, D. W. 1977. Species diversity and community organization in desert seed-eating ants. *Ecology* 58:711–24.

Davidson, N. A., and N. D. Stone. 1989. Imported fire ants. Pp. 196–217 in *Eradication of exotic pests*, ed. D. L. Dahlsten and R. Garcia. New Haven, Conn.: Yale University Press.

Davis, W. L., R. G. Jones, and G. R. Farmer. 1989. Insect hemolymph factor promotes muscle histolysis in *Solenopsis. Anat. Rec.* 224:473–78.

Davis-Carter, J. G., and D. C. Sheppard. 1993. Redistribution of metals and nutrients by fire ants in a flue dust contaminated pasture. *Soil Biol. Biochem.* 25:747–50.

DeHeer, C. J., M. A. D. Goodisman, and K. G. Ross. 1999. Queen dispersal strategies in the multiple-queen form of the fire ant *Solenopsis invicta. Amer. Nat.* 153:660–75.

DeHeer, C. J., and K. G. Ross. 1997. Lack of detectable nepotism in multiple-queen colonies of the fire ant *Solenopsis invicta* (Hymenoptera: Formicidae). *Behav. Ecol. Sociobiol.* 40:27–33.

DeHeer, C. J., and W. R. Tschinkel. 1998. The success of alternative reproductive tactics in mono-gyne populations of the ant *Solenopsis invicta:* Significance for transitions in social organization. *Behav. Ecol.* 9:130–35.

Delabie, J. H. C., and H. G. Fowler. 1995. Soil and litter cryptic ant assemblages of Bahian cocoa plantations. *Pedobiologia* 39:423–33.

deShazo, R. D., and W. A. Banks. 1994. Medical consequences of multiple fire ant stings occurring indoors. *J. Allergy Clin. Immunol.* 93:847–50.

deShazo, R. D., B. T. Butcher, and W. A. Banks. 1990. Reactions to the stings of the imported fire ant. *New Eng. J. Med.* 323:462–46.

deShazo, R. D., C. Griffing, T. H. Kwan, W. A. Banks, and H. F. Dvorak. 1984. Dermal hypersensitivity reactions to imported fire ants. *J. Allergy Clin. Immunol.* 74:841–47.

Detroit Free Press. July 10, 1997. Fire ants attacked! (web page).

Dhandapandi, N., S. Jayaraj, and R. J. Rabindra. 1994. Activity of ants on cotton plants sprayed with nuclear polyhedrosis virus and adjuvants against *Heliothis armigera* (Hübner). *J. Entomol. Res.* 18:65–68.

Dickinson, V. M. 1995. Red imported fire ant predation on Crested Caracara nestlings in South Texas. *Wilson Bull.* 107:761–62.

Dickinson, V. M., and K. A. Arnold. 1996. Breeding biology of the Crested Caracara in South Texas. *Wilson Bull.* 108:516–23.

Diffie, S., and M. H. Bass. 1994. Densities of monogynous red imported fire ant (Hymenoptera: Formicidae) colonies in Georgia pastures. *J. Entomol. Sci.* 29:367–69.

Diffie, S., M. H. Bass, and K. Bondari. 1997. Winter survival of *Solenopsis invicta* and the *Solenopsis* hybrid (Hymenoptera: Formicidae) in Georgia. *J. Agric. Entomol.* 14:93–101.

Diffie, S. K., and D. C. Sheppard. 1989. Supercooling studies on the imported fire ants: *Solenopsis in-*

victa and *Solenopsis richteri* (Hymenoptera: Formicidae) and their hybrid. *J. Entomol. Sci.* 24:361–64.

Diffie, S., R. K. Vander Meer, and M. H. Bass. 1988. Discovery of hybrid fire ant populations in Georgia and Alabama. *J. Entomol. Sci.* 23:187–91.

Disney, R. H. L. 1994. *Scuttle flies: The Phoridae.* New York : Chapman and Hall.

Donaldson, W., A. H. Price, and J. Morse. 1994. The current status and future prospects of the Texas horned lizard *(Phrynosoma cornutum)* in Texas. *Tex. J. Sci.* 46:97–113.

Dorough, H. W., and G. W. Ivie. 1974. Fate of mirex-^{14}C during and after a 28-day feeding period to a lactating cow. *Envir. Entomol.* 3:65–67.

Drees, B. M. 1994. Red imported fire ant predation on nestlings of colonial waterbirds. *Southwest. Entomol.* 19:355–59.

———. 1995. Red imported fire ant multiple stinging incidents to humans indoors in Texas. *Southwest. Entomol.* 20:383–85.

———. 1998. Fire ant trails: News from the Texas Imported Fire Ant Research & Management Plan 1(1):1–2.

Drees, B. M., C. L. Barr, and S. B. Vinson. 1992a. Effects of spot treatments of Logic® (fenoxycarb) on polygynous red imported fire ants: An introduction of resource sharing? *Southwest. Entomol.* 17:313–17.

Drees, B. M., C. L. Barr, S. B. Vinson, R. E. Gold, M. E. Merchant, and D. Kostroun. 1996. Managing red imported fire ants in urban areas. Publication 15M-9-96 (revised). Texas Agric. Ext. Serv.

Drees, B. M., L. A. Berger, R. Cavazos, and S. B. Vinson. 1991. Factors affecting sorghum and corn seed predation by foraging red imported fire ants (Hymenoptera: Formicidae). *J. Econ. Entomol.* 84:285–89.

Drees, B. M., R. Cavazos, L. A. Berger, and S. B. Vinson. 1992b. Impact of seed-protecting insecticides on sorghum and corn seed feeding by red imported fire ants (Hymenoptera: Formicidae). *J. Econ. Entomol.* 85:993–97.

Drees, B. M., R. W. Miller, S. B. Vinson, and R. Georgis. 1992c. Susceptibility and behavioral response of red imported fire ant (Hymenoptera: Formicidae) to selected entomogenous nematodes (Rhabditida: Steinernematidae & Heterorhabditidae). *J. Econ. Entomol.* 85:365–70.

Drees, B. M., and S. B. Vinson. 1990. Comparison of the control of monogynous and polygynous forms of the red imported fire ant (Hymenoptera: Formicidae) with a chlorpyrifos mound drench. *J. Entomol. Sci.* 25:317–24.

Dubois, B. R., and M. B. Dubois. 1994. Colony founding by queens of *Solenopsis molesta* (Hymenoptera: Formicidae). *Entomol. News* 105:61–68.

DuBois, M. B. 1979. New records of ants in Kansas. *Tech. Publ. State Biol. Surv. Kans.* 8:47–55.

DuBois, M. B., and W. E. LaBerge. 1988. Annotated list of ants in Illinois (Hymenoptera: Formicidae). Pp. 133–56 in *Advances in myrmecology,* ed. J. C. Trager. New York: E. J. Brill.

Dunton, R., S. B. Vinson, and J. S. Johnston. 1991. Unique isozyme electromorphs in polygynous red imported fire ant populations. *Biochem. Syst. Ecol.* 19:453–60.

Duplantier, J. A., and J. J. Bernard. 1998. Fatal anaphylaxis due to fire ant stings. *Am. J. Forensic Med. & Path.* 19:137–42.

Dutcher, J. D., P. M. Estes, and M. J. Dutcher. 1999. Interactions in entomology: Aphids, aphidophaga, and ants in pecan orchards. *J. Entomol. Sci.* 34:40–56.

Dutcher, J. D., and D. C. Sheppard. 1981. Predation of pecan weevil *(Curculio caryae)* larvae by red imported fire ants *(Solenopsis invicta). J. Georgia Entomol. Soc.* 16:210–13.

Eagleson, C. 1940. Fire ants causing damage to telephone equipment. *J. Econ. Entomol.* 33:700.

Eden, W. G., and F. S. Arant. 1949. Control of the imported fire ant in Alabama. *J. Econ. Entomol.* 42:976–79.

Eisenberg, R. M. 1972. Partition of space among colonies of the fire ant, *Solenopsis saevissima.* I. Spatial arrangement. *Tex. J. Sci.* 24:39–43.

Ellis, M. H., R. S. Jacobson, and D. R. Hoffman. 1992. Allergy to *Solenopsis aurea*, an uncommon native fire ant. *J. Allergy Clin. Immunol.* 89:293.

Ellsbury, M. M., and F. M. Davis. 1982. Front-mounted motor cycle net for mass collection of clover insects. *J. Econ. Entomol.* 75:251–53.

Elsey, K. D. 1980. Pickleworm: Mortality on cucumbers in the field. *Environ. Entomol.* 9:806–809.

Elton, C. S. 1958. *The ecology of invasions by animals and plants.* London: Methuen.

Elvin, M. K., J. L. Stimac, and W. H. Whitcomb. 1983. Estimating rates of arthropod predation on velvetbean caterpillar *[Anticarsia gemmatalis]* larvae in soybeans. *Florida Entomol.* 66: 319–30.

Elzen, G. W. 1986. Oxygen consumption and water loss in the imported fire ant *Solenopsis invicta* Buren. *Comp. Biochem. Physiol. A Comp. Physiol.* 84:13–18.

Emery, C. 1921. Fam. Formicidae, Subfam. Myrmicinae. Wytsman's *Genera Insectorum* (Brussels, Belgium: V. Vertenevil and L. Desmet; Fascicule). 174.

Ervin, R. T., and W. T. Tennant, Jr. 1990. Red imported fire ants' *(Solenopsis invicta)* impact on Texas outdoor recreation. Pp. 504–10 in *Applied myrmecology: A world perspective,* ed. R. K. Vander Meer, K. Jaffe, and A. Cedeno. Westview studies in insect biology. Boulder, Colo.: Westview Press.

Erwin, T. 1981. A synopsis of the immature stages of Pseudomorphini (Coleoptera: Carabidae) with notes on tribal affinities and behavior in relation to life with ants. *Coleop. Bull.* 35:53–68.

Escala, M., and N. X. de Enrech. 1991. Morphoanatomical study of myrmecochoral seeds on a semiarid Venezuelan ecosystem. ORSIS 6:45–60.

Escoubas, P., and M. S. Blum. 1990. The biological activities of ant-derived alkaloids. Pp. 482–89 in *Applied myrmecology: A world perspective,* ed. R. K. Vander Meer, K. Jaffe, and A. Cedeno. Westview studies in insect biology. Boulder, Colo.: Westview Press.

Eskafi, F. M., and M. M. Kolbe. 1990. Predators on larval and pupal *Ceratitis capitata* (Diptera: Tephritidae) by the ant *Solenopsis geminata* (Hymenoptera: Formicidae) and other predators in Guatemala. *Environ. Entomol.* 19:148–53.

Esquivel, D. M. S., D. Acosta-Avalos, L. J. El-Jaick, A. D. M. Cunha, M. G. Malheiros, and E. Wajnberg. 1999. Evidence for magnetic material in the fire ant *Solenopsis* sp. by electron paramagnetic resonance measurements. *Naturwissenschaften* 86:30–32.

Essig, E. O. 1926. *Insects of western North America.* New York: Macmillan.

Ettershank, G. 1966. A generic revision of the world Myrmicinae related to *Solenopsis* and *Pheidologeton* (Hymenoptera: Formicidae). *Austral. J. Zool.* 14:73–171.

Extoxnet: Extension Toxicology Network. 1993. A pesticide information project of cooperative extension offices. Oregon State University, Corvallis, Ore.

Fabricius, J. C. 1804. *Systema Piezatorum.* Reprint edition 1974, Graz, Austria: Akademische Druck–Verlagsanstalt.

Fall, H. C. 1928. *Alaudes. Pan-Pacific Entomol.* 4:145–50.

Farry, S. C., S. E. Henke, S. L. Beasom, and M. G. Fearneyhough. 1998. Efficacy of bait distributional strategies to deliver canine rabies vaccines to coyotes in southern Texas. *J. Wildl. Dis.* 34:23–32.

Favorite, F. G. 1958. The imported fire ant. *Publ. Health Repts.* 73:445–48.

Federal Code of Regulations (section 301). 1999.

Feener, D. H., Jr. 1986. Alarm-recruitment behavior in *Pheidole militicida* (Hymenoptera: Formicidae). *Ecol. Entomol.* 11:67–74.

———. 1987a. Size-selective oviposition in *Pseudacteon crawfordi* (Diptera: Phoridae), a parasite of fire ants. *Ann. Entomol. Soc. Amer.* 80:148–51.

———. 1987b. Response of *Pheidole morrisi* to two species of enemy ants, and a general model of defense behavior in *Pheidole* (Hymenoptera: Formicidae). *J. Kansas Entomol. Soc.* 60:569–75.

Feener, D. H., Jr., and B. V. Brown. 1992. Reduced foraging of *Solenopsis geminata* (Hymenoptera: Formicidae) in the presence of parasitic *Pseudacteon* spp. (Diptera: Phoridae). *Ann. Entomol. Soc. Amer.* 85:80–84.

Feger, T. A., W. K. Dolen, J. L. Ford, R. D. Ponder, and D. R. Hoffman. 1995. Laboratory evaluation of a commercial immunoassay for fire ant allergen-specific IgE antibodies. *J. Allergy Clin. Immunol.* 96:182–87.

Ferguson, D. E. 1962. Fish feeding on imported fire ants. *J. Wildlife Man.* 26:206–207.

Ferguson, J. S., A. J. Hosmer, and M. E. Green. 1996. Rate of removal of fenoxycarb (Logic) fire ant bait by red imported fire ants (Hymenoptera: Formicidae) from treated pastures. *J. Entomol. Sci.* 31:20–32.

Ferris, D. K., M. J. Killion, K. P. Ferris, W. E. Grant, and S. B. Vinson. 1998. Influence of relative abundance of red imported fire ants *(Solenopsis invicta)* on small mammal captures. *Southwest. Nat.* 43:97–100.

Fincher, G. T., and H. O. Lund. 1967. Notes on the biology of the imported fire ant, *Solenopsis saevissima richteri* Forel (Hymenoptera: Formicidae) in Georgia. *J. Georgia Entomol. Soc.* 2:91–94.

Fisher, T. H., W. E. McHenry, E. G. Alley, C. S. Lofgren, and D. F. Williams. 1983. Some phosphorothionate imported fire ant toxicants with delayed kill. *J. Agric. Food Chem.* 31:730–33.

Fleetwood, S. C., P. D. Teel, and G. Thompson. 1984. Impact of imported fire ant on lone star tick mortality in open and canopied pasture habitats of east central Texas. *Southwest. Entomol.* 9:158–63.

Fletcher, D. J. C. 1983. Three newly-discovered polygynous populations of the fire ant, *Solenopsis invicta*, and their significance. *J. Georgia Entomol. Soc.* 18:538–43.

———. 1986. Perspectives on some queen pheromones of social insects with special reference to the fire ant, *Solenopsis invicta*. Pp. 184–91 in *Fire ants and leaf-cutting ants: Biology and management*, ed. C. S. Lofgren and R. K. Vander Meer. Westview studies in insect biology. Boulder, Colo.: Westview Press.

Fletcher, D. J. C., and M. S. Blum. 1981a. Pheromonal control of dealation and oogenesis in virgin queen fire ants. *Science* 212:73–75.

———. 1981b. A bioassay technique for an inhibitory primer pheromone of the fire ant, *Solenopsis invicta* Buren. *J. Georgia Entomol. Soc.* 16:352–56.

———. 1983a. Regulation of queen number by workers in colonies of social insects. *Science* 219:312–14.

———. 1983b. The inhibitory pheromone of queen fire ants *[Solenopsis invicta]*: Effects of disinhibition on dealation and oviposition by virgin queens. *J. Comp. Physiol. A Sens. Neural Behav. Physiol.* 153:467–76.

Fletcher, D. J. C., M. S. Blum, T. V. Whitt, and N. Temple. 1980. Monogyny and polygyny in the fire ant, *Solenopsis invicta*. *Ann. Entomol. Soc. Amer.* 73:658–61.

Fletcher, D. J. C., D. Cherix, and M. S. Blum. 1983. Some factors influencing dealation by virgin queen fire ants. *Insectes Sociaux* 30:443–54.

Fletcher, T. B. 1914. *Some south Indian insects and other animals of importance.* Dehra Dun, India: Bishen Singh Mahendra Pal Singh.

Fluker, S. S., and J. W. Beardsley. 1970. Sympatric associations of three ants: *Iridomyrmex humilis, Pheidole megacephala,* and *Anoplolepis longipes* in Hawaii. *Ann. Entomol. Soc. Amer.* 63:1290–96.

Folgarait, P. J., and L. E. Gilbert. 1999. Phorid parasitoids affect foraging activity of *Solenopsis richteri* under different availability of food in Argentina. *Ecol. Entomol.* 24:163–73.

Fontenla Rizo, J. L. 1993. Composición y estructura de comunidades de hormigas en un sistema de formaciones vegetales costeras. *Poeyana* no. 441:1–19.

Fontenla Rizo, J. L., and L. M. Hernandez. 1993. Relaciones de coexistencia en comunidades de hormiga en un agroecosistema de caña de azúcar. *Poeyana* no. 438:1–16.

Ford, J. H., J. C. Hawthorne, and G. P. Markin. 1973. Residues of mirex and certain other chlorinated hydrocarbon insecticides in beef fat, 1971. *Pestic. Monit. J.* 7:87–94.

Forel, A. 1893. Formicides de l'Antille St. Vincent. *Trans. Entomol. Soc. London.* 41:333–418.

Fowler, H. G. 1984. Recruitment, group retrieval and major worker behavior in *Pheidole oxyops* (Hymenoptera: Formicidae). *Rev. Brasil. Biol.* 44:21–24.

———. 1993. Experimental incipient nest transplants and survivorship of *Solenopsis invicta* Buren (Hymenoptera: Formicidae) in Brazil. *J. Appl. Entomol.* 116:212–14.

———. 1997. Morphological prediction of worker size discrimination and relative abundance of sympatric species of *Pseudacteon* (Dipt., Phoridae) parasitoids of the fire ant, *Solenopsis saevissima* (Hym., Formicidae) in Brazil. *J. Appl. Entomol.* 121:37–40.

Fowler, H. G., J. V. E. Bernardi, and L. F. T. di Romagnano. 1990. Community structure and *Solenopsis invicta* in São Paulo. Pp. 199–207 in *Applied myrmecology: A world perspective,* ed. R. K. Vander Meer, K. Jaffe, and A. Cedeno. Westview studies in insect biology. Boulder, Colo.: Westview Press.

Fowler, H. G., S. Campiolo, M. A. Pesquero, and S. D. Porter. 1995a. Notes on a southern record for *Solenopsis geminata* (Hymenoptera: Formicidae). *Iheringia,* Ser. Zool. (Porto Alegre, Brasil), no. 79:173.

Fowler, H. G., and J. H. C. Delabie. 1995. Resource partitioning among epigaeic and hypogaeic ants (Hymenoptera: Formicidae) of a Brazilian cocoa plantation. *Ecologia Austral* 5:117–24.

Fowler, H. G., M. A. Pesquero, S. Campiolo, and S. D. Porter. 1995b. Seasonal activity of species of *Pseudacteon* (Diptera: Phoridae) parasitoids of fire ants *(Solenopsis saevissima)* (Hymenoptera: Formicidae) in Brazil. *Científica* 23:367–71.

Francke, O. F. 1983. Efficacy tests of single-mound treatments for control of red imported fire ants, *Solenopsis invicta* Buren. *Southwest. Entomol.* 8:42–45.

Francke, O. F., and J. C. Cokendolpher. 1986. Temperature tolerances of the red imported fire ant. Pp. 104–13 in *Fire ants and leaf-cutting ants: Biology and management,* ed. C. S. Lofgren and R. K. Vander Meer. Westview studies in insect biology. Boulder, Colo.: Westview Press.

Francke, O. F., J. C. Cokendolpher, A. H. Horton, S. A. Phillips, Jr., and L. R. Potts. 1983. Distribution of fire ants in Texas. *Southwest. Entomol.* 8:32–41.

Francke, O. F., J. C. Cokendolpher, and L. R. Potts. 1986. Supercooling studies on North American fire ants (Hymenoptera: Formicidae). *Southwest. Nat.* 31:87–94.

Francke, O. F., L. R. Potts, and J. C. Cokendolpher. 1985. Heat tolerances of four species of fire ants (Hymenoptera: Formicidae: *Solenopsis*). *Southwest. Nat.* 30:59–68.

Frank, J. H. 1977. *Myrmecosaurus ferrugineus,* an Argentinian beetle from fire ant nests in the United States. *Florida Entomol.* 60:31–36.

Frank, W. A. 1988. Report of limited establishment of red imported fire ant, *Solenopsis invicta* Buren in Arizona. *Southwest. Entomol.* 13:307–308.

Freeman, T. M., R. Hylander, A. Ortiz, and M. E. Martin. 1992. Imported fire ant immunotherapy: Effectiveness of whole body extracts. *J. Allergy Clin. Immunol.* 90:210–15.

Fritz, G. N. 1985. A consideration of alternative intermediate hosts for *Moniezia expansa* (Cestoda: Anoplocephalidae). *Proc. Helminth. Soc. Wash.* 52:80–84.

Fuentes, J. E., S. Herrera, and R. G. Medel. 1996. Preliminary observations on resource use and activity temperature in harvester ant assemblages in northern Chile. *Acta Ent. Chilena* 20:13–17.

Fuller, B. W., S. B. Hays, and D. Stanley. 1984. Relocation of red imported fire ant *[Solenopsis invicta]* colonies. *J. Agric. Entomol.* 1:185–90.

Fuller, B. W., T. E. Reagan, J. L. Flynn, and M. A. Boetel. 1997. Predation on fall armyworm (Lepidoptera: Noctuidae) in sweet sorghum. *J. Agric. Entomol.* 14:151–55.

Gehring, W. J. 1998. *Master control genes in development and evolution: The homeobox story.* New Haven, Conn.: Yale University Press.

George, J. L. 1958. *The program to eradicate the imported fire ant.* New York: Conservation Foundation.

George, R. P., and T. C. Narendran. 1987. Ecology of *Solenopsis geminata* Fabr., a dominant species of ants in Malabar [India]. *Geobios* 14:200–204.

Georgia House of Representatives. 1998. HR 842—Red imported fire ant; urge federal govt increase funds to eradicate. www.doas.state.ga.us.

Gilbert, L. E. 1996. Prospects of controlling fire ants with parasitoid flies: The perspective from research based at Brackenridge Field Laboratory. www.utexas.edu.

———. 1997. Ecology and conservation biology of common species in Texas: Behavioral and community interaction of phorid flies and fire ants. lgilbert@mail.utexas.edu.

Gilbert, L. E., and L. W. Morrison. 1997. Patterns of host specificity in *Pseudacteon* parasitoid flies (Diptera: Phoridae) that attack *Solenopsis* fire ants (Hymenoptera: Formicidae). *Environ. Entomol.* 26:1149–54.

Gillespie, J. H. 1998. *Population genetics: A concise guide.* Baltimore, Md.: Johns Hopkins University Press.

Giuliano, W. M., C. R. Allen, R. S. Lutz, and S. Demarais. 1996. Effects of red imported fire ants on northern bobwhite chicks. *J. Wildlife Man.* 60:309–13.

Glancey, B. M. 1986a. The queen recognition pheromone of *Solenopsis invicta.* Pp. 223–30 in *Fire ants and leaf-cutting ants: Biology and management,* ed. C. S. Lofgren and R. K. Vander Meer. Westview studies in insect biology. Boulder, Colo.: Westview Press.

———. 1986b. Research highlights for 1985. Pp. 17–28 in *Proceedings of the 1986 imported fire ant conference,* comp. M. E. Mispagel. Athens, Ga.: Texas Department of Agriculture and Veterinary Medical Experiment Station, University of Georgia.

Glancey, B. M., and W. A. Banks. 1988. Effect of the insect growth regulator fenoxycarb on the ovaries of queens of the red imported fire ant (Hymenoptera: Formicidae). *Ann. Entomol. Soc. Amer.* 81:642–48.

Glancey, B. M., W. A. Banks, and M. S. Obin. 1989a. The effect of fenoxycarb on alates of the red imported fire ant. *J. Entomol. Sci.* 24:290–97.

Glancey, B. M., C. H. Craig, C. E. Stringer, and P. M. Bishop. 1973c. Multiple fertile queens in colonies of the imported fire ant, *Solenopsis invicta. J. Georgia Entomol. Soc.* 8:237–38.

Glancey, B. M., and J. C. Dickens. 1988. Behavioral and electrophysiological studies with live larvae and larval rinses of the red imported fire ant, *Solenopsis invicta* Buren (Hymenoptera: Formicidae). *J. Chem. Ecol.* 14:463–74.

Glancey, B. M., and C. S. Lofgren. 1985. Spermatozoon counts in males and inseminated queens of the imported fire ants, *Solenopsis invicta* and *Solenopsis richteri* (Hymenoptera: Formicidae). *Florida Entomol.* 68:162–68.

———. 1988. Adoption of newly-mated queens: A mechanism for proliferation and perpetuation of polygynous red imported fire ants, *Solenopsis invicta* Buren. *Florida Entomol.* 71:581–87.

Glancey, B. M., C. S. Lofgren, J. R. Rocca, and J. H. Tumlinson. 1983. Behavior of disrupted colonies of *Solenopsis invicta* towards queens and pheromone-treated surrogate queens placed outside the nest. *Sociobiology* 7:283–88.

Glancey, B. M., C. S. Lofgren, and D. F. Williams. 1982. Avermectin B_1a: Effects on the ovaries of red imported fire ant queens (Hymenoptera: Formicidae). *J. Med. Entomol.* 19:743–47.

Glancey, B. M., N. Reimer, and W. A. Banks. 1990. Effects of IGR fenoxycarb and Sumitomo S-31183 on the queens of two myrmicine ant species. Pp. 604–13 in *Applied myrmecology: A world perspective*, ed. R. K. Vander Meer, K. Jaffe, and A. Cedeno. Westview studies in insect biology. Boulder, Colo.: Westview Press.

Glancey, B. M., J. Rocca, C. S. Lofgren, and J. Tumlinson. 1984a. Field tests with synthetic components of the queen recognition pheromone of the red imported fire ant, *Solenopsis invicta*. *Sociobiology* 9:19–30.

Glancey, B. M., C. E. Stringer, and P. M. Bishop. 1973a. Trophic egg production in the imported fire ant *Solenopsis invicta. J. Georgia Entomol. Soc.* 8:217–20.

Glancey, B. M., C. E. Stringer, C. H. Craig, and P. M. Bishop. 1975. An extraordinary case of polygyny in the red imported fire ant. *Ann. Entomol. Soc. Amer.* 68:922.

Glancey, B. M., C. E. Stringer, Jr., C. H. Craig, P. M. Bishop, and B. B. Martin. 1970a. Pheromone may induce brood tending in the fire ant *Solenopsis saevissima. Nature* 226:863–64.

———. 1973b. Evidence of a replete caste in the fire ant *Solenopsis invicta. Ann. Entomol. Soc. Amer.* 66:233–34.

Glancey, B. M., M. K. St. Romain, and R. H. Crozier. 1976c. Chromosome numbers of the red and the black imported fire ants, *Solenopsis invicta* and *S. richteri. Ann. Entomol. Soc. Amer.* 69:469–70.

Glancey, B. M., M. K. Vandenburgh, and M. K. St. Romain. 1976a. Testes degeneration in the red imported fire ant, *Solenopsis invicta. J. Georgia Entomol. Soc.* 11:83–88.

Glancey, B. M., R. K. Vander Meer, A. Glover, C. S. Lofgren, and S. B. Vinson. 1981. Filtration of microparticles from liquids ingested by the red imported fire ant *Solenopsis invicta. Insectes Sociaux* 28:395–401.

Glancey, B. M., R. K. Vander Meer, and D. P. Wojcik. 1989b. Polygyny in hybrid imported fire ants. *Florida Entomol.* 72:632–36.

Glancey, B. M., D. P. Wojcik, C. H. Craig, and J. A. Mitchell. 1976b. Ants of Mobile county, AL, as monitored by bait transects. *J. Georgia Entomol. Soc.* 11:191–97.

Glancey, M. L., W. Roberts, and J. Spence. 1970b. Honey-bee populations exposed to bait containing mirex applied for control of imported fire ants. *Am. Bee J.* 110:134.

Glasgow, L. L. 1958. Studies on the effect of the imported fire ant control program on wildlife in Louisiana. Pp. 24–29 in *Proceedings symposium: The fire ant eradication program and how it affects wildlife.* Proc. Ann. Conf. Southeastern Assoc. Game and Fish Comm.

———. 1959. Wildlife and the fire ant program. *Trans. Twenty-fourth North Amer. Wildlife Conf.*, ed. J. B. Trefethen (Washington, D.C.: Wildlife Management Institute): 142–49.

Glover, P. M. 1930. Entomological aspects of lac research in India. *Bull. Entomol. Res.* 21:261–66.

Glunn, F. J., D. F. Howard, and W. R. Tschinkel. 1981. Food preference in colonies of the fire ant, *Solenopsis invicta. Insectes Sociaux* 28:217–22.

Goetsch, W., and R. Grüger. 1942. Pilzzuchet und Pilznahrung staatenbildenden Insekten. *Biologia Generalis* (Vienna) 16:41–112.

Gonçalves, C. R. 1940. Observações sobre *Pseudococcus comstocki* (Kuw., 1902) atacando Citrus na Baixada Fluminense. *Rodriguésia* (Rio de Janeiro) 4:179–98.

Goni, B., L. C. de Zolessi, and H. T. Imai. 1983. Karyotypes of 13 ant species from Uruguay (Hymenoptera: Formicidae). *Caryologia* (Pisa, Italy) 36:363–72.

Gonzalez Perez, J. L. 1987. Ethnoecological study of some Cuban ants. I. *Cienc. Biol. Acad. Cienc. Cuba* no. 18:53–63.

Goodisman, M. A. D., P. D. Mack, D. E. Pearse, and K. G. Ross. 1999. Effects of a single gene on worker and male body mass in the fire ant *Solenopsis invicta* (Hymenoptera: Formicidae). *Ann. Entomol. Soc. Am.* 92:563–70.

Goodisman, M. A. D., and K. G. Ross. 1996. Relationship of queen number and worker size in polygyne colonies of the fire ant *Solenopsis invicta*. *Insectes Sociaux* 43:303–307.

———. 1997. Relationship of queen number and queen relatedness in multiple-queen colonies of the fire ant *Solenopsis invicta*. *Ecol. Entomol.* 22:150–57.

———. 1998. A test of queen recruitment models using nuclear and mitochondrial markers in the fire ant *Solenopsis invicta*. *Evolution* 52:1416–22.

———. 1999. Queen recruitment in a multiple-queen population of the fire ant *Solenopsis invicta*. *Behav. Ecol.* 10:428–35.

Goodisman, M. A. D., D. D. Shoemaker, and M. A. Asmussen. 1998. Cytonuclear theory for haplodiploid species and x-linked genes. II. stepping stone models of gene flow and application to a fire ant hybrid zone. *Evolution* 52:1423–40.

Gorman, J. S. T., T. H. Jones, T. F. Spande, R. R. Snelling, J. A. Torres, and H. M. Garraffo. 1998. 3-hexyl-5-methylindolizidine isomers from thief ants, *Solenopsis (Diplorhoptrum)* species. *J. Chem. Ecol.* 24:933–43.

Gorsuch, C. S., and R. E. McWhorter. 1997a [date of printout]. Evaluation of AWARD bait formulations for control of red imported fire ants on commercial turfgrass. Cooperative Agriculture Pest Survey & NAPIS' webpage on Imported Fire Ant.

———. 1997b [date of printout]. Efficacy of the entomopathogenic nematode #355 on red imported fire ant, *Solenopsis invicta*, infesting turfgrass. Cooperative Agriculture Pest Survey & NAPIS' webpage on Imported Fire Ant.

Gravena, S., and W. L. Sterling. 1983. Natural predation on the cotton leafworm *[Alabama argillacea]* (Lepidoptera: Noctuidae). *J. Econ. Entomol.* 76:779–84.

Green, H. B. 1952. Biology and control of the imported fire ant in Mississippi. *J. Econ. Entomol.* 45:593–97.

———. 1959. Imported fire ant mortality due to cold. *J. Econ. Entomol.* 52:347.

———. 1962. On the biology of the imported fire ant. *J. Econ. Entomol.* 55:1003–1004.

———. 1967. The imported fire ant in Mississippi. Bull. 737. Miss. State University Agric. Exp. Sta.

Green, H. B., and R. E. Hutchins. 1960. Laboratory study of toxicity of imported fire ants to bluegill fish. *J. Econ. Entomol.* 53:1137–38.

Green, W. P., D. E. Pettry, and R. E. Switzer. 1998. Impact of imported fire ants on the texture and fertility of Mississippi soils. *Commun. Soil Sci. Plant Anal.* 29:447–57.

———. 1999. Impact of imported fire ants on Mississippi soils. *Tech. Bull.* 223: Miss. Agric. and Forestry Exp. Sta.

Greenberg, L., D. J. C. Fletcher, and S. B. Vinson. 1985. Differences in worker size and mound distribution in monogynous and polygynous colonies of the fire ant *Solenopsis invicta*. *J. Kansas Entomol. Soc.* 58:9–18.

Greenberg, L., and S. B. Vinson. 1986. A long-term study of a single-queen/multiple-queen transect. P. 6 in *Proceedings of the 1986 imported fire ant conference,* comp. M. E. Mispagel. Athens, Ga.: Texas Department of Agriculture and Veterinary Medical Experiment Station, University of Georgia.

Greenberg, L., S. B. Vinson, and S. Ellison. 1992. Nine year study of a field containing both monogyne and polygyne red imported fire ants (Hymenoptera: Formicidae). *Ann. Entomol. Soc. Amer.* 85:686–95.

Greenberg, L., H. J. Williams, and S. B. Vinson. 1990. A comparison of venom and hydrocarbon profiles from alates in Texas monogyne and polygyne fire ants, *Solenopsis invicta.* Pp. 95–101 in *Applied myrmecology: A world perspective,* ed. R. K. Vander Meer, K. Jaffe, and A. Cedeno. Westview studies in insect biology. Boulder, Colo.: Westview Press.

Greenblatt, J. A., J. A. Norton, R. A. Dybas, and D. P. Harlan. 1986. Control of the red imported fire ant with abamectin (Affirm), a novel insecticide in individual mound trials. *J. Agric. Entomol.* 3:233–41.

Griffitts, S. D. 1942. Ants as probable agents in the spread of *Shigella* infections. *Science* 96:271–72.

Grissell, E. E. 1975. Ethology and larva of *Pterocheilus texanus* (Hymenoptera: Eumenidae). *J. Kansas Entomol. Soc.* 48:244–53.

Gross, H. R., Jr., and W. T. Spink. 1969. Responses of striped earwigs following applications of heptachlor and mirex, and predator-prey relationships between imported fire ants and striped earwigs. *J. Econ. Entomol.* 62:686–89.

Hangartner, W. 1969a. Structure and variability of the individual odor trail in *Solenopsis geminata* Fabr. (Hymenoptera: Formicidae). *Z. Vergl. Physiol.* (Berlin) 62:111–20.

———. 1969b. Carbon dioxide, a releaser for digging behavior in *Solenopsis geminata* (Hymenoptera: Formicidae). *Psyche* 76:58–67.

Hannan, C. J., Jr., C. T. Stafford, R. B. Rhoades, B. B. Wray, H. Baer, and M. C. Anderson. 1986. Seasonal variation in antigens of the imported fire ant *Solenopsis invicta. J. Allergy Clin. Immunol.* 78:331–36.

Harlan, D. P., W. A. Banks, H. L. Collins, and C. E. Stringer. 1981. Large area tests of AC-217,300 bait for control of imported fire ants in Alabama, Louisiana, and Texas. *Southwest. Entomol.* 6:150–57.

Harris, W. G., and E. C. Burns. 1972. Predation on the lone star tick by the imported fire ant. *Environ. Entomol.* 1:362–65.

Haug, G. W. 1934. Effect of Argentine ant poison on the ant fauna of Mississippi. *Ann. Entomol. Soc. Amer.* 27:621–32.

Hays, K. L. 1958. The present status of the imported fire ant in Argentina. *J. Econ. Entomol.* 51:111–12.

———. 1959. Ecological observations on the imported fire ant, *Solenopsis saevissima richteri* Forel, in Alabama. *J. Alabama Acad. Sci.* 30:14–18.

Hays, S. B., and F. S. Arant. 1960. Insecticidal baits for control of the imported fire ant, *Solenopsis saevissima richteri. J. Econ. Entomol.* 53:188–91.

Hays, S. B., and K. L. Hays. 1959. Food habits of *Solenopsis saevissima richteri* Forel. *J. Econ. Entomol.* 52:455–57.

Hays, S. B., P. M. Horton, J. A. Bass, and D. Stanley. 1982. Colony movement of imported fire ants *(Solenopsis invicta). J. Georgia Entomol. Soc.* 17:266–74.

Helenius, J. 1998. Enhancement of predation through within-field diversification. Pp. 121–60 in *Enhancing biological control: Habitat management to promote natural enemies of agricultural pests,* ed. C. H. Pickett and R. L. Bugg. Berkeley: University of California Press.

Helmly, R. B. 1970. Anaphylactic reaction to fire ant. *Hawaii Med. J.* 29:368–69.

Heraty, J. M. 1994. Pp. 104–20 in *Exotic Ants,* ed. D. F. Williams. Boulder: Colo.: Westview Press.

Hermann, H. R., Jr., and M. S. Blum. 1965. Morphology and histology of the reproductive system of the imported fire ant queen, *Solenopsis saevissima richteri*. *Ann. Entomol. Soc. Amer.* 58:81–89.

Herzog, D. C., T. E. Reagan, D. C. Sheppard, K. M. Hyde, S. S. Nilakhe, M. Y. B. Hussein, M. L. McMahon, R. C. Thomas, and L. D. Newsom. 1976. *Solenopsis invicta* Buren: Influence on Louisiana pasture soil chemistry. *Environ. Entomol.* 5:160–62.

Hickling, R. 1998. Stridulation sounds of black fire ants *(Solenopsis richteri)* in different situations. http://home.olemiss.edu/~hickling/

Hill, D. S. 1975. *Agricultural insect pests of the tropics and their control*. Cambridge, U.K.: Cambridge University Press.

———. 1987. *Agricultural insect pests of temperate regions and their control*. Cambridge, U.K.: Cambridge University Press.

———. 1990. *Pests of stored products and their control*. Boca Raton, Fla.: CRC Press.

Hoffman, D. R. 1987. Allergens in Hymenoptera venom. XVII: Allergenic components of *Solenopsis invicta* (imported fire ant) venom. *J. Allergy Clin. Immunol.* 80:300–306.

———. 1993. Allergens in Hymenoptera venom. XXIV: The amino acid sequences of imported fire ant venom allergens Sol i II, Sol i III, and Sol i IV. *J. Allergy Clin. Immunol.* 91:71–78.

———. 1995. Fire ant venom allergy. *Allergy* 50:535–44.

———. 1997. Reactions to less common species of fire ants. *J. Allergy Clin. Immunol.* 100:679–93.

Hoffman, D. R., D. E. Dove, and R. S. Jacobson. 1988a. Allergies in Hymenoptera venom. XX: Isolation of four allergens from imported fire ant *(Solenopsis invicta)* venom. *J. Allergy Clin. Immunol.* 82:818–27.

Hoffman, D. R., D. E. Dove, J. E. Moffitt, and C. T. Stafford. 1988b. Allergies in Hymenoptera venom. XXI: Cross-reactivity and multiple reactivity between fire ant venom and bee and wasp venoms. *J. Allergy Clin. Immunol.* 82:828–34.

Hoffman, D. R., R. S. Jacobson, M. Schmidt, and A. M. Smith. 1991. Allergens in Hymenoptera venoms. XXIII: Venom content of imported fire ant whole body extracts. *Ann. Allergy* 66:29–31.

Hoffman, D. R., A. M. Smith, M. Schmidt, J. E. Moffitt, and M. Guralnick. 1990. Allergens in Hymenoptera venom. XXII: Comparisons of venoms from two species of imported fire ants, *Solenopsis invicta* and *richteri*. *J. Allergy Clin. Immunol.* 85:988–95.

Hogue, C. L. 1993. *Latin American insects and entomology*. Berkeley: University of California Press.

Hölldobler, B., and E. O. Wilson. 1990. *The ants*. Cambridge, Mass.: Harvard University Press.

———. 1994. *Journey to the ants: A story of scientific exploration*. Cambridge, Mass.: Harvard University Press.

Hölldobler, K. 1928. Zur Biologie der diebischen Zwergameise *(Solenopsis fugax)* und ihrer Gäste. *Biol. Zentralbl.* (Erlangen) 48:129–42.

Hollingshaus, J. G. 1987. Inhibition of mitochondrial electron transport by hydramethylnon: A new amidinohydrazone insecticide. *Pestic. Biochem. Physiol.* 27:61–70.

Holtcamp, W. N., W. E. Grant, and S. B. Vinson. 1997. Patch use under predation hazard: Effect of the red imported fire ant on deer mouse foraging behavior. *Ecology* 78:308–17.

Hook, A. W., and S. D. Porter. 1990. Destruction of harvester ant colonies by invading fire ants in south-central Texas (Hymenoptera: Formicidae). *Southwest Nat.* 35:477–78.

Hooper, L. M., and M. K. Rust. 1997. Food preference and patterns of foraging activity of the southern fire ant (Hymenoptera: Formicidae). *Ann. Entomol. Soc. Amer.* 90:246–53.

Horton, P. M., and S. B. Hays. 1974. Occurrence of brood stages and adult castes in field colonies of the red imported fire ant in South Carolina. *Environ. Entomol.* 3:656–58.

Horton, P. M., S. B. Hays, and J. R. Holman. 1975. Food carrying ability and recruitment time of the red imported fire ant. *J. Georgia Entomol. Soc.* 10:207–13.

Horton, P. M., J. B. Kissam, S. B. Hays, and G. W. Query. 1982. Chlorpyrifos aerosol mound injections for the control of the red imported fire ant *(Solenopsis invicta)*. *J. Georgia Entomol. Soc.* 17:478–84.

Horvitz, C. C. 1981. Analysis of how ant behaviors affect germination in a tropical myrmecochore *Calathea microcephala* (P. & E.) Koernicke (Marantaceae): Microsite selection and aril removal by neotropical ants, *Odontomachus, Pachycondyla,* and *Solenopsis* (Formicidae). *Oecologia* 51 : 47–52.

Horvitz, C. C., and D. W. Schemske. 1986. Seed dispersal of a neotropical myrmecochore: Variation in removal rates and dispersal distance. *Biotropica* (St. Louis) 18:319–23.

Horvitz, C. C., C. Turnbull, and D. J. Harvey. 1987. Biology of immature *Eurybia elvina* (Lepidoptera: Riodinidae), a myrmecophilous metalmark butterfly. *Ann. Entomol. Soc. Amer.* 80:513–19.

Howard, D. F., and W. R. Tschinkel. 1976. Aspects of necrophoric behavior in the red imported fire ant, *Solenopsis invicta. Behaviour* 56:157–80.

———. 1981a. Internal distribution of liquid foods in isolated workers of the fire ant, *Solenopsis invicta. J. Insect Physiol.* 27:67–74.

———. 1981b. The flow of food in colonies of the fire ant, *Solenopsis invicta:* A multifactorial study. *Physiol. Entomol.* 6:297–306.

Howard, F. W., and A. D. Oliver. 1979. Field observation of ants (Hymenoptera: Formicidae) associated with red imported fire ants, *Solenopsis invicta,* in Louisiana, USA pastures. *J. Georgia Entomol. Soc.* 14:259–63.

Howard, R. A., and T. A. Zanoni. 1989. Two atypical examples of seed distribution in the Dominican Republic. *Moscosoa* (Santo Domingo) 5:216–25.

Hoyt, E. 1996. *The earth dwellers: Adventures in the land of ants.* New York: Simon and Schuster.

Hu, G. Y., and J. H. Frank. 1996. Effect of the red imported fire ant (Hymenoptera: Formicidae) on dung-inhabiting arthropods in Florida. *Environ. Entomol.* 25:1290–96.

Hubbard, M. D. 1974. Influence of nest material and colony odor on digging in the ant *Solenopsis invicta* (Hymenoptera: Formicidae). *J. Georgia Entomol. Soc.* 9:127–32.

Hubbard, M. D., and W. G. Cunningham. 1977. Orientation of mounds in the ant *Solenopsis invicta* (Hymenoptera, Formicidae, Myrmicinae). *Insectes Sociaux* 24:3–7.

Huddleston, E. W., and S. S. Fluker. 1968. Distribution of ant species of Hawaii. *Proc. Hawaiian Entomol. Soc.* 20:45–69.

Hull, D. A., and A. J. Beattie. 1988. Adverse effects on pollen exposed to *Atta texana* and other North American ants: Implications for ant pollination. *Oecologia* 75:153–55.

Hung, A. C. F. 1985. Isozymes of two fire ant species and their hybrid. *Biochem. Syst. Ecol.* 13:337–40.

Hung, A. C. F., M. R. Barlin, and S. B. Vinson. 1977. *Identification, distribution, and biology of fire ants in Texas.* Publication B-1185. College Station: Texas Agricultural Experiment Station.

Hung, A. C. F., W. N. Norton, and S. B. Vinson. 1975. Gynandromorphism in the red imported fire ant, *Solenopsis invicta* Buren (Hymenoptera: Formicidae). *Entomol. News* 86:45–46.

Hung, A. C. F., and S. B. Vinson. 1975. Notes on the male reproductive system in ants (Hymenoptera: Formicidae). *J. New York Entomol. Soc.* 83:192–97.

———. 1977. Interspecific hybridization and caste specificity of protein in fire ant. *Science* 196:1458–460.

———. 1978. Factors affecting the distribution of fire ants in Texas (Myrmicinae: Formicidae). *Southwest. Nat.* 23:205–14.

Hung, A. C. F., S. B. Vinson, and J. W. Summerlin. 1974. Male sterility in the red imported fire ant, *Solenopsis invicta. Ann. Entomol. Soc. Amer.* 67:909–12.

Hunt, A. N., and H. R. Hermann. 1973. Insect envenomization: Some hematological reactions in guinea pigs to three hymenopterous venoms. *J. Georgia Entomol. Soc.* 8:249–64.

Hunter, J. E., III, and M. H. Farrier. 1976a. Mites of the genus *Oplitis* Berlese (Acarina: Uropodidae) associated with ants (Hymenoptera: Formicidae) in the southeastern United States. Part 1. *Acarologia* 17:595–624.

———. 1976b. Mites of the genus *Oplitis* Berlese (Acarina: Uropodidae) associated with ants (Hymenoptera: Formicidae) in the southeastern United States. Part 2. *Acarologia* 18:20–50.

Hunter, P. E., and M. Costa. 1971. Description of *Gymnolaelaps shealsi* n. sp. (Acarina: Mesostigmata) associated with the imported fire ant. *J. Georgia Entomol. Soc.* 6:51–53.

Huxley, J. 1943. *Evolution: The modern synthesis.* New York: Harper and Brothers.

Jaffe, K. 1986. Nestmate recognition and territorial marking in *Solenopsis geminata* and in some Attini. Pp. 211–22 in *Fire ants and leaf-cutting ants: Biology and management,* ed. C. S. Lofgren and R. K. Vander Meer. Westview studies in insect biology. Boulder, Colo.: Westview Press.

Jaffe, K., and H. Puche. 1984. Colony-specific territorial marking with the metapleural gland secretion in the ant *Solenopsis geminata* (Fabr.). *J. Insect Physiol.* 30:265–70.

Jaffe, K., G. Villegas, O. Colmenares, H. Puche, N. A. Zabala, M. I. Alvarez, J. G. Navarro, and E. Pino. 1985. Two different decision-making systems in recruitment to food in ant societies. *Behaviour* 92:9–21.

Javors, M. A., W. Zhou, J. W. Maas, Jr., S. Han, and R. W. Keenan. 1993. Effects of fire ant venom alkaloids on platelet and neutrophil function. *Life Sciences* 53:1105–12.

Jeanne, R. L. 1991. The swarm-founding Polistinae. Pp. 191–231 in *The social biology of wasps,* ed. K. G. Ross and R. W. Matthews. Ithaca, N.Y.: Cornell University Press.

Jemal, A., and M. Hugh-Jones. 1993. A review of the red imported fire ant (*Solenopsis invicta* Buren) and its impacts on plant, animal, and human health. *Prev. Veter. Med.* 17:19–32.

Jerome, C. A., D. A. McInnes, and E. S. Adams. 1998. Group defence by colony-founding queens in the fire ant *Solenopsis invicta. Behav. Ecol.* 9:301–308.

Johnson, C. 1988. Colony structure and behavioral observations in *Pheidole morrisi* (Hymenoptera: Formicidae). Pp. 371–83 in *Advances in myrmecology,* ed. J. C. Trager. New York: E. J. Brill.

Jones, D., and W. L. Sterling. 1979. Manipulation of red imported fire ants in a trap crop for boll weevil suppression. *Environ. Entomol.* 8:1073–77.

Jones, D. B., L. C. Thompson, and K. W. Davis. 1997. Use of fenoxycarb followed by acephate for spot eradication of imported fire ants. *J. Kansas Entomol. Soc.* 70:169–74.

Jones, R. G., and W. L. Davis. 1985. Leupeptin, a protease inhibitor, blocks insemination-induced flight muscle histolysis in the fire ant *Solenopsis. Tissue and Culture* 17:111–16.

Jones, R. G., W. L. Davis, A. C. F. Hung, and S. B. Vinson. 1978. Insemination-induced histolysis of the flight musculature in fire ants (*Solenopsis,* spp.): An ultrastructural study. *Amer. J. Anat.* 151:603–10.

Jones, R. G., W. L. Davis, and S. B. Vinson. 1982. A histochemical and X-ray microanalysis study of calcium changes in insect flight muscle degeneration in *Solenopsis,* the fire ant. *J. Histochem. Cytochem.* 30:293–304.

Jones, S. R., and S. A. Phillips, Jr. 1987. Aggressive and defensive propensities of *Solenopsis invicta* (Hymenoptera: Formicidae) and three indigenous ant species in Texas. *Tex. J. Sci.* 39:107–16.

———. 1989. Superiority of *Aphaenogaster occidentalis* in confrontation with *Solenopsis invicta* (Hymenoptera: Formicidae). *Entomol. News* 100:173–75.

———. 1990. Resource collecting abilities of *Solenopsis invicta* (Hymenoptera: Formicidae) compared with those of three sympatric Texas ants. *Southwest. Nat.* 35:416–22.

Jones, T. H., J. S. T. Gorman, R. R. Snelling, J. H. C. Delabie, M. S. Blum, H. M. Garraffo, P. Jain,

J. W. Daly, and T. F. Spande. 1999. Further alkaloids common to ants and frogs: Decahydroquinolines and a quinolizidine. *J. Chem. Ecol.* 25:1179–193.

Jones, T. H., R. J. Highet, M. S. Blum, and H. M. Fales. 1984. (5Z, 9Z)-3-alkyl-5-methylindolizidines from *Solenopsis (Diplorhoptrum)* species. *J. Chem. Ecol.* 10:1233–50.

Jones, T. H., J. A. Torres, T. F. Spande, H. M. Garraffo, M. S. Blum, and R. R. Snelling. 1996. Chemistry of venom alkaloids in some *Solenopsis (Diplorhoptrum)* species from Puerto Rico. *J. Chem. Ecol.* 22:1221–36.

Jouvenaz, D. P. 1986. Diseases of fire ants: Problems and opportunities. Pp. 327–38 in *Fire ants and leaf-cutting ants: Biology and management*, ed. C. S. Lofgren and R. K. Vander Meer. Westview studies in insect biology. Boulder, Colo.: Westview Press.

———. 1990. Approaches to biological control of fire ants in the United States. Pp. 620–27 in *Applied myrmecology: A world perspective*, ed. R. K. Vander Meer, K. Jaffe, and A. Cedeno. Westview studies in insect biology. Boulder, Colo.: Westview Press.

Jouvenaz, D. P., G. E. Allen, W. A. Banks, and D. P. Wojcik. 1977. A survey for pathogens of fire ants, *Solenopsis* spp., in the southeastern United States. *Florida Entomol.* 60:275–79.

Jouvenaz, D. P., and D. W. Anthony. 1979. *Mattesia geminata* sp. n. (Neogregarinida: Ophrocystidae) a parasite of the tropical fire ant, *Solenopsis geminata* (Fabricius). *J. Protozool.* 26:354–56.

Jouvenaz, D. P., W. A. Banks, and C. S. Lofgren. 1974. Fire ants: Attraction of workers to queen secretions. *Ann. Entomol. Soc. Amer.* 67:442–44.

Jouvenaz, D. P., M. S. Blum, and J. G. MacConnell. 1972. Antibacterial activity of venom alkaloids from the imported fire ant, *Solenopsis invicta* Buren. *Antimicrobial Agents and Chemotherapy* 21:291–93.

Jouvenaz, D. P., and E. A. Ellis. 1986. *Vairimorpha invictae* n. sp. (Microspora: Microsporida), a parasite of the red imported fire ant, *Solenopsis invicta* Buren (Hymenoptera: Formicidae). *J. Protozool.* 33:457–61.

Jouvenaz, D. P., and E. I. Hazard. 1978. New family, genus, and species of Microsporidia (Protozoa: Microsporida) from the tropical fire ant, *Solenopsis geminata* (Fabricius) (Insecta: Formicidae). *J. Protozool.* 25:24–29.

Jouvenaz, D. P., and J. W. Kimbrough. 1991. *Myrmecomyces annellisae* gen. nov., sp. nov. (Deuteromycotina: Hyphomycetes), an endoparasitic fungus of fire ants, *Solenopsis* spp. (Hymenoptera: Formicidae). *Mycol. Res.* 95:1395–1401.

Jouvenaz, D. P., C. S. Lofgren, and G. E. Allen. 1981. Transmission and infectivity of spores of *Burenella dimorpha* (Microsporida: Burenellidae). *J. Invert. Pathol.* 37:265–68.

Jouvenaz, D. P., J. C. Lord, and A. H. Undeen. 1996. Restricted ingestion of bacteria by fire ants. *J. Invert. Pathol.* 68:275–77.

Kaakeh, W., and J. D. Dutcher. 1992. Foraging preference of red imported fire ants (Hymenoptera: Formicidae) among three species of summer cover crops and their extracts. *J. Econ. Entomol.* 85:389–94.

Kaiser, K. L. E. 1978. The rise and fall of mirex. *Environ. Sci. Tech.* 12:520–28.

Kaspar, M., and E. L. Vargo. 1994. Nest site selection by fire ant queens. *Insectes Sociaux* 41:331–33.

———. 1995. Colony size as a buffer against seasonality: Bergmann's rule in social insects. *Amer. Nat.* 145:610–32.

Kathirithamby, J., and J. S. Johnston. 1992. Stylopization of *Solenopsis invicta* (Hymenoptera: Formicidae) by *Caenocholax fenyesi* (Strepsiptera: Myrmecolacidae) in Texas. *Ann. Entomol. Soc. Amer.* 85:293–97.

Keall, J. B. 1980. Some arthropods recently intercepted entering New Zealand in orchids from Honduras. *New Zealand Entomol.* 7:127–29.

Kearney, G. P., P. M. Toom, and G. J. Blomquist. 1977. Induction of de-alation in virgin female *Solenopsis invicta* with juvenile hormones. *Ann. Entomol. Soc. Amer.* 70:699–701.

Keller, L., and M. Genoud. 1997. Extraordinary lifespans in ants: A test of evolutionary theories of ageing. *Nature* 389:958–60.

Keller, L., and P. Nonacs. 1993. The role of queen pheromones in social insects: Queen control or queen signal? *Animal Behav.* 45:787–94.

Keller, L., and K. G. Ross. 1993a. Phenotypic basis of reproductive success in a social insect: Genetic and social determinants. *Science* 260:1107–10.

———. 1993b. Phenotypic plasticity and "cultural transmission" of alternative social organizations in the fire ant *Solenopsis invicta*. *Behav. Ecol. Sociobiol.* 33:121–29.

———. 1995. Gene by environment interaction: Effects of a single gene and social environment on reproductive phenotypes of fire ant queens. *Functional Ecol.* 9:667–76.

———. 1998. Selfish genes: A green beard in the red fire ant. *Nature* 394:573–75.

Kendall, R. J., R. Noblet, J. D. Hair, and H. B. Jackson. 1977. Mirex residues in bobwhite quail after aerial application of bait for fire ant control, South Carolina, 1975–1976. *Pestic. Monit. J.* 11: 64–68.

Khan, A. R., H. B. Green, and J. R. Brazzel. 1967. Laboratory rearing of the imported fire ant. *J. Econ. Entomol.* 60:915–17.

Kidd, K. A., and C. S. Apperson. 1984. Environmental factors affecting relative distribution of foraging red imported fire ants *[Solenopsis invicta]* in a soybean field on soil and plants. *J. Agric. Entomol.* 1:212–18.

Kidd, K. A., C. S. Apperson, and L. A. Nelson. 1985. Recruitment of the red imported fire ant, *Solenopsis invicta,* to soybean oil baits. *Florida Entomol.* 68:253–61.

Killion, M. J., and W. E. Grant. 1995. A colony-growth model for the imported fire ant: Potential geographic range of an invading species. *Ecol. Model.* 77:73–84.

Killion, M. J., W. E. Grant, and S. B. Vinson. 1995. Response of *Baiomys taylori* to changes in density of imported fire ants. *J. Mammal.* 76:141–47.

King, T. G., and S. A. Phillips, Jr. 1992. Destruction of young colonies of the red imported fire ant by the pavement ant (Hymenoptera: Formicidae). *Entomol. News* 103:72–77.

Kistner, D. H. 1982. The social insects' bestiary. Pp. 1–244 in *Social insects,* ed. H. R. Hermann. New York: Academic Press.

Klotz, J. H., J. R. Mangold, K. M. Vail, L. R. Davis, Jr., and R. S. Patterson. 1995. A survey of the urban pest ants (Hymenoptera: Formicidae) of peninsular Florida. *Florida Entomol.* 78:109–18.

Klotz, J. H., K. M. Vail, and D. F. Williams. 1997a. Toxicity of a boric acid–sucrose water bait to *Solenopsis invicta* (Hymenoptera: Formicidae). *J. Econ. Entomol.* 90:488–91.

Klotz, J. H., L. L. Van Zandt, B. L. Reid, and G. W. Bennett. 1997b. Evidence lacking for magnetic compass orientation in fire ants (Hymenoptera: Formicidae). *J. Kansas Entomol. Soc.* 70:64–65.

Knapp, J. L., J. W. Noling, L. W. Timmer, and D. P. H. Tucker. 1996. Florida citrus IPM. Pp. 317–47 in *Pest management in the subtropics: Integrated pest management—a Florida perspective,* ed. D. R. Rosen, F. D. Bennett, and J. L. Capinera. Andover, U.K.: Intercept Limited.

Knell, J. D., G. E. Allen, and E. I. Hazard. 1977. Light and electron microscope study of *Thelohania solenopsae* n. sp. (Microsporida: Protozoa) in the red imported fire ant, *Solenopsis invicta. J. Invert. Pathol.* 29:192–200.

Knight, P. 1944. Insects associated with the Palay rubber vine in Haiti. *J. Econ. Entomol.* 37:100–102.

Knight, R. L., and M. K. Rust. 1990. The urban ants of California with distribution notes of imported species. *Southwest. Entomol.* 15:167–78.

Koch, R. B., and D. Desaiah. 1974. Inhibition of *Escherichia coli* Mg^{2+}ATPase: Synergism between a fire ant *Solenopsis richteri* (Forel) abdomen factor and a photoreduction product of mirex. *Biochim. Biophys. Acta* 367:259–63.

Kochansky, J. P., W. E. Robbins, C. S. Lofgren, and D. F. Williams. 1979. Design of some delayed-action toxicants for baits to control red imported fire ants. *J. Econ. Entomol.* 72:655–58.

Korzukhin, M. D., and S. D. Porter. 1994. Spatial model of territorial competition and population dynamics in the fire ant *Solenopsis invicta* (Hymenoptera: Formicidae). *Environ. Entomol.* 23:912–22.

Kral, R. M., Jr., H.-S. Liu, S. A. Phillips, Jr., D. P. Bartell, and S. L. Bilimoria. 1986. *In vitro* maintenance of ovaries and ovarian cells from *Solenopsis invicta* (Hymenoptera: Formicidae). *J. Kansas Entomol. Soc.* 59:737–40.

Krieger, M. J. B., K. G. Ross, C. W. Y. Chang, and L. Keller. 1999. Frequency and origin of triploidy in the fire ant *Solenopsis invicta. Heredity* 82:142–50.

Krispyn, J. W., and J. W. Todd. 1982. The red imported fire ant *(Solenopsis invicta)* as a predator of the southern green stink bug *(Nezara viridula)* on soybeans in Georgia, USA. *J. Georgia Entomol. Soc.* 17:19–26.

Kundrotas, L. 1993. Sting of the fire ant *(Solenopsis). New Eng. J. Med.* 329:1317. (Color photos of ant, sting, pustules on skin.)

Laan, P. A. 1952. Epidemiology of some tobacco pests in Deli Sumatra. *Int. Cong. Ent., Trans. IXth* 1:795–99.

Lake, P. S., and D. J. O'Dowd. 1991. Red crabs in rain forest, Christmas Island: Biotic resistance to invasion by an exotic snail. *Oikos* 62:25–29.

Lakshmikantha, B. P., N. G. Lakshminarayan, T. M. Musthak Ali, and G. K. Veeresh. 1996. Fire-ant damage to potato in Bangalore. *J. Indian Potato Assoc.* 23:75–76.

Lamb, K. P. 1974. *Economic entomology in the tropics.* New York: Academic Press.

Lamon, B., and H. Topoff. 1985. Social facilitation of eclosion in the fire ant, *Solenopsis Invicta. Dev. Psychobiol.* 18:367–74.

Landry, C. E., and S. A. Phillips, Jr. 1996. Potential of ice-nucleating bacteria for management of the red imported fire ant (Hymenoptera: Formicidae). *Environ. Entomol.* 25:859–66.

Lanza, J. 1991. Response of fire ants (Formicidae: *Solenopsis invicta* and *S. geminata*) to artificial nectars with amino acids. *Ecol. Entomol.* 16:203–10.

Lanza, J., E. L. Vargo, S. Pulim, and Y. Z. Chang. 1993. Preferences of the fire ants *Solenopsis invicta* and *S. geminata* (Hymenoptera: Formicidae) for amino acid and sugar components of extrafloral nectars. *Environ. Entomol.* 22:411–17.

Larsen, K. J., F. E. Vega, G. Moya-Raygoza, and L. R. Nault. 1991. Ants (Hymenoptera: Formicidae) associated with the leafhopper *Dalbulus quinquenotatus* (Homoptera: Cicadellidae) on gamagrasses in Mexico. *Ann. Entomol. Soc. Amer.* 84:498–501.

Laskey, A. R. 1940. The 1939 nesting season of bluebirds at Nashville, Tennessee. *Wilson Bull.* 52:183–90.

Lateef, S. S., and W. Reed. 1990. Insect pests on pigeon pea. Pp. 193–242 in *Insect pests of tropical food legumes,* ed. S. R. Singh. New York: John Wiley and Sons.

Lay, D. W. 1958a. Count three for trouble. *Texas Game and Fish,* July, 4–7.

―――. 1958b. Fire ant eradication and wildlife. Pp. 22–24 in *Proceedings symposium: The fire ant eradication program and how it affects wildlife.* Proc. Ann. Conf. Southeastern Assoc. Game and Fish Comm.

Lechner, K. A., and D. O. Ribble. 1996. Behavioral interactions between red imported fire ants *(Solenopsis invicta)* and three rodent species of south Texas. *Southwest. Entomol.* 21:123–28.

Leclercq, S., J. C. Braekman, D. Daloze, J. M. Pasteels, and R. K. Vander Meer. 1996. Biosynthesis of the Solenopsins, venom alkaloids of the fire ants. *Naturwissenschaften* 83:222–25.

Leclercq, S., I. Thirionet, F. Broeders, D. Daloze, R. Vander Meer, and J. C. Braekman. 1994. Absolute configuration of the solenopsins, venom alkaloids of the fire ants. *Tetrahedron* 50:8465–78.

Lee, D. K., A. P. Bhatkar, S. B. Vinson, and J. K. Olson. 1994. Impact of foraging red imported fire ants *(Solenopsis invicta)* (Hymenoptera: Formicidae) on *Psorophora columbiae* eggs. *J. Am. Mosq. Contr. Assoc.* 10:163–73.

Lee, D. S., and M. K. Clark. 1993. Notes on post-breeding American swallow-tailed kites *Elanoides forficatus* (Falconiformes: Accipitridae), in North Central Florida. *Brimleyana* no. 19:185–203.

Lee, J. H., S. J. Johnson, and V. L. Wright. 1990. Quantitative survivorship analysis of the velvetbean caterpillar (Lepidoptera: Noctuidae) pupae in soybean fields in Louisiana. *Environ. Entomol.* 19:978–86.

Lemke, L. A., and J. B. Kissam. 1987. Evaluation of various insecticides and home remedies for control of individual red imported fire ant colonies. *J. Entomol. Sci.* 22:275–81.

———. 1988. Impact of red imported fire ant (Hymenoptera: Formicidae) predation on horn flies (Diptera: Muscidae) in a cattle pasture treated with Pro-Drone. *J. Econ. Entomol.* 81:855–58.

———. 1989. Public attitudes on red imported fire ant (Hymenoptera: Formicidae) infestations in homes and recreational areas. *J. Entomol. Sci.* 24:446–53.

Levins, R., and H. Heatwole. 1973. Biogeography of the Puerto Rican bank: Introduction of species onto Palominitos Island. *Ecology* 54:1056–64.

Levy, R., J. F. Carroll, Y. J. Chiu, and W. A. Banks. 1974a. Toxicity of chemical baits against the red imported fire ant, *Solenopsis invicta. Florida Entomol.* 57:155–59.

Levy, R., Y. J. Chiu, and W. A. Banks. 1973. Laboratory evaluation of candidate bait toxicants against the imported fire ant, *Solenopsis invicta. Florida Entomol.* 56:141–46.

Levy, R., H. L. Cromroy, and H. A. Van Rinsvelt. 1979. Comparisons in major and trace elements between adult and immature stages of 2 species of fire ants. *Florida Entomol.* 62:260–66.

Levy, R., D. P. Jouvenaz, and H. L. Cromroy. 1974b. Tolerance of three species of insects to prolonged exposures to ozone. *Environ. Entomol.* 3:1184–85.

Lewin, R. 1996. All for one, one for all. *New Scientist,* 14 December, 8–33.

Li, J., and K. M. Heinz. 1998. Genetic variation in desiccation resistance and adaptability of the red imported fire ant (Hymenoptera: Formicidae) to arid regions. *Ann. Entomol. Soc. Amer.* 91:726–29.

Lind, N. K. 1982. Mechanism of action of fire ant *(Solenopsis)* venoms. I: Lytic release of histamine from mast cells. *Toxicon* 20:831–40.

Lindquist, A. W. 1942. Ants as predators of *Cochliomyia americana* C. & P. *J. Econ. Entomol.* 35:850–52.

Lobdell, G. H. 1930. Twelve new mealybugs from Mississippi. (Homoptera: Coccoidea). *Ann. Entomol. Soc. Amer.* 23:209–36.

Lockaby, B. G., and J. C. Adams. 1985. Pedoturbation of a forest soil by fire ants *[Solenopsis invicta]. Soil Sci. Soc. Am. J.* 49:220–23.

Lockey, R. F. 1974. Systemic reactions to stinging ants. *J. Allergy Clin. Immunol.* 54:132–46.

Lockley, T. C. 1995a. Observations of predation on alate queens of the red imported fire ant (Hymenoptera: Formicidae) by the black and yellow garden spider (Araneae: Araneidae). *Florida Entomol.* 78:609–10.

———. 1995b. Effect of imported fire ant predation on a population of the least tern: An endangered species. *Southwest. Entomol.* 20:517–19.

Lockwood, J. A., and L. D. DeBrey. 1990. A solution for the sudden and unexplained extinction of the Rocky Mountain grasshoppers (Orthoptera: Acrididae). *Environ. Entomol.* 19:1194–1205.

Lockwood, J. A., and R. N. Story. 1986. Adaptive functions of nymphal aggregation in the southern green stink bug, *Nezara viridula* (L.) (Hemiptera: Pentatomidae). *Environ. Entomol.* 15:739–49.

Löding, H. P. 1929. An ant (*Solenopsis saevissima richteri* Forel). Insect pest survey bulletin no. 6 [p. 241]. Washington, D.C.: Bureau of Entomology.

Lofgren, C. S. 1962. Imported fire ant toxic bait studies: GC-1283, a promising toxicant. *J. Econ. Entomol.* 55:405–407.

———. 1986a. History of imported fire ants in the United States. Pp. 36–47 in *Fire ants and leaf-cutting ants: Biology and management*, ed. C. S. Lofgren and R. K. Vander Meer. Westview studies in insect biology. Boulder, Colo.: Westview Press.

———. 1986b. The search for chemical bait toxicants. Pp. 369–77 in *Fire ants and leaf-cutting ants: Biology and management*, ed. C. S. Lofgren and R. K. Vander Meer. Westview studies in insect biology. Boulder, Colo.: Westview Press.

———. 1986c. The economic importance and control of imported fire ants in the United States. Pp. 227–56 in *Economic impact and control of social insects*, ed. S. B. Vinson. New York: Praeger Publishers.

Lofgren, C. S., and C. T. Adams. 1982. Economic aspects of the imported fire ant in the United States. Pp. 124–29 in *The biology of social insects*, ed. M. D. Breed, C. D. Michener, and H. E. Evans. Boulder, Colo.: Westview Press.

Lofgren, C. S., V. E. Adler, W. A. Banks, and N. Pierce. 1964a. Control of imported fire ants with chlordane. *J. Econ. Entomol.* 57:331–33.

Lofgren, C. S., V. E. Adler, and W. F. Barthel. 1961a. Effect of some variations in formulation or application procedure on control of the imported fire ant with granular heptachlor. *J. Econ. Entomol.* 54:45–47.

Lofgren, C. S., W. A. Banks, and B. M. Glancey. 1975. Biology and control of imported fire ants. *Ann. Rev. of Entomol.* 20:1–30.

Lofgren, C. S., F. J. Bartlett, and C. E. Stringer. 1961b. Imported fire ant toxic bait studies: The evaluation of various food materials. *J. Econ. Entomol.* 54:1096–1100.

———. 1963. Imported fire ant toxic bait studies: Evaluation of carriers for oil baits. *J. Econ. Entomol.* 56:62–66.

———. 1964b. The acceptability of some fats and oils as food to imported fire ants. *J. Econ. Entomol.* 57:601–602.

Lofgren, C. S., F. J. Bartlett, C. E. Stringer, Jr., and W. A. Banks. 1964c. Imported fire ant bait studies: Further tests with granulated mirex-soybean oil bait. *J. Econ. Entomol.* 57:695–98.

Lofgren, C. S., B. M. Glancey, A. Glover, J. Rocca, and J. Tumlinson. 1983. Behavior of workers of *Solenopsis invicta* (Hymenoptera: Formicidae) to the queen recognition pheromone: Laboratory studies with an olfactometer and surrogate queens. *Ann. Entomol. Soc. Amer.* 76:44–50.

Lofgren, C. S., and C. E. Stringer, Jr. 1964. The effect of heptachlor and chlordane on the foraging activity of imported fire ants. *J. Econ. Entomol.* 57:235–37.

Lofgren, C. S., C. E. Stringer, Jr., F. J. Bartlett, W. A. Banks, and W. F. Barthel. 1965. Dual low dosage applications of heptachlor for control of the imported fire ant. *Florida Entomol.* 48:265–70.

Lofgren, C. S., and D. E. Weidhass. 1972. On the eradication of imported fire ants: A theoretical appraisal. *Bull. Entomol. Soc. Am.* 18:17–20.

Lofgren, C. S., and D. F. Williams. 1982. Avermectin B_1a: Highly potent inhibitor of reproduction by queens of the red imported fire ant *(Solenopsis invicta)* (Hymenoptera: Formicidae). *J. Econ. Entomol.* 75:798–803.

Lok, J. B., E. W. Cupp, and G. J. Blomquist. 1975. Cuticular lipids of the imported fire ants, *Solenopsis invicta* and *richteri. Insect Biochem.* 5:821–29.

Long, W. H., E. A. Cancienne, E. J. Concienne, R. N. Dopson, and L. D. Newsom. 1958. Fire ant eradication program increases damage by the sugarcane borer. *Sugar Bulletin* 37:62–63.

Lopez, J. D., Jr. 1982. Emergence pattern of an overwintering population of *Cardiochiles nigriceps* in Central Texas. *Environ. Entomol.* 11:838–42.

Lubin, Y. D. 1984. Changes in the native fauna of the Galápagos Islands following invasion by the little red fire ant *Wasmannia auropunctata. Biol. J. Linn. Soc.* 21:229–42.

Lucas, J. R., and H. J. Brockmann. 1981. Predatory interactions between ants and antlions (Hymenoptera: Formicidae and Neuroptera: Myrmeleontidae). *J. Kansas Entomol. Soc.* 54:228–32.

Lyle, C. 1952. Can insects be eradicated?. Pp. 197–99 in *Insects: The Yearbook of Agriculture, 1952*. Washington, D.C.: Government Printing Office.

Lyle, C., and I. Fortune. 1948. Notes on an imported fire ant. *J. Econ. Entomol.* 41:833–34.

McAlpine, J. F., B. V. Peterson, G. E. Shewell, H. J. Teskey, J. R. Vockeroth, and D. M. Wood (coordinators). 1987. *Manual of Nearctic Diptera*, vol. 2. Monograph no. 28. Research Branch Agriculture Canada.

McCluskey, E. S., and D. K. McCluskey. 1984. Hour of mating flight in three species of ants (Hymenoptera: Formicidae). *Pan-Pacific Entomol.* 60:151–54.

MacConnell, J. G., and M. S. Blum. 1970. Alkaloid from fire ant venom: Identification and synthesis. *Science* 168:840–41.

MacConnell, J. G., M. S. Blum, W. F. Buren, R. N. Williams, and H. M. Fales. 1976. Fire ant venoms: Chemotaxonomic correlations with alkaloidal compositions. *Toxicon* 14:69–78.

MacConnell, J. G., M. S. Blum, and H. M. Fales. 1971. The chemistry of fire ant venom. *Tetrahedon* 26:1129–39.

McCook, H. C. 1879. Formicariae. Pp. 182–89 in *Report upon cotton insects*, ed. J. H. Comstock. Washington, D.C.: Government Printing Office.

McDaniel, S. G., and W. L. Sterling. 1979. Predator determination and efficiency on *Heliothis virescens* eggs in cotton using ^{32}P. *Environ. Entomol.* 8:1083–87.

———. 1982. Predation of *Heliothis virescens* (F.) eggs on cotton in East Texas. *Environ. Entomol.* 11:60–66.

McDaniel, S. G., W. L. Sterling, and D. A. Dean. 1981. Predators of tobacco budworm larvae in Texas cotton. *Southwest. Entomol.* 6:102–108.

McDonald, D. 1993. Insect pest control in urban areas: Some novel approaches. *Int. Pest Control* 35:151–52.

McHenry, W. E., R. M. Stiffin, T. H. Fisher, and E. G. Alley. 1982. O,O-dialkyl-O-[p-(N-Alkylcarbamoyl)phenyl]phosphorothionate: A promising new series of toxicants for the control of imported fire ants. *J. Agric. Food Chem.* 30:1042–45.

McInnes, D. A., and W. R. Tschinkel. 1995. Queen dimorphism and reproductive strategies in the fire ant *Solenopsis geminata* (Hymenoptera: Formicidae). *Behav. Ecol. Sociobiol.* 36:367–75.

———. 1996. Mermithid nematode parasitism of *Solenopsis* ants (Hymenoptera: Formicidae) of northern Florida. *Ann. Entomol. Soc. Amer.* 89:231–37.

Mack, T. P., A. G. Appel, C. B. Backman, and P. J. Trichilo. 1988. Water relations of several arthropod predators in the peanut agroecosystem. *Environ. Entomol.* 17:778–81.

MacKay, W. P., and R. Fagerlund. 1997. Range expansion of the red imported fire ant, *Solenopsis invicta* Buren (Hymenoptera: Formicidae), into New Mexico and extreme western Texas. *Proc. Entomol. Soc. Wash.* 99:757–58.

MacKay, W. P., L. Greenberg, and B. Vinson. 1994. A comparison of bait recruitment in monogynous and polygynous forms of the red imported fire ant, *Solenopsis invicta* Buren. *J. Kansas Entomol. Soc.* 67:133–36.

MacKay, W. P., D. Lowrie, A. Fisher, E. MacKay, F. Barnes, and D. Lowrie. 1988. The ants of Los Alamos County, New Mexico (Hymenoptera: Formicidae). Pp. 79–131 in *Advances in myrmecology*, ed. J. C. Trager. New York: E. J. Brill.

MacKay, W. P., S. Majdi, J. Irving, S. B. Vinson, and C. Messer. 1992a. Attraction of ants (Hymenoptera: Formicidae) to electric fields. *J. Kansas Entomol. Soc.* 65:39–43.

MacKay, W. P., S. Porter, D. Gonzalez, A. Rodriguez, H. Armendedo, A. Rebeles, and S. B. Vinson. 1990. A comparison of monogyne and polygyne populations of the tropical fire ant, *Solenopsis geminata* (Hymenoptera: Formicidae), in Mexico. *J. Kansas Entomol. Soc.* 63:611–15.

MacKay, W. P., and S. B. Vinson. 1989a. Two new ants of the genus *Solenopsis (Diplorhoptrum)* from eastern Texas (Hymenoptera: Formicidae). *Proc. Entomol. Soc. Wash.* 91:175–78.

———. 1989b. Evaluation of the spider *Steatoda triangulosa* (Araneae: Theridiidae) as a predator of the red imported fire ant (Hymenoptera: Formicidae). *J. New York Entomol. Soc.* 97:232–33.

———. 1990. Control of the red imported fire ant *Solenopsis invicta* in electrical equipment. Pp. 614–19 in *Applied myrmecology: A world perspective*, ed. R. K. Vander Meer, K. Jaffe, and A. Cedeno. Westview studies in insect biology. Boulder, Colo.: Westview Press.

MacKay, W. P., S. B. Vinson, J. Irving, S. Majdi, and C. Messer. 1992b. Effect of electrical fields on the red imported fire ant (Hymenoptera: Formicidae). *Environ. Entomol.* 21:866–70.

McLain, D. K. 1983. Ants, extrafloral nectaries and herbivory on the passion vine, *Passiflora incarnata. Am. Midland. Nat.* 110:433–39.

Macom, T. E., and S. D. Porter. 1995. Food and energy requirements of laboratory fire ant colonies (Hymenoptera: Formicidae). *Environ. Entomol.* 24:387–91.

———. 1996. Comparison of polygyne and monogyne red imported fire ant (Hymenoptera: Formicidae) population densities. *Ann. Entomol. Soc. Amer.* 89:535–43.

Mallipudi, N. M., S. J. Stout, A. Lee, and E. J. Orloski. 1986. Photolysis of Amdro fire ant insecticide active ingredient hydramethylnon (AC 217300) in distilled water. *J. Agric. Food Chem.* 34:1050–57.

Mallis, A. 1938. The California fire ant and its control. *Pan-Pacific Entomol.* 14:87–91.

———. 1941. *A list of the ants of California with notes on their habits and distribution.* Los Angeles: Southern California Academy of Sciences.

de Manero Estela, A., and H. Vilte. 1982. Morphological study of *Rhigopsidius tucumanus* (Coleoptera: Curculionidae): A potato pest in the Quebrada de Humahuaca and Puna of the province of Jujuy, Argentina. *Rev. Agron. Noreoeste Argent.* 19:5–42.

Manley, D. G. 1981. Fire ants observed moving poison with colony. *J. Georgia Entomol. Soc.* 16:440.

———. 1982. Efficacy of Amdro bait on fire ants in South Carolina, *(Solenopsis invicta). J. Georgia Entomol. Soc.* 17:410–12.

Mann, W. M. 1916. The ants of Brazil. *Bull. Mus. Comp. Zool. Harv.* 60:399–490.

———. 1920. Additions to the ant fauna of the West Indies and Central America. *Bull. Am. Mus. Nat. Hist.* 42:403–39.

Marak, G. E., Jr., and J. J. Wolken. 1965. An action spectrum for the fire ant *(Solenopsis saevissima). Nature* 205:1328–29.

Marcus, H. 1953. Estudios mirmecologicos. *Folia Universitaria* 6:17–68.

Marikovsky, P. I. 1962. On some features of behavior of the ants *Formica rufa* L. infected with fungous disease. *Insectes Sociaux* 9:173–79.

Markin, G. P. 1981. Translocation and fate of the insecticide mirex within a bahia grass pasture ecosystem. *Environ. Pollut. Ser. A, Ecol. Biol.* 26:227–41.

Markin, G. P., H. L. Collins, and J. Davis. 1974a. Residues of the insecticide mirex in terrestrial and aquatic invertebrates following a single aerial application of mirex bait, Louisiana: 1971–72. *Pestic. Monit. J.* 8:131–34.

Markin, G. P., H. L. Collins, and J. H. Dillier. 1972. Colony founding by queens of the red imported fire ant, *Solenopsis invicta. Ann. Entomol. Soc. Amer.* 65:1053–58.

Markin, G. P., and J. H. Dillier. 1971. The seasonal life cycle of the imported fire ant, *Solenopsis saevissima richteri,* on the Gulf Coast of Mississippi. *Ann. Entomol. Soc. Amer.* 64:562–65.

Markin, G. P., J. H. Dillier, and H. L. Collins. 1973. Growth and development of colonies of the red imported fire ant, *Solenopsis invicta. Ann. Entomol. Soc. Amer.* 66:803–808.

Markin, G. P., J. H. Dillier, S. O. Hill, M. S. Blum, and H. R. Hermann. 1971. Nuptial flight and flight ranges of the imported fire ant, *Solenopsis saevissima richteri* (Hymenoptera: Formicidae). *J. Georgia Entomol. Soc.* 6:145–56.

Markin, G. P., and S. O. Hill. 1971. Microencapsulated oil bait for control of the imported fire ant. *J. Econ. Entomol.* 64:193–96.

Markin, G. P., J. O'Neal, and H. L. Collins. 1974b. Effects of mirex on the general ant fauna of a treated area in Louisiana. *Environ. Entomol.* 3:895–98.

————. 1975a. Control of the red imported fire ant with microencapsulated baits containing reduced amounts of mirex. *J. Georgia Entomol. Soc.* 10:281–84.

Markin, G. P., J. O'Neal, and J. Dillier. 1975b. Foraging tunnels of the red imported fire ant, *Solenopsis invicta* (Hymenoptera: Formicidae). *J. Kansas Entomol. Soc.* 48:83–89.

Markin, G. P., J. O'Neal, J. H. Dillier, and H. L. Collins. 1974c. Regional variation in the seasonal activity of the imported fire ant, *Solenopsis saevissima richteri. Environ. Entomol.* 3:446–52.

Martin, J. B., B. M. Drees, W. E. Grant, E. K. Pedersen, C. L. Barr, and S. B. Vinson. 1998. Foraging range of the polygynous form of the red imported fire ant, *Solenopsis invicta* Buren. *Southwest. Nat.* 23:221–28.

Matthews, R. W., R. A. Saunders, and J. R. Matthews. 1981. Nesting behavior of the sand wasp *Stictia maculata* (Hymenoptera: Sphecidae) in Costa Rica. *J. Kansas Entomol. Soc.* 54:249–54.

Maynard Smith, J., and E. Szathmáry. 1995. *The major transitions in evolution.* New York: W. H. Freeman and Co.

Mayr, E. 1963. *Animal species and evolution.* Cambridge, Mass.: Harvard University Press.

Medel, R. G., and J. E. Fuentes. 1995. Notes on the individual activity, diet, and abundance of the ants *Pogonomyrmex vermiculatus* and *Solenopsis gayi* (Hymenoptera: Formicidae) in a semiarid ecosystem on northern Chile. *Rev. Chilena Entomol.* 22:81–84.

Meier, R. E. 1994. Coexisting patterns and foraging behavior of introduced and native ants (Hymenoptera: Formicidae) in the Galápagos Islands (Ecuador). Pp. 44–62 in *Exotic ants,* ed. D. F. Williams. Boulder, Colo.: Westview Press.

Metcalf, R. L., and R. A. Metcalf. 1993. *Destructive and useful insects: Their habits and control.* 5th ed. New York: McGraw-Hill Book Company.

Mettler, L. E., T. G. Gregg, and H. E. Schaffer. 1988. *Population genetics and evolution.* 2nd ed. Englewood Cliffs, N.J.: Prentice-Hall.

Miami Herald. June 4, 1998. Texas river trout die after eating fire ants. [From www.herald.com.]

Milio, J., C. S. Lofgren, and D. F. Williams. 1988. Nuptial flight studies of field-collected colonies of *Solenopsis invicta* Buren. Pp. 419–31 in *Advances in myrmecology,* ed. J. C. Trager. New York: E. J. Brill.

Miller, N. C. E. 1971. *The biology of the Heteroptera.* 2nd ed. Hampton, U.K.: E. W. Classey Ltd.

Mirenda, J. T., D. G. Eakins, K. Gravelle, and H. Topoff. 1980. Predatory behavior and prey selection by army ants in a desert-grassland habitat. *Behav. Ecol. Sociobiol.* 7:119–27.

Mirenda, J. T., and S. B. Vinson. 1981. Division of labour and specification of castes in the red imported fire ant *Solenopsis invicta* Buren. *Animal Behav.* 29:410–20.

———. 1982. Single and multiple queen colonies of imported fire ants in Texas. *Southwest. Entomol.* 7:135–41.

Mispagel, M. E. 1986. The effect of Abamectin on female alate fertility of the red imported fire ant *(Solenopsis invicta)*. Pp. 51–55 in *Proceedings of the 1986 imported fire ant conference,* comp. M. E. Mispagel. Athens, Ga.: Texas Department of Agriculture and Veterinary Medical Experiment Station, University of Georgia.

Mitchell, G. B., and D. P. Jouvenaz. 1985. Parasitic nematode observed in the tropical fire ant, *Solenopsis geminata* (F.) (Hymenoptera: Formicidae). *Florida Entomol.* 68:492–93.

Mitchell, J. D., and W. D. Pierce. 1912. The ants of Victoria County, Texas. *Proc. Entomol. Soc. Wash.* 14:67–76.

Mitchell, M. S., R. A. Lanica, and E. J. Jones. 1996. Use of insecticide to control destructive activity of ants during trapping of small mammals. *J. Mammal.* 77:1107–13.

Moody, J. V., and O. F. Francke. 1982. *The ants (Hymenoptera: Formicidae) of western Texas, Part 1: Subfamily Myrmicinae.* Graduate Studies no. 27. Lubbock: Texas Tech Press.

Moody, J. V., O. F. Francke, and F. W. Merickel. 1981. The distribution of fire ants, *Solenopsis (Solenopsis)* in western Texas (Hymenoptera: Formicidae). *J. Kansas Entomol. Soc.* 54:469–80.

Morel, L., R. K. Vander Meer, and C. S. Lofgren. 1990. Comparison of nestmate recognition between monogyne and polygyne populations of *Solenopsis invicta* (Hymenoptera: Formicidae). *Ann. Entomol. Soc. Amer.* 83:642–47.

Mori, K., and Y. Nakazono. 1986. Synthesis of both the enantiomers of invictolide, a pheromone component of the red imported fire ant. *Tetrahedron* 42:6459–64.

Morrill, W. L. 1974a. Production and flight of alate red imported fire ants. *Environ. Entomol.* 3:265–71.

———. 1974b. Dispersal of red imported fire ants by water. *Florida Entomol.* 57:38–42.

———. 1976a. Red imported fire ant control with mound drenches. *J. Econ. Entomol.* 69:542–44.

———. 1976b. A caliper for measuring fire ant mound dimensions. *J. Georgia Entomol. Soc.* 11:346–48.

———. 1977a. Overwinter survival of the red imported fire ant in central Georgia. *Environ. Entomol.* 6:50–52.

———. 1977b. Red imported fire ant foraging in a greenhouse. *Environ. Entomol.* 6:416–18.

———. 1977c. Red imported fire ant control with diazinon and chlorpyrifos drenches. *J. Georgia Entomol. Soc.* 12:96–100.

———. 1978. Red imported fire ant predation on the alfalfa weevil and pea aphid. *J. Econ. Entomol.* 71:867–68.

Morrill, W. L., and J. A. Bass. 1976. Flight and survival of alate red imported fire ants after mirex treatment. *J. Georgia Entomol. Soc.* 11:203–208.

Morrill, W. L., and G. L. Greene. 1975. Reduction of red imported fire ant populations by tillage. *J. Georgia Entomol. Soc.* 10:162–64.

Morrill, W. L., P. B. Martin, and D. C. Sheppard. 1978. Overwinter survival of the red imported fire ant: Effects of various habitats and food supply. *Environ. Entomol.* 7:262–64.

Morris, J. R., and K. L. Steigman. 1993. Effects of polygyne fire ant invasion on native ants of a blackland prairie in Texas. *Southwest. Nat.* 38:136–40.

Morrison, J. E., Jr., D. F. Williams, and D. H. Oi. 1999c. Effect of crop seed water content on the rate of seed damage by red imported fire ants (Hymenoptera: Formicidae). *J. Econ. Entomol.* 92:215–19.

Morrison, J. E., Jr., D. F. Williams, D. H. Oi, and K. N. Potter. 1997a. Damage to dry crop seed by red imported fire ant (Hymenoptera: Formicidae). *J. Econ. Entomol.* 90:218–22.

Morrison, L. W. 1997. Polynesian ant (Hymenoptera: Formicidae) species richness and distribution: A regional survey. *Acta Oecologica* 18:685–95.

Morrison, L. W., C. G. Dall'Aglio Holvorcem, and L. E. Gilbert. 1997. Oviposition behavior and development of *Pseudacteon* flies (Diptera: Phoridae), parasitoids of *Solenopsis* fire ants (Hymenoptera: Formicidae). *Environ. Entomol.* 26:716–24.

Morrison, L. W., and L. E. Gilbert. 1998. Parasitoid-host relationships when host size varies: The case of *Pseudacteon* flies and *Solenopsis* fire ants. *Ecol. Entomol.* 23:409–16.

Morrison, L. W., E. A. Kawazoe, R. Guerra, and L. E. Gilbert. 1999b. Phenology and dispersal in *Pseudacteon* flies (Diptera: Phoridae), parasitoids of *Solenopsis* fire ants (Hymenoptera: Formicidae). *Ann. Entomol. Soc. Amer.* 92:198–207.

Morrison, L. W., S. D. Porter, and L. E. Gilbert. 1999a. Sex ratio variation as a function of host size in *Pseudacteon* flies (Diptera: Phoridae), parasitoids of *Solenopsis* fire ants (Hymenoptera: Formicidae). *Biol. J. Linn. Soc.* 66:257–67.

Moser, J. C. 1970. Pheromones of social insects. Pp. 161–78 in *Control of insect behavior by natural products,* ed. D. L. Wood, R. M. Silverstein, and M. Nakajima. New York: Academic Press.

Moulis, R. A. 1997. Predation by the imported fire ant *(Solenopsis invicta)* on loggerhead sea turtle *(Caretta caretta)* nests on Wassaw National Wildlife Refuge, Georgia. *Chelonian Cons. Biol.* 2:433–36.

Moutia, L. A., and R. Mamet. 1946. A review of twenty-five years of economic entomology in the island of Mauritius. *Bull. Entomol. Res.* 36:439–72.

Muckenfuss, A. E., B. M. Shepard, and E. R. Ferrer. 1992. Natural mortality of diamondback moth in coastal South Carolina. Pp. 27–36 in *Diamondback moths and other crucifer pests,* ed. N. S. Talekar. Taipei, Taiwan: Asian Vegetable Research and Development Center.

Mullens, B. A., J. A. Meyer, and J. D. Mandeville. 1986. Seasonal and diel activity of filth fly parasites (Hymenoptera: Pteromalidae) in caged-layer poultry manure in southern California. *Environ. Entomol.* 15:56–60.

Muniappan, R., and M. Marutani. 1992. Pest management for head cabbage production on Guam. Pp. 541–49 in *Diamondback moth and other crucifer pests,* ed. S. Talekar. Taipei, Taiwan: Asian Vegetable Research and Development Center.

Munroe, P. D., H. G. Thorvilson, and S. A. Phillips, Jr. 1996. Comparison of desiccation rates among three species of fire ants. *Southwest. Entomol.* 21:173–79.

Murthy, D. V. 1959. A preliminary note on the control of red ant (*Solenopsis geminata* Fabr.) on some of the vegetable crops. *Mysore Agric. J.* 34:9–14.

Myers, J. G. 1927. Ethological observations on some Pyrrhocoridae of Cuba (Hemiptera—Heteroptera). *Ann. Entomol. Soc. Amer.* 20:279–300.

Nafus, D. M., and I. H. Schreiner. 1988. Parental care in a tropical nymphalid butterfly *Hypolimnas anomala. Animal Behav.* 36:1425–31.

Nair, M. R. G. K. 1975. *Insects and mites of crops in India.* New Delhi: Indian Council of Agricultural Research.

Nash, M. S., W. G. Whitford, J. Van Zee, and K. Havstad. 1998. Monitoring changes in stressed ecosystems using spatial patterns of ant communities. *Envir. Monitoring and Assess.* 51:201–10.

Neal, T. M., and W. H. Whitcomb. 1972. Odonata in the Florida Soybean agroecosystem. *Florida Entomol.* 55:107–14.

Neece, K. C., and D. P. Bartell. 1981. Insects associated with *Solenopsis* spp. in southeastern Texas. *Southwest. Entomol.* 6:307–11.

————. 1982. *A faunistic survey of the organisms associated with ants of western Texas.* Graduate Studies no. 25. Lubbock: Texas Tech Press.

Nelson, D. R., C. L. Fatland, R. W. Howard, C. A. McDaniel, and G. J. Blomquist. 1980. Re-analysis of the cuticular methylalkanes of *Solenopsis invicta* and *S. richteri. Insect Biochem.* 10:409–18.

Nesom, G. L. 1981. Ant dispersal in *Wedelia hispida* Hbk. (Heliantheae: Compositae). *Southwest. Nat.* 26:5–12.

Nestel, D. and F. Dickschen. 1990. The foraging kinetics of ground ant communities in different Mexican coffee agroecosystems. *Oecologia* 84:58–63.

Newsom, J. D. 1958. A preliminary progress report of fire ant eradication program Concordia Parish, Louisiana, June 1958. Pp. 29–31 in *Proceedings symposium: The fire ant eradication program and how it affects wildlife.* Proc. Ann. Conf. Southeastern Assoc. Game and Fish Comm.

Nichols, B. J., and R. W. Sites. 1989. A comparison of arthropod species within and outside the range of *Solenopsis invicta* Buren in Central Texas. *Southwest. Entomol.* 14:345–50.

————. 1991. Ant predators of founder queens of *Solenopsis invicta* (Hymenoptera: Formicidae) in Central Texas. *Environ. Entomol.* 20:1024–29.

Nickerson, J. C., C. A. R. Kay, L. L. Buschman, and W. H. Whitcomb. 1977. The presence of *Spississ-tilus festinus* as a factor affecting egg predation by ants in soybeans. *Florida Entomol.* 60:193–99.

Nickerson, J. C., W. H. Whitcomb, A. P. Bhatkar, and M. A. Naves. 1975. Predation on founding queens of *Solenopsis invicta* by workers of *Conomyrma insana. Florida Entomol.* 58:75–82.

Nickle, W. R., and D. P. Jouvenaz. 1987. *Tetradonema solenopsis* n. sp. (Nematoda: Tetradonematidae) parasitic on the red imported fire ant *Solenopsis invicta* Buren from Brazil. *J. Nematol.* 19:311–13.

Nyffeler, M., D. A. Dean, and W. L. Sterling. 1987. Evaluation of the importance of the striped lynx spider *Oxyopes salticus* (Araneae: Oxyopidae), as a predator in Texas cotton. *Environ. Entomol.* 16:1114–23.

————. 1988. The southern black widow spider, *Latrodectus mactans* (Araneae: Theridiidae), as a predator of the red imported fire ant, *Solenopsis invicta* (Hymenoptera: Formicidae), in Texas cotton fields. *J. Appl. Entomol.* 106:52–57.

Oberheu, J. C. 1972. The occurrence of mirex in starlings collected in seven southeastern states: 1970. *Pestic. Monit. J.* 6:41–42.

Obin, M. S. 1986. Nestmate recognition cues in laboratory and field colonies of *Solenopsis invicta* Buren (Hymenoptera: Formicidae) Effect of environment and role of cuticular hydrocarbons. *J. Chem. Ecol.* 12:1965–76.

Obin, M. S., B. M. Glancey, W. A. Banks, and R. K. Vander Meer. 1988. Queen pheromone production and its physiological correlates in fire ant queens (Hymenoptera: Formicidae) treated with fenoxycarb. *Ann. Entomol. Soc. Amer.* 81:808–15.

Obin, M. S., L. Morel, and R. K. Vander Meer. 1993. Unexpected, well-developed nestmate recognition in laboratory colonies of polygyne imported fire ants (Hymenoptera: Formicidae). *J. Insect Behav.* 6:579–89.

Obin, M. S., and R. K. Vander Meer. 1985. Gaster flagging by fire ants (*Solenopsis* spp.): Functional significance of venom dispersal behavior. *J. Chem. Ecol.* 11:1757–68.

————. 1989a. Mechanism of template-label matching in fire ant, *Solenopsis invicta* Buren, nestmate recognition. *Animal Behav.* 38:430–35.

————. 1989b. Between- and within-species recognition among imported fire ants and their hybrids (Hymenoptera: Formicidae): Application to hybrid zone dynamics. *Ann. Entomol. Soc. Amer.* 82:649–52.

————. 1994. Alate semiochemicals release worker behavior during ant nuptial flights. *J. Entomol. Sci.* 29:143–51.

Oi, D. H., R. M. Pereira, J. L. Stimac, and L. A. Wood. 1994. Field applications of *Beauveria bassiana* for control of the red imported fire ant (Hymenoptera: Formicidae). *J. Econ. Entomol.* 87:623–30.

Oi, D. H., and D. F. Williams. 1996. Toxicity and repellency of potting soil treated with bifenthrin and tefluthrin to red imported fire ants (Hymenoptera: Formicidae). *J. Econ. Entomol.* 89:1526–30.

Olive, A. T. 1960. Infestation of the imported fire ant, *Solenopsis saevissima* v. *richteri* at Fort Benning, Georgia. *J. Econ. Entomol.* 53:646–48.

Oliver, B. 1997 [date of printout from webpage]. Queen Invicta (Fire Ant Invincible). Austin, Tex.: Morris Media Associates, Inc.

O'Neal, J., and G. P. Markin. 1973. Brood nutrition and parental relationships of the imported fire ant *Solenopsis invicta*. *J. Georgia Entomol. Soc.* 8:294–303.

————. 1975a. Brood development of the various castes of the imported fire ant, *Solenopsis invicta* Buren (Hymenoptera: Formicidae). *J. Kansas Entomol. Soc.* 48:152–59.

————. 1975b. The larval instars of the imported fire ant, *Solenopsis invicta* Buren (Hymenoptera: Formicidae). *J. Kansas Entomol. Soc.* 48:141–51.

Ordelheide, C. H. 1929. Een nieuwe bestrijdingswijze van de roode tabaksmier *(Solenopsis geminata)* op zaadbedden. Publication 64. *Proefstation voor Vorstenlandsche Tabak.* 5 pp.

Orr, M. R., S. H. Seike, and L. E. Gilbert. 1997. Foraging ecology and patterns of diversification in dipteran parasitoids of fire ants in south Brazil. *Ecol. Entomol.* 22:305–14.

Osborn, F. and K. Jaffe. 1998. Chemical ecology of the defense of two nymphalid butterfly larvae against ants. *J. Chem. Ecol.* 24:1173–85

Osburn, M. R. 1948. Comparison of DDT, chlordane, and chlorinated camphene for control of the little fire ant. *Florida Entomol.* 31:11–15.

Oster, G. F., and E. O. Wilson. 1978. *Caste and ecology in the social insects.* Monographs in Population Biology no. 12. Princeton, N.J.: Princeton University Press.

Pair, S. D., and H. R. Gross. 1989. Seasonal incidence of fall armyworm (Lepidoptera: Noctuidae) pupal parasitism in corn by *Diapetimorpha introita* and *Cryptus albitarsis* (Hymenoptera: Ichneumonidae). *J. Entomol. Sci.* 24:339–43.

Patton, W. S. 1931. *Insects, ticks, mites and venomous animals of medical and veterinary importance. Part II: Public health.* Croydon, U.K.: H. R. Grubb, Ltd.

Patton, W. S., and A. W. Evans. 1929. *Insects, ticks, mites and venomous animals. Part I: Medical.* Croydon, U.K.: H. R. Grubb, Ltd.

Paull, B. R., T. H. Coghlan, and S. B. Vinson. 1983. Fire ant venom hypersensitivity. I: Comparison of fire ant venom and whole body extract in the diagnosis of fire ant allergy. *J. Allergy Clin. Immunol.* 71:448–53.

Pavis, C., C. Malosse, P. H. Ducrot, and C. Descoins. 1994b. Dorsal abdominal glands in nymphs of southern green stink bug, *Nezara viridula* (L.) (Heteroptera: Pentatomidae): Chemistry of secretions of five instars and role of (E)-4-oxo-2-decenal, compound specific to first instars. *J. Chem. Ecol.* 20:2213–27.

Pavis, C., C. Malosse, P. H. Ducrot, F. Howse, K. Jaffe, and C. Descoins. 1992. Defensive secretion of first-instar larvae of rootstalk borer weevil, *Diaprepes abbreviatus* L. (Coleoptera: Curculionidae), to the fire-ant *Solenopsis geminata* (F.) (Hymenoptera: Formicidae). *J. Chem. Ecol.* 18:2055–68.

Pavis, C., H. Mauleon, N. Barre, and M. Maibeche. 1994a. Dermal gland secretions of tropical bont tick, *Amblyomma variegatum* (Acarina: Ixodidae): Biological activity on predators and pathogens. *J. Chem. Ecol.* 20:1495–1503.

Pearse, V., J. Pearse, M. Buchsbaum, and R. Buchsbaum. 1987. *Living invertebrates.* Palo Alto/ Pacific Grove, Calif.: Blackwell Scientific Publications and Boxwood Press.

Peck, S. B., J. Heraty, B. Landry, and B. J. Sinclair. 1998. Introduced insect fauna of an oceanic island: The Galápagos Islands, Ecuador. *Amer. Entomol.* 44:218–37.

Pedersen, E. K., W. E. Grant, and M. T. Longnecker. 1996. Effects of red imported fire ants on newly-hatched northern bobwhite. *J. Wildlife Man.* 60:164–69.

Pereira, R. M., and J. L. Stimac. 1992. Transmission *of Beauveria bassiana* within nests of *Solenopsis invicta* (Hymenoptera: Formicidae) in the laboratory. *Environ. Entomol.* 21:1427–32.

Perfecto, I. 1990. Indirect and direct effects in a tropical agroecosystem: The maize-pest-ant system in Nicaragua. *Ecology* 71:2125–34.

———. 1991. Dynamics of *Solenopsis geminata* in a tropical fallow field after ploughing. *Oikos* 62:139–44.

———. 1992. Observations of a *Labidus coecus* (Latreille) underground raid in the central highlands of Costa Rica. *Psyche* 99:214–20.

———. 1994. Foraging behavior as a determinant of asymmetric competitive interaction between two ant species in a tropical agroecosystem. *Oecologia* 98:184–92.

Perfecto, I., and A. Sediles. 1992. Vegetational diversity, ants (Hymenoptera: Formicidae) and herbivorous pests in a neotropical agroecosystem. *Environ. Entomol.* 21:61–67.

Perfecto, I., and R. R. Snelling. 1995. Biodiversity and the transformation of a tropical agroecosystem: Ants in coffee plantations. *Ecol. Appl.* 5:1084–97.

Perfecto, I., and J. Vander Meer. 1996. Microclimatic changes and the indirect loss of ant diversity in a tropical agroecosystem. *Oecologia* 108:577–82.

Pergande, T. 1901. The ant-decapitating fly. *Proc. Entomol. Soc. Wash.* 4:497–502.

Permenter, P., and J. Bigley. 1994. Pining for Bastrop. *Austin American-Statesman,* June 18, D1, D6.

Pesquero, M. A., S. Campiolo, H. G. Fowler, and S. D. Porter. 1996. Diurnal patterns of ovipositional activity in two *Pseudacteon* fly parasitoids (Diptera: Phoridae) of *Solenopsis* fire ants (Hymenoptera: Formicidae). *Florida Entomol.* 79:455–57.

Pesquero, M. A., H. G. Fowler, and S. D. Porter. 1998. The social parasitic ant, *Solenopsis (= Labauchena) daguerrei* (Hymenoptera: Formicidae) in São Paulo, Brazil. *Rev. Biol. Trop.* 46:464–65.

Pesquero, M. A., S. D. Porter, H. G. Fowler, and S. Campiolo. 1995. Rearing of *Pseudacteon* spp. (Dipt., Phoridae), parasitoids of fire ants (*Solenopsis* spp.) (Hym., Formicidae). *J. Appl. Entomol.* 119: 677–78.

Petralia, R. S., A. A. Sorensen, and S. B. Vinson. 1980. The labial gland system of larvae of the imported fire ant, *Solenopsis invicta* Buren. *Cell and Tissue Res.* 206:145–56.

Petralia, R. S., and S. B. Vinson. 1978. Feeding in the larvae of the imported fire ant, *Solenopsis invicta:* Behavior and morphological adaptations. *Ann. Entomol. Soc. Amer.* 71:643–48.

———. 1979. Developmental morphology of larvae and eggs of the imported fire ant, *Solenopsis invicta. Ann. Entomol. Soc. Amer.* 72:472–84.

———. 1980. Internal anatomy of the fourth instar larva of the imported fire ant, *Solenopsis invicta* Buren (Hymenoptera: Formicidae). *Int. J. Insect Morphol. Embryol.* 9:89–106.

Phillips, J. S. 1934. The biology and distribution of ants in Hawaiian pineapple fields. Bull. no. 15. University of Hawaii, Experiment Station of the Pineapple Producers' Cooperative Association, Limited.

Phillips, S. A., Jr., D. M. Claborn, and O. F. Francke. 1984. Comparison of aerial application and single-mound drenches of fenvalerate against the red imported fire ant, *Solenopsis invicta* Buren, in Texas. *Southwest. Entomol.* 9:164–68.

Phillips, S. A., Jr., D. M. Claborn, and H. G. Thorvilson. 1985. An insect growth regulator (Pro-Drone) for effective management of the red imported fire ant *[Solenopsis invicta]* (Hymenoptera: Formicidae). *J. Entomol. Sci.* 20:194–98.

Phillips, S. A., S. R. Jones, and D. M. Claborn. 1986a. Temporal foraging patterns of *Solenopsis invicta* and native ants of Central Texas. Pp. 114–15 in *Fire ants and leaf-cutting ants: Biology and management*, ed. C. S. Lofgren and R. K. Vander Meer. Westview studies in insect biology. Boulder, Colo.: Westview Press.

Phillips, S. A., Jr., S. R. Jones, D. M. Claborn, and J. C. Cokendolpher. 1986b. Effect of Pro-Drone, an insect growth regulator, *on Solenopsis invicta* Buren and nontarget ants. *Southwest. Entomol.* 11:287–94.

Phillips, S. A., Jr., R. Jusino-Atresino, and H. G. Thorvilson. 1996. Desiccation resistance in populations of the red imported fire ant (Hymenoptera: Formicidae). *Environ. Entomol.* 25:460–64.

Phillips, S. A., Jr., and H. G. Thorvilson. 1986. The effect of an insect growth regulator (Pro-Drone) on *Solenopsis invicta* Buren (Hymenoptera: Formicidae) and non-target ants. Pp. 88–101 in *Proceedings of the 1986 imported fire ant conference,* comp. M. E. Mispagel. Athens, Ga.: Texas Department of Agriculture and Veterinary Medical Experiment Station, University of Georgia.

———. 1989. Use of fenoxycarb for area-wide management of red imported fire ants (Hymenoptera: Formicidae). *J. Econ. Entomol.* 82:1646–49.

Phillips, S. A., Jr., and S. B. Vinson. 1980. Comparative morphology of glands associated with the head among castes of the red imported fire ant, *Solenopsis invicta. J. Georgia Entomol. Soc.* 15:215–26.

Picanco, M., V. W. D. Casali, I. R. de Oliviera, and G. L. D. Leite. 1997. Hymenoptera associated to *Solanum gila* (Solanaceae). *Rev. Brasil. Zool.* 14:821–29.

Pimentel, D. 1955. Relationships of ants to fly control in Puerto Rico. *J. Econ. Entomol.* 48:28–30.

Pimm, S. L., and D. P. Bartell. 1980. Statistical model for predicting range expansion of the red imported fire ant, *Solenopsis invicta,* in Texas. *Environ. Entomol.* 9:653–58.

Pinson, C. K., J. D. Edwig, Jr., and J. K. Wangberg. 1980. Sampling technique for monitoring within mound distribution of the red imported fire ant *(Solenopsis invicta). J. Econ. Entomol.* 73:111–12.

Planck, H. K., and M. R. Smith. 1940. A survey of the pineapple mealybug in Puerto Rico and preliminary studies of its control. *J. Agric. University Puerto Rico* 24:49–76.

Porter, S. D. 1988. Impact of temperature on colony growth and developmental rates of the ant, *Solenopsis invicta. J. Insect Physiol.* 34:1127–34.

———. 1989. Effects of diet on the growth of laboratory fire ant colonies (Hymenoptera: Formicidae). *J. Kansas Entomol. Soc.* 62:288–91.

———. 1990. Overview. Pp. 187–89 in *Applied myrmecology: A world perspective*, ed. R. K. Vander Meer, K. Jaffe, and A. Cedeno. Westview studies in insect biology. Boulder, Colo.: Westview Press.

———. 1991. Origins of new queens in polygyne red imported fire ant colonies (Hymenoptera: Formicidae). *J. Entomol. Sci.* 26:474–78.

———. 1992. Frequency and distribution of polygyne fire ants (Hymenoptera: Formicidae) in Florida. *Florida Entomol.* 75:248–57.

———. 1993. Stability of polygyne and monogyne fire ant populations (Hymenoptera: Formicidae: *Solenopsis invicta*) in the United States. *J. Econ. Entomol.* 86:1344–47.

Porter, S. D., and L. E. Alonso. 1999. Host specificity of fire ant decapitating flies (Diptera: Phoridae) in laboratory oviposition tests. *J. Econ. Entomol.* 92:110–14.

Porter, S. D., A. Bhatkar, R. Mulder, S. B. Vinson, and D. J. Clair. 1991. Distribution and density of polygyne fire ants (Hymenoptera: Formicidae) in Texas. *J. Econ. Entomol.* 84:866–74.

Porter, S. D., H. G. Fowler, S. Campiolo, and M. A. Pesquero. 1995a. Host specificity of several *Pseudacteon* (Diptera: Phoridae) parasites of fire ants (Hymenoptera: Formicidae). *Florida Entomol.* 78:70–75.

Porter, S. D., H. G. Fowler, and W. P. MacKay. 1992. Fire ant mound densities in the United States and Brazil (Hymenoptera: Formicidae). *J. Econ. Entomol.* 85:1154–61.

Porter, S. D., M. A. Pesquero, S. Campiolo, and H. G. Fowler. 1995b. Growth and development of *Pseudacteon* phorid fly maggots (Diptera: Phoridae) in the heads of *Solenopsis* fire ant workers (Hymenoptera: Formicidae). *Environ. Entomol.* 24:474–79.

Porter, S. D., and D. A. Savignano. 1990. Invasion of polygyne fire ants decimates native ants and disrupts arthropod community. *Ecology* 71:2095–2106.

Porter, S. D., and W. R. Tschinkel. 1985a. Fire ant polymorphism (Hymenoptera: Formicidae): Factors affecting worker size. *Ann. Entomol. Soc. Amer.* 78:381–86.

———. 1985b. Fire ant polymorphism: The ergonomics of brood production. *Behav. Ecol. Sociobiol.* 16:323–36.

———. 1986. Adaptive value of nanitic workers in newly founded red imported fire ant colonies (Hymenoptera: Formicidae). *Ann. Entomol. Soc. Amer.* 79:723–26.

———. 1987. Foraging in *Solenopsis invicta* (Hymenoptera: Formicidae): Effects of weather and season. *Environ. Entomol.* 16:802–808.

———. 1992. Frequency and distribution of polygyne fire ants (Hymenoptera: Formicidae) in Florida. *Florida Entomol.* 75:248–57.

———. 1993. Fire ant thermal preferences: Behavioral control of growth and metabolism. *Behav. Ecol. Sociobiol.* 32:321–29.

Porter, S. D., R. K. Vander Meer, M. A. Pesquero, S. Campiolo, and H. G. Fowler. 1995c. *Solenopsis* (Hymenoptera: Formicidae) fire ant reactions to attacks of *Pseudacteon* flies (Diptera: Phoridae) in southeastern Brazil. *Ann. Entomol. Soc. Amer.* 88:570–75.

Porter, S. D., B. Van Eimeren, and L. E. Gilbert. 1988. Invasion of red imported fire ants (Hymenoptera: Formicidae): Microgeography of competitive replacement. *Ann. Entomol. Soc. Amer.* 81:913–18.

Porter, S. D., D. F. Williams, and R. S. Patterson. 1997a. Rearing the decapitating fly *Pseudacteon tricuspis* (Diptera: Phoridae) in imported fire ants (Hymenoptera: Formicidae) from the United States. *J. Econ. Entomol.* 90:135–38.

———. 1997b. Intercontinental differences in the abundance of *Solenopsis* fire ants (Hymenoptera: Formicidae): Escape from natural enemies? *Environ. Entomol.* 26:373–84.

Potts, L. R., O. F. Francke, and J. C. Cokendolpher. 1984. Humidity preferences of four species of fire ants (Hymenoptera: Formicidae: *Solenopsis*). *Insectes Sociaux* 31:335–39.

Prahlow, J. A., and J. J. Barnard. 1998. Fatal anaphylaxis due to fire ant stings. *Am. J. Forensic Med. & Path.* 19:137–42.

Prins, A. J. 1985. Formicoidea. Pp. 443–51 in *Insects of southern Africa*, ed. C. H. Scholtz and E. Holm. Durban, South Africa: Butterworths.

Prins, A. J., H. G. Robertson, and A. Prins. 1990. Pest ants in urban and agricultural areas of southern Africa. Pp. 25–33 in *Applied myrmecology: A world perspective*, ed. R. K. Vander Meer, K. Jaffe, and A. Cedeno. Westview studies in insect biology. Boulder, Colo.: Westview Press.

Propp, G. D., and P. B. Morgan. 1985. Mortality of eggs and first-stage larvae of the house fly, *Musca domestica* (Diptera: Muscidae), in poultry manure. *J. Kansas Entomol. Soc.* 58:442–47.

Ramos, M. G., ed. *1998–1999 Texas Almanac*. Dallas, Tex.: Dallas Morning News.

Rao, S. R. M. 1942. Life-history and bionomics *of Pseudococcus saccharina* Takh. (Homoptera: Coccidae): A new pest of sugarcane in India. *Proc. Indian Acad. Sci. Sect. B* 16:79–85.

Read, G. W., N. K. Lind, and C. S. Oda. 1978. Histamine release by fire ant *(Solenopsis)* venom. *Toxicon* 16:361–67.

Ready, C. C., and S. B. Vinson. 1995. Seed selection by the red imported fire ant (Hymenoptera: Formicidae) in the laboratory. *Environ. Entomol.* 24:1422–31.

Reagan, T. E. 1986. Beneficial aspects of the imported fire ant: A field ecology approach. Pp. 58–71 in *Fire ants and leaf-cutting ants: Biology and management*, ed. C. S. Lofgren and R. K. Vander Meer. Westview studies in insect biology. Boulder, Colo.: Westview Press.

Reagan, T. E., G. Coburn, and S. D. Hensley. 1972. Effects of mirex on the arthropod fauna of a Louisiana sugarcane field. *Environ. Entomol.* 1:588–91.

Reaumur, R. A. F. de. 1926. *The natural history of ants*. Trans. by W. M. Wheeler. New York: Alfred A. Knopf. (From ms. of ca. 1743.)

Reddell, J. R. 1981. *A review of the cavernicole fauna of Mexico, Guatemala, and Belize*. Texas Memorial Museum Bull. 27. Austin: University of Texas.

Reed, J. T., and D. B. Smith. 1999. Comparison of two treatment methods and four insecticides for control of individual fire ant mounds. Miss. Agric. Forest Exp. Sta. Bull. 1080.

Rehn, J. A. G. 1904. Notes on Orthoptera from northern and central Mexico. *Proc. Acad. Nat. Sci. Phil.* 56:513–49.

Reichensperger, A. 1927. Eigenartiger Nestbefund und neue Gastarten neotropischer *Solenopsis*-Arten. *Folia Myrmecologica et Termitologica* 1:47–51.

———. 1935. Beitrag zur Kenntnis der Myrmekophilenfauna Brasiliens und Costa Rica. III: (Col. Staphyl. Hist.). *Arb. Morphol. Taxon. Entomol. Berlin-Dahlem* 2:188–217.

———. 1936. Beitrag zur Kenntnis der Myrmecophilen- und Termitophilenfauna Brasiliens und Costa Rica. IV: (Col. Hist. Staphyl. Pselaph.). *Rev. Entomol.* (Rio de Janeiro) 6:222–42.

Reimer, N., J. W. Beardsley, and G. Jahn. 1990. Pp. 40–50 in *Applied myrmecology: A world perspective*, ed. R. K. Vander Meer, K. Jaffe, and A. Cedeno. Westview studies in insect biology. Boulder, Colo.: Westview Press.

Reinert, J. A. 1978. Natural enemy complex of the southern chinch bug in Florida. *Ann. Entomol. Soc. Amer.* 71:728–31.

Rhoades, R. B. 1977. *Medical aspects of the imported fire ant*. Gainesville: University Press of Florida.

Rhoades, R. B., W. L. Schafer, W. H. Schmid, P. F. Wubbena, R. M. Dozier, A. W. Townes, and H. J. Wittig. 1975. Hypersensitivity to the imported fire ant. *J. Allergy Clin. Immunol.* 56:84–93.

Rhoades, R. B., C. T. Stafford, and F. K. James, Jr. 1989. Survey of fatal anaphylactic reactions to imported fire ant stings. *J. Allergy Clin. Immunol.* 84:159–62.

Rhoades, W. C. 1962. A synecological study of the effects of the imported fire ant eradication program. *Florida Entomol.* 45:161–73.

Rhoades, W. C., and D. R. Davis. 1967. Effects of meteorological factors on the biology and control of the imported fire ant. *J. Econ. Entomol.* 60:554–58.

Richards, O. W. 1953. *The social insects*. New York: Philosophical Library.

Ricks, B. L., and S. B. Vinson. 1970. Feeding acceptability of certain insects and various water-soluble compounds to two varieties of the imported fire ant. *J. Econ. Entomol.* 63:145–49.

———. 1972a. Changes in nutrient content during one year in workers of the imported fire ant. *Ann. Entomol. Soc. Amer.* 65:135–38.

———. 1972b. Digestive enzymes of the imported fire ant, *Solenopsis richteri* (Hymenoptera: Formicidae). *Entomol. Exp. Appl.* 15:329–34.

Ridley, M. 1996. *Evolution.* 2nd ed., Cambridge, Mass.: Blackwell Science.

Risch, S. 1981. Ants as important predators of rootworm eggs in the neotropics. *J. Econ. Entomol.* 74:88–90.

Risch, S. J., and C. R. Carroll. 1982a. Effect of a keystone predaceous ant, *Solenopsis geminata,* on arthropods in a tropical agroecosystem. *Ecology* 63:1979–83.

———. 1982b. The ecological role of ants in two Mexican agroecosystems. *Oecologia* 55:114–19.

———. 1986. Effects of seed predation by a tropical ant on competition among weeds. *Ecology* 67:1319–27.

Robeau, R. M., and S. B. Vinson. 1976. Effects of juvenile hormone analogues on caste differentiation in the imported fire ant, *Solenopsis invicta. J. Georgia Entomol. Soc.* 11:198–202.

Robinson, D. A., C. T. Stafford, B. L. Crosby, and D. R. Hoffman. 1992. Safety and efficacy of fire ant venom in the diagnosis of fire ant allergy. *J. Allergy Clin. Immunol.* 89:293.

Roe, R. A., II, 1974. A biological study of *Solenopsis invicta* Buren, the red imported fire ant, in Arkansas with notes on related species. M.S. thesis, University of Arkansas, Fayetteville.

Rosene, W., Jr. 1958. Whistling-cock counts of bobwhite quail on areas treated with insecticide and on untreated areas, Decatur County, Georgia. Pp. 14–18 in *Proceedings symposium: The fire ant eradication program and how it affects wildlife.* Proc. Ann. Conf. Southeastern Assoc. Game and Fish Comm.

Ross, K. G. 1988a. Population and colony-level genetic studies of ants. Pp. 189–215 in *Advances in myrmecology,* ed. J. C. Trager. New York: E. J. Brill.

———. 1988b. Differential reproduction in multiple queen colonies of the fire ant *Solenopsis invicta* (Hymenoptera: Formicidae). *Behav. Ecol. Sociobiol.* 23:341–56.

———. 1989. Reproductive and social structure in polygynous fire ant colonies. Pp. 149–62 in *The genetics of social evolution,* ed. M. D. Breed and R. E. Page, Jr. Boulder, Colo.: Westview Press.

———. 1992. Strong selection on a gene that influences reproductive competition in a social insect. *Nature* 355:347–49.

———. 1993. The breeding system of the fire ant *Solenopsis invicta:* Effects on colony genetic structure. *Amer. Nat.* 141:554–76.

———. 1997. Multilocus evolution in fire ants: Effects of selection, gene flow and recombination. *Genetics* 145:961–74.

Ross, K. G., and D. J. C. Fletcher. 1985a. Genetic origin of male diploidy in the fire ant, *Solenopsis invicta* (Hymenoptera: Formicidae), and its evolutionary development. *Evolution* 39:888–903.

———. 1985b. Comparative study of genetic and social structure in two forms of the fire ant *Solenopsis invicta* (Hymenoptera: Formicidae). *Behav. Ecol. Sociobiol.* 17:349–56.

———. 1986. Diploid male production: A significant colony mortality factor in the fire ant *Solenopsis invicta* (Hymenoptera: Formicidae). *Behav. Ecol. Sociobiol.* 19:283–92.

Ross, K. G., D. J. C. Fletcher, and B. May. 1985. Enzyme polymorphisms in the fire ant, *Solenopsis invicta* (Hymenoptera: Formicidae). *Biochem. Syst. Ecol.* 13:29–34.

Ross, K. G., and L. Keller. 1995. Joint influence of gene flow and selection on a reproductively important genetic polymorphism in the fire ant *Solenopsis invicta. Amer. Nat.* 146:325–48.

Ross, K. G., M. J. B. Krieger, D. D. Shoemaker, E. L. Vargo, and L. Keller. 1997. Hierarchical analysis of genetic structure in native fire ant populations: Results from three classes of molecular markers. *Genetics* 147:643–55.

Ross, K. G., and J. L. Robertson. 1990. Developmental stability, heterozygosity, and fitness in two introduced fire ants *(Solenopsis invicta* and *S. richteri)* and their hybrid. *Heredity* 64:93–104.

Ross, K. G., and D. D. Shoemaker. 1993. An unusual pattern of gene flow between the two social forms of the fire ant *Solenopsis invicta*. *Evolution* 47:1595–1605.

———. 1997. Nuclear and mitochondrial genetic structure in two social forms of the fire ant, *Solenopsis invicta*: Insights into transitions to an alternate social organization. *Heredity* 78:590–602.

Ross, K. G., D. D. Shoemaker, M. J. B. Krieger, C. J. DeHeer, and L. Keller. 1999. Assessing genetic structure with multiple cases of molecular markers: A case study involving the introduced fire ant *Solenopsis invicta*. *Mol. Biol. Evol.* 16:525–43.

Ross, K. G., and J. C. Trager. 1990. Systematics and population genetics of fire ants (*Solenopsis saevissima* complex) from Argentina. *Evolution* 44:2113–34.

Ross, K. G., R. K. Vander Meer, D. J. C. Fletcher, and E. L. Vargo. 1987a. Biochemical phenotypic and genetic studies of two introduced fire ants and their hybrid (Hymenoptera: Formicidae). *Evolution* 41:280–93.

Ross, K. G., E. L. Vargo, and D. J. C. Fletcher. 1987b. Comparative biochemical genetics of three fire ant species in North America, with special reference to the two social forms of *Solenopsis invicta* (Hymenoptera: Formicidae). *Evolution* 41:979–90.

Ross, K. G., E. L. Vargo, and L. Keller. 1988. Colony genetic structure and queen mating frequency in fire ants of the subgenus *Solenopsis* (Hymenoptera: Formicidae). *Biol. J. Linn. Soc.* 34:105–17.

———. 1996a. Simple genetic basis for important social traits in the fire ant *Solenopsis invicta*. *Evolution* 50:2387–99.

———. 1996b. Social evolution in a new environment: The case of introduced fire ants. *Proc. Nat. Acad. Sci.* 93:3021–25.

Ross, K. G., E. L. Vargo, L. Keller, and J. C. Trager. 1993. Effect of a founder event on variation in the genetic sex-determining system of the fire ant *Solenopsis invicta*. *Genetics* 135:843–54.

Roth, W. 1998. Ask the Watson Clinic. www.watsonclinic.com.

Russell, C. E. 1981. Predation on the cowpea curculio *(Chalcodermus aeneus)* by the red imported fire ant *(Solenopsis invicta)*. *J. Georgia Entomol. Soc.* 16:13–15.

Ryckman, D. M., and R. V. Stevens. 1987. Stereoselective syntheses cis-2-alkyl-6-methylpiperidines. *J. Org. Chem.* 52:4274–4279.

Sánchez-Peña, S. R., and H. G. Thorvilson. 1992. Two fungi infecting red imported fire ant founding queens from Texas. *Southwest. Entomol.* 17:181–82.

San Martin, P. R. 1966a. Nota sobre *Anommatocoris coleopteratus* Kormilev, 1955 (Vianaidina, Tingidae, Hemiptera). *Rev. Brasil. Biol.* 26:327–28.

———. 1966b. Notas sobre *Neoblissus parasitaster* Bergroth, 1903 (Blissinae, Lygaeidae, Hemiptera). *Rev. Brasil. Biol.* 26:247–51.

———. 1968. Nuevo hallazgo de *Metopioxys gallardoi* Bruch, 1917 (Coleoptera, Pselaphidae, Metopiinae). *Rev. Brasil. Biol.* 28:27–28.

———. 1971. The venomous ants of the genus *Solenopsis*. Pp. 95–101 in *Venomous animals and their venoms*, ed. W. Bücherl and E. E. Buckley. New York: Academic Press.

Santschi, F. 1916. Formicides sudamericaines nouveaux ou peu connus. *Physis* 2:365–99.

———. 1923. *Solenopsis* et autres fourmis néotropicales. *Rev. Suisse de Zoologie* 30:18–273.

———. 1930. Un nouveau genre de fourmi parasite sans ouvrières de l'Argentina. *Rev. Soc. Entomol. Argentina* 3:81–83.

Scheffrahn, R. H., L. K. Gaston, J. J. Sims, and M. K. Rust. 1984. Defensive ecology of *Forelius foetidus* and its chemosystematic relationship to *F.* (= *Iridomyrmex*) *pruinosus* (Hymenoptera: Formicidae: Dolichoderinae). *Environ. Entomol.* 13:1502–1506.

Schmidt, C. D. 1984. Influence of fire ants on horn flies and other dung-breeding Diptera in Bexar County, Texas. *Southwest. Entomol.* 9:174–77.

Schmidt, G. D., and L. S. Roberts. 1981. *Foundations of parasitology.* 2nd ed. St. Louis, Mo.: C. V. Mosby Co.

Schmidt, K. 1995. A new ant on the block. *New Scientist,* 4 November, 28–31.

Schmidt, M., T. J. McConnell, and D. R. Hoffman. 1996. Production of a recombinant imported fire ant venom allergen, Sol i 2, in native and immunoreactive form. *J. Allergy Clin. Immunol.* 98:82–88.

Schmidt, M., R. B. Walker, D. R. Hoffman, and T. J. McConnell. 1993. Nucleotide sequence of cDNA encoding the fire ant venom protein Sol i II. *FEBS Letters* 319:138–40.

Schoor, W. P., and S. M. Newman. 1976. The effect of mirex on the burrowing activity of the lugworm *(Arenicola cristata). Trans. Am. Fish. Soc.* 6:700–703.

Scott, M. P., J. F. A. Traniello, and I. A. Fetherston. 1987. Competition for prey between ants and burying beetles (*Nicrophorus* spp.): Differences between northern and southern temperate sites. *Psyche* 94:325–32.

Severin, H. H. P. 1923. "Fire Ant" injurious to potatoes in California. *J. Econ. Entomol.* 16:96–97.

Shanahan, G. J. 1946. The toxicity of "666" to prepupae of *Lucilia cuprina. J. Austral. Inst. Agric. Sci.* 12:148–49.

Shattuck, S. O., Porter, S. D., and D. P. Wojcik. 1999. *Solenopsis invicta* Buren, 1972 (Insecta, Hymenoptera): Proposed conservation of the specific name. *Bull. Zool. Nomen.* 56:27–30.

Sheppard, C. 1982. Effects of broadcast Diazinon sprays on populations of red imported fire ants *(Solenopsis invicta). J. Georgia Entomol. Soc.* 17:177–83.

Sheppard, C., P. B. Martin, and F. W. Mead. 1979. A planthopper (Homoptera: Cixiidae) associated with red imported fire ant (Hymenoptera: Formicidae) mounds. *J. Georgia Entomol. Soc.* 14:140–44.

Sheppard, D. C. 1984. Toxicity of citrus peel liquids to the housefly *(Musca domestica)* and red imported fire ant *(Solenopsis invicta). J. Agric. Entomol.* 1:95–100.

Shigesada, N., and K. Kawasaki. 1997. *Biological invasions: Theory and practice.* New York: Oxford University Press.

Shoemaker, D. D., J. T. Costa, III, and K. G. Ross. 1992. Estimates of heterozygosity in two social insects using a large number of electrophoretic markers. *Heredity* 69:573–82.

Shoemaker, D. D., and K. G. Ross. 1996: Effects of social organization on gene flow in the fire ant *Solenopsis invicta. Nature* 383:613–16.

Shoemaker, D. D., K. G. Ross, and M. L. Arnold. 1994. Development of RAPD markers in two introduced fire ants, *Solenopsis invicta* and *S. richteri,* and their application to the study of a hybrid zone. *Molec. Ecol.* 3:531–39.

———. 1996. Genetic structure and evolution of a fire ant hybrid zone. *Evolution* 50:1958–76.

Showler, A. T., R. M. Knaus, and T. E. Reagan. 1989. Foraging territoriality of the imported fire ant, *Solenopsis invicta* Buren, in sugarcane as determined by neutron activation analysis. *Insectes Sociaux* 36:235–39.

Sidhu, D. S., D. Mukesh, and R. Garg. 1979. Comparative studies on the total glycogen reserves of some adult insects. *Indian J. Zool.* 7:1–6.

Siebeneicher, S. R., S. B. Vinson, and C. M. Kenerley. 1992. Infection of the red imported fire ant by *Beauveria bassiana* through various routes of exposure. *J. Invert. Pathol.* 59:280–85.

Silveira Guido, A., J. C. Bruhn, C. Crisci, and P. San Martin. 1968. *Labauchena daguerrei* Santschi como parasito social de la hormiga *Solenopsis saevissima richteri* Forel. *Agronomia Tropical* 18:207–209.

Singh, T., and B. Singh. 1982. Comparative morphological studies on the mandibular gland and mandibular groove in Hymenoptera Apocrita. *J. Anim. Morphol. Physiol.* 29:78–84.

Sinski, J. T., G. A. Adrouny, V. J. Derbes, and R. C. Jung. 1959. Further characterization of hemolytic component of fire ant venom, mycological aspects. *Proc. Soc. Exper. Biol. Med.* 102:659–60.

Sison, P. 1938. Some observations on the life history, habits, and control of the rice caseworm, *Nymphala depunctalis* Guen. *Phil. J. Agric.* 9:273–301.

Sittig, M. 1991. *Handbook of toxic and hazardous chemicals and carcinogens.* 3d ed. Vol. 2. Westwood, N.J.: Noyes Publications.

Sivapragasam, A., and T. H. Chua. 1997. Natural enemies for the cabbage webworm, *Hellula undalis* (Fabr.) (Lepidoptera: Pyralidae) in Malaysia. *Res. Pop. Ecol.* 39:3–10.

Slater, J. A., and P. D. Ashlock. 1966. *Atrazonotus,* a new genus of Gonianotini from North America (Hemiptera: Lygaeidae). *Proc. Entomol. Soc. Wash.* 68:152–56.

Slowik, T. J., B. L. Green, and H. G. Thorvilson. 1997a. Detection of magnetism in the red imported fire ant *(Solenopsis invicta)* using magnetic resonance imaging. *Bioelectromagnetics* 18:396–99.

Slowik, T. J., and H. G. Thorvilson. 1996. Localization of subcuticular iron-containing tissue in the red imported fire ant. *Southwest. Entomol.* 21:247–54.

Slowik, T. J., H. G. Thorvilson, and B. L. Green. 1996. Red imported fire ant (Hymenoptera: Formicidae) response to current and conductive material of active electrical equipment. *J. Econ. Entomol.* 89:347–52.

———. 1997b. Response of red imported fire ant to magnetic fields in the nest environment. *Southwest. Entomol.* 22:301–306.

Smith, A. M., and D. R. Hoffman. 1992. Further characterization of imported fire ant venom allergens. *J. Allergy Clin. Immunol.* 89:292.

Smith, B. J., and T. C. Lockley. 1993. Control of red imported fire ant in blueberries with fenoxycarb. *J. Entomol. Sci.* 28:236–39.

Smith, C. F., and H. A. Denmark. 1984. Life history and synonymy of *Grylloprociphilus imbricator* new combination (Homoptera: Aphididae). *Florida Entomol.* 67:430–34.

Smith, J. D., and E. B. Smith. 1971. Multiple fire ant stings: A complication of alcoholism. *Arch. Dermat.* 103:438–41.

Smith, J. W., Jr., and J. T. Pitts. 1974. Pest status of *Pangaeus bilineatus* attacking peanuts in Texas. *J. Econ. Entomol.* 67:111–13.

Smith, M. R. 1924. An annotated list of the ants of Mississippi. *Entomol. News* 35:77–85.

———. 1928. *Plastophora crawfordi* Coq. and *Plastophora spatulata* Malloch (Diptera: Phoridae), parasitic on *Solenopsis geminata* Fabr. *Proc. Entomol. Soc. Wash.* 30:105–108.

———. 1936a. A list of the ants of Texas. *J. New York Entomol. Soc.* 44:155–70.

———. 1936b. The ants of Puerto Rico. *J. Agric. University Puerto Rico* 20:819–75.

———. 1942. The relationship of ants and other organisms to certain scale insects on coffee in Puerto Rico. *J. Agric. University Puerto Rico* 26:21–27.

———. 1947. A generic and subgeneric synopsis of the United States ants, based on the workers (Hymenoptera: Formicidae). *Am. Midland Nat.* 37:521–647.

———. 1965. House-infesting ants of the eastern United States. USDA Tech. Bull. no. 1326. 105 pp.

Smittle, B. J., C. T. Adams, W. A. Banks, and C. S. Lofgren. 1988. Red imported fire ants: Feeding on radiolabeled citrus trees. *J. Econ. Entomol.* 81:1019–21.

Smittle, B. J., C. T. Adams, and C. S. Lofgren. 1983. Red imported fire ants *[Solenopsis invicta]:* Detection of feeding on corn, okra and soybeans with radioisotopes. *J. Georgia Entomol. Soc.* 18:78–82.

Snelling, R. R. 1963. The United States species of the fire ants of the genus *Solenopsis,* subgenus

Solenopsis Westwood with synonyms on *Solenopsis aurea* Wheeler. Occ. Pap. 3. Calif. Dept. Agr. Bur. Entomol., 15 pp.

———. 1997. The social Hymenoptera (Insecta) of Lakekamu. www.lam.mus.ca.us.

Sonnet, P. E. 1967. Fire ant venom: Synthesis of a reported component of solenamine. *Science* 156:1759–60.

Sorensen, A. A., T. M. Busch, and S. B. Vinson. 1983a. Behaviour of worker subcastes in the fire ant, *Solenopsis invicta*, in response to proteinaceous food. *Physiol. Entomol.* 8:83–92.

———. 1983b. Factors affecting brood cannibalism in laboratory colonies of the imported fire ant, *Solenopsis invicta* (Hymenoptera: Formicidae). *J. Kansas Entomol. Soc.* 56:140–50.

———. 1985a. Trophallaxis by temporal subcastes in the fire ant, *Solenopsis invicta*, in response to honey. *Physiol. Entomol.* 10:105–12.

———. 1985b. Control of food influx by temporal subcastes in the fire ant, *Solenopsis invicta. Behav. Ecol. Sociobiol.* 17:191–98.

Sorensen, A. A., and D. J. C. Fletcher. 1985. Techniques for studying the execution of foreign queens by temporal subcastes in fire ants *(Solenopsis invicta). Entomol. Exp. Appl.* 37:289–95.

Sorensen, A. A., D. J. C. Fletcher, and S. B. Vinson. 1985c. Distribution of inhibitory queen pheromone among virgin queens of an ant, *Solenopsis invicta. Psyche* 92:57–70.

Sorensen, A. A., R. S. Kamas, and S. B. Vinson. 1983. The influence of oral secretions from larvae on levels of proteinases in colony members of *Solenopsis invicta* Buren (Hymenoptera: Formicidae). *J. Insect Physiol.* 29:163–68.

Sorensen, A. A., and M. Trostle. 1986. Answers to your questions about imported fire ants. Pp. 44–50 in *Proceedings of the 1986 imported fire ant conference,* comp. M. E. Mispagel. Athens, Ga.: Texas Department of Agriculture and Veterinary Medical Experiment Station, University of Georgia.

Sorensen, A. A., and S. B. Vinson. 1982. Dynamics of food flow in the imported fire ant, *Solenopsis invicta* Buren. P. 411 in *The biology of social insects,* ed. M. D. Breed, C. D. Michener, and H. E. Evans. Boulder, Colo.: Westview Press.

———. 1985. Behavior of temporal subcastes of the fire ant, *Solenopsis invicta*, in response to oil (Hymenoptera: Formicidae). *J. Kansas Entomol. Soc.* 58:586–96.

Southeastern Association of Game and Fish Commissioners. 1958. *Proceeding symposium: The fire ant eradication program and how it affects wildlife.* Proc. Ann. Conf. Southeastern Assoc. Game and Fish Comm. 12:1–34.

Spence, J. H., and G. P. Markin. 1974. Mirex residues in the physical environment following a single bait application, 1971–72. *Pestic. Monit. J.* 135–39.

Stafford, C. T., J. E. Moffitt, A. Bunker-Soler, D. R. Hoffman, and W. O. Thompson. 1990. Comparison of *in vivo* and *in vitro* tests in the diagnosis of imported fire ant sting allergy. *Ann. Allergy* 64:368–72.

Stafford, C. T., R. B. Rhoades, A. L. Bunker-Soler, W. O. Thompson, and L. K. Impson. 1989. Survey of whole body–extract immunotherapy for imported fire ant- and other Hymenoptera-sting allergy. *J. Allergy Clin. Immunol.* 83:1107–11.

Stafford, C. T., S. L. Wise, D. A. Robinson, B. L. Crosby, and D. R. Hoffman. 1992. Safety and efficacy of fire ant venom in the diagnosis of fire ant allergy. *J. Allergy Clin. Immunol.* 90:653–61.

Stahl, C. F., and L. C. Scaramuzza. 1929. Soil insects attacking sugar cane in Cuba. *Trop. Plant Res. Found. Bull.* (Washington, D.C.) 10:1–19.

Stam, P. A., L. D. Newsom, and E. N. Lambremont. 1987. Predation and food as factors affecting survival of *Nezara viridula* (L.) (Hemiptera: Pentatomidae) in a soybean ecosystem. *Environ. Entomol.* 16:1211–16.

Stamps, W. T., and S. B. Vinson. 1991. Raiding in newly founded colonies of *Solenopsis invicta* Buren (Hymenoptera: Formicidae). *Environ. Entomol.* 20:1037–41.

Stein, M. B., and H. G. Thorvilson. 1989. Ant species sympatric with the red imported fire ant in southeastern Texas. *Southwest. Entomol.* 14:225–32.

Stein, M. B., H. G. Thorvilson, and J. W. Johnson. 1990. Seasonal changes in bait preference by red imported fire ant, *Solenopsis invicta* (Hymenoptera: Formicidae). *Florida Entomol.* 73:117–23.

Steiner, W. E., Jr. 1982. *Poecilocrypticus formicophilus* Gebien, a South American beetle established in the United States (Coleoptera: Tenebrionidae). *Proc. Entomol. Soc. Wash.* 84:232–39.

Sterling, W. L. 1978. Fortuitous biological suppression of the boll weevil by the red imported fire ant. *Environ. Entomol.* 7:564–68.

Sterling, W. L., D. Jones, and D. A. Dean. 1979. Failure of the red imported fire ant to reduce entomophagous insect and spider abundance in a cotton agroecosystem. *Environ. Entomol.* 8:976–81.

Stiles, J. H., and R. H. Jones. 1998. Distribution of the red imported fire ant, *Solenopsis invicta*, in road and powerline habitats. *Landscape Ecology* 13:335–46.

Stimac, J. L., and S. B. Alves. 1994. Ecology and biological control of fire ants. Pp. 353–80 in *Pest management in the subtropics: Biological control—a Florida perspective*, ed. D. Rosen, F. D. Bennett, and J. L. Capinera. Andover, U.K.: Intercept Limited.

Stimac, J. L., S. B. Alves, and M. T. Vieira Camargo. 1987. Susceptibility of *Solenopsis* spp. to different species of entomopathogenic fungi. *An. Soc. Entomol. Brasil* 16:377–88.

Stimac, J. L., R. M. Pereira, S. B. Alves, and L. A. Wood. 1993. *Beauveria bassiana* (Balsamo) Vuillemin (Deuteromycetes) applied to laboratory colonies of *Solenopsis invicta* Buren (Hymenoptera: Formicidae) in soil. *J. Econ. Entomol.* 86:348–52.

Stoker, R. L., D. K. Ferris, W. E. Grant, and L. J. Folse. 1994. Simulating colonization by exotic species: A model of the red imported fire ant *(Solenopsis invicta)* in North America. *Ecol. Model.* 73:281–92.

Stoker, R. L., W. E. Grant, and S. B. Vinson. 1995. *Solenopsis invicta* (Hymenoptera: Formicidae) effect on invertebrate decomposers of carrion in Central Texas. *Environ. Entomol.* 24:817–22.

Storey, G. K., R. K. Vander Meer, D. G. Boucias, and C. W. McCoy. 1991. Effect of fire ant *(Solenopsis invicta)* venom alkaloids on the in vitro germination and development of selected entomogenous fungi. *J. Invert. Pathol.* 58:88–95.

Stratton, L. O., and W. P. Coleman. 1973. Maze learning and orientation in the fire ant *(Solenopsis saevissima)*. *J. Compar. Physiol. Psychol.* 83:7–12.

Stringer, C. E., Jr., W. A. Banks, B. M. Glancey, and C. S. Lofgren. 1976. Red imported fire ants: Capability of queens from established colonies and of newly-mated queens to establish colonies in the laboratory. *Ann. Entomol. Soc. Amer.* 69:1004–1006.

Stringer, C. E., W. A. Banks, and J. A. Mitchell. 1980. Effects of chlorpyrifos and acephate on populations of red imported fire ants *(Solenopsis invicta)* in cultivated fields. *J. Georgia Entomol. Soc.* 15:413–17.

Stringer, C. E., B. M. Glancey, P. M. Bishop, C. H. Craig, and B. B. Martin. 1973a. A device for sampling the distribution patterns of granules dispersed from aircraft. *Florida Entomol.* 56:15–17.

Stringer, C. E., Jr., B. M. Glancey, and B. B. Martin. 1973b. A simple method for separating alate imported fire ants from workers and soil. *J. Econ. Entomol.* 66:295–97.

Stringer, C. E., Jr., C. S. Lofgren, and F. J. Bartlett. 1964. Imported fire ant toxic bait studies: Evaluation of toxicants. *J. Econ. Entomol.* 57:941–45.

Sturm, M. M., and W. L. Sterling. 1990. Geographical patterns of boll weevil mortality: Observations and hypothesis. *Environ. Entomol.* 19:59–65.

Sullender, B. 1998. A natural history of extrafloral nectar-collecting ants in the Sonoran Desert. www.ruf.rice.edu/~bws/spiders.html.

Summerlin, J. W. 1976. Polygyny in a colony of the southern fire ant. *Ann. Entomol. Soc. Amer.* 69:54.

———. 1978. Beetles of the genera *Myrmecaphodius, Rhyssemus,* and *Blapstinus* in Texas fire ant nests. *Southwest. Entomol.* 3:27–29.

Summerlin, J. W., W. A. Banks, and K. H. Schroeder. 1975. Food exchange between mounds of the red imported fire ant. *Ann. Entomol. Soc. Amer.* 68:863–66.

Summerlin, J. W., and L. R. Green. 1977. Red imported fire ant: A review on invasion, distribution, and control in Texas. *Southwest. Entomol.* 2:94–101.

Summerlin, J. W., R. L. Harris, and H. D. Petersen. 1984b. Red imported fire ant (Hymenoptera: Formicidae): Frequency and intensity of invasion of fresh cattle droppings. *Environ. Entomol.* 13:1161–63.

Summerlin, J. W., A. C. F. Hung, and S. B. Vinson. 1977a. Residues in nontarget ants, species simplification and recovery of populations following aerial applications of mirex. *Environ. Entomol.* 6:193–97.

Summerlin, J. W., and S. E. Kunz. 1978. Predation of the red imported fire ant on stable flies. *Southwest. Entomol.* 3:260–62.

Summerlin, J. W., J. K. Olson, R. R. Blume, A. Aga, and D. E. Bay. 1977b. Red imported fire ant: Effects on *Onthophagus gazella* and the horn fly. *Environ. Entomol.* 6:440–42.

Summerlin, J. W., J. K. Olson, and J. O. Fick. 1976. Red imported fire ant: Levels of infestation in different land management areas of the Texas coastal prairies and an appraisal of the control program in Fort Bend County, Texas. *J. Econ. Entomol.* 69:73–78.

Summerlin, J. W., H. D. Petersen, and R. L. Harris. 1984a. Red imported fire ant (Hymenoptera: Formicidae): Effects on the horn fly (Diptera: Muscidae) and coprophagous scarabs. *Environ. Entomol.* 13:1405–10.

Taber, S. W. 1998. *The world of the harvester ants.* College Station: Texas A&M University Press.

———. 1999. Opinion. In Comments on the proposed conservation of the specific name of *Solenopsis invicta* Buren, 1972 (Insecta, Hymenoptera). *Bull. Zool. Nomen.* 56:198–99.

Taber, S. W., and J. C. Cokendolpher. 1988. Karyotypes of a dozen ant species from the southwestern U.S.A. (Hymenoptera: Formicidae). *Caryologia* 41:93–102.

Taber, S. W., J. C. Cokendolpoher, and O. F. Francke. 1987. Supercooling points of red imported fire ants, *Solenopsis invicta* (Hymenoptera: Formicidae) from Lubbock, Texas. *Entomol. News* 98:153–58.

Talice, R. V., S. L. de Mosera, A. M. S. de Sprechmann, and A. F. Spiritosa. 1978. Note on the behavior in carrying away and depositing the dead among *Camponotus punctulatus* Mayr and *Solenopsis richteri* Forel. *Rev. Biol. Uruguay* 6:87–88.

Tarzwell, C. M. 1958. The toxicity of some organic insecticides to fishes. Pp. 7–13 in *Proceedings symposium: The fire ant eradication program and how it affects wildlife.* Proc. Ann. Conf. Southeastern Assoc. Game and Fish Comm.

Taubes, G. 1998. Tales of a bloodsucker. *Discover* 19(7):124–30.

Taylor, P. 1977. Foraging behavior of ants: Experiments with two species of myrmicine ants. *Behav. Ecol. Sociobiol.* 2:147–67.

———. 1978. Foraging behavior of ants: Theoretical considerations. *J. Theor. Biol.* 71:541–65.

Tedders, W. L., C. C. Reilly, B. W. Wood, R. K. Morrison, and C. S. Lofgren. 1990. Behavior of *Solenopsis invicta* (Hymenoptera: Formicidae) in pecan orchards. *Environ. Entomol.* 19:44–53.

Teel, P. D., S. W. Hopkins, W. A. Donahue, and O. F. Strey. 1998. Population dynamics of immature

Amblyomma maculatum (Acari: Ixodidae) and other ectoparasites on meadowlarks and northern bobwhite quail resident to the coastal prairie of Texas. *J. Med. Entomol.* 35:483–88.

Teli, V. S., and G. N. Salunkhe. 1994. Biology of sweet potato weevil. *J. Maharashtra Agric. University* 19:381–84.

Tennant, L. E., and S. D. Porter. 1991. Comparison of diets of two fire ant species (Hymenoptera: Formicidae): Solid and liquid components. *J. Entomol. Sci.* 26:450–65.

Texas Parks and Wildlife Department, June 1, 1998. Trout in Guadalupe River die from ingesting fire ants. www.tpwd.state.tx.us.

Thompson, M. J., B. M. Glancey, W. E. Robbins, C. S. Lofgren, S. R. Dutky, J. Kochansky, R. K. Vander Meer, and A. R. Glover. 1981. Major hydrocarbons of the post-pharyngeal glands of mated queens of the red imported fire ant *Solenopsis invicta. Lipids* 16:485–95.

Thompson, T. E., and M. S. Blum. 1967. Structure and behavior of spermatozoa of the fire ant *Solenopsis saevissima* (Hymenoptera: Formicidae). *Ann. Entomol. Soc. Amer.* 60:632–42.

Thorvilson, H. G., J. C. Cokendolpher, and S. A. Phillips, Jr. 1992. Survival of the red imported fire ant (Hymenoptera: Formicidae) on the Texas High Plains. *Environ. Entomol.* 21:964–68.

Thorvilson, H. G., S. A. Phillips, Jr., and A. A. Sorensen. 1989. An innovative thermofumigation technique for control of red imported fire ants (Hymenoptera: Formicidae). *J. Agric. Entomol.* 6:31–36.

Thorvilson, H., S. A. Phillips, Jr., A. Sorensen, and M. Trostle. 1986. Straw itch mites as a biocontrol agent of red imported fire ants. Pp. 70–75 in *Proceedings of the 1986 imported fire ant conference,* comp. M. E. Mispagel. Athens, Ga.: Texas Department of Agriculture and Veterinary Medical Experiment Station, University of Georgia.

———. 1987. The straw itch mite, *Pyemotes tritici* (Acari: Pyemotidae), as a biological control agent of red imported fire ants, *Solenopsis invicta* (Hymenoptera: Formicidae). *Florida Entomol.* 70:439–44.

Tomalski, M. D., M. S. Blum, T. H. Jones, H. M. Fales, D. F. Howard, and L. Passera. 1987. Chemistry and functions of exocrine secretions of the ants *Tapinoma melanocephalum* and *T. erraticum. J. Chem. Ecol.* 13:253–63.

Toom, P. M., E. W. Cupp, and C. P. Johnson. 1976a. Amino acid changes in newly inseminated queens of *Solenopsis invicta. Insect Biochem.* 6:327–31.

Toom, P. M., E. W. Cupp, C. P. Johnson, and I. Griffin. 1976b. Utilization of body reserves for minim brood development by queens of the imported fire ant, *Solenopsis invicta. J. Insect Physiol.* 22:217–20.

Toom, P. M., C. P. Johnson, and E. W. Cupp. 1976c. Utilization of body reserves during preoviposition activity by *Solenopsis invicta. Ann. Entomol. Soc. Amer.* 69:145–48.

Trabanino, C. R., H. N. Pitre, K. L. Andrews, and D. H. Meckenstock. 1989. Effect of seed size, color, number of seeds per hill and depth of planting on sorghum seed survival and stand establishment: Relationships to phytophagous insects. *Trop. Agric.* 66:225–29.

Tracy, M. J., J. G. Demain, J. M. Quinn, D. R. Hoffman, D. W. Goetz, and T. M. Freeman. 1995. The natural history of exposure to the imported fire ant *(Solenopsis invicta). J. Allergy Clin. Immunol.* 95:824–28.

Trager, J. C. 1991. A revision of the fire ants, *Solenopsis geminata* group (Hymenoptera: Formicidae: Myrmicinae). *J. New York Entomol. Soc.* 99:141–98.

Travis, B. V. 1938. The fire ant (*Solenopsis* spp.) as a pest of quail. *J. Econ. Entomol.* 31:649–52.

———. 1939. Tests of soil treatments for the control of the fire ant, *Solenopsis geminata* (F.). *J. Econ. Entomol.* 32:645–50.

———. 1941. Notes on the biology of the fire ant *Solenopsis geminata* (F.) in Florida and Georgia. *Florida Entomol.* 24:15–22.

————. 1942. Poisoned-bait tests against the fire ant, with special reference to thallium sulfate and thallium acetate. *J. Econ. Entomol.* 35:706–13.

————. 1943. Further tests with thallium baits for control of the fire ant. *J. Econ. Entomol.* 36:55–58.

Troisi, S. J., and L. M. Riddiford. 1974. Juvenile hormone effects on metamorphosis and reproduction of the fire ant, *Solenopsis invicta. Environ. Entomol.* 3:112–16.

Tschinkel, W. R. 1986. The ecological nature of the fire ant: Some aspects of colony foundation and some unanswered questions. Pp. 72–87 in *Fire ants and leaf-cutting ants: Biology and management,* ed. C. S. Lofgren and R. K. Vander Meer. Westview studies in insect biology. Boulder, Colo.: Westview Press.

————. 1987. Fire ant queen longevity and age: Estimation by sperm depletion. *Ann. Entomol. Soc. Amer.* 80:263–66.

————. 1988a. Distribution of the fire ants *Solenopsis invicta* and *S. geminata* (Hymenoptera: Formicidae) in northern Florida in relation to habitat and disturbance. *Ann. Entomol. Soc. Amer.* 81:76–81.

————. 1988b. Colony growth and the ontogeny of worker polymorphism in the fire ant, *Solenopsis invicta. Behav. Ecol. Sociobiol.* 22:103–16.

————. 1988c. Social control of egg-laying rate in queens of the fire ant, *Solenopsis invicta. Physiol. Entomol.* 13:327–350.

————. 1992a. Brood raiding and the population dynamics of founding and incipient colonies of the fire ant, *Solenopsis invicta. Ecol. Entomol.* 17:179–88.

————. 1992b. Brood raiding in the fire ant, *Solenopsis invicta* (Hymenoptera: Formicidae): Laboratory and field observations. *Ann. Entomol. Soc. Amer.* 85:638–46.

————. 1993a. Sociometry and sociogenesis of the fire ant *Solenopsis invicta* during one annual cycle. *Ecol. Monographs* 63:425–57.

————. 1993b. Resource allocation, brood production, and cannibalism during colony founding in the fire ant, *Solenopsis invicta. Behav. Ecol. Sociobiol.* 33:209–23.

————. 1995. Stimulation of fire ant queen fecundity by a highly specific brood stage. *Ann. Entomol. Soc. Amer.* 88:876–82.

————. 1996. A newly-discovered mode of colony founding among fire ants. *Insectes Sociaux* 43:267–76.

————. 1998a. The reproductive biology of fire ant societies. *Bioscience* 48:593–605.

————. 1998b. An experimental study of pleometrotic colony founding in the fire ant, *Solenopsis invicta:* What is the basis for association? *Behav. Ecol. Sociobiol.* 43:247–57.

Tschinkel, W. R., E. S. Adams, and T. Macom. 1995. Territory area and colony size in the fire ant *Solenopsis invicta. J. Anim. Ecol.* 64:473–80.

Tschinkel, W. R., and D. F. Howard. 1978. Queen replacement in orphaned colonies of the fire ant, *Solenopsis invicta. Behav. Ecol. Sociobiol.* 3:297–310.

————. 1980. A simple, nontoxic home remedy against fire ants *(Solenopsis invicta). J. Georgia Entomol. Soc.* 15:102–105.

————. 1983. Colony founding by pleometrosis in the fire ant, *Solenopsis invicta. Behav. Ecol. Sociobiol.* 12:103–43.

Tschinkel, W. R., and N. C. E. Nierenberg. 1983. Possible importance of relatedness in the fire ant, *Solenopsis invicta* Buren (Hymenoptera: Formicidae) in the United States. *Ann. Entomol. Soc. Amer.* 76:989–91.

Tschinkel, W. R., and S. D. Porter. 1988. Efficiency of sperm use in queens of the fire ant, *Solenopsis invicta* (Hymenoptera: Formicidae). *Ann. Entomol. Soc. Amer.* 81:777–81.

Turner, W. D. 1891. Red ants in California. *Insect Life* 4:203.

Van den Berg, H., A. Bagus, K. Hassan, A. Muhammad, and S. Zega. 1995. Predation and parasitism on eggs of two pod-sucking bugs, *Nezara viridula* and *Piezodorus hybneri,* in soybean. *Int. J. Pest Manag.* 41:134–42.

Vander Meer, R. K. 1986a. The trail pheromone complex of *Solenopsis invicta* and *Solenopsis richteri*. Pp. 201–10 in *Fire ants and leaf-cutting ants: Biology and management,* ed. C. S. Lofgren and R. K. Vander Meer. Westview studies in insect biology. Boulder, Colo.: Westview Press.

———. 1986b. Chemical taxonomy as a tool for separating *Solenopsis* spp. Pp. 316–26 in *Fire ants and leaf-cutting ants: Biology and management,* ed. C. S. Lofgren and R. K. Vander Meer. Westview studies in insect biology. Boulder, Colo.: Westview Press.

———. 1996. Potential role of pheromones in fire ant control. Pp. 223–32 in *Pest management in the subtropics: Integrated pest management—a Florida perspective,* ed. D. R. Rosen, F. D. Bennett, and J. L. Capinera. Andover, U.K.: Intercept Limited.

Vander Meer, R. K., and L. E. Alonso. 1998. Pheromone directed behavior in ants. Pp. 159–92 in *Pheromone communication in social insects: Ants, wasps, bees, and termites.* ed. R. K. Vander Meer, M. D. Breed, K. E. Espelie, and M. L. Winston. Boulder, Colo.: Westview Press.

Vander Meer, R. K., F. Alvarez, and C. S. Lofgren. 1988. Isolation of the trail recruitment pheromone of *Solenopsis invicta. J. Chem. Ecol.* 14:825–38.

Vander Meer, R. K., B. M. Glancey, and C. S. Lofgren. 1982a. Biochemical changes in the crop, oesophagus and postpharyngeal gland of colony-founding red imported fire ant queens *(Solenopsis invicta). Insect Biochem.* 12:123–28.

Vander Meer, R. K., B. M. Glancey, C. S. Lofgren, A. Glover, J. H. Tumlinson, and J. Rocca. 1980. The poison sac of red imported fire ant queens: Source of a pheromone attractant. *Ann. Entomol. Soc. Amer.* 73:609–12.

Vander Meer, R. K., D. P. Jouvenaz, and D. P. Wojcik. 1989a. Chemical mimicry in a parasitoid (Hymenoptera: Eucharitidae) of fire ants (Hymenoptera: Formicidae). *J. Chem. Ecol.* 15:2247–62.

Vander Meer, R. K., and C. S. Lofgren. 1989. Biochemical and behavioral evidence for hybridization between fire ants, *Solenopsis invicta* and *Solenopsis richteri* (Hymenoptera: Formicidae). *J. Chem. Ecol.* 15:1757–65.

———. 1990. Chemotaxonomy applied to fire ant systematics in the United States and South America. Pp. 75–84 in *Applied myrmecology: A world perspective,* ed. R. K. Vander Meer, K. Jaffe, and A. Cedeno. Westview studies in insect biology. Boulder, Colo.: Westview Press.

Vander Meer, R. K., C. S. Lofgren, and F. M. Alvarez. 1990. The orientation inducer pheromone of the fire ant *Solenopsis invicta. Physiol. Entomol.* 15:483–88.

Vander Meer, R. K., C. S. Lofgren, B. M. Glancey, and D. F. Williams. 1982b. The trail pheromone of the red imported fire ant, *Solenopsis invicta* chemistry, behavior and potential for control. P. 333 in *The biology of social insects,* ed. M. D. Breed, C. D. Michener, and H. E. Evans. Boulder, Colo.: Westview Press.

Vander Meer, R. K., C. S. Lofgren, and D. F. Williams. 1985. Fluoroaliphatic sulfones: A new class of delayed-action insecticides for control of *Solenopsis invicta* (Hymenoptera: Formicidae). *J. Econ. Entomol.* 78:1190–97.

———. 1986. Control of *Solenopsis invicta* with delayed-action fluorinated toxicants. *Pestic. Sci.* 17:449–55.

Vander Meer, R. K., and L. Morel. 1988. Brood pheromones in ants. Pp. 491–513 in *Advances in myrmecology,* ed. J. C. Trager. New York: E. J. Brill.

———. 1995. Ant queens deposit pheromones and antimicrobial agents on eggs. *Naturwissenschaften* 82:93–95.

———. 1998. Nestmate recognition in ants. Pp. 79–103 in *Pheromone communication in social insects: Ants, wasps, bees, and termites*, ed. R. K. Vander Meer, M. D. Breed, K. E. Espelie, and M. L. Winston. Boulder, Colo.: Westview Press.

Vander Meer, R. K., L. Morel, and C. S. Lofgren. 1992. A comparison of queen oviposition rates from monogyne and polygyne fire ant, *Solenopsis invicta*, colonies. *Physiol. Entomol.* 17:384–90.

Vander Meer, R. K., D. Saliwanchik, and B. Lavine. 1989b. Temporal changes in colony cuticular hydrocarbon patterns of *Solenopsis invicta*. Implications for nestmate recognition. *J. Chem. Ecol.* 15:2115–25.

Vander Meer, R. K., D. F. Williams, and C. S. Lofgren. 1982c. Degradation of the toxicant AC-217,300 [tetrahydro-5,5-dimethyl-2-(1H)-pyrimidinone-[3-[4-(trifluoro=methyl]phenyl]-1-[2-[4-(trifluoromethyl)phenyl]ethenyl]-2-propenylidene]=hydrazone) in Amdro imported fire ant *(Solenopsis invicta)* bait under field conditions. *J. Agric. Food Chem.* 30:1045–48.

Vander Meer, R. K., and D. P. Wojcik. 1982. Chemical mimicry in the myrmecophilous beetle *Myrmecaphodius excavaticollis*. *Science* 218:806–808.

Van Pelt, A. F. 1958. The ecology of the ants of the Welaka Reserve, Florida (Hymenoptera: Formicidae). *Am. Midland Nat.* 59:1–57.

Van Zee, J. W., W. G. Williams, and W. E. Smith. 1997. Mutual exclusion by dolichoderine ants on a rich food source. *Southwest. Nat.* 42:229–31.

Vargo, E. L. 1982. Factors influencing the production of sexuals in the fire ant, *Solenopsis invicta*. P. 256 in *The biology of social insects*, ed. M. D. Breed, C. D. Michener, and H. E. Evans. Boulder, Colo.: Westview Press.

———. 1988a. Effect of pleometrosis and colony size on the production of sexuals in monogyne colonies of the fire ant *Solenopsis invicta*. Pp. 217–25 in *Advances in myrmecology*, ed. J. C. Trager. New York: E. J. Brill.

———. 1988b. A bioassay for a primer pheromone of queen fire ants *(Solenopsis invicta)* which inhibits the production of sexuals. *Insectes Sociaux* 35:382–92.

———. 1990. Social control of reproduction in fire ant colonies. Pp. 158–72 in *Applied myrmecology: A world perspective*, ed. R. K. Vander Meer, K. Jaffe, and A. Cedeno. Westview studies in insect biology. Boulder, Colo.: Westview Press.

———. 1992. Mutual pheromonal inhibition among queens in polygynous colonies of the fire ant *Solenopsis invicta*. *Behav. Ecol. Sociobiol.* 31:205–10.

———. 1993. Colony reproductive structure in a polygyne population of *Solenopsis geminata* (Hymenoptera: Formicidae). *Ann. Entomol. Soc. Amer.* 86:441–49.

———. 1996. Sex investment ratios in monogyne and polygyne populations of the fire ant *Solenopsis invicta*. *J. Evol. Biol.* 9:783–802.

———. 1997. Poison gland of queen fire ants *(Solenopsis invicta)* is the source of a primer pheromone. *Naturwissenschaften* 84:507–10.

Vargo, E. L., and D. J. C. Fletcher. 1986a. Queen number and the production of sexuals in the fire ant, *Solenopsis invicta* (Hymenoptera: Formicidae). *Behav. Ecol. Sociobiol.* 19:41–48.

———. 1986b. Evidence of pheromonal queen control over the production of male and female sexuals in the fire ant, *Solenopsis invicta*. *J. Comp. Physiol. A Sens. Neural Behav. Physiol.* 159:741–50.

———. 1987. Effect of queen number on the production of sexuals in natural populations of the fire ant, *Solenopsis invicta*. *Physiol. Entomol.* 12:109–16.

———. 1989. On the relationship between queen number and fecundity in polygyne colonies of the fire ant *Solenopsis invicta*. *Physiol. Entomol.* 14:223–32.

Vargo, E. L., and M. Laurel. 1994. Studies on the mode of action of a queen primer pheromone of the fire ant *Solenopsis invicta*. *J. Insect Physiol.* 40:601–10.

Vargo, E. L., and S. D. Porter. 1989. Colony reproduction by budding in the polygyne form of *Solenopsis invicta* (Hymenoptera: Formicidae). *Ann. Entomol. Soc. Amer.* 82:307–13.

———. 1993. Reproduction by virgin queen fire ants in queenless colonies: Comparative study of three taxa *(Solenopsis richteri,* hybrid *S. invicta/richteri, S. geminata)* (Hymenoptera: Formicidae). *Insectes Sociaux* 40:283–93.

Vargo, E. L., and K. G. Ross. 1989. Differential viability of eggs laid by queens in polygyne colonies of the fire ant, *Solenopsis invicta. J. Insect Physiol.* 35:587–94.

Veeresh, G. K. 1990a. Pest ants of India. Pp. 15–24 in *Applied myrmecology: A world perspective,* ed. R. K. Vander Meer, K. Jaffe, and A. Cedeno. Westview studies in insect biology. Boulder, Colo.: Westview Press.

———. 1990b. Pest ants of India and their management. Pp. 267–68 in *Social insects and the environment,* ed. G. K. Veeresh, B. Mallik, and C. A. Viraklimath. New Delhi, India: Oxford and IBH.

Vilhelmsen, L. 1997. The phylogeny of lower Hymenoptera (Insecta), with a summary of the early evolutionary history of the order. *J. Zool. Syst. Evol. Res.* 35:49–70.

Vinson, S. B. 1968. The distribution of an oil, carbohydrate, and protein food source to members of the imported fire ant colony. *J. Econ. Entomol.* 61:712–14.

———. 1970. Gustatory response by the imported fire ant to various electrolytes. *Ann. Entomol. Soc. Amer.* 63:932–35.

———. 1972. Imported fire ant feeding on *Paspalum* seeds. *Ann. Entomol. Soc. Amer.* 65:988.

———. 1986. The physiology of the imported fire ants: Basic gaps in our understanding. Pp. 289–301 in *Fire ants and leaf-cutting ants: Biology and management,* ed. C. S. Lofgren and R. K. Vander Meer. Westview studies in insect biology. Boulder, Colo.: Westview Press.

———. 1991. Effect of the red imported fire ant (Hymenoptera: Formicidae) on a small plant-decomposing arthropod community. *Environ. Entomol.* 20:98–103.

———. 1997. Invasion of the red imported fire ant (Hymenoptera: Formicidae): Spread, biology, and impact. *Amer. Entomol.* 43:23–39.

Vinson, S. B., and S. Ellison. 1996. An unusual case of polygyny in *Solenopsis invicta* Buren. *Southwest. Nat.* 21:387–93.

Vinson, S. B., and W. P. MacKay. 1990. Effects of the fire ant, *Solenopsis invicta,* on electrical circuits and equipment. Pp. 496–503 in *Applied myrmecology: A world perspective,* ed. R. K. Vander Meer, K. Jaffe, and A. Cedeno. Westview studies in insect biology. Boulder, Colo.: Westview Press.

Vinson, S. B., S. A. Phillips, Jr., and H. J. Williams. 1980. The function of the post-pharyngeal glands of the red imported fire ant, *Solenopsis invicta* Buren. *J. Insect Physiol.* 26:645–50.

Vinson, S. B., and R. Robeau. 1974. Insect growth regulator effects on colonies of the imported fire ant. *J. Econ. Entomol.* 67:584–87.

Vinson, S. B., R. Robeau, and L. Dzuik. 1974. Bioassay and activity of several insect growth regulators on the imported fire ant. *J. Econ. Entomol.* 67:325–28.

Vinson, S. B., and T. A. Scarborough. 1989. Impact of the imported fire ant on laboratory populations of cotton aphid, *(Aphis gossypii)* predators. *Florida Entomol.* 72:107–11.

———. 1991. Interactions between *Solenopsis invicta* (Hymenoptera: Formicidae), *Rhopalosiphum maidis* (Homoptera: Aphididae), and the parasitoid *Lysiphlebus testaceipes* Cresson (Hymenoptera: Aphidiidae). *Ann. Entomol. Soc. Amer.* 84:158–64.

Vinson, S. B., and A. A. Sorensen. 1986. *Imported fire ants: Life history and impact.* College Station/Austin: Texas A&M University Department of Entomology and Texas Department of Agriculture.

Vinson, S. B., J. L. Thompson, and H. B. Green. 1967. Phagostimulants for the imported fire ant, *Solenopsis saevissima* var. *richteri*. *J. Insect Physiol.* 13:1729–36.

Vogt, J. T. 1996. Founding queen of the red imported fire ant *(Solenopsis invicta)* (Hymenoptera: Formicidae) observed in carnivorous plant. *Entomol. News* 107:141–42.

Vogt, J. T., and A. G. Appel. 1999. Standard metabolic rate of the fire ant, *Solenopsis invicta* Buren: Effects of temperature, mass, and caste. *J. Insect Physiol.* 45:655–66.

Voss, S. H. 1981. Trophic egg production in virgin fire ant queens. *J. Georgia Entomol. Soc.* 16:437–40.

Voss, S. H., J. F. McDonald, J. H. D. Bryan, and C. H. Keith. 1987. Abnormal mitotic spindles: Developmental block in fire ant trophic eggs. *Eur. J. Cell Biol.* 45:9–15.

Voss, S. H., J. F. McDonald, and C. H. Keith. 1988. Production and abortive development of fire ant trophic eggs. Pp. 517–34 in *Advances in myrmecology*, ed. J. C. Trager. New York: E. J. Brill.

Walker, J. R., and D. F. Clower. 1961. Morphology and histology of the alimentary canal of the imported fire ant queen *(Solenopsis saevissima richteri)*. *Ann. Entomol. Soc. Amer.* 54:92–99.

Wallace, J. B. 1970. The defensive function of a case on a chrysomelid larva. *J. Georgia Entomol. Soc.* 5:19–24.

Waller, D. A., and J. P. La Fage. 1986a. *Solenopsis* predation on subterranean termites. Pp. 3–4 in *Proceedings of the 1986 imported fire ant conference*, comp. M. E. Mispagel. Athens, Ga.: Texas Department of Agriculture and Veterinary Medical Experiment Station, University of Georgia.

———. 1986b. Fire ant predation on subterranean termites: Relative effectiveness of *Reticulitermes* sp. and *Coptotermes formosanus* Shiraki defenses (Isoptera: Rhinotermitidae). *Mater. Organ.* 21:291–300.

Walsh, C. T., J. H. Law, and E. O. Wilson. 1965. Purification of the fire ant trail substance. *Nature* 207:320–21.

Walsh, J. P., and W. R. Tschinkel. 1974. Brood recognition by contact pheromone in the red imported fire ant, *Solenopsis invicta*. *Animal Behav.* 22:695–704.

Wangberg, J. K., J. D. Ewig, Jr., and C. K. Pinson. 1980. The relationship of *Solenopsis invicta* Buren to soils of East Texas. *Southwest. Entomol.* 5:16–18.

Ward, M. 1998. There's an ant in my phone . . . . *New Scientist*, 24 January, pp. 32–35.

Ward, P. S. 1989. Genetic and Social changes associated with ant speciation. Pp. 123–48 in *The genetics of social evolution*, ed. M. D. Breed and R. E. Page, Jr. Boulder, Colo.: Westview Press.

Waters, E. M., J. E. Huff, and H. B. Gerstner. 1977. Mirex: An overview. *Environ. Res.* 14:212–22.

Way, M. J., Z. Islam, K. L. Heong, and R. C. Joshi. 1998. Ants in tropical irrigated rice: Distribution and abundance, especially of *Solenopsis geminata* (Hymenoptera: Formicidae). *Bull. Entomol. Res.* 88:467–76.

Weber, N. A. 1948. Ants from the Leeward Group and some other Caribbean localities. *Studies on the Fauna of Curaçao, Aruba, Bonaire and the Venezuelan Islands* 14:78–85.

Wells, H. G. 1905. The empire of the ants. *Strand Magazine* 30:685–93.

Wells, J. D., and B. Greenberg. 1994. Effect of the red imported fire ant (Hymenoptera: Formicidae) and carcass type on the daily occurrence of postfeeding carrion-fly larvae (Diptera: Calliphoridae, Sarcophagidae). *J. Med. Entomol.* 31:171–74.

Wells, J. D., and G. Henderson. 1993. Fire ant predation on native and introduced subterranean termites in the laboratory: Effect of high soldier number in *Coptotermes formosanus*. *Ecol. Entomol.* 18:270–74.

Wendel, L. E., and S. B. Vinson. 1978. Distribution and metabolism of a juvenile hormone analogue within colonies of the red imported fire ant. *J. Econ. Entomol.* 71:561–65.

Wernick, S. 1976. *The fire ants.* New York: Award Books.

Wheeler, D. E. 1990. The developmental basis of worker polymorphism in fire ants. *J. Insect Physiol.* 36:315–21.

Wheeler, G. C., and E. W. Wheeler. 1937: New hymenopterous parasites of ants (Chalcidoidea: Eucharidae). *Ann. Entomol. Soc. Amer.* 30:163–75.

Wheeler, G. C., and J. N. Wheeler. 1955. The ant larvae of the myrmicine tribe Solenopsidini. *Am. Midland Nat.* 54:119–41.

———. 1973. *Ants of Deep Canyon.* Riverside: Philip L. Boyd Deep Canyon Desert Research Center, University of California.

———. 1986. *The ants of Nevada.* Los Angeles: Natural History Museum of Los Angeles County.

Wheeler, W. B., D. P. Jouvenaz, D. P. Wojcik, W. A. Banks, C. H. Vanmiddelem, C. S. Lofgren, S. Nesbitt, L. Williams, and R. Brown. 1977. Mirex residues in nontarget organisms after application of 10-5 bait for fire ant control, northeast Florida: 1972–74. *Pestic. Monit. J.* 11:146–56.

Wheeler, W. M. 1900. The habits of *Myrmecophila nebrascensis* Bruner. *Psyche* 9:111–15.

———. 1906. The ants of the Grand Cañon. *Bull. Am. Mus. Nat. Hist.* 22:329–45.

———. 1908a. The ants of Texas, New Mexico and Arizona. Part I. *Bull. Am. Mus. Nat. Hist.* 24:399–485.

———. 1908b. Ants from Moorea, Society Islands. *Bull. Am. Mus. Nat. Hist.* 24:165–66.

———. 1908c. Ants of Jamaica. *Bull. Am. Mus. Nat. Hist.* 24:159–63.

———. 1908d. Ants of Porto Rico and Virgin Islands. *Bull. Am. Mus. Nat. Hist.* 24:117–58.

———. 1910. *Ants: Their structure, development and behavior.* New York: Columbia University Press.

———. 1915. Some additions to the North American ant-fauna. *Bull. Am. Mus. Nat. Hist.* 34:389–421.

———. 1928. The evolution of ants. Pp. 210–24 in *Creation by evolution,* ed. F. Mason. New York: Macmillan.

Whitcomb, W. H. 1994. Environment and habitat management to increase predator populations. Pp. 149–79 in *Pest management in the subtropics: Biological control—a Florida perspective,* ed. D. Rosen, F. D. Bennett, and J. L. Capinera. Andover, U.K.: Intercept Limited.

Whitcomb, W. H., A. Bhatkar, and J. C. Nickerson. 1973. Predators of *Solenopsis invicta* queens prior to successful colony establishment. *Environ. Entomol.* 2:1101–1103.

Whitcomb, W. H., H. A. Denmark, A. P. Bhatkar, and G. L. Greene. 1972. Preliminary studies on the ants of Florida soybean fields. *Florida Entomol.* 55:129–42.

Whitcomb, W. H., T. D. Gowan, and W. F. Buren. 1982. Predators of *Diaprepes abbreviatus* (Coleoptera: Curculionidae) larvae. *Florida Entomol.* 65:150–58.

Whitford, W. G. 1978. Structure and seasonal activity of Chihuahua desert ant communities. *Insectes Sociaux* 23:79–88.

Whiting, M. J. 1994. *Pseudemys texana* (Texas river cooter). Nesting interference. *Herpet. Rev.* 25:25.

Whitworth, S. T., M. S. Blum, and J. Travis. 1998. Proteolytic enzymes from larvae of the fire ant, *Solenopsis invicta:* Isolation and characterization of four serine endopeptidases. *J. Biol. Chem.* 273:14430–34.

Whitworth, S. T., T. Kordula, and J. Travis. 1999. Molecular cloning of Soli E2: An elastase-like serine proteinase from the red imported fire ant *(Solenopsis invicta). Insect Biochem. Mol. Biol.* 29:249–54.

Wilkinson, R. C., A. P. Bhatkar, W. J. Kloft, W. H. Whitcomb, and E. S. Kloft. 1978. *Formica integra:* 2. Feeding, trophallaxis, and interspecific confrontation behavior. *Florida Entomol.* 61:179–87.

Willer, D. E., and D. J. C. Fletcher. 1986. Differences in inhibitory capability among queens of the ant *Solenopsis invicta. Physiol. Entomol.* 11:475–82.

Williams, D. F. 1986a. Chemical baits: Specificity and effects on other ant species. Pp. 378–86 in *Fire ants and leaf-cutting ants: Biology and management*, ed. C. S. Lofgren and R. K. Vander Meer. Westview studies in insect biology. Boulder, Colo.: Westview Press.

———. 1986b. Effects of two bait toxicants on natural populations of nontarget ants. Pp. 83–87 in *Proceedings of the 1986 imported fire ant conference*, comp. M. E. Mispagel. Athens, Ga.: Texas Department of Agriculture and Veterinary Medical Experiment Station, University of Georgia.

———. 1990. Oviposition and growth of the fire ant *Solenopsis invicta*. Pp. 150–57 in *Applied myrmecology: A world perspective*, ed. R. K. Vander Meer, K. Jaffe, and A. Cedeno. Westview studies in insect biology. Boulder, Colo.: Westview Press.

Williams, D. F., and W. A. Banks. 1987. *Pseudacteon obtusus* (Diptera: Phoridae) attacking *Solenopsis invicta* (Hymenoptera: Formicidae) in Brazil. *Psyche* 94:9–13.

Williams, D. F., W. A. Banks, and C. S. Lofgren. 1997. Control of *Solenopsis invicta* (Hymenoptera: Formicidae) with teflubenzuron. *Florida Entomol.* 80:84–91.

Williams, D. F., G. J. Knue, and J. J. Becnel. 1998. Discovery of *Thelohania solenopsae* from the red imported fire ant, *Solenopsis invicta*, in the United States. *J. Invert. Pathol.* 71:175–76.

Williams, D. F., and C. S. Lofgren. 1981. EL-468, a new bait toxicant for control of the red imported fire ant *(Solenopsis invicta). Florida Entomol.* 64:472–77.

———. 1983. Imported fire ant *[Solenopsis invicta]* (Hymenoptera: Formicidae) control: Evaluation of several chemicals for individual mound treatments. *J. Econ. Entomol.* 76:1201–1205.

———. 1988. Nest castings of some ground-dwelling Florida ant species using dental labstone. Pp. 433–43 in *Advances in myrmecology*, ed. J. C. Trager. New York: E. J. Brill.

Williams, D. F., C. S. Lofgren, W. A. Banks, C. E. Stringer, and J. K. Plumley. 1980a. Laboratory studies with 9 amidinohydrazones, a promising new class of bait toxicants for control of red imported fire ants *(Solenopsis invicta). J. Econ. Entomol.* 73:798–802.

Williams, D. F., C. S. Lofgren, and A. Lemire. 1980b. A simple diet for rearing laboratory colonies of the red imported fire ant *(Solenopsis invicta). J. Econ. Entomol.* 73:176–77.

Williams, D. F., C. S. Lofgren, and R. K. Vander Meer. 1987a. The red imported fire ant, *Solenopsis invicta:* Control with fluoroaliphatic sulfone bait toxicants. *J. Agric. Entomol.* 4:41–47.

———. 1990. Fly pupae as attractant carriers for toxic baits for red imported fire ants (Hymenoptera: Formicidae). *J. Econ. Entomol.* 83:67–73.

Williams, D. F., D. H. Oi, and G. J. Knue. 1999. Infection of red imported fire ant (Hymenoptera: Formicidae) colonies with the entomopathogen *Thelohania solenopsae* (Microsporidia: Thelohaniidae). *J. Econ. Entomol.* 92:830–36.

Williams, D. F., R. K. Vander Meer, and C. S. Lofgren. 1987b. Diet-induced nonmelanized cuticle in workers of the imported fire ant *Solenopsis invicta* Buren. *Arch. Insect Biochem. Physiol.* 4:251–59.

Williams, H. J., M. R. Strand, G. W. Elzen, S. B. Vinson, and S. J. Merritt. 1986. Nesting behavior, nest architecture, and use of Dufour's gland lipids in nest provisioning by *Megachile integra* and *Mendica mendica mendica* (Hymenoptera: Megachilidae). *J. Kansas Entomol. Soc.* 59:588–97.

Williams, H. J., M. R. Strand, and S. B. Vinson. 1981. Trail pheromone of the red imported fire ant *Solenopsis invicta* (Buren). *Experientia* (Basel) 37:1159–60.

Williams, R. N. 1980. Insect natural enemies of fire ants in South America with several new records. *Proc. Tall Timber Confer.* 7:123–34.

Williams, R. N., J. Strand, D. Gallo, and W. H. Whitcomb. 1973. Fire ants attacked by phorid flies. *Florida Entomol.* 56:259–62.

Wilson, E. O. 1951. Variation and adaptation in the imported fire ant. *Evolution* 5:68–79.

———. 1952. The *Solenopsis saevissima* complex in South America (Hymenoptera: Formicidae). *Mem. Inst. Oswaldo Cruz* (Rio de Janeiro) 50:60–68.

———. 1953. Origin of the variation in the imported fire ant. *Evolution* 7:262–63.

———. 1958. The fire ant. *Scientific American* 198(3):36–41.

———. 1959a. Source and possible nature of the odor trail of fire ants. *Science* 129:643–44.

———. 1959b. Invader of the South. *Nat. Hist.* 68:276–81.

———. 1962. Chemical communication among workers of the fire ant *Solenopsis saevissima* (Fr. Smith). *Animal Behav.* 10:134–64.

———. 1971. *The insect societies.* Cambridge, Mass.: Harvard University Press.

———. 1975. Enemy specification in the alarm-recruitment system of an ant. *Science* 190:798–800.

———. 1976. The organization of colony defense in the ant *Pheidole dentata* Mayr (Hymenoptera: Formicidae). *Behav. Ecol. Sociobiol.* 1:63–81.

———. 1978. Division of labor in fire ants based on physical castes (Hymenoptera: Formicidae: *Solenopsis*). *J. Kansas Entomol. Soc.* 51:615–36.

———. 1986. The defining traits of fire ants and leaf-cutting ants. Pp. 1–9 in *Fire ants and leaf-cutting ants: Biology and management*, ed. C. S. Lofgren and R. K. Vander Meer. Westview studies in insect biology. Boulder, Colo.: Westview Press.

———. 1994. *Naturalist.* New York: Warner Books.

Wilson, E. O., and W. L. Brown. 1958. Recent changes in the introduced population of the fire ant *Solenopsis saevissima* (Fr. Smith). *Evolution* 12:211–18.

Wilson, E. O., and J. H. Eads. 1949. Special report to Alabama Department of Conservation: A report on the imported fire ant *Solenopsis saevissima* var. *richteri* Forel in Alabama. 55 pp. + 8 plates.

Wilson, E. O., and R. W. Taylor. 1967. The ants of Polynesia (Hymenoptera: Formicidae). *Pacific Insects Monographs* 14. 109 pp.

Wilson, N. L., J. H. Dillier, and G. P. Markin. 1971. Foraging territories of imported fire ants. *Ann. Entomol. Soc. Amer.* 64:660–65.

Wilson, N. L., and A. D. Oliver. 1969. Food habits of the imported fire ant in pasture and pine forest areas in southeastern Louisiana. *J. Econ. Entomol.* 62:1268–71.

———. 1970. Relationship of the imported fire ant to Nantucket pine tip moth infestations. *J. Econ. Entomol.* 63:1250–52.

Wisdom, W. A., and W. G. Whitford. 1981. Effects of vegetation change on ant communities of arid rangelands. *Environ. Entomol.* 10:893–97.

Wojcik, D. P. 1980. Fire ant myrmecophiles: Behavior of *Myrmecosaurus ferrugineus* Bruch (Coleoptera: Staphylinidae) with comments on its abundance. *Sociobiology* 5:63–68.

———. 1986. Observations on the biology and ecology of fire ants in Brazil. Pp. 88–103 in *Fire ants and leaf-cutting ants: Biology and management*, ed. C. S. Lofgren and R. K. Vander Meer. Westview studies in insect biology. Boulder, Colo.: Westview Press.

———. 1990. Behavioral interactions of fire ants and their parasites, predators and inquilines. Pp. 329–44 in *Applied myrmecology: A world perspective*, ed. R. K. Vander Meer, K. Jaffe, and A. Cedeno. Westview studies in insect biology. Boulder, Colo.: Westview Press.

Wojcik, D. P., W. A. Banks, and D. H. Habeck. 1978. Fire ant myrmecophiles: Flight periods of *Myrmecaphodius excavaticollis* (Blanchard) and *Euparia castanea* Serville (Coleoptera: Scarabaeidae). *Coleop. Bull.* 32:59–64.

Wojcik, D. P., W. A. Banks, D. M. Hicks, and J. W. Summerlin. 1977. Fire ant myrmecophiles: New hosts and distribution of *Myrmecaphodius excavaticollis* (Blanchard) and *Euparia castanea* Serville (Coleoptera: Scarabaeidae). *Coleop. Bull.* 31:329–34.

Wojcik, D. P., W. A. Banks, W. B. Wheeler, D. P. Jouvenaz, C. H. Van Middelem, and C. S. Lofgren. 1975. Mirex residues in nontarget organisms after application of experimental baits for fire ant control, southwest Georgia: 1971–72. *Pestic. Monit. J.* 9:124–33.

Wojcik, D. P., B. J. Smittle, and H. L. Cromroy. 1991. Fire ant myrmecophiles: Feeding relationships of *Martinezia dutertrei* and *Euparia castanea* (Coleoptera: Scarabaeidae) with their host ants, *Solenopsis* spp. (Hymenoptera: Formicidae). *Insectes Sociaux* 38:273–81.

Wolcott, G. N. 1933. Recent experiments in the control of two Puerto Rican ants. *J. Agric. University Puerto Rico* 17:223–39.

———. 1951. The present status of economic entomology in Puerto Rico. University of Puerto Rico Agric. Exp. Sta. Bull. No. 99.

Wong, M. A., and T. T. Y. Wong. 1988. Predation of the Mediterranean fruit fly and the Oriental fly (Diptera: Tephritidae) by the fire ant (Hymenoptera: Formicidae) in Hawaii [USA]. *Proc. Hawaiian Entomol. Soc.* 28:169–78.

Wood, H. P. 1917. The chicken mite: Its life history and habits. USDA Tech. Bull. no. 553. 14 pp.

Wood, L. A., and W. R. Tschinkel. 1981. Quantification and modification of worker size variation in the fire ant *Solenopsis invicta*. *Insectes Sociaux* 28:117–28.

Worthing, C. R., and R. J. Hance, eds. 1991. *The pesticide manual.* 9th ed. Farnham, Surrey, U.K.: British Crop Protection Council.

Wray, D. L. 1962. An unusual record of the southern fire ant, *Solenopsis xyloni*, in North Carolina. *J. Econ. Entomol.* 55:145.

Wright, S. 1932. The roles of mutation, inbreeding, crossbreeding and selection in evolution. *Proc. 6th Int. Congr. Genet.* 1:356–66.

———. 1949. Adaptation and selection. Pp. 365–89 in *Genetics, paleontology, and evolution,* ed. G. L. Jepsen, E. Mayr, and G. G. Simpson. Princeton, N.J.: Princeton University Press.

Yeh, J. Z., T. Narahashi, and R. R. Almon. 1975. Characterization of neuromuscular blocking action of piperidine derivatives. *J. Pharmacol. Exp. Ther.* 194:373–83.

Yoder, J. A. 1995. Allomonal defence secretions of the American dog tick *Dermacentor variabilis* (Acari: Ixodidae) promote clustering. *Exp. & Appl. Acar.* 19:695–705.

Yoffe, E. 1988. The ants from hell. *Texas Monthly,* August, 80–84, 142–46.

Yosef, R., and F. E. Lohrer. 1995. Loggerhead shrikes, red fire ants and red herrings. *Condor* 97:1053–56.

Young, O. P. 1984. Utilization of dead insects on the soil surface in row crop situations. *Environ. Entomol.* 13:1346–51.

Zak, B. 1984. *A field guide to Texas critters.* Dallas: Taylor Publishing Company.

Zakharov, A. A., and L. C. Thompson. 1998a. Effects of repeated use of fenoxycarb and hydramethylnon baits on nontarget ants. *J. Entomol. Sci.* 33:212–20.

———. 1998b. Tunnels and territorial structure in polygyne fire ants, *Solenopsis wagneri* (Hymenoptera: Formicidae). *Zoologicheskii Zhurnal* 77:911–22.

Zalkow, L. H., R. W. Howard, L. T. Gelbaum, M. M. Gordon, H. M. Deutsch, and M. S. Blum. 1981. Chemical ecology of *Reticulitermes flavipes* (Kollar) and *R. virginicus* (Banks) (Rhinotermitidae). *J. Chem. Ecol.* 7:717–31.

Zalom, F. G., and W. J. Bentley. 1985. Southern fire ant (Hymenoptera: Formicidae) damage to harvested almonds in California. *J. Econ. Entomol.* 78:339–41.

Zenner de Polania, I., and N. R. Bolaños. 1985. Habitos alimenticios y relaciones simbioticas de la "hormiga loca" *Nylanderia fulva* con otros artropodos. *Rev. Colomb. Entomol.* 11:3–10.

Zimmerman, E. C. 1948. *Insects of Hawaii,* Vol. 2. Honolulu, Hawaii: Bernice P. Bishop Museum.

Index

Scientific names and pages containing relevant figures appear in italics.

abamectin, 153
Abananote hylonome (butterfly), 189–90
abnormalities, 57
Acanthaspis concinnula (assassin bug), 188
acephate, 153
Affirm, 153
African land snail *(Achatina fulica)*, 212
aggregation, 78
alarm pheromone, 41, 46
aldrex, 157
aldrin, 18, 142, 143, 149, 157
alkaloids, 13, 107, 134–35, 137, 138–39, 140
allergens (protein), 134, 135–37
allergy to stings. *See* anaphylactic shock
almonds, 213
amber fossils, 106
Amblyomma americanum (tick), 203
Amblyomma maculatum (tick), 203–204
Amblyomma variegatum (tick), 75, 189
Amdro bait, 111, 134, 150–51, 153, 154, 157, 210
amidinohydrazone. *See* hydramethylnon
anaphylactic shock, 128–33, 138
Anax junius (dragonfly), *172*
Anillus affabilis (ground beetle), *124*
Anommatocoris coleopteratus (lace bug), 121
anteaters, 176
antenna, 62, 78, 231
ant-lion, 172, *173*
Anurogryllus muticus (cricket), 118
Aphaenogaster occidentalis (ant), 165
Apocellus (rove beetle), 127
Apocellus schmidtii (rove beetle), *124*
Apocephalus coquilleti (phorid fly), 191
Apocephalus normenti (phorid fly), 180
Apodicrania termophila (phorid fly), 104
apoptosis, 49
Apterophora attophila (phorid fly), 126

Araeoschizus decipiens (darkling beetle), 127
Argentine ant *(Linepithema humile)*, 12, 158, 160, 180, 184, 190
Argiope aurantia (spider), 173
aril, *74*, 76
Arizona: invasion of, 219, 222
Arkansas, 219
armadillo, 176
arsenic, 138, 156
artificial insemination, 53
Ascend, 153
asexual reproduction, 54
ashes, 154
Aspergillus flavus (fungus), 177, 181
Atrazonotus umbrosus (seed bug), 124, *125*
autotomy, 135
avermectins, 152–53
Award, 152. *See also* fenoxycarb

Bacillus sphaericus (bacterium), 191
Bacillus thuringiensis (bacterium), 178
bait, 142, 145, 146, 150, 152
Bant, 154
Beauveria bassiana (fungus), 176–77, 178, 181
behavioral aging, 56
bendiocarb, 158
benefits from fire ants, 18–19, 20. *See also* individual species
Bengal Fire Ant Killer, 154
Bergmann's rule, 113
BIFA. *See* black imported fire ant
bifenthrin, 154
biocontrol, 17, 159–93.
birds: killed by chemicals, 145; killed by fire ants, 21, 197, 208–209, 214; killers of fire ants, 175
bite, 131. *See also* sting

black imported fire ant (BIFA; *Solenopsis richteri*): biocontrol, 180–81; biology, 58–65; chemical control, 156; communication 62; development, 65; expansion in United States, 225; identification of, *231, 232, 233*; invasion of United States, xv, 15–16; in list of fire ants, 229; medical importance, 137; nesting sites, 60; nest population, foraging behavior, diet, feeding behavior, 61–62; nests, 60–61; nest symbionts, 120–23; pest status, 205; polygyny, 114; reproduction, 62–63; sting, *5*; worker, *9*; world distribution, 59
black widow (spider), *173*
Blapstinus (darkling beetle), 118, 127
bleach, 132, 154
Blissus parasigaster. See Neoblissus parasitaster
blueberry, 195
Bolton, B., 14, 25
Boophilus microplus (tick), 212
boric acid, 154, 158
Bothriocera (bug), 127
Brachynemurus nebulosus (ant-lion), 172
brood–raiding, 56–57
Buckley, S. B., 68
Buren, W. F., 25, 26, 58
Burenella dimorpha (microsporidian), 178, 189, 191
Bushwhacker, 154

Caenocholax fenyesi (twisted-wing insect), 168–69, 188
Calathea microcephala (plant), 73–74
Calathea ovandensis (plant), 74
calcium cyanide, 156
California: invasion of, 217, 219, 222–23
Callows, 55
Calytodesmus schubarti (millipede), 118, 124
Camponotus floridanus (ant), 184
Canada: possible invasion of, 223
cancer: and venom chemistry, 140
Candida (fungus), 178
cannibalism, 37–38
carbaryl, 153, 154
carbolic acid, 157
carbon dioxide. *See* aggregation
carbon disulfide, 158
carbon tetrachloride, 158
Carolina mantis, 172
carrion beetles, 199, 205
Carson, R., 158
castes, 227. *See also* queens; workers
cattle, 196, 197, 209

chemical control, 18, 76, 91, 131, 138, 141–58. *See also individual chemicals and baits*
chlordane, 18, 143, 149, 156, 157
chlorinated hydrocarbons. *See individual chemicals*
chlorpyrifos, 153, 156, 158
Cicindella punctulata (tiger beetle), 166
citrus, 195, 206, 207, 211
citrus oils, 154
claustral nest founding, 31
Cleland, M., 217
Cnemodus mavortius (seed bug), 118
cold-hardiness, 20–21, 223, 225
Commoptera solenopsidis (phorid fly), 124–25
Conibius (darkling beetle), 127
Conidiobolus (fungus), 178
contact poisons, 141, 153
Convolvulus arvensis (plant), 200
Coptotermes formosanus (termite), 168
corn, 195, 196, 206
corn earworm *(Heliothis zea)*, 36
cotton, 201–202, 210, 214
cotton rat, 196
coyotes, 199
culturing ovaries, 54
cyanide, 157. *See also* calcium cyanide
cypermethrin, 158

Daguerre's fire ant. *See Solenopsis daguerrei*
Dalmatian insect flower, 154
Darwin, C., 108
DDT, 18, 104, 142, 146, 148, 149
Dechlorane. *See* mirex
deer, 196–97
deltamethrin, 154
Dermacentor variabilis (tick), 174
Dermanyssus gallinae (chicken mite), 215
desert fire ant. *See* golden fire ant
development of imported fire ants, 22–23. *See also individual species*
Diaprepes abbreviatus (weevil), 189
diatomaceous earth, 155
diazinon, 153, 154, 157, 158
dieldrin, 18, 142, 143, 144, 149, 157
diet, 17, 18, 21, 51. *See also individual fire ant species*
Dinardopsis plaumanni (rove beetle), 121, 122
Dinardopsis solenopsidicola (rove beetle), 121
Dinusella convexicollis (rove beetle), 121
Dinusella santschii (rove beetle), 121
Dinusella solenopsidis (rove beetle), 121
Dione junio (butterfly), 189–90

diploid males, 81. *See also* sterile males
Discoderus (ground beetle), 118
disease transmission, 139
dispersal, *23–24*
Dorymyrmex flavopectus (ant), 162
Dorymyrmex insanus (ant), 162
Dorymyrmex pyramicus (ant), 162, 184
Dufour's gland, 33, 34, 41, 44, 62
Dursban, 153, 154

eggs, 49, 51, 52, 55, 63, *82–83*
elaiosomes, *73–74*
electrical equipment, damage to, 34, 200, 214
electromagnetic attraction, 34
emigration of colony, 24, 61, 71, 72, 95, 157
enemies of fire ants. *See* biocontrol
Ephebomyrmex imberbiculus (ant), 162
Ephebomyrmex naegelii (ant), 162
epsom salts, 154
eradication efforts, xv, 217, 225. *See also* chemical control
Erodium cicutarium (plant), 102
eucharitid wasps, 193. *See also* Orasema
Euparia castanea (scarab beetle), 127, 166, 188
Euryopis (spider), 191
Euthorax pictipennis (rove beetle), *123–24*
evolution, 11, 105–16, 226
evolutionary tree, *106*, 226

Fabricius, J. C., xvi, 66
farnesene, 34
fatalities from stings, 130–33, 139
Federal Code of Regulations (Section 301), 219
Federal Imported Fire Ant Quarantine, 217
fenoxycarb, 151–52, 155
ferriamicide, 142
Ficam, 154
fire: as fire ant control, 190
Fire Ant Control (product), 154
fire ants: chemistry, 21–22; common names, 3, 7–8; nest defense, 3–7; origin, 3, 105–106; United States species, 8. *See also* individual fire ant species
fish: killed by chemicals, 144; killed by fire ants, 144, 198–99, 205
Forelius mccooki (ant), 190–91
Forelius pruinosus (ant), 191
forensic entomology, 199
Fustiger elegans (beetle), 121

gamma benzene hexachloride ("666," gamma-BHC), 18, 157

gaster-flagging, 35, 41
Gastrophysa cyanea (leaf beetle), 166
genetic diversity, 108, 109, 115
GFA. *See* golden fire ant
giant mounds, 60–61
golden fire ant (GFA; *Solenopsis aurea*): biology, 93–97; communication, reproduction, development, 97; enemies, 191; foraging behavior, diet, feeding behavior, 95, 97; identification of, *230*, *231*, *233*; in list of fire ants, 229; medical importance, 140; name, 13; nesting sites, 93; nest population, 95; nests, 95; nest symbionts, 127; pest status, 194; worker, *10*; world distribution, *94*
golf courses, 201
Gramm, P., 217
grand mal seizure, 129
Grassiella (silverfish), 118, 127
Grassiella praestans (silverfish), 124
Green, H. B., 21
green-beard, 44, 52
grits, 155
group foraging, 91
Gymnolaelaps shealsi (mite), 122
gynandromorphs, 57, 97
gypsy moth, 16, 168

habitat conservation (as biocontrol), 181
Haematobia irritans (horn fly), 203, *204*
Hamearis epulis signatus (butterfly), 120
Harvester Bait 300, 142
harvesting machinery (damage to) 195
heptachlor, 141–42, 143–45, 149, 157, 158
Heterorhabditis heliothidis (worm), 192
Hippeutister solenopsidis (beetle), *122*, 123
Hirsutella (fungus), 178
histamine, 134, 138
Holostaspis (mite), 127
homosesquiterpene, 34
horned lizard, 175–76, 190
hot water: as fire ant control, 154
household pests, 28, 70, 158, 201, 209, 214
Houston toad, 198
humpbacked flies. *See* phorid flies; *individual species*
Huxley, J., 105
hybrid fire ants: biocontrol question, 227; characteristics of RIFA x BIFA, 113–14; characteristics of TFA x SFA, 115; cold-tolerance, 223; enemies, 114, 190, 225; existence of RIFA x BIFA, 16, 26; facilitation of RIFA x BIFA, 107–108; identification, 233; in list of

hybrid fire ants (*continued*)
   fire ant species, 229; United States distribution, *224;* venom, 137
hydramethylnon, 150–51, 153, 155, 157, 158
hydroprene, 151
Hypolimnas anomala (butterfly), 75–76

IGRs (insect growth regulators), 151–52. *See also individual IGRs*
imported fire ant, xvi, 3, 17–24, *218. See also* black imported fire ant; red imported fire ant
infestation (means of), 24
insect growth regulators. *See* IGRs
instars, 55
intercaste, 57
invasion of North America, xv, 11, 16
invictolides, 42
Iridomyrmex humilis. See Argentine ant
isofenphos, 154

juvenile hormones, 51, 151. *See also* IGRs

Kentucky: predicted invasion, 60
Kepone, 142–43, 145
"killer bee," 16
kin selection, 108–109
kitchen middens, 21
klamboe, 157
Knox-Out, 154

Labidura riparia (earwig), 172
Labidus coecus (ant), *164,* 183–84
lac insects, 212
lactones, 42
larvae, *51,* 55, *64, 82–84*
Lasius neoniger (ant), 162, 165–66
lead, 156
leaf-cutter ants, 9–10
lime dust, 158
Linepithema humile. See Argentine ant
little red fire ant *(Wasmannia auropunctata),* 8
Löding, H. P., 15
Logic, 151–52. *See also* fenoxycarb

McCook, H. C., 87
macrogyne, 81, 115, 189
Malachra (plant), 75
malathion, 153
male fire ants: black imported fire ant, *64;* flight conditions, 48; golden fire ant, *96, 97;* lack of sting, 37; mating strategy, 45; red imported fire ants, *46, 47,* 53, *56; Solenop-*sis amblychila, *99;* southern fire ant, *92;* sperm production, 53–54; tropical fire ant, *79*
Martinezia dutertrei (scarab beetle), 118, 120, 121, 127, 166
Maryland: invasion of, 219
mating flight. *See* nuptial (mating) flights
Mattesia geminata (protozoan), 189
medical importance of fire ants, 128–40
Melanoplus spretus (grasshopper), 216
Melocactus communis (plant), 74
Memphis, Tenn.: invasion of, 60
mercuric chloride, 138
mercury, 156
Mesostigmata (mite), 174
Messor pergandei (ant), 191
metapleural gland, 44, 77
Metarhizium anisopliae (fungus), *177, 178,* 181
methoprene, 151
methyl bromide, 156
methylchloroform, 154
Metopioxys gallardoi (beetle), *121,* 122
Mexico: possible invasion of, 220
microgyne, 81, 115
microsporidians, 176. *See also individual species*
Mima mounds, 61
minims, 22
mirex, 141–42, 145–49, 150, 156, 157, 158, 210
Mirolepisma (silverfish), 127
mitochondrial DNA, 109
Mobile, Ala., xv, 11, 15, 16, 18, 24
monarch butterfly, 199
mongoose, 209
Moniezia expansa (tapeworm), 174
monogyne colonies: 32, *42;* backup queens, 51; compared to polygyne colonies, 80, 110–13; physogastric queens, 52; queen fecundity, 43–44; queen types, 81; relative lack of sterile males, 48; social parasites, 49; southern fire ant, 116; trophallaxis 76
Monomorium minimum (ant), 162, *163,* 184, 191
mosquitoes, 203
mounds: *7, 19;* near roadkills, 204; nuisances, 201; seasonal construction, 18; structure and function, 17, 21, *29–32,* 55, *70,* 71, 90, 95, 103, 107
multiple-queen colonies. *See* polygyne colonies
Myrmecaphodius excavaticollis (scarab beetle), 118, 122, 127, 188
Myrmecochara tricuspidis (beetle), 121
myrmecochory, 73

Myrmecomyces annellisae (fungus), 178, 181
Myrmecophila nebrascensis (cricket), 118, *119*, 127
Myrmecophila pergandei (cricket), 118, 124
Myrmecophila quadrispina (cricket), 124
myrmecophiles. *See* nest symbionts
Myrmecosaurus ferrugineus (rove beetle), 118, *119*, 120, 121
Myrmecosaurus gallardoi (rove beetle), 121

Nebraska: invasion of, 219
necrophoric behavior, 22, 45, 62
Neivamyrmex harrisii (army ant), 191
Neivamyrmex nigrescens (army ant), *184*
nematodes, *64*, 188–89. *See also individual species*
Neoblissus (seed bug), 121
Neoblissus parasitaster (seed bug), 121, 188
nestmate recognition, 44, 62, 77, 91, 149
nest symbionts, 117–27. *See also individual species*
New Mexico (invasion of), 219, 222
Nezara viridula (stink bug), 189
nocturnal fire ant, 95
Nosema (microsporidian), 192
nuptial (mating) flights: details of, 45–48, 62–63, 78, 80–81, 92–93; fish kills, 144; functions, 23; infestations, 24; open questions, 226–27; unsuccessful, 112; wingless sexuals, *47*, 57
nurse workers, 55

okra, 195
oleic acid, 190
Oliarus vicarius (bug), 120
Oplitis arborcavi (mite), 126
Oplitis carteretensis (mite), 118
Oplitis communis (mite), 118, 126
Oplitis exopodi (mite), 127
Oplitis moseri (mite), 120
Oplitis virgilinus (mite), 120
Orasema (wasp), *166*, 181, 190
organophosphorus chemicals, 153, 154. *See also individual chemicals*
origin of fire ants, 105–106
Orthene 75S, 153
Oxyepoecus (ants), 106
Oxyopes salticus (spider), 173
Oxypoda (rove beetle), 124

Pachybrachius bilobatus (seed bug), 118
Pachydiplax longipennis (dragonfly), 172
Paecilomyces fumosoroseus (fungus), 178

Paederus littoreus (rove beetle), 124
Pantanal region (South America), 109
Paraponera clavata (bullet ant), 140
Parasitus (mite), 127
Paratrechina arenivaga (ant), 164
Paratrechina fulva (ant), 183
park visitation: effects of fire ants on, 201
pecans, 196
pesticides. *See* chemical control; *individual chemicals*
pest status of fire ants, 15, 17–18. *See also individual species*
phagostimulant, 22
Pheidole dentata (ant), *164*, 182, *183*, 187
Pheidole gilvescens (ant), 191
Pheidole hyatti (ant), 190
Pheidole megacephala (ant), 74, 182, 207
Pheidole militicida (ant), 190
Pheidole morrisii (ant), 182
Pheidole oxyops (ant), 182
Pheidole radoszkowskii (ant), 183
Phenacoccus solenopsis (mealybug), 126
phloxin B, 156
phorid flies, 104, 107, 124–26, 169–72, 180–81, 186–88, 191. *See also individual species*
physogastric queen, 51–52, 112
pineapples, 208
piperonyl butoxide, 156
Placophorina obtecta (phorid fly), 126
Plantago hispidula (plant), 102
pleometrosis, 49, 81, 109–10
Poecilocrypticus formicophilus (darkling beetle), 122–23
Pogonomyrmex badius (ant), 162
Pogonomyrmex barbatus (ant), 162
Pogonomyrmex californicus (ant), 191
Pogonomyrmex comanche (ant), 162, *163*
Pogonomyrmex rugosus (ant), 191
pollination, 77
Polybia occidentalis (wasp), *192*
polygyne colonies: budding, 24, 54, 82, 143, 201; cold-tolerant, 225; compared to monogyne colonies, 110–13; food exchange, 41, 76; "green-beard," 52; indoor attacks by, 131; mound density, 71–72; open questions, 226; queen number, 51, 80, 93; queen recognition pheromone, 43; in South America, 61, 114; of South American endemics, 103; southern fire ant, 116; sterile males, 48, 160; working against a species, 171–72
postpharyngeal gland, 77
potatoes, 195–96, 205, 207
praesaepium (food basket), 39–40

Prenolepis (ants), 184
preserving fire ants for study, 234–35
Pro-Drone, 152
Prolepismina (silverfish), 127
Pseudacteon antiguensis (phorid fly), 186
Pseudacteon arcuatus (phorid fly), 186
Pseudacteon bifidus (phorid fly), 186
Pseudacteon browni (phorid fly), 186
Pseudacteon crawfordi (phorid fly), 186, *187*,
    188, 191
Pseudacteon curriei (phorid fly), 191
Pseudacteon curvatus (phorid fly), 169, 180, 186
Pseudacteon grandis (phorid fly), 186
Pseudacteon litoralis (phorid fly), 169, *170*, 171,
    180
Pseudacteon longicauda (phorid fly), 186
Pseudacteon obtusus (phorid fly), 169, 180
Pseudacteon solenopsidis (phorid fly), 169, 186
Pseudacteon spatulatus (phorid fly), 191
Pseudacteon tricuspis (phorid fly), 169, 170,
    171, 180, 186
Pseudacteon wasmanni (phorid fly), 169, 186
Pseudococcus comstocki (bug), 103
Pseudomonas (bacterium), 176, 192
Pseudomonas aeruginosa (bacterium), 191
Pseudomonas chlororaphis (bacterium), 191
Pseudomonas syringae (bacterium), 178–79
Pseudomorpha (ground beetle), 166, *167*
Pterocheilus texanus (wasp), 73
Puerto Rico: invasion of, 218, 219, 223
Puliciphora incerta (phorid fly), 126
pupa, 55, *85*
pustule: absence of, 139, 140; appearance, 3,
    5–6, 128; on birds, 197; on reptiles, 198;
    secondary infection, 129; unusual types,
    132, 138
Pyemotes tritici (fire mite), 174
pygidial gland, 33
pygmy mouse, 196
pyrethrins, 154
pyrethroids, 154
pyriproxyfen, 152

queen execution, 52, 160
queen longevity, 53
queen recognition pheromone, 42, 77–78
queens: black imported fire ant, *63*, *64*; char-
    acteristics, 22; execution of, 52, 160; golden
    fire ant, 96, 97; identification of, 230; nup-
    tial flight, *47*; queen recognition pheromone,
    42; rate of egg-laying, 51; red imported fire
    ant, 46, 47, 50, 56, 163; response to aver-
    mectins, 153; response to IGRs, 152; *Solenop-*

sis amblychila, 99; southern fire ant, 92;
    spermatheca, 54; tropical fire ant, 79, *82*,
    232; use of sting, 37, 42

Raid Fire Ant Killer, 153
RAST (radioallergosorbent testing), 136
recruitment pheromone, 33, 34, 72, 77
red imported fire ant (RIFA; *Solenopsis invicta*):
    beneficial predator and benefactor, 201–
    205; biocontrol of, 160–80; biology, 25–57;
    chemical control of, 141–56; communica-
    tion, 41–45; crop pest, 195–96; develop-
    ment, 54–57; diet, 37–39; feeding behavior,
    39–41; foraging behavior, 32–37; identifi-
    cation, *231–33*; infestation of United States,
    216–25; in list of fire ants, 229; livestock
    and wildlife pest, 196–200; medical impor-
    tance, 128–37; names of, 12; nesting sites,
    26–*29*; nest population, 32; nest structure,
    29–32; nest symbionts, 117–20; origin and
    evolution, 109–14; property damage, 200–
    201; reproduction, 45–54; sting, *4*; TFA as
    enemy, 185–86; trails and tunnels, *31, 33*;
    worker, *8*; world distribution, 27
replete, 40
reptiles, 197–98
reserve workers, 56
resmethrin, 154
Reticulitermes flavipes (termite), 188
Reticulitermes virginicus (termite), 188
Rhigopsidius tucumanus (weevil), 104
Rhyssemus neglectus (scarab beetle), 118, 127
RIFA. *See* red imported fire ant
RIT (rush immunotherapy), 131
road damage, *200*
robber fly, 172
rodents, 196
rose bengal, 156
rotenone, 154, 156

Santschi, F., 25
scavengers, 213
scuttle flies. *See* phorid flies; *individual species*
Scytodes (spider), 174
seed-harvesting, 205–206, 207, 210
Serratia (bacterium), 192
Serratia marcescens (bacterium), 191
Sesbania (plant), *179*
sesquiterpene, 34
Sevin RP-2, 154
Sevin SL, 154
SFA. *See* southern fire ant
Shigella flexneri (bacterium), 139

single-queen colonies. *See* monogyne colonies
skin tests, 131, 136
soap, 154
social parasites, 49, 115. *See also Solenopsis daguerrei*
sodium fluoride, 157
Solanum gilo (plant), 103
solenopsins. *See* alkaloids
Solenopsis, 12–14
Solenopsis amblychila: biology, 99–100; identification, 230, *231*, 233; in list of fire ant species, 229; medical importance, 140; pest status, 194; worker, *11*; world distribution, *98*
Solenopsis aurea. See golden fire ant
Solenopsis bruesi, 101, 229
Solenopsis daguerrei: biology and hosts, 102, 104, 115, *161*–62, 180; in list of fire ant species, 229
Solenopsis electra, 102, 229
Solenopsis gayi, 102, 229
Solenopsis geminata. See tropical fire ant
Solenopsis hostilis, 229
Solenopsis interrupta, 102, 229
Solenopsis invicta. See red imported fire ant
Solenopsis macdonaghi, 102, 162, 229
Solenopsis megergates, 102, 229
Solenopsis molesta (thief ant), 126, 162
Solenopsis pusillignis, 103, 229
Solenopsis pythia, 103, 229
Solenopsis quinquecuspis, 103, 108, 114, 229
Solenopsis richteri. See black imported fire ant
Solenopsis saevissima: biology, 103–104; chromosome number, 108; early confusion with imported fire ants, 17, 25; host of *Solenopsis daguerrei*, 102, 162; in list of fire ant species, 229
Solenopsis saevissima richteri, 15, 17
Solenopsis solenopsidis, 229
Solenopsis wagneri. See red imported fire ant
Solenopsis weyrauchi, 104, 229
Solenopsis xyloni. See southern fire ant
Somatochlora provocans (dragonfly), 172
sorghum, 195
southern fire ant (SFA; *Solenopsis xyloni*): beneficial predator, 214–15; biology, 87–93; chemical control, 157–58; communication, 91; development, 93; diet, feeding behavior, 91; enemies, 190–91; enemy of RIFA queens, 162; evolution, 115–16; foraging behavior, 90–91; identification, 233; in list of fire ant species, 229; medical importance, 139; nesting sites, 89–90; nest population, 90; nests, 90; nest symbionts, 126–27; pest status,

213–14; reproduction, 92–93; worker, *10*; world distribution, *88*
soybeans, 195, 202
sperm, 53–54
spermatheca, 54
starvation, 77
Steinernema carpocapsae (worm), 174–75
Steinernema riobravis (worm), 174
sterile males, 160. *See also* diploid males
Stictia maculata (wasp), 73
sting: capturing prey, 75; dispersal as aerosol, 35; laying recruitment pheromone, 33, 72; medical importance, 128–40; presence in colony, 36–37; red imported fire ant, 3–7
stomach poisons, 141
Streptomyces avermitilis (bacterium), 152–53
stridulation, 45
sugarcane, 201, 202
sulfluramid, 154

Tapinoma melanocephalum (ant), 184
teflubenzuron, 152
tefluthrin, 154
tending insects: black imported fire ants, 62; imported fire ants, 18, 21; red imported fire ants, *19*, 196, 202; southern fire ant, 214; tropical fire ants; 207–208
Tetradonema solenopsis (worm), 174, *175*
Tetramorium caespitum (ant), 165
Texas: history of invasion, 219–20, 222, 225
Texas Imported Fire Ant Research and Management Plan, 217
TFA. *See* tropical fire ant
thallium acetate, 156–57
thallium sulfate, 156–57
Thelohania hereditaria (microsporidian), 178
Thelohania solenopsae (microsporidian), 121, 178, 181
therapy for sting victims, 130–33, 135–37
thief ants, *13*, 107, 126, 162
thysanurans (silverfish), *118*, 120, 172. *See also individual species*
ticks, 203–204, 212. *See also individual species*
tiger beetle, 166, *167*
tomatoes, 206
toxaphene, 18, 149
trail pheromone. *See* recruitment pheromone
Tramea carolina (dragonfly), 172
Travis, B. V., 68
triolein, 44
Triumph 1G, 153
trophallaxis, 39, 76
trophic egg, 38, 40

tropical fire ant (TFA; *Solenopsis geminata*): beneficial predator, 210–12; biology, 66–86; chemical control, 156–57; communication, 77–78; competing with RIFA, 28, 213; crop pest, 205–208; development, 82–86; diet, 75–76; enemies, 162, 181–90; evolution, 114–15; feeding behavior, 76–77; foraging behavior, 72–75; identification, 230–33; in list of fire ants, 229; medical importance, 137–39; nesting sites, 68–70; nest population, 72; nests, 70–72; nest symbionts, 123–26; origin, 11; pest of livestock, wildlife, home, 208–209; possible benefits, 212–13; property damage, 209–210; reproduction, 78–82; worker, 9; world distribution, 67
Tschinkel, W. R., 26, 28
tucandeira. *See Paraponera clavata*
Tyrophagus putrescentiae (mite), 174
Tyta luctosa (moth), 200

Vairimorpha invictae (microsporidian), 178, 181
Vairimorpha "undeeni" (microsporidian), 189
venom, 107, 128–29, 133–37, 138–39, 140.
    See also medical importance of fire ants
Vicia graminea (plant), 120

Vinson, S. B., xv
violets, 74
Virginia (invasion of), 219, 223
vision, 22

Wagner, E. R., 25, 26
Washington, D.C. (invasion of), 219
Wedelia hispida (plant), 73
Westwood, J. O., 12
wheat, 195
Wheeler, W. M., 93, 95, 100, 105
Wilson, E. O., 18, 20, 26, 33, 155, 160
wolf spiders, 172
worker lifespan, 57
workers: black imported fire ant, 9, 65; golden fire ant, 10, 96; identification, 230–33; red imported fire ant, 4, 7, 8, 35, 36, 42, 43; *Solenopsis amblychila*, 11, 99; southern fire ant, 10; subcastes, 55–56; thief ant, 13; tropical fire ant, 9, 79, 82; weight, 86

yeasts, 39

Zikania schmidti (phorid fly), 126
zinc, 155